Donated to
VB Co. Library
in memory
Erma Metcar
by Sue Blakeney

2016
DATE DUE

This item is Due on
or before Date shown.

JONBENÉT

JONBENÉT

INSIDE THE RAMSEY MURDER INVESTIGATION

STEVE THOMAS

WITH DON DAVIS

ST. MARTIN'S PRESS
NEW YORK

ISBN 0-312-25326-5

First Edition: April 2000

10   9   8   7   6   5   4   3   2   1

To a little girl I never met
who caused so many to reflect
within themselves

And to those cops and prosecutors
across the country
who do the right thing
day in, day out

CONTENTS

AUTHOR'S NOTE

To certain members of the Boulder Police Department, cops who still cannot speak out publicly and who know this story all too well, I appreciate your continued support and the confidences you provided me in the preparation of this book. To John Eller, who tried to do the right thing, I respect your efforts in the case. To Bob Keatley, the most ethical man I know. To John Lang, a cop's cop, and the entire Georgia Bureau of Investigation team. To Don Foster, a true professional. To Dan Caplis and the Dream Team, who stepped up when asked. To members of the FBI and those law enforcement experts who assisted us in seeking justice, thank you.

To the A-Team cops who have left the BPD, the likes of Haukeness, Idler, Schunk, Joy, Kolar, Ross, Ready, Finn, Sears, Ramos, Aguilar, Riggs, and Humphrey—Boulder doesn't realize what it lost. And to the cops of the Wheat Ridge Police Department, who taught me so much about real police work.

To all those who were wrongly accused in this case, and there are so many of you, such as Mike Glynn, Jeff Merrick, and Bill McReynolds, I respect your decency and honor. To Fleet and Priscilla White, the most principled of people, who quietly fought hard for justice and were forsaken not only by friends but by a criminal justice system.

To my friend and attorney, Peg Miller, for never allowing those who opposed me to silence my right to speak and who never wavered as a loyal friend in the face of spiteful opposition.

To Shelley Ross, whose integrity and professionalism is without parallel and whom I admire tremendously.

To the group at St. Martin's Press, Charles Spicer, John Murphy, and Heather Florence, and to my agent, Barbara Lowenstein, my sincere thanks. And to Don and Robin Davis for your hard work.

To my friends Todd Sears, Richard Setian, Steve Headley, and Danny Nutt, guys who never wavered in their support and whose friendships I value most of all.

To my family, Pop, Cathie, Amanda, and Christine, in Arkadelphia and elsewhere, and the Jesaitis family, my deepest gratitude.

And most of all, to my wife, Karena. You endured a tremendous burden and supported me throughout. I am forever grateful.

———

The true name of John Ramsey's former mistress has not been used in the book. The name Jodi Roberts is a pseudonym. All other names are real.

Just remember that one thing does not abide by majority rule, Scout—
it's your conscience.

—HARPER LEE, *To Kill a Mockingbird*

PART ONE

LITTLE MISS CHRISTMAS

PROLOGUE

There was not another little girl in America with her name. Jon-Benét—a combination of her father's first and middle names, John and Bennett—was more of a title created just for her, similar to those of the four daughters of her mother's best friend who also bore classy Francophile names. At home she was called Johnni-B.

JonBenét Ramsey entered the world on August 6, 1990, in Atlanta's Northside Hospital, weighing six pounds, nine ounces. She was able to fall asleep easily with a bottle and the background noise of a television set, but she also had a grumpy side, and her grandmother would recall that after her second birthday, JonBenét could indeed be a Terrible Two. At three and a half, she still regularly drank her milk from the bottle.

The family moved from Georgia to Colorado, into a huge house at the foot of the Rocky Mountains, after her first birthday. Her lavishly decorated bedroom was originally built for her two much older stepsisters, Beth and Melinda, but a double tragedy made it hers. Beth was killed in an automobile accident, and JonBenét's mother was diagnosed with cancer.

The little girl was moved into the bigger bedroom to be closer to her mother, who, ravaged by chemical treatments, temporarily gave up sleeping in the master bedroom in favor of one more convenient to a bathroom. Mother and daughter were right next door. Her room was so warm that even on the coldest winter night, when the outside temperature would dip below zero, JonBenét would kick off her covers and sleep with only a sheet and blanket.

Her education began with early home schooling and then a church preschool program but did not stop at the classroom door. The little girl traveled widely, to New York several times and as far away as Italy. She was a member of Daisy Troop 2349 of the Girl Scouts in Boulder.

Summers were spent at a sprawling white house that had been expensively remodeled in Charlevoix, Michigan, where JonBenét loved to swing on the tire at the bottom of the hill, swim in the lake, go roller-blading and biking, and be a tomboy who didn't care about getting dirt under her fingernails.

Her hair, which would go dishwater dirty during the Colorado winter, would blaze back blond in the Michigan sunshine, with some help from a bottle, and she wore it in a ponytail or a braid. Her favorite foods were macaroni and cheese and fresh fruit, and she loved pineapple.

The entrance of JonBenét into the peculiar and competitive world of children's beauty pageants was destined from the very start. Her mom, Patsy Ramsey, and her aunt Pam Paugh had both won the Miss West Virginia crown and competed for Miss America. JonBenét seemed to have what it took to carry on that family tradition. Patsy and her mother, Nedra, were inspired to put JonBenét into pageants during a visit to a Little Miss America contest in 1994, and a career was set.

JonBenét was only four years old, not yet in kindergarten, when she hit the circuit, and the judges immediately knew that the sparkling beginner in the white dress still needed a lot of work, but they said she was a natural. In the summer of 1994 JonBenét was accidentally hit on the left cheek by a golf club swung by her brother, Burke, and her mother rushed the child to see a plastic surgeon, who thought Patsy was overreacting. The doctor apparently didn't understand the importance of an imperfection on a budding beauty queen.

Her first major win came in Michigan. After a thorough "pageant scrub" to clean up dirty knees and elbows, a good hair wash, and a French manicure for those dirty nails, JonBenét performed a patriotic song and tap routine and was crowned Little Miss Charlevoix.

The child radiated star power, but there was a brain inside that pretty head. She listened attentively to adults talk in the evening, nestled on someone's lap in a big chair, and her vocabulary and sense of logic were remarkable. When her aunt found her running barefoot on the Charlevoix dock and asked, "Why don't you put your shoes on?" Jon-

Benét answered, "Aunt Pam, I want to feel the rhythm of the earth under my feet." She was a free spirit.

In October 1995, she became Little Miss Colorado Sunburst and qualified for a national pageant the next year. In the 1995 Boulder Christmas parade, she sang and waved from a float called the *Good Ship Lollipop*, which was built by her grandfather. "Quite a performer," the judges said, the payoff for the hundred-dollar-per-hour lessons.

She blossomed as a beauty, loving everything about the pageants and making sure to tell her mother, who was leaving for London, to bring her back some hats. The natural prissiness of a little girl came forth as she expressed her strong will, not hesitating to tell an adult doing her hair, "I don't like that, I want it this way."

On many nights, JonBenét would fall asleep watching videotapes of Patsy and Pam in the Miss America pageant. She wanted to stroll that Atlantic City Boardwalk someday, and it was drummed into her that the coveted sash, trophy, and tiara would come only through total dedication. Once, when she balked, her grandmother groused, "JonBenét, you *will* do it. This is your job. There are no excuses." A family friend recalled JonBenét being chilly in a restaurant after a pageant and her mother not allowing the child to put on a sweater because "You're still on show."

JonBenét did not need a professional trainer with a couple of former Miss West Virginias in the family. They would be her mentors instead of some professional who might turn her into a rigid automaton, with nothing but boring ten- and two-o'clock stances, flashing the collar and cuffs, never touching the dress, and perhaps, her grandmother warned, even using the sleazy shoulder shake that homosexuals taught. The strategy was for Johnni-B to go beyond the ordinary and bring her natural friendliness and a touch of class to the shows. In pageants from Rome, Georgia, to Elk Rapids, Michigan, the plan worked.

Daddy had money, a great advantage because the pageant world is not for the miserly. Talent lessons were expensive, and her spectacular handmade costumes cost even more. JonBenét would not go out there in K-Mart dresses, and she regularly brought home "Best Wardrobe" titles.

But there were some dark secrets. She had a continuing problem with wetting her bed, regressing in her toilet training in the months before her death. Occasionally she would even defecate in the bed and at one point was wetting or soiling her underpants during the day. She would not wipe adequately after a bowel movement. This would never do for a beauty queen.

Her intelligence kept pace with her almost flawless beauty, and she kept a list on her night table of books that had been read to her. Her father insisted that knowledge and talent were much more important than looking good. She was truly beautiful but still was only a child beginning to read and write, even though her mother created a more impressive résumé on pageant entry forms by claiming that JonBenét played the violin, spoke French, and wanted to be an Olympic ice-skating champion.

Confidence came with experience, and when the family returned from a trip to Mexico, JonBenét made them all do the sinuous macareña dance. "That's not the way you do it," she scolded, then led it herself. "There. That's the way it's done."

Like lots of kids, although she suffered from colds and coughs, her sinus infections were eventually diagnosed as allergic rhinitis, not unlike a problem that had once plagued her father. In 1995 she tripped in a grocery store, landed on her nose, and the doctor treated her with ice and Popsicles. Six months later she fell again, bonking herself over the left eye. In the twenty-four months before her death, she visited the doctor eighteen times.

Her last year was a rainbow ride. In July she won the title of America's Royale Tiny Miss, and the five-year-old took home $500 in prize money. The next month, the Sunburst National Pageant at the Airport Marriott Hotel in Atlanta was a disappointment because she was only second runner-up in the beauty competition, and by now people expected JonBenét to win everything, all the time. They were usually right. Titles were bagged with frequency, and the professional touches of makeup, perfect hair, and a portfolio of glamour photographs gave the child a sultry look that was part angel, part Lolita. Best-in-show trophies were just over the horizon.

In two trips to New York, she saw five Broadway shows and ate a $125 lobster dinner in a fancy restaurant. People waiting in line to see the Statue of Liberty asked permission to take her picture. After turning six that August, JonBenét entered private school, and her stage training made oral reports a snap, although her writing skills were minimal. She went to see the school nurse twice in December, both times on a Monday after a weekend.

Before the Christmas break, her mother arranged to have JonBenét perform as a holiday treat for her classmates, and in pageant finery she sang and danced all day while class after class came through to watch. She went home exhausted. Her lesson in school that day was that perfection and celebrity carried a price. On December 17 she picked up still another crown, Colorado's Little Miss Christmas.

Six days later, during a party at her parents' home, a family friend came across a JonBenét who was seldom seen. The child was immaculate in a holiday frock, and her platinum blond hair was done perfectly, but she sat alone on a staircase in the butler's kitchen, crying softly. The friend sat beside her.

"What's wrong, honey?"

Little Miss Christmas sobbed, "I don't feel pretty."

1

It felt good to put down my detective's badge, at least for a while, because being a cop in Boulder, Colorado, can be like patrolling Fantasyland. The city, with its alternative lifestyles and bizarre counterculture, was Mickey Mouse, with Goofy and Dopey in charge. A dozen years on the job, and the surprises just kept coming.

I had come into police work with total admiration for the men and women who wore the blue uniform. Born in the small town of Arkadelphia, Arkansas, with a horoscope that said I was "extremely tenacious," I grew up respecting the law. My mother died when I was a small boy, and my father moved my sisters and me to Dallas in 1969. While he roamed the nation raising funds for the March of Dimes, my sisters and I grew up under the guidance of a wonderful black woman named Lee Bass, who taught me to treat all people equally.

After graduating from the University of Colorado in Boulder, I spent a few years with the nearby Wheat Ridge Police Department, learning my trade, and was awarded a medal for rescuing an elderly couple from a burning building. Eventually I was assigned to a special investigations unit that introduced me to undercover work. But when the opportunity came in 1991 to join the Boulder PD, with its high salaries and top-of-the-line equipment, I took it and, like Alice in the fairy tale, tumbled through the mirror and into another world.

Not long after arriving in Boulder, I noticed the huge number of escort services advertising in the local papers and set up a prostitution sting in the city's nicest hotel. The department had not worked such an operation in twenty years. In no time we nabbed several girls, some pimps, cocaine, cash, and guns. When the newspapers reported the story, city officials quickly declared there was no prostitution problem in Boulder. When I tried to arrange another such sting, a memo was posted mandating that unless there were public complaints, we were not to work prostitution. It taught me the early lesson that Boulder did not want its boat rocked.

After my first year with the department, I was among several officers who confronted an enraged, psychotic suspect who was waving two butcher knives in a busy downtown intersection on a hot summer day and screaming that "someone is going to die." Ranting and out of control, he charged at me, and the decision was textbook. I shot him twice and still had a struggle putting handcuffs on the fighting, bleeding man.

I had become the first BPD officer in over a decade to be involved in a shooting, and got my first real taste of the Boulder County District Attorney's office. Pete Hofstrom, chief of the felony division, asked me, "Couldn't you have just hit him with a stick or something?" Using any sort of force against a suspect in Boulder was viewed as extraordinary.

Hofstrom's response was typical of the distance between a cop on the street and a prosecutor in the entrenched bureaucracy of the Office of the Boulder County District Attorney. We dealt with the law on real terms, while to me they seemed more concerned with justice as some kind of test-tube experiment. In many other jurisdictions, an assistant DA would have been among the first to support a street cop in such a life-or-death situation. In Boulder, they wanted me to bop him with a stick.

Less than a year later, I had to do it again. As a member of the SWAT team, I was covering fellow officers trying to apprehend a suicidal, armed suspect who had already shot at his wife. He charged, pointing a pistol right at me, and again I had no choice, and brought him down with three quick shots. I was hustled back to the police department for an internal investigation while Police Chief Tom Koby rushed to the emergency room bedside of the suspect, consoled him, and told him everything was going to be all right. Officers were embarrassed by the chief's action. I did not expect a commendation, because Koby would not award a decoration to any officer who used deadly force against a citizen. Instead I was sent off to "verbal judo" school to learn how to resolve critical situations with words.

By then I had begun to understand the locker-room talk. When we traded war stories, we shrugged and said, "Hey, this is Boulder." We were subjected to Internal Affairs investigations for raising our voices to suspects, and the beads-and-sandal types were in command positions. Cops hesitated to be confrontational.

Still, I found a niche in police work that I thoroughly enjoyed, working on a small undercover narcotics team. We did our own thing and were mostly left alone, but being a drug cop in a city where drugs were almost universally accepted had its moments, too. One day, in my beard and long hair, I drove an unmarked pickup truck loaded with tall marijuana plants through downtown Boulder to the police department, cheered along the way by honking motorists. "Dude, you're far too brave!" called one fan. The police received not a single tip about the load of dope being hauled through the city streets.

Shortly thereafter, the local paper printed a letter to the editor denouncing the War on Drugs. It was written by a judge who often signed my narcotics warrants.

Of course, this was Boulder, where drugs were a very, very low priority. Two of us went to the office of the district attorney one day to discuss a search warrant for a drug bust and listened to a couple of the prosecutors mock our operation and joke about their own previous drug use. Cases involving substantial quantities of heroin and cocaine were routinely plea-bargained, including one in which the arrested suspect was a deputy district attorney found with syringes in her bathrobe and what appeared to be cocaine in her dresser drawers. Claiming the drugs and paraphernalia belonged to her live-in boyfriend, she was allowed to plead to lesser crimes. But plea bargains weren't handed out just in drug cases, for even people accused of the most heinous crimes could negotiate a deal. Defense attorneys were big fans of the DA. It was the way business was done.

More than once, when I insisted on contesting a plea, a prosecutor would ask me, "Why do you want to ruin somebody's life?" I made hundreds of arrests in Boulder but went to court exactly twice in seven years.

I couldn't help but compare passive Boulder to the hard-charging task force I worked with in neighboring Jefferson County for most of 1996. There, we were about to bring home more than a dozen grand jury indictments in a racketeering case. An assistant Jeffco DA was even assigned full-time to the drug task force to give the cops on-the-spot guidance and legal advice and expedite needed warrants, a usual practice in many counties where the DA actively supports the police investigative process. That was not the usual practice in Boulder, where the DA's office usually waited on the sidelines until we "presented" a case to them.

In December 1996 I laid the badge aside for a while and went off to hunt quail with my father on a plantation in south Georgia. Days in the field with the sunshine, the dogs, and the quiet were a pleasant respite from the peculiarities of Boulder. The holiday over, we returned to Atlanta and boarded the plane for home.

There was no way to know that these would be some of my last idle moments for the next two years. In a few weeks my life would be turned upside down, and I would be flying back to Atlanta as a detective investigating the terrible murder of a little girl named JonBenét.

2

There was no television camera watching or videotape running in the house at 755 Fifteenth Street in Boulder on the night of December 25, 1996, so only two people really know what happened when JonBenét Ramsey was murdered: the victim and the killer. JonBenét took whatever she knew to her grave, and the person who killed her has remained stone silent. It is often that way with murder.

But rarely is there such a thing as a perfect homicide, and a wise man once told me, "Murders are usually what they seem." After spending twenty months in the churning cauldron of the Ramsey investigation, after examining all the evidence, I now agree with him. Others disagree, but to me the simplest explanation for what has gone into the books as one of the most perplexing and notorious murders of the decade is also the truth.

At one point my partner, Detective Ron Gosage, stood in the dark of the former Ramsey home, after we had spent almost a week searching it, and voiced the central question that had baffled everyone: "What the hell happened in this house?" Short of a confession, which is unlikely, the actual events will never be known.

But there are only two possible answers. One is that an intruder, known or unknown to the family, crept into the house, killed JonBenét in a botched kidnapping attempt while the family slept, then vanished, leaving behind what has been called the *War and Peace* of ransom notes, and then disappeared. The other scenario is that the little girl was killed by a family member, whom I believe to have been her panicked mother, Patsy Ramsey, and that her father, John Ramsey, opted to protect his wife in the investigation that followed.

The district attorney and his top prosecutor, two police chiefs, and a large number of cops, although so at odds on some points that they almost came to blows, all agreed on one thing—that probable cause existed to arrest Patsy Ramsey in connection with the death of her daughter. But due to a totally inept justice system in Boulder, no one was ever put in handcuffs, and the Ramseys were never really in serious jeopardy.

What follows is the story of how someone got away with murder.

————

The first word of what had happened came at 5:52 A.M. on the morning after Christmas Day, when Patsy Ramsey dialed the 911 emergency number.

PATSY RAMSEY: (inaudible) police.
BOULDER POLICE DISPATCHER: (inaudible)
PATSY RAMSEY: Seven fifty-five Fifteenth Street.
DISPATCHER: What's going on there, Ma'am.
PATSY RAMSEY: We have a kidnapping . . . Hurry, please.
DISPATCHER: Explain to me what's going on, OK?
PATSY RAMSEY: There we have a . . . There's a note left and our daughter's gone.
DISPATCHER: A note was left and your daughter is gone?
PATSY RAMSEY: Yes.
DISPATCHER: How old is your daughter?
PATSY RAMSEY: She's six years old . . . she's blond . . . six years old.
DISPATCHER: How long ago was this?
PATSY RAMSEY: I don't know. I just found the note and my daughter's (inaudible).
DISPATCHER: Does it say who took her?
PATSY RAMSEY: What?
DISPATCHER: Does it say who took her?
PATSY RAMSEY: No. . . . I don't know it's there . . . there's a ransom note here.
DISPATCHER: It's a ransom note.
PATSY RAMSEY: It says SBTC Victory. . . . Please.
DISPATCHER: OK, what's your name? Are you . . .
PATSY RAMSEY: Patsy Ramsey. I'm the mother. Oh my God, please . . .

DISPATCHER: I'm . . . OK, I'm sending an officer over, OK?

PATSY RAMSEY: Please.

DISPATCHER: Do you know how long she's been gone?

PATSY RAMSEY: No, I don't. Please, we just got up and she's not here. Oh my God, please.

DISPATCHER: OK.

PATSY RAMSEY: Please send somebody.

DISPATCHER: I am, honey.

PATSY RAMSEY: Please.

DISPATCHER: Take a deep breath (inaudible).

PATSY RAMSEY: Hurry, hurry, hurry (inaudible).

DISPATCHER: Patsy? Patsy? Patsy? Patsy? Patsy?

The telephone call gave us a cornerstone of evidence, not so much for what was easily heard but for what was found when experts washed out the background noise. It has been my experience as a police officer that such emergency calls are virtually unchallengeable. They are tape-recorded, and either something was said or it was not. Tapes can be so powerful that prosecutors regularly play them so a jury can hear the actual voices and emotions of the participants.

In preliminary examinations, detectives thought they could hear some more words being spoken between the time Patsy Ramsey said, "Hurry, hurry, hurry" and when the call was terminated. However, the FBI and the U.S. Secret Service could not lift anything from the background noise on the tape. As a final effort several months later, we contacted the electronic wizards at the Aerospace Corporation in Los Angeles and asked them to try and decipher the sounds behind the noise.

Their work produced a startling conclusion. Patsy apparently had trouble hanging up the telephone, and before it rested in the cradle she was heard to moan, "Help me, Jesus. Help me, Jesus." Her husband was heard to bark, "We're not talking to you." And in the background was a young-sounding voice: "What *did* you find?" It was JonBenét's brother, Burke.

The Ramseys would repeatedly tell us that their son did not wake up at any point throughout the night of the crime. We knew differently.

3

Watch III, the graveyard shift, was almost over when the dispatcher called for patrol unit 273 of the Boulder Police Department to respond to 755 Fifteenth Street. A ransom note had been found, and a six-year-old girl was missing. With little traffic on the roads an hour before sunrise, Officer Rick French got to the house on University Hill within minutes. His mere arrival was the first of many mistakes that police would make in the coming hours. An unmarked car or undercover officers should have responded to the kidnapping call, not a black-and-white, but French had no idea of the warnings in the ransom note. If the alleged kidnappers were watching the house, they would have known police had been contacted.

French walked up a curving sidewalk lined with Christmas decorations and large candy canes, small lights glittering in the darkness, and was met at the front door by a distraught dark-haired woman in black pants and a red sweater. He noted that although it was still before dawn, her hair was neatly done and her makeup was in place. They were joined at the door by a man in a long-sleeved blue-and-white–striped shirt and khaki slacks. Patsy and John Ramsey told the officer that their daughter, JonBenét, was missing and their nine-year-old son was asleep upstairs. They escorted French through a foyer and kitchen area to a back hallway, where three pages of white legal tablet paper covered with blocky handwriting were spread out on the wooden floor. The note read:

Mr. Ramsey,

Listen carefully! We are a group of individuals that represent a small foreign faction. We ~~do~~ respect your bussiness [sic] but not the country that it serves. At this time we have your daughter in our posession [sic]. She is safe and unharmed and if you want her to see 1997, you must follow our instructions to the letter.

You will withdraw $118,000.00 from your account. $100,000 will be in $100 bills and the remaining $18,000 in $20 bills. Make sure that you bring an adequate size attache to the bank. When you get home you will put the money in a brown paper bag. I will call you between 8 and 10 am tomorrow to instruct you on delivery. The delivery will be exhausting so I advise you to be rested. If we monitor you getting the money early, we might call you early to arrange an earlier delivery of the money and hence a [sic] earlier ~~delivery~~ pick-up of your daughter.

Any deviation of my instructions will result in the immediate execution of your daughter. You will also be denied her remains for proper burial. The two gentlemen watching over your daughter do not particularly like you so I advise you not to provoke them. Speaking to anyone about your situation, such as Police, F.B.I., etc., will result in your daughter being beheaded. If we catch you talking to a stray dog, she dies. If you alert bank authorities, she dies. If the money is in any way marked or tampered with, she dies. You will be scanned for electronic devices and if any are found, she dies. You can try to deceive us but be warned that we are familiar with Law enforcement countermeasures and tactics. You stand a 99% chance of killing your daughter if you try to out smart us. Follow our instructions and you stand a 100% chance of getting her back. You and your family are under constant scrutiny as well as the authorities. Don't try to grow a brain John. You are not the only fat cat around so don't think that killing will be difficult. Don't underestimate us John. Use that good southern common sense of yours. It is up to you now John!

Victory!
S.B.T.C.

At the Boulder PD, Sergeant Paul Reichenbach, the patrol supervisor, pushed aside his end-of-shift paperwork when he heard the dispatcher's unusual call and headed for his car.

While Reichenbach drove to the house, Mrs. Ramsey was telling

Officer French that she had gone into JonBenét's bedroom at 5:45 A.M. to awaken her daughter because the family planned to fly to Michigan that morning. The bedroom was empty, and when she descended a spiral staircase, she found the note on a lower rung. John Ramsey said he had checked the house, and it appeared to still be locked as he had left it the night before. He saw no sign of a forced entry or a struggle. The alarm system had not been engaged, their small dog had spent the night at a neighbor's home, and the Ramseys had heard nothing unusual during the night.

French stepped away from them to meet Sergeant Reichenbach at the front door and confirmed that it looked as if there might have been a kidnapping. But, he observed, "Something isn't right."

———

Patsy Ramsey had made two more telephone calls immediately after contacting the police, despite the explicit warning in the ransom note that her child would be "beheaded" if she so much as spoke to a stray dog. She called her friends Fleet and Priscilla White, at whose home the family had attended a party the night before, then also alerted two other close friends, John and Barbara Fernie. All four were asked to hurry over, and they did. If kidnappers had been watching, the sudden arrival of two police cars and a covey of friends would have told them the dire warnings in their note were being disregarded.

———

Reichenbach thought about his next move as he read the ransom note. The patrol sergeant knew he was going to need a lot more help, and on this day, of all days, that could be a problem.

Not only did the discovery of the note hit almost exactly when the shifts were about to change, but it caught the police department at one of its weakest staffing periods—Christmas. Every cop who could arrange it was off for the holidays, leaving a minimum of officers on duty.

He called for more officers, crime scene technicians to search for evidence, and victim advocates to comfort and help the Ramseys; alerted the phone company to put a trap on the Ramsey telephone; and notified the on-call detective supervisor, Sergeant Bob Whitson. Further radio traffic was ordered to cease to prevent the kidnappers from picking up police broadcasts with a scanner. Communication would be by phone, and therefore less effective. As other police arrived, they considered the behavior of the parents. While the father seemed calm and composed, he was not comforting the mother, who had dissolved into an emotional mess, lying alone on the floor in a nearby room, hugging pillows, clutching a crucifix, and wailing.

Reichenbach and John Ramsey went up to the second floor to look into the missing child's bedroom. Two beds were parallel and about three feet apart. One was made, and the other's peach comforter was pulled back toward a pillow at the foot, exposing a white fitted sheet printed with cartoon characters. A small blue fanny pack was looped over a bedpost, a white steamer trunk gaped slightly, and a large Christmas tree decorated with angels and snowflakes stood beside green curtains and a closed door to a covered balcony that was glazed with undisturbed frost. Dolls and clothes lay about the room. Folding closet doors on the opposite wall stood open, revealing more clothes on hangars and in heaps. Strewn amid the toys were trophies and little tiaras. On a wall above a white chest of drawers was a formal portrait of the missing girl, a beautiful child with a bright smile, chin resting on lace-gloved hands.

The father lifted the dust ruffle to peer beneath his daughter's bed and was told not to touch anything else. They left the room as a telephone rang, and Ramsey answered. "JonBenét's been kidnapped," he said and began crying. The lights were off in the nearby bedroom of the second child, and Reichenbach looked in on Burke Ramsey, who appeared asleep, then closed that door.

The sergeant found no evidence of forced entry during a walk through the house, then went outside. A light dusting of snow and frost lay atop an earlier crusty snow in spotty patches on the grass. He saw no fresh shoe impressions, found no open doors or windows, nothing to indicate a break-in, but walking on the driveway and sidewalks left no visible prints. It was frigid, about nine degrees, and Reichenbach returned inside.

He went down into the sprawling basement and walked through it. At the far end was a white door secured at the top by a block of wood that pivoted on a screw. Reichenbach tried to open the door, stopped when he felt resistance, then returned upstairs. Reichenbach, Officer French, and one of the friends Patsy had called, Fleet White, would all check that white door in the basement during the morning, and White would even open it. They found nothing.

———————

By the time the sun rose at 6:30, the Whites and Fernies had arrived to comfort their friends. Their admittance to the house was also a mistake, for the place had become the scene of a crime, apparently a kidnapping.

Good police procedure would have been to empty the house immediately and take the inhabitants to the police station, post a patrol officer inside the front door, and allow entry only to authorized personnel. Another perimeter should have been established some distance away to preserve the grounds. No one knew at this point what evidence, such as footprints or fibers, might yet be found, and the crime scene was put at risk by allowing the friends to come inside.

As if to demonstrate that problem, Fleet White stepped away from the little group attending the Ramseys and took a walk inside the house, certainly with the best of intentions. No one had told him not to. His own little girl, JonBenét's best friend, had temporarily disappeared the year before, and he vividly remembered the fear he endured until Daphne was found hiding. Maybe JonBenét was doing the same thing, just playfully hiding somewhere.

White went downstairs. The lights were on, and shadows danced in the big basement. A small broken window in a large room where a model railroad was laid out caught his attention, and on the floor beneath the window he found a piece of glass, which he placed on the ledge. He dropped to his hands and knees, searching for other pieces, and moved a suitcase in doing so.

Unknowingly, he was altering a vital part of the crime scene. In coming months, claims would be made that a mysterious intruder came through that window and used the suitcase as a step.

Moving deeper into the basement, he found the same white door that had been checked by Sergeant Reichenbach. Fleet White turned the makeshift latch and pulled the door open, toward him. It was totally dark inside, and when he could find neither of two light switches, he closed the door, relatched it, and went back upstairs. He never saw JonBenét.

By 6:45 two victim advocates from the police department had arrived, and the population inside the house continued to swell. Five minutes later, as a crime scene tech dusted for fingerprints, one of the advocates followed along, tidying up with a spray cleaner and a cloth. It was a terrible breach of procedure—possible trace evidence was being erased in the name of neatness.

Another tech saw the ransom note on the bottom step of the spiral staircase and photographed it there. But the photograph lied. The note had traveled from the stairs, possibly into Patsy's hands, then had been spread out on the hallway floor where John Ramsey and the police had read it, and French had put it back on the stairs. The photograph, which was supposed to show exactly where evidence had been discovered, was inaccurate.

The Reverend Rol Hoverstock, pastor of St. John's Episcopal Church, arrived as an officer left to take the ransom note to police headquarters. The minister was also allowed into the home, adding to the crowd.

Police mistakes piled up at an alarming rate, the crime scene was disintegrating, and no one had taken firm control. Instead of shutting the place down tight and preserving evidence, police were treading gingerly in the lavish home of a wealthy couple. The scene was seriously compromised before the investigation even really started.

———

Sergeant Whitson summoned Detectives Fred Patterson and Linda Arndt, then called other relevant personnel from the sheriff's department and the FBI, along with Deputy District Attorney Pete Hofstrom and the city's public information officer, Leslie Aaholm. He requested that the senior command staff be alerted by pager.

At 7:33 a K-9 unit with a tracking dog was put on standby, but not used. Had the dog been put to work immediately, there was a strong chance it would have followed the scent of the missing child from her bed right to the basement room where her body was. Another error.

One minute after that, an available officer who had just come onto the day shift headed for the scene, but radio silence was broken when she was told en route that no more officers were necessary. Cops were being turned away instead of summoned.

———

Detectives Patterson and Arndt linked up at headquarters, where Arndt picked up a photocopy of the ransom note. Then they drove to the parking lot of the Basemar shopping center, only six blocks from the Ramsey residence. Sergeant Reichenbach pulled alongside in his own car and gave them an overview of what was known so far.

———

At the house, another peculiar scene unfolded that left police bewildered. Burke Ramsey was awakened by his father and Fleet White, dressed, and was being taken from the house. Burke was one of only three people in the house at the time of the crime and therefore a witness who needed to be closely questioned about the disappearance of his sister. Perhaps he had heard or seen something during the night that could help investigators find JonBenét. So when Officer Rick French saw him being taken away, he went over to talk to the boy. But John Ramsey intervened. The father told the policeman that Burke didn't know anything and had slept through it all, and he hustled the boy to a waiting vehicle. It was one of the poignant moments of the morning. His sister was thought to be the victim of a terrorist kidnapping, but Burke was exiled to the White's home, an unprotected location, where he would be watched over by friends instead of police. Whatever he knew went away with him. I would later wonder why the parents had not awakened the boy immediately upon discovering that JonBenét was missing.

––––––––

At 8:03 Sergeant Whitson telephoned John Eller, the detective division commander, who was in the midst of a two-week vacation with family members from Florida, celebrating the holidays and his grandson's first birthday. The Christmas spirit faded when he learned that the six-year-old daughter of a local business owner had been kidnapped. There was no sign of struggle or a forced entry, a long ransom note was asking for $118,000, and the kidnappers would call. Detectives Patterson and Arndt were on the way, and the FBI and the DA's office had been alerted. The money was being arranged, and the phones were being trapped. No details had been given about delivering the ransom.

Eller gave Whitson a list of things to do: Put a detective on the Ramseys, never to leave their side, and get undercover narcotics detectives out for surveillance. Confirm that the phones were tapped, and contact the sheriff's office. Have a helicopter on standby, get a recent photo of the child, and put a transponder on a car that would deliver the ransom. Check the victim's medical records, and determine if there were any custody disputes. Get scanners and cell phones, and make early preparations for a possible major media broadcast. Eller wrote down each point as he spoke.

As he hung up, he realized that the sergeant he had been talking to was from the narcotics squad, not Sergeant Larry Mason, the acting commander in the detective division during Eller's absence. On the margin of his Daytimer, Eller wrote and circled, "Where is Mason?"

––––––––

Detectives Arndt and Patterson arrived at the Ramsey house at 8:10 A.M., and Officer Rick French gave them an updated briefing. Then, with detectives finally on the scene to handle the witnesses, French checked the garage and lower levels of the house, looking for places through which a kidnapper might have carried off the child. He found none. The house was messy, but he saw no sign of a struggle.

In the basement he also came to the white door at the far end that was closed and secured at the top by the wooden block on a screw. French was looking for exit points from the house, and the door obviously was not one. No one could have gone through that door, closed it behind them, and locked it on the opposite side by turning the wooden latch, so he did not open it.

When he went back upstairs, the patrolman noticed Patsy Ramsey watching him through parted fingers that covered her face. "Eyeballing" him, he would later recall.

———

Things quieted somewhat in the house following the shock of the kidnapping and the sudden arrival of police and the Ramseys' friends.

It had been difficult to get information from the parents at first, but now several officers and detectives were speaking with them, pulling together elements of what had happened.

It soon became clear that Patsy Ramsey had changed a very important part of her story and that her statements about her initial movements were inconsistent. It raised some doubts when investigators compared their notes. She originally told Officer French that she checked the bedroom *before* finding the note on the stairs, but she later told Detective Arndt that she went downstairs and found the note first and only then hurried to the bedroom and found JonBenét gone.

An equally important point, made by John Ramsey, was repeated to three different officers. He told French, Arndt, and later Sergeant Whitson that he had personally checked the doors the previous night and all were secure. When three cops get the same information during separate conversations with the same person, I view it as a consistent story. Months later, in an official interview, Ramsey would deny saying it to any of them.

Patsy also told officers she thought the house was locked when they went to bed. No keys had been lost or stolen, John Ramsey told both French and Arndt, and the only people who had keys other than the immediate family were Patsy's mother and his oldest son, both of whom were out of state, and the housekeeper, Linda Hoffmann-Pugh.

Officers reconstructed some of the timeline of the previous night from the parents' recollections. John Ramsey said the family returned home from the party about ten o'clock, and he read to both children before they went to sleep. He confirmed to Arndt that he had read to JonBenét after tucking her in. He would later deny those statements as well.

The parents said that everyone was in bed by ten-thirty because they had to be up early for a flight to Michigan, where they had planned to spend a belated Christmas at their vacation home with Ramsey's older children, then go to Florida for a cruise on Disney's Big Red Boat.

Patsy said that JonBenét went to sleep wearing long white underwear and a red turtleneck top.

———

Police were puzzled by the irregular ransom sum demanded by the kidnappers. The two friends, Fleet White and John Fernie, were equally mystified, for such an amount was relatively insignificant in comparison with the overall fortune of John Ramsey, who was a millionaire several times over. He was president and chief executive officer of Access Graphics, a local computer company with worldwide customers, more than 330 employees, and over a billion dollars in sales. Both John and Patsy told police they were unaware of any significance concerning the $118,000 figure.

At the suggestion of police, arrangements were made with the La-fayette State Bank to prepare the ransom cash but to hold it until further notice.

Detective Arndt instructed John Ramsey on how to handle the phone call expected from the kidnapper: Demand to speak to the child. Get specific instructions for a meeting to deliver the ransom. Say he could not get the money until five o'clock that afternoon. Write down what the caller said. Ramsey seemed distracted, but his manner re-mained cordial, and she felt he understood her.

While Ramsey's language was clear and articulate, and he even smiled and joked, his overwrought wife was in the care of Priscilla White and Barbara Fernie. She looked vacant and dazed, repeatedly asking in a soft, empty voice, "Why didn't I hear my baby?" Despite her obvious distress, her husband did not go to her. It was as if the house had separated into two camps, His and Hers, with the friends dividing their time between the two. Patsy stayed in the sunroom, and John paced the dining room and den. It has been my experience that in situations where a child has been injured or killed, the parents cling to each other, so police considered the physical distance between John and Patsy Ramsey to be remarkable under the stressful conditions.

When detectives asked the parents who might be responsible for the disappearance of JonBenét, Patsy promptly gave the name of her house-keeper for the past two years, Linda Hoffmann-Pugh, who had recently asked for a $2,000 loan. The handwriting in the ransom note, the mother said, also looked a little like the housekeeper's.

The Reverend Rol Hoverstock told police about a phone call made that morning to Patsy's parents, Nedra and Don Paugh, in Atlanta. Mrs. Paugh, he said, mentioned that Linda Hoffmann-Pugh had commented about how beautiful JonBenét was and expressed the fear that someone might kidnap her. The housekeeper's name had come up several times in a short period, and police had already been told she had a key. She became the first suspect, and police made plans to contact her immediately.

A second name offered was that of Jeff Merrick, who had been terminated by Ramsey's company several months before in an unpleasant parting. They wrote his name down too.

Detective Arndt asked Ramsey, White, and Fernie for their opinions of the ransom note. White and Fernie commented that it seemed to reveal a familiarity with John Ramsey. The use of such words as *hence* and *attache* indicated the writer was educated. John Ramsey had little to say about it and was unusually quiet. None had any idea what SBTC meant.

In the sunroom, Patsy Ramsey examined a second-generation photocopy of the ransom note, a smeary version that showed little more than the dark printed words. Rather than commenting on the words and content, she told one of her friends that the note was written on the same kind of paper she had in her kitchen. Police would wonder how she could tell, since they saw no similarities.

Detectives also drove through the neighborhood with a video camera, documenting people and vehicles in the area and looking for anything suspicious. Sergeant Larry Mason, the acting detective division commander, was finally alerted at his home by the staff page and telephoned headquarters to find out what was happening. A few minutes later he went to the police department.

Time was passing swiftly, and the two-hour window during which the kidnappers had said they would call was about to expire.

Ten o'clock came and went. Detective Arndt thought it strange that no one, including the Ramseys, seemed to pay any attention to the deadline.

The ransom note had been unclear about the contact date, saying only that the kidnappers would call "between 8 and 10 am tomorrow." When that would was would depend on the "today" when it was written. It could mean December 27 as easily as December 26. But why would parents desperate to contact their child not assume that it meant the current day?

Thirty minutes later the bedroom of JonBenét was sealed with yellow tape. More than four hours elapsed before any part of the big house was officially designated as a crime scene.

Since no call had been received from the kidnappers, police began moving back to the department for a strategy session that would involve the various agencies now working the kidnapping. The two victim advocates soon left for lunch.

Detective Linda Arndt was now alone with seven adults—the Ramseys, the Whites, the Fernies, and the minister. There was no way only one officer could keep track of them all, and Arndt would realize she had lost John Ramsey.

Patsy moved into the rear den and lay on the couch, attended by her friends. She said she was having second thoughts about the housekeeper being the author of the note.

Around noon Arndt used a cell phone to page Sergeant Mason, now at police headquarters, for an update and to get more cops back at the house, but she received no response. Thirty minutes later she repeated the page, and it too went unanswered. The order for radio silence denied her the direct communication she needed. She had not carried a radio pack set with her.

————

Detective Arndt could not account for John Ramsey until about noon. She found him reading some correspondence, and she incorrectly assumed he had stepped out to get his mail. She was unaware that the house did not have an exterior mail box and that the mail came in through a front door slot. Ramsey had been out of contact for over an hour. In coming months, we realized that the time lapse would have allowed Ramsey plenty of time to roam his house.

Arndt noted a marked change in Ramsey's attitude when she saw him again. Whereas he had been calm and collected earlier, he now sat alone in the dining room, preoccupied in thought, his leg bouncing nervously.

At one o'clock that afternoon, Arndt enlisted Fleet White to help keep Ramsey's mind occupied. Making a decision for which she would later be heavily criticized, she suggested they go through the house "from top to bottom" to see if they could find anything belonging to the missing girl. No police officer was available to escort them, which meant the two civilians would be roaming the house unsupervised.

John Ramsey was on the move at once and headed immediately for the basement, starting at the bottom of the house instead of the top as the detective had suggested. Fleet White followed him down.

———

The basement was a warren of rooms, closets, nooks, and crawl spaces. When Ramsey and White reached the bottom of the stairs, they had several choices of which way to go.

To their left was a tiny bathroom, only a sink and a toilet with a little window above it. To their right was a narrow closet, a laundry room with washer and dryer, and a storage area.

Straight ahead were a pair of open doors. The left one went into a hallway that led to the boiler and freezer area. At the end of this corridor was the white door that had been checked earlier by two police officers and Fleet White.

Ramsey and White walked through the right-hand door instead, which led into a large, oddly shaped room containing a model train setup and a couple of small closets. Weak winter sunlight filtered through the triple window, which was set into the west wall below ground level, looking out on a window well and protected by a metal grate.

Each window had four panes, and Fleet White, having been down there earlier, pointed out the baseball-sized hole in the upper left pane of the middle window. "Damn it, I had to break that," John Ramsey said, adding that it had happened the previous summer when he kicked in the window to get into the house after locking himself out. Should have fixed it then, he noted, tapping his forehead. The window was closed but unlatched.

They moved out of the train room, turned into the other hallway, and John Ramsey headed toward the white door at the far end. Fleet White was several steps behind. Ramsey turned the wooden latch, opened the door, and screamed, "Oh my God, oh my God!"

Fleet ran to him and saw the body of JonBenét lying on her back in the small windowless room. Her arms were straight above the top of her head.

Earlier, when White had opened that same door, he had been unable to see anything in the stygian darkness. John Ramsey was kneeling beside his daughter, feeling her ashen face. A piece of black duct tape lay on the blanket, and a long cord was attached to her right wrist. Nearby was a pink nightgown. White, who had never before touched a dead person, felt JonBenét's cold ankle, turned, and ran for help. John Ramsey picked up his daughter, who had been carefully wrapped, papoose-like, in a white blanket, and followed.

———

Detective Linda Arndt, still working with a cell telephone instead of a police radio, was waiting for her pages to be returned when she heard a shout. The panicked Fleet White ran up the stairs, grabbed a telephone and punched in a few numbers, then hung up. He ran back toward the basement, yelling for someone to call an ambulance, as if he had forgotten a detective was standing right there.

Patsy Ramsey was in the den with her friends, and when White shouted, Priscilla White and Barbara Fernie hurried toward the sound. Patsy did not move from the couch.

John Ramsey emerged from the basement carrying the body of Jon-Benét, not cradled close but held away from him, his hands gripping her waist. The child's head was above his, facing him, her arms were raised high, stiffened by rigor mortis, and her lips were blue. The child was obviously dead.

Arndt ordered Ramsey to put the body down on the floor near the front door and told Fleet White to guard the basement door. Instead, White ran back down to the little cellar room, picked up the black tape, and stared at it. By doing so, White unknowingly mishandled a critical piece of evidence.

Linda Arndt felt the body for a neck pulse, noticed the odor of decay, and chose to move the body into the living room herself. She lay the dead child on her back, on a rug before the Christmas tree.

This was another huge error. In a normal murder investigation, the body should have been left untouched as it was found in the basement. Now it had been moved upstairs by the father, then moved again by a detective who should have known better than to touch it at all. Each time it was moved, the crime scene changed and potential evidence was put in jeopardy.

The detective and the father were face-to-face over the body, and he asked if his daughter was alive. When Arndt confirmed that she was dead, John Ramsey groaned softly. He told Arndt, "It has to be an inside job."

Three years later Arndt described the event differently on national television, revealing information she never put in her police reports. "As we looked at each other, I wore a shoulder holster, I remember tucking my gun right next to me and consciously counting I've got eighteen bullets," she said. "I didn't know if we'd all be alive when people showed up. . . . Everything made sense in that instant, and I knew what happened."

A guttural wail came from Patsy on the far side of the house, and the detective told Ramsey to call 911, then go to his wife. He was back within two minutes, grabbed a blanket from a chair, and tossed it over the body before Arndt could react.

It was one of the most damaging things that could have been done and created a forensics nightmare. By covering the body, Ramsey compromised the already despoiled crime scene even more. Now the possibility existed that any fibers left on the blanket by some unknown person's clothing might have been transferred from the blanket to the body. Arndt compounded the error by adjusting the quilt so the body was covered from the neck down. When someone else spread a gray Colorado Avalanche sweatshirt over the exposed feet a few minutes later, it became virtually impossible to prove the origin of almost any fiber that might be found on the clothing and much of the body.

And the mistakes continued. The body itself was now a crime scene and should have been declared totally off-limits, even to the distraught parents, until it could be professionally examined. But Ramsey knelt beside his daughter and stroked her hair, then lay down and put his arm around her. Arndt thought he was crying but saw no tears. He came to his knees, peered around, then hugged JonBenét and called her his little angel. No matter what his motive, he was altering things that should have been left untouched.

The others were coming down the hallway, Patsy Ramsey being held upright by her friends. On reaching the body, she fell across her daughter, substantially adding to the possibility of fiber transfers. The blanket, the sweatshirt, the personal close contact of the parents—all were extraordinarily damaging to the future evidence collection process.

Arndt simply could not control this many people, and her calls for help had not yet been returned. Barbara Fernie tugged at her arm, pleading with her not to leave them, and a shaken Fleet White was in the next room. To restore some order, the detective asked Father Hoverstock to lead a prayer, and she stood beside the piano to watch. *"Our Father, Who art in Heaven . . ."*

Patsy Ramsey rose to her knees, her arms straight overhead, and called out, "Jesus! You raised Lazarus from the dead, raise my baby from the dead!" The woman seemed ready to swoon.

Arndt used the cell phone to call 911. The absence of a police radio created another crisis, for had she been able to broadcast "156. Code 10. 755 Fifteenth Street," the cavalry would instantly have been on the way. But instead of reaching Boulder, her cell call bounced to neighboring Weld County, which was uninvolved in the case, and a few minutes later she saw an ambulance cruise past the house. The paramedics had been given the wrong address.

Arndt placed a second 911 call, this time got Boulder, reported the child's death, and requested detectives, the coroner, and an ambulance. The dispatcher issued a Code Black to designate the call as a homicide, and a few minutes later, at 1:20 P.M., Officer Barry Weiss rushed in through a rear door, calling her name.

4

The case was breaking wide open on two different fronts. About the same time Ramsey found the body of his daughter, a detective discovered what would mark a turning point in the investigation, the existence of a possible practice ransom note in a tablet belonging to Patsy Ramsey.

When Sergeant Bob Whitson had arrived at the house, he asked for handwriting samples of John and Patsy Ramsey, standard procedure to begin eliminating people as possible authors of the ransom note. Without hesitation John Ramsey had picked up two tablets of white lined paper—one from a countertop and the other from a hallway table a few steps from the spiral staircase—and handed them to the policeman. Whitson scribbled *John* across the top of one, which contained business notes Ramsey said he had made, and *Patsy* atop the second, on which the first four pages were covered with doodles, lists, and other writing in a feminine hand. Both pads were taken to the police department and given to Detective Jeff Kithcart, our forgery and fraud investigator, who put them aside while he completed more pressing jobs.

Just before the big briefing was to begin, Kithcart reviewed the tablets. They seemed ordinary enough, apparently the same kind of paper on which the ransom note had been written. He flipped through the one bearing the word *Patsy* and, in the middle, noticed a page with a partial salutation written by a black felt-tip pen.

Mr. and Mrs. I

The single vertical line seemed as if it could be the downstroke that would start the capital letter R. To Kithcart it looked like the start of another ransom note, and it was in a tablet belonging to the mother of the missing child. *How did it get in there?* He quickly headed toward the conference room, thinking that perhaps something more than a kidnapping was at work, but before he could share his find, the Code Black came in.

———

Police cars, fire trucks, and an ambulance swarmed around 755 Fifteenth Street. A Santa Claus doll watched blankly from a small sleigh on the snowy lawn as uniformed officers walked between the giant candy canes and paper-bag luminarias. Green vines gripped the Tudor brick facade, and a giant wreath hung on the front door that led into the living room where the dead body of a little girl lay beside a gaily decorated Christmas tree.

Sergeant Larry Mason, the acting detective bureau commander, and a supervisory agent from the Denver FBI office arrived as paramedics tended to the distraught Patsy Ramsey, who was clinging to her child. Mason and the FBI agent went downstairs and surveyed the small dank room in which the body had been discovered.

Commander John Eller received his second telephone call on the case when a detective advised him that a body had been found. Just after hanging up, Eller heard the phone ring again, and Police Chief Tom Koby said, "John, I think they need your help in there." Eller was out the door. He would not see his family again for five days.

At the Ramsey house a detective overheard John Ramsey on the telephone at 1:40 P.M., telling his pilot to ready his plane for a flight to Atlanta. Ramsey was soon told to cancel that flight, but police would consider the action suspicious. Why would a father whose child had just been murdered be readying an airplane to get out of town? It made no sense.

With the discovery of the murder, a comprehensive search of the house was imperative, but warrants take time, and a legal shortcut was considered. When signed by the property owner, a "consent to search" form grants the needed permission but carries the risk that the owner might later claim coercion because of police pressure. Warrants are infinitely better.

Detective Tom Trujillo arrived on Fifteenth Street with the consent form at 2:15 P.M., just as the parents emerged from the house. He gave the form to Sergeant Mason, who handed it to John Ramsey, who read and signed it. Ramsey would eventually say he thought he had been signing an authorization for an autopsy.

John Ramsey's adult children, John Andrew Ramsey and Melinda Ramsey, along with Melinda's fiancé, Stewart Long, had just arrived by taxi from the Denver airport. They had flown from Atlanta to Minneapolis that morning en route to meeting the family at the vacation place in Charlevoix, Michigan, but the tragic news caught up with them at the Minneapolis airport. They made an emergency flight to Colorado.

Patsy Ramsey, wearing a long fur coat, walked out sobbing uncontrollably and still leaning on her friends. She climbed into a car and was driven away. Her husband got into a van, and the coterie of family and friends relocated to the Fernie residence in South Boulder, on Tin Cup Circle.

It was perhaps the most critical moment of the investigation. The crime had abruptly changed from kidnapping to murder, the place was surrounded by police, a detective sergeant and an FBI agent were there, yet the parents simply walked away. No one said a word to stop them, and they were not even going to police headquarters to be questioned. Important questions ranging from why that unexplained partial note was in Patsy's tablet to why John wanted to fly away from Boulder were left unanswered. In most child murders, parents resist leaving the body.

The parents had been treated with quiet respect throughout the morning, when it was thought their little girl had been kidnapped. Murder is treated much differently, and when a child dies, authorities *must* look at the parents. The FBI would tell us that only about 6 percent of all child murders are committed by strangers, while an overwhelming 54 percent are committed by family members. The investigation of such murders normally begins with those who live inside the home. Not this time.

By 2:35 P.M. the house was empty except for the body of JonBenét. Much too late, police officers were finally assigned to guard the doors.

————

At the police department ten minutes later, John Eller hung up his overcoat and headed for the Situation Room, where his detectives and various officers were gathering for a briefing.

A pair of Denver FBI agents wanted a word. Things had changed, they said, since the agency had first been notified that a federal crime, kidnapping, had been committed. "This is now a homicide," said one. "It's local, so it's not our case." Agent Ron Walker added, "Look at the parents. No bullshit, that's where you need to be." They promised future FBI assistance and left. A third agent, from Boulder, stuck around to help.

Eller got the briefing moving by giving Detective Mike Everett total crime scene responsibility for gathering physical evidence and assigning another detective to draft a search warrant for the house. The commander did not want his people going in with only a consent order that might blow up when challenged. He was also uncomfortable to learn that Tom Trujillo and Linda Arndt had already been designated as co–lead detectives at the scene. For some unknown personal reason, the two detectives were not on speaking terms. I knew both of them and thought they were a most unlikely match.

Eller looked around the room and saw not only cops but Pete Hofstrom and another prosecutor from the DA's office, more victim's advocates, and the city's public information officer. He noted that arrangements had to be made as soon as possible to interview the Ramseys individually at police headquarters.

The briefing was guided by what little was known. A warrant was suggested for the housekeeper's home in nearby Ft. Lupton, which the local cops had under surveillance, and another warrant was discussed for John Ramsey's office at Access Graphics. Police wanted handwriting samples, notes, pens and paper, tape, and cord. Within minutes they were off and running.

As hours passed, Commander Eller asked where the search warrants were and was told the district attorney's office was demanding a string of rewrites and revisions. He knew that a detective could normally hammer together such a warrant in an hour, but this one was stalled until the DA's office would turn it loose.

It was a dangerous and early indication that once again the Boulder Police Department and the Office of the Boulder County District Attorney were not going to mesh well on a major investigation, as the result of long-ingrained philosophical differences. That happened frequently in Boulder, and in this case it would have devastating consequences. In other jurisdictions where I've worked, prosecutors worked in the trenches alongside the cops, many of them even carrying badges and guns, putting on raid jackets when necessary, and getting their hands and boots dirty. Over the years in Boulder, however, the cops and prosecutors had learned it was best that they not work together, for their goals seldom seemed to be the same. Police were charged to apprehend suspects, while to the police, it seemed the prosecutors were more intent on refining a system of politically correct justice in a small, highly educated, mostly white town with a low crime rate. We were not a team.

Therefore the prosecutors had not gone to the Ramsey house immediately to give the police legal advice while a major felony investigation—the kidnapping of a child—was unfolding. But they were forever afterward highly critical of every mistake the officers made. My question about their twenty-twenty hindsight during the coming months was "Where were you when you were needed?" Had a deputy district attorney been on the scene supervising the legal points, perhaps things would have turned out differently.

———

Instead of focusing on the family, the police investigation was headed another way, toward Linda Hoffmann-Pugh, the Ramseys' housekeeper. Despite being overcome with grief, she furnished the startling information that the little girl had a problem wetting her bed. That was of great interest to the police. Often the fouling of a bed is seen in cases of incest, as a child tries to appear undesirable to an offender.

For the first six months Hoffmann-Pugh worked there, she said, JonBenét wet the bed every night, and Patsy even had the girl in pull-up diapers. Then the bed-wetting had stopped, but it had resumed about a month ago. When Hoffmann-Pugh arrived for work, she said, Patsy already had the bed stripped and the sheets going in the washing machine.

She told the police that the problem also extended to JonBenét soiling the bed, and recalled once finding fecal matter the size of a grapefruit on the sheets.

Hoffmann-Pugh had fallen apart with emotion at her home on Valle Drive in Ft. Lupton when two detectives told her that JonBenét was dead. This was what she had dreaded and warned the family about! The gorgeous child was allowed to roller-skate and ride her bike all alone, and the nightmare had come true. "My poor Patsy," she sobbed. "I love Patsy like my daughter."

Patsy had hired her away from a cleaning service crew known as Merry Maids about fourteen months earlier and had befriended her new housekeeper. Hoffmann-Pugh had dropped out of high school as a sophomore, married at age fifteen, and had six children. She was wearing a pair of Patsy's old shoes as she spoke to police.

The detectives quickly cleared up the question of the $2,000 loan she had recently requested from the Ramseys. Patsy had agreed to recover the loan from future weekly paychecks of $200. Hoffmann-Pugh was to use part of the money to pay the rent, and the rest would go for truck parts and some family dental work. Christmas dinner had been soft tacos because her husband had no teeth.

Mervin Pugh, the husband, was visibly intoxicated when he was interviewed, and the detectives knew he had had a few brushes with the law back in Michigan. "Is she missing or dead?" he asked. "How did she die, was it natural, strangulation, or what?" The questions were awfully close to the truth, close enough to raise police suspicion.

A blunt-spoken man in his fifties, Pugh had been in the Ramsey home a few times to help his wife, including a recent weekend when they spent three hours hauling Christmas decorations up from the basement. He said he didn't know the Ramseys but had been inside the house. "All you gotta do is turn around in that goddamn place and you don't know where you're going." His wife agreed it would be difficult to locate the storage room in which the body was found.

Both were cooperative and gave fingerprints, and unaware that she had been the first person named as a murder suspect, the housekeeper scratched out a compassionate note of condolence to Patsy. It was only a first interview. Police would be back.

The search warrant for the Ramsey residence was authorized at eight o'clock that night, and twenty-three minutes later, Dr. John Meyer, the coroner, put on protective booties and latex gloves and entered to perform the job of officially pronouncing the child dead.

The blanket was removed from the upper torso and the sweatshirt from the feet. The child wore a white long-sleeved shirt with a star of silver sequins on the chest, and long-john pants that appeared urine stained. When the body was turned over, police saw that a garrote was knotted tight around her neck. It had been fashioned from a thin cord tied to a narrow wooden stick about four inches long and splotched with colors, broken at one end, which had been used as a handle. A gold necklace and cross—a Christmas present—were entwined in the garrote. Abrasions were noted below the right earlobe and right jawline, and there was a small amount of blood around the nasal passages. White cord similar to the garrote was still tied around the right wrist. Small bits of lint and dust were on her bare feet, and her blond hair was done in two ponytails. The little body was zippered inside two plastic bags and taken away by the coroner's wagon. Meyer stayed only seven minutes, not taking the time to perform two routine procedures that would have helped establish the time of death—taking vitreous fluid from the eye and obtaining the internal body temperature. Determining the time frame in which death occurred is extraordinarily important in a murder investigation and would present a problem for months to come.

The body was taken to the coroner's facility in the basement of the Boulder Community Hospital and placed in a refrigerated drawer. The morgue log noted the arrival.

––––––––

Technicians began a ten-day search of the rambling house, but the crime scene had been thoroughly polluted by having so many people go in and out during the kidnap phase. Evidence such as the ransom note, the body, the suitcase in the basement, and the tape that covered the victim's mouth had all been moved. Who could tell what was real and what had been disturbed? The photographs that were taken were of a house, not a pristine crime scene.

Still, a technician went through the darkened house slowly with a video camera before the body was moved, producing a tape that was eerie in its juxtaposition of death amid the debris of what had been a happy Christmas.

On the stair landing just outside the victim's bedroom were a washer and dryer and some wall cabinets, and the door of one cabinet stood wide open, with a large package of pull-up diapers hanging halfway off the shelf. Police were struck by the oddity of diapers being used in a household with kids aged nine and six, particularly when viewed in light of the bed-fouling report about JonBenét. We had to determine if that was somehow related to her death.

On the bathroom counter lay a balled-up child's red turtleneck sweater. Although Patsy said JonBenét had gone to bed wearing a red turtleneck, the body was discovered in the same white pullover she had worn the evening before. Who had changed her clothes?

Downstairs in the basement, another technician examined the broken window. Three windows, each eighteen-by-thirty-inch rectangles, were in a row. The top left pane in the center window was broken, and the screen was off. The tech noticed pieces of glass outside the window and a scuff mark on the wall. The dust, film, and debris on the window-sill were undisturbed.

Outside, a detective examined the steel grate that covered the window well and found undisturbed cobwebs still attached from the grate to the bricks. The foliage around the grate also appeared undisturbed.

In the far corner of the basement, just outside the small room where the body had lain, Detective Mike Everett discovered a half-dozen oil paintings on canvas and an artist's plastic tote box belonging to Patsy. In the tote was a broken brush splotched by paint. Splinters were on the floor beside the tote. It was a major find because the broken brush matched the fractured end of the multicolored stick used in the garrote. The detective had found the source of part of the murder weapon and where it had been broken.

Because Detective Arndt had touched the body, another tech collected her jeans and black silk blouse, but not her footwear. It was important to take those garments because fibers from Arndt's clothing could be used for elimination purposes against any fiber discovered on the body. In another astonishing lapse of procedure, however, no one had collected the clothing worn by either of the Ramseys, both of whom had been in direct contact with the body as it lay in the living room. A huge legal fight would ensue over the coming months as we sought to retrieve their clothing, particularly Patsy's red turtleneck sweater, her black-and-red–checked blazer, and any fur garments. They would eventually assume tremendous importance.

Police officers also canvassed the neighborhood. An elderly couple across the street said they had seen John Ramsey's older son and Jon-Benét's half-brother, John Andrew Ramsey, at the Ramsey home on Christmas Day. Another neighbor, Melody Stanton, whose bedroom faced the Ramsey home from across the street, did not want to get involved with the investigation and told police that she heard nothing unusual during the night. She would soon revise her statement to say that she had heard a child scream.

———

While the Ramseys were at the Fernies' home on Tin Cup Circle, John Eller sought the opportunity to put cops with the family around the clock so the officers could report what they saw and heard. Throughout the night of December 26 they watched John and Patsy alternately sleeping, roaming the halls, and just sitting around, seemingly lost to the world. The parents said little to each other.

Patsy was in a stupor on the living room floor after taking a Valium issued by Dr. Francesco Beuf, her children's pediatrician and a family friend. John Ramsey also took a couple of Valium and walked through the house drinking scotch, occasionally stumbling. Once, a police officer overheard him cry softly, "I'm sorry. . . . I'm so very sorry." John Fernie and Dr. Beuf took him for a short walk outside.

———

Months would pass before we learned that only a few hours after the body of JonBenét was found, an attorney representing the Ramseys was already on the scene making calls.

Fleet and Priscilla White had returned to their home by six o'clock, and after telling their children that JonBenét had gone to heaven, they received a call from a local lawyer named Mike Bynum. He wanted to know if they were OK and had everything they needed. That evening, Bynum joined the family and friends gathered at Tin Cup Circle.

Later the Whites told us they were interviewed the following day, December 27, by a three-person team of private investigators and attorneys representing the Ramseys. While police were barely getting the investigation cranked up and had yet to have any serious interviews with John or Patsy Ramsey, legal help was being summoned and was in the field, locking crucial witnesses into their stories.

At about 9 P.M. John lay beside Patsy for about ten minutes but then got up and left her again. Nothing was said between them. He went to the Denver airport with friends to pick up other family members. Patsy awakened an hour later and asked where her son and husband were, then sobbed, "Why did they do this? Why did they do this?" She wanted more pills but was told she had to wait.

Patsy's two sisters, Pam and Polly, arrived from Atlanta about 11 P.M., and instantly demanded to know from a police officer if suspects had been found and if the FBI was involved. The two sisters settled in beside Patsy and read the Bible to her, all three waving their arms in the air and moaning. One said she had a vision in which JonBenét was an angel. A police officer later noticed that the Bible verses dealt with forgiveness.

John Ramsey returned at midnight. He and Patsy took more Valium and fell asleep on the floor. Family members stayed close, praying. Patsy would awaken occasionally and ask for more Valium, declaring she just wanted "to stay asleep." She said she no longer had a reason to live.

The worst thing that could happen to the Boulder Police Department had just exploded and there was going to be hell to pay.

At police headquarters, John Eller weighed the damage. He had worked in Boulder for many years since working for the big-city police department in Miami, and knew what it took to handle a case such as this.

He knew there was a lack of tough front-line experience in this city where nonconfrontation with citizens was almost insisted upon. Since the appointment of Tom Koby as a New Age police chief in 1991, Eller had watched with dismay as the Boulder Police Department became divided into "meat eaters," who took care of business, and "grazers," who organized ice cream socials and shied away from real street police work. Boulder had just the kind of gentle justice system it wanted, but it was woefully unprepared to handle a monster homicide case.

The timidity of the officers was further complicated by a district attorney's office that was tightly connected to the community of defense lawyers and plea-bargained almost everything. Many cops didn't trust the prosecutors. And some of us felt you almost had to have a videotape of a murder, a full confession, and an affidavit from the victim to get a homicide case to go forward in Boulder. Eller expected little help from the DA.

Eller also realized that the officers who responded to the Ramsey home that morning were all products of Boulder-style policing, which had them trained not to be assertive or confrontational. The lack of aggressiveness in those early hours may have doomed the investigation before it started. As a future police chief would observe some months down the line, "Our department wasn't ready for something like this."

All of that was irrelevant, however, for no matter what the situation, the case was now Eller's to pursue. He examined the roster. He had a couple of gold circle detectives already on the job but decided he needed a few more meat-eaters.

At this point in the Ramsey homicide case I was not involved. I was working as an undercover narcotics cop, with a uniform of unshaven face, long hair, and jeans. Furthermore, I was on vacation.

I first heard about it that evening as my new wife and I ferried a bed (a Christmas gift from my father) back home from Denver. Driving west toward the Rocky Mountains as night fell, I heard a grim radio report about the murder of a six-year-old girl in the Boulder home of her wealthy parents, apparently the victim of a kidnapping attempt gone bad.

I wondered who had caught it, because a police department is a pretty lonely place during the holidays. But every detective is intrigued by a murder in his town, and something didn't sound right. Why would a kidnapper who wanted ransom money murder his victim and leave the body at the crime scene? Even dead, the body was valuable collateral because the family, unaware of the death, might still pay the money.

5

The coroner, Dr. John Meyer, hardly noticed the detectives, other investigators, and DA staff members who stood in the autopsy room in the basement of the Boulder Community Hospital as he began trying to determine how JonBenét had died. In most murders a single cause of death, such as a gunshot wound, is relatively obvious before the first autopsy cut is made. Meyer was about to uncover not one but two possible causes of death, heightening the mystery surrounding the little girl's murder.

It was the morning of December 27. The little body was first removed from a locked yellow outer covering, then from an inner black bag. The paper sacks were removed from the hands and feet, and Meyer began describing his findings.

The victim weighed forty-five pounds, was three feet, eleven inches tall, and had green eyes, and some green garland was caught in her blond hair. A single loop of white cord was around the right wrist, tied on top of the sleeve but so loosely the doctor easily slid it free. There were 15½ inches between that loop and a loop on the other end, which once apparently had bound the left wrist. A white cord of the same type was wrapped so tightly around the throat and neck that a deep horizontal furrow had been dug into the skin. A gold chain and cross were tangled in that ligature, which was tied behind the neck to a broken stick. Blond hair was snared in the knot, and the coroner had to cut the hair in order to remove the cord, which was tied more like a noose than a twisting garrote. The broken paintbrush used as the garrote handle had *Korea* printed on it.

When Meyer clipped the nails of each finger, no blood or tissue was found that would indicate a struggle. He used the same clippers for all the fingers, although doing so created an issue of cross-contamination. For optimal DNA purposes, separate and sterile clippers should have been used for each finger. Furthermore, we later learned that the coroner's office sometimes used the same clippers on different autopsy subjects.

A heart was drawn in red ink on the palm of the victim's left hand, she wore a gold ring on her right middle finger, and a gold bracelet was on her wrist. It was a gift from her Aunt Pam, engraved "JonBenét 12-25-96."

The long underwear and a pair of oversized floral panties with *Wednesday* printed on them were both stained by urine, and the panties had red stains in the crotch. Meyer found the vagina slightly discolored and noted an abrasion at the seven o'clock position of the hymeneal opening, along with some red liquid consistent with blood. It appeared that the vaginal area had been wiped, and small dark fibers were collected from her pubic region.

Detective Trujillo then scanned the body with ultraviolet light and saw fluorescent markings along the thighs. Such light is useful in observing fluid not visible to the naked eye, and Trujillo thought he saw traces of semen. Samples were taken for testing. Any presence of semen on the victim would indicate a male attacker.

The stomach was empty, but the coroner found what appeared to be chunks of pineapple in the upper digestive tract. This also would be tested in an effort to determine to what extent the food had been digested, a key indicator in helping establish the time of death. Police would need to identify what she had eaten the day before, when, and where.

Abrasions were noted on the face and shoulder, as were two small rectangular ones on the back, a triangular abrasion on the neck, and a scratch on the lower left leg.

There had been a surprising lack of blood for such a violent murder. The child did not seem to have been beaten, and when the coroner examined the eyelids, he found the pinpoint petechial hemorrhaging that indicated she was still alive and her heart pumping when she was choked. The garrote was the most obvious cause of death.

So the viewers at the autopsy were astonished when Meyer peeled back the scalp and discovered that the entire upper right side of her skull had been crushed by some enormous blow that left a well-defined rectangular pattern. The brain had massively hemorrhaged, but the blood had been contained within the skull. The caved-in skull was a second, and totally unexpected, possible cause of death.

Meyer concluded that JonBenét was alive at the time her head was struck and was still alive when she was choked. Either attack would have been fatal, but he officially called it asphyxia due to strangulation associated with massive head trauma. He could not establish a time of death.

———

In the police department's Community Room, the press was gathered in force as Commander Eller prepared for his first and only news conference on the Ramsey case. Few crimes had ever attracted the kind of media attention this one was drawing. It had already spread beyond the circulation area of the local newspaper and beyond the sphere of the two big papers in Denver, just down Highway 36. The murder had become national news, more out-of-town reporters were arriving by the hour, and the deluge was just beginning. For weeks, months, and years to come, the media would promote JonBenét Ramsey to the postmortem status usually reserved for celebrities.

Eller needed a photograph of the child but thought most of the pictures in a stack he was handed were rather unseemly. Instead of a glamour shot, he chose one in which JonBenét looked like a little girl: a nice smile on a pretty face that was framed by golden hair touching the shoulders of a pink sweater. He pinned it to the wall of the conference room, and it soon became a national icon, one of the most recognizable photos in a story that was awash with pictures.

The commander faced a room filled with reporters and photographers swaddled in lights, flashguns, tape recorders, television cameras, notepads, and microphones. Never had he seen such a turnout in Boulder. He kept it short—confirming the death, the identity, the victim's age, and the location. No specifics.

Afterward he met with Chief Tom Koby, who decided that since this was to be a national show, a professional spokeperson like himself would henceforth personally represent the Boulder Police Department. That was fine by Eller, who had plenty to do running the investigation. Koby, who did not particularly like the press even in the best of times, took over the BPD media relations. I couldn't think of a worse person for the job.

I was at the kitchen table that morning, reading newspaper reports about the murder, when my telephone rang. My former SWAT partner, Detective Ron Gosage, said that Eller was putting together a team to handle the Ramsey case and wanted me. Did I want in? Absolutely.

With that one phone call, my life was forever altered.

I checked to be sure my good suit was clean and looked in the mirror at the bearded face of an undercover narc. Cut the long hair? Not yet. Shave the beard.

After the autopsy, the police spent five hours working up a new warrant for 755 Fifteenth Street, based upon the coroner's findings, to search for additional items not specified in the original warrant. The detectives felt the long delay was again due to difficulty in getting the DA's office to sign off on what should have been a routine search warrant addendum.

Among the items police now sought were the possible bludgeon that caused the head wound and any dark fabric that might account for the fibers found on the body. A red clay brick that appeared to have fibers stuck to it was retrieved from the living room fireplace, and a baseball bat with a blond hair on it was found in the backyard. They were also looking for traces of semen, and in the victim's bedroom, ultraviolet light showed stains on the bed and surrounding carpet. The mattress was wrapped in plastic.

Detectives going through the house noted cobwebs in the tracks of various windows and found some windows painted closed. Dust and debris had gathered on other sills, giving no indication of forced entry. Some curious pry marks were found on a back door, but more and more, except for the broken window in the basement, it looked as though the big house had been locked up tight the night before.

A New International Version Study Bible was photographed on the desk of John Ramsey, open to the pages of Psalms 35 and 36. There was no way to know it at the time, but those verses were to play a critical role in the unfolding case. Beside the Bible was a greeting card JonBenét had made for her father, on which she had printed, "The best gift I can give is me."

While the house search went on, other cops fanned out to canvass the neighborhood and conduct more interviews. A resident directly to the south reported that the light was off in the southeast corner sunroom of the Ramsey home and thought that odd because it was the only time she was aware in the past few years that it did not burn all night. A neighbor to the north would say that the butler kitchen lights were on around midnight and considered that unusual since it was the first time he had noticed that light being on in the Ramsey home. A third neighbor, to the west, said that her dogs, who barked at anyone walking in the alley, just as they did when the police officer came to question her, made no noise Wednesday night. It was impossible to make a 100 percent sweep because some people were away on holiday vacations, other houses had caretakers, and some just stood empty.

Additional interviews filled in small pieces of the Ramsey puzzle. An acquaintance said that JonBenét was rebelling against appearing in the child beauty contests. She was being pushed into the pageants by her mother and grandmother, said the witness. Someone else, who knew the family through the private school JonBenét attended, said the girl so routinely presented gifts to her teachers on holidays that Patsy was asked to be more discreet because the feelings of other students were being hurt.

In-depth interviews were held with three important figures—former nanny Suzanne Savage, Ramsey's personal pilot Mike Archuleta, and the housekeeper, Linda Hoffmann-Pugh.

Savage, a religious person who had spent eighteen months on a mission for her church, had no idea that she was among the first people the Ramseys had mentioned as a possible murder suspect. She had worked as a nanny and done some light housekeeping for the family from 1992 until 1994, when the children were small, but had not worked there full-time for three years.

Savage told police that she seldom stayed overnight at the Ramsey home but had occasionally slept in JonBenét's bed and still had a house key. The Ramseys, she said, were very careful about locking their doors.

JonBenét usually slept with her door open in those days, said the nanny. This contrasted with Patsy's earlier statements that the door had been closed when she reached the room and found it empty the previous morning.

Savage had only complimentary things to say about the Ramseys and the kids. You could make Burke behave by telling him no, she said, but sometimes JonBenét had to be given a "time-out" for doing things such as stomping on Burke's Lego creations. JonBenét enjoyed riding her bike and loved cats and dogs and having people read to her. The little girl also liked to play and paint pictures in the basement, and Patsy had recently taken a class and was painting in oils.

Savage was puzzled about where the body had been hidden. The former nanny had been in the basement many times and said that someone would have to know the house well just to find the little room.

————

John Ramsey had two planes, a 1972 twin-engine Beechcraft King Air C-90, white with red stripes and with the name of his first daughter, *Beth*, stenciled below the left window, and a smaller single-engine Beechcraft. A radio scanner in his home office was kept tuned to 126.25, the Jefferson County airport channel.

Mike Archuleta, Ramsey's private pilot, confirmed that Ramsey had telephoned him about leaving for Atlanta the previous day, but Archuleta attached no significance to the call since he had been readying the plane to fly to Michigan that morning anyway. He figured the man was under tremendous stress and just wanted to get his family out of Boulder. Ramsey had called him twice, once about the girl being missing and the second time when the body was found, and asked how long it would take to be ready to leave for Atlanta. Two hours, the pilot had said. Another man, Fleet White, called a short time later to cancel the flight.

————

Ramsey housekeeper Linda Hoffmann-Pugh and her husband, Mervin, managed to focus suspicion on themselves by being as cooperative in their second interview as they had been in the first. They even helped police succeed in a macabre scavenger hunt. When the detectives asked if the couple had any black tape, Mervin dug three rolls from his garage, only one unused. Then the detectives said they wanted white lined notepads, and Linda handed over one that seemed to be a visual match of the ransom notepaper and admitted it had come from the Ramsey house. A key? Two. Any felt-tip pens of the sort that probably wrote the ransom note? Three. Police found a two-foot piece of narrow nylon rope, then another length wrapped around a stick! The detectives left with an armful of potential evidence.

Savage, Archuleta, Hoffmann-Pugh, and her husband had all been forthcoming and helpful when questioned. As a detective, that was what I would have expected when investigating the murder of a child.

————

By midafternoon, after studying the autopsy results, Eller still had unanswered questions about the body. What about the massive skull fracture? What and where was the murder weapon? What about the vaginal trauma? A lot of points needed to be covered.

Chief Koby pointed out to him that the body itself had become evidence, and to release it at this point could affect the investigation. Eller and the coroner agreed.

But only a few minutes passed before Deputy District Attorney Pete Hofstrom called to say that the Ramseys were asking about burial. His appearance raised an important question that was not addressed: Why were the Ramseys already communicating through the DA's people rather than directly to the investigating detectives? That indicated they were talking through a private lawyer, and with the strong links between the DA's office and the defense attorneys in Boulder, that could only mean trouble for the police.

Eller told Hofstrom that Koby, the coroner, and he had decided to hold the body for further evidentiary tests, and thought no more of it.

His attention at the moment was focused on setting up formal Q-and-A sessions with the Ramseys. The police expected that both the Ramseys would want to cooperate as soon as possible in the hunt for the killer of their child. We had hundreds of questions, questions only they could answer, because the situation had changed so dramatically from the time police first arrived on the scene of what had been thought to be a kidnapping. Eller assigned Detective Arndt to arrange a formal interview.

A short time later an agitated Pete Hofstrom came into Eller's office.

"Pete, we need to talk to the Ramseys," the commander told the prosecutor.

"You can't ransom the body for an interview," Hofstrom shot back.

"We are not 'ransoming' the body. It's just premature to release it."

"You can't ransom the body," Hofstrom repeated, as if he had not heard Eller's words.

"I'm not suggesting that," the commander said, laying out the forensic and evidentiary concerns.

"You can't ransom the body," Hofstrom insisted for a third time.

Eller grew irritable. "Pete, they are unrelated issues. Go make your deal with them, that's what you do. We need an interview."

We would later learn that Hofstrom went to see Mike Bynum, who was already representing the Ramseys behind the scenes, and announced, "We've got a problem." *We* was the word that shook us.

———

That evening, John Ramsey went to Crist Mortuary to discuss funeral arrangements. In addition to the usual rites, transportation was needed for burial in Atlanta.

Patsy awoke while he was gone and staggered from the bedroom to a couch, barely able to speak, and told her sisters she needed some things from Fifteenth Street. John was overheard to ask someone quietly, "Did you get my golf bag?" When I learned of that statement, it seemed totally out of order. There had been two golf bags in the house, but he had not specified which one he wanted. Neither bag was collected by police. Moreover, it was winter in Colorado, Michigan, and Georgia, not exactly optimal golfing conditions. Why would a man whose daughter had just been murdered be wanting his golf clubs anyway? I wondered what else might have been in the bag that was so important that Ramsey would even think to ask about it.

––––––––––

On the night of December 27, the day after the debacle on Fifteenth Street, Detective Arndt and Sergeant Larry Mason arrived at Tin Cup Circle at 9:30 P.M. to schedule the formal interviews. But instead of stepping forward to cooperate, the Ramseys seemed to be fast fading from view.

John Ramsey was there but would not talk to them alone. Also present were his brother, Jeff Ramsey; Dr. Beuf, the pediatrician; Rod Westmoreland, Ramsey's financial adviser from Atlanta, who introduced himself as an attorney; and the influential local lawyer Mike Bynum, who had once worked in the DA's office. Bynum made his role official when he said he would be providing John Ramsey with legal advice.

It was the first time police had had a chance to speak with Ramsey since he had left his house the previous afternoon, yet he sat there with two lawyers.

The session lasted only forty minutes, during which time the detectives learned little. Ramsey asked no questions about the murder, the autopsy, or how JonBenét was killed. I later considered this very peculiar behavior. Parents usually want to provide information as soon as possible to help police find who harmed their child before the trail goes cold.

He confirmed that he had been locked out of the house about four months earlier and had removed the metal grate over the window well and kicked in the pane to gain entrance. That explained the broken window. But he made a point of mentioning that the grate was not secured by a lock and that the window had never been fixed.

Giving some family background, Ramsey mentioned how Patsy had conquered cancer over the last few years, then added that this was a tough time of year for his family. His eldest daughter, Beth, had died in a car accident on January 8, 1992. JonBenét was to be buried next to her in Atlanta. A private memorial service was planned in Boulder on Sunday, then the family would fly to Georgia for the funeral on Tuesday, December 31.

Ramsey said he was considering posting a reward. When he was asked again about possible suspects, he repeated the name of Jeff Merrick, who had been through a messy firing from Access Graphics. Then he added another ex-employee, whose name he had forgotten but who had been fired for lying on his application by saying he did not smoke. The company had paid a $15,000 settlement when he sued.

When the detectives asked to speak to Patsy, Dr. Beuf said she was too medicated to talk to anyone tonight. The two police officers insisted that early interviews were imperative. Perhaps tomorrow morning? The pediatrician hedged, saying that Patsy's emotional state was very fragile. John Ramsey was noncommittal about when he would talk with police again.

Months would pass before he did, and when it happened, I would be asking the questions.

6

Thirty-third Street in front of the police department was jammed with television satellite trucks, and reporters swarmed. At noon on December 28, I ducked into headquarters through the Bat Cave, a hidden back entrance used by undercover cops who did not want to be seen. I could not risk having my photograph taken because I might be back working narcotics in a few days.

The square two-story building was a hive of activity. Uniformed cops, detectives, civilians from the department of social services, deputy sheriffs, and people I had never seen before were coming and going, all looking tired. Framed explosions of bizarre modern art flashed from the walls, reminders that I was back in the New and Improved Boulder Police Department, which had no place for traditional cop decor such as plaques and photos of decorated officers.

I went straight to a corral of offices, cubicles, and government desks that occupied the southeast ground floor, where the line of authority was along one wall. The office of Bob Keatley, the department's legal adviser, divided the patrol and detective divisions. In line away from him were the offices of Sergeant Tom Wickman, Commander John Eller, and Sergeant Larry Mason. I found Eller standing at his desk, fatigue etched on his face.

"There's a briefing this afternoon," he said by way of a terse greeting. "Be there." He had every available officer and detective working the case and a to-do list that was growing by the minute. "This is going to be big, Steve. It's an APE." I nodded at the police jargon—acute political emergency.

The detective bureau folded away across industrial gray carpet, with the newest detectives having the desks closest to the sergeants and being the most likely to catch a "Hey, get in here" call. The veterans gravitated to the far side of the bureau, and Ron Gosage had one of the most distant desks of all, putting a lot of bodies between himself and the bosses. I found him coming around the corner with a cup of coffee in his hand and the usual wad of chewing tobacco in his mouth. We had known each other since we were patrol officers together in Wheat Ridge, and I considered him one of the best detectives in the house. He was assigned to crimes against persons.

"We've got some problems with this thing," he said, in perhaps one of the biggest understatements he had ever made. He described how the crime scene had been compromised big time and said we had not yet even interviewed the parents about the murder.

It took me a moment to comprehend what he was saying. To a detective, the crime scene is Ground Zero in any investigation, the place from which we start piecing together the story of what happened. It is the source of evidence, and it changes from the moment the first police officer sets foot in it. The destruction of a crime scene puts the entire subsequent investigation at great risk because errors made in protecting it can never be undone. To hear that the Ramsey homicide scene had been wrecked was like a punch in the stomach. And it was just as bad to learn that forty-eight hours into this, we had not interviewed the parents. I felt that we were already in deep trouble.

———

It was about to get much worse. As Gosage and I sat in police headquarters, Pam Paugh, one of Patsy Ramsey's sisters who had flown in from Atlanta, was staging a one-woman raid on the crime scene that I could only compare to burning the damned place down. And she did it with the help of the cops!

Patrol Officer Angie Chromiak told me later that when she showed up to pull a security shift at Tin Cup Circle, she was ordered by police headquarters to ferry Pam Paugh over to Fifteenth Street to collect some clothing that John, Patsy, and Burke Ramsey could wear to the funeral. Even that decision, as kind as it might have been to grieving parents, was questionable, for *nothing* should be removed from an active crime scene.

To disguise her identity from the media, Pam donned a Boulder Police jacket, complete with badge and patches. When they parked behind the house to dodge the media out front, Pam psyched herself up for the job ahead: "I can do this, I can do this, I can do this," she panted as she pulled on latex gloves. Then she headed into the house, accompanied by Detective Mike Everett. She spent an hour on her first trip through the crime scene and emerged with a big cardboard box filled to the brim, which she plopped into the trunk of the police car. For the next several hours, Pam made about half a dozen trips through the house, often spending an hour or more inside, and hauled out suitcases, boxes, bags, and loose items until the backseat of the police car was stuffed like a steamer trunk.

Like me, the patrol officer understood how far out of the ordinary the visit was. "Are you checking all this? It's way more than just funeral clothes," Chromiak asked Detective Everett. "You don't worry about it," Everett replied. I listened with total disbelief when I interviewed Chromiak about the incident. It was too crazy to be true—what had begun as a courteous gesture to allow some funeral clothes to be fetched had turned, probably without intention, into a scorched earth assault. The officer said she was told by a police intern on duty not to be concerned because "The detectives already know who did it."

Pam's last trip was into the bedroom of JonBenét, and she pumped herself up again: "I can do this, I can do this, I can do this." She came back carrying an armload of stuffed animals and other items from the first room in the house to have been sealed off by police.

Everett kept only a general inventory of what was removed, and even that abbreviated listing was astonishing. Stuffed animals, tiaras, three dresses for JonBenét, pageant photo portfolios, toys and clothes for Burke, John Ramsey's Daytimer, the desk Bible, and clothing. For Patsy, there were black pants, dress suits, boots, and the contents of a curio cabinet. Bills, credit cards, a black cashmere trench coat, jewelry that included her grandmother's ring and an emerald necklace, bathrobes, a cell phone, personal papers, bank records, Christmas stockings, her Nordstrom's credit card, and even their passports! The patrol car was loaded with zipped bags, boxes, sacks, and luggage, the true contents unknown. This, to my mind, was madness. Once those items were gone, they weren't coming back, and the police were only in their second day of the official search of the house. Pam Paugh should never have been allowed in there at all. The removal of so much potential evidence, with police assistance, was more like an earthquake than a mere procedural error.

Pam finally got into the front seat, clutching some stuffed animals, and Chromiak drove off, only to have Pam thrust out her arms and scream as if spiders were crawling on her. "Get these gloves off of me! Get them off! Get them *off!* Get them *OFF!*" The puzzled cop removed the latex gloves, and Pam immediately felt better. "I need a large Diet Coke with a lot of ice," she demanded. "Right now!"

On the way to a fast-food restaurant, Chromiak told me, her passenger described making her first million dollars before the age of thirty-two and not knowing what to do with all her money. In reality, she worked at a department store cosmetics counter. The patrol car, stuffed with Ramsey belongings, went to a drive-up window, and Pam (still wearing the BPD jacket) settled down with a Happy Meal. Chromiak paid the bill.

————

The afternoon briefing began when John Eller walked into the Situation Room, where four long tables had been pushed together to form an empty square. The photo of JonBenét in her pink sweater was tacked to a wall, where it remained throughout the investigation. Gosage and I were at one corner, and every chair was filled, with more people standing. The SitRoom was to become my home for the next year and a half.

Detective Linda Arndt reported that Ramsey lawyer Mike Bynum said the parents of the victim were willing to cooperate with the police, but that any further communication with John and Patsy Ramsey would be with their attorney, Bryan Morgan, present.

Bynum also said the pediatrician, Dr. Beuf, had determined that Burke Ramsey could not be interviewed by police.

Detective Arndt asked Bynum to schedule an interview with John and Patsy Ramsey.

————

Later that afternoon, Detectives Arndt and Trujillo were advised by Deputy DA Pete Hofstrom that the Ramseys had now both retained counsel and would not consent to an interview with the police at this time. Hofstrom then suggested the detectives submit *written* questions. I did not believe the proposal should even be considered, for it would tip off the people being questioned, and their attorneys, to topics the police considered important.

Hofstrom further advised that the Ramsey attorneys wanted to review all case information before allowing cops access to their clients.

All case information? People we wanted to question in connection with the murder of JonBenét wanted an advance look at our case? Any investigator should refuse that demand. The suggestion was preposterous.

But by now, it was plain that the newly hired Ramsey attorneys preferred to talk to the DA's office instead of to the investigating detectives.

When Detective Arndt was prepared to reply to Hofstrom, she dialed a telephone number where he said he could be located. It was the law office of Ramsey attorney Mike Bynum.

The law is an adversarial process, and in most jurisdictions across the nation, the district attorney and his prosecutors are firmly on the other side of the fence from defense lawyers. Indeed, some are barely civil to each other because their jobs demand such different allegiances. No law-and-order prosecutor, who represents the public, should want to appear too cozy with defense lawyers. The way the justice system worked in Boulder was an anomoly, not the rule. For Deputy DA Pete Hofstrom, the prosecutor, to be making house calls on the defense lawyers was truly an ominous sign to the police.

We were then brought up to date on a new discovery. Crime scene techs at the house had recovered three Sharpie felt-tip pens from an orange metal container on the kitchen counter beneath the telephone from which Patsy had made her 911 call, not far from where the ransom note tablet was found.

That was exactly the sort of physical evidence we needed, and I thank God that Pam Paugh didn't carry it away, because the U.S. Secret Service eventually determined that one of those pens, a pre-November 1992 water-based ink Sharpie, was used to write both the practice and actual ransom notes. The Secret Service, which maintains a huge database on inks because of its federally mandated assignment to chase forgers, told us, "The ink [on the notes] is unique in the collection of approximately 7,000 standards from the Ink Library."

That meant that whoever wrote the notes used that exact pen from that cup. They not only left the pad behind but, when they finished, neatly put the felt-tip pen in its container.

Eller gave out new assignments. Gosage and I were to get over to the Criminal Justice Center and collect from the Ramsey family what is known as "nontestimonial evidence"—blood and hair samples, photographs, and fingerprints that could be compared with whatever might come from the crime scene. This is such a standard procedure that it cannot be avoided.

I was anxious to see these people. It had been my experience in thirteen years as a police officer that victims tend to act like victims, so I expected to find a grief-stricken family demanding investigative results. Instead they were flanked by a squadron of attorneys and private investigators and saying absolutely nothing to police.

We set up shop in a narrow room with a sink and long counter, and the family members were escorted in one by one.

John Ramsey, in khakis and a dark sweater, looked unsure of himself as he sat in a plastic chair to have his photo snapped. He nervously put an elbow on the counter, then took it off, leaned over, elbows on knees, then sat up straight again, searching for elusive comfort. He uttered not an unsolicited word, and I could not understand how someone whose child had been killed would not at least ask detectives what progress was being made.

A few minutes after he left the room, he was back, shepherding Burke, a month shy of turning ten years old and apparently oblivious to the gravity of the situation. Gosage and I went gently about our business while Ramsey held and hugged the boy, almost smothering him and speaking quietly in his ear.

Patsy Ramsey came in next, looking as if she had just crawled off a shipwreck. Her dark hair was pulled back sharply and capped by a pair of sunglasses atop her head. Without makeup, she in no way resembled the effervescent beauty about whom I had been hearing. Tear trails stained her cheeks as she stood between us with her ink-smeared fingers ready to be rolled for prints. One of her attorneys leaned against the wall and watched.

Patsy was unsteady as I had her lift the sleeves of her loose denim blouse so I could check for bruises or scratches on the fronts and backs of her hands and arms. Then I checked her face and neck and found nothing unusual. We were standing in a row at the counter, with Patsy in the middle, when she shifted slightly and whispered to Gosage, "Will this help find who killed my baby?"

He carefully replied, equally softly, "I hope so."

Patsy looked at her inked fingers and spoke again. "I didn't kill my baby." The lawyer apparently did not hear her, but my head snapped around as if on a swivel. Colorado Revised Statute Procedure 41.1 spelled out that we couldn't ask investigative questions during this evidence collection, but we could certainly listen if anything was said voluntarily, and the mother of the murder victim had blurted out something totally unexpected. I directed my comment to Gosage. "What did she just say?"

Patsy Ramsey repeated, to me this time, "I didn't kill my baby."

The lawyer launched away from the wall, placed his hands on her shoulders, brought his face to within inches of her ear, and whispered emphatically. She didn't say another word during the entire session, but what she had already said hung like thunder. *I didn't kill my baby.*

No one suggested that she had.

––––––––

Detective Arndt took the handwriting samples from John, Patsy, and Burke, and when a private investigator asked for copies, she gave them to him. She later would be criticized for giving them a copy of the ransom note. All that information was evidence and should not have been handed over. But the handwriting and the ransom note were mere drops in the bucket.

We didn't know it then, but one of the most disheartening aspects of the entire case would be the incredible amount of evidence given to the Ramseys and their lawyers. It went out the door, drop by drop, page by page, until the police and prosecutors had few secrets left. In my opinion, Team Ramsey had it all, and that cold fact sickened me.

––––––––

The Ramseys were among dozens of people who would give handwriting exemplars in the case. To keep the comparisons accurate, we had them all write a mock business document, called the London Letter, which incorporates a variety of characters and punctuation. They also wrote a series of words from the ransom note—*Mr. Ramsey, John, withdraw, family, attache, daughter, S.B.T.C., your, delivery, 100%, killing, instructions, countermeasures, $118,000, difficult, authorities,* and *bank.*

While Arndt handled the writing samples, the elder kids of John Ramsey from his first marriage were made available for interviews and evidence samples.

Melinda Ramsey, twenty-two, wore a white pullover and jeans, and her eyes were puffy from weeping. She was attractive and polite when a detective and a sheriff's investigator began questioning her, but by the time the interview was done she was left with her head buried in her arms, crying. They had pressed her hard about the possibility of inappropriate sexual behavior in the family. Melinda vehemently denied that, and in fact revealed nothing of significance, since she was in Atlanta at the time of the murder. She had been caught in a web not of her own making, and the interview left her with a bad taste about dealing with police.

Gosage and I interviewed twenty-year-old John Andrew Ramsey. He was a lanky young man with dark eyes and short dark hair, who wore a checkered shirt, a winter jacket, and an attitude. When the blood tech moved close with her needle, the former Eagle Scout, who was now a third-semester sophomore at the University of Colorado, whispered, "I may pass out."

Although he also claimed to have been in Atlanta when the crime occurred, we had to check him out because of the neighbor who had reported seeing him on Christmas Day. We had to determine who was right.

We asked him to put his thoughts on paper, and he wrote a document that brimmed with feelings about his little stepsister being murdered, giving us a glimpse into his world. He caught our attention immediately by writing, "I think it was someone that had intimate knowledge of my family and how we lived day to day. Why would they leave the ransom note on the back staircase instead of the front?"

Good question, I thought. How would a stranger know which stairway Patsy Ramsey would come down that morning?

He ridiculed the idea of a small foreign faction being involved, was certain the crime had nothing to do with his father's company, and questioned why a ransom note was left at all. "Why did they ask for $118,000? I could pay that amount," he wrote. Someone was envious of their wealth and thought of the Ramseys as "rich bastards," he said.

John Andrew told us that whoever did this was probably uneducated, were amateurs at kidnapping, and had seen the movie *Ransom*, in which the family of Mel Gibson's character was a "spitting image" of his own. He did not believe anyone came in through the broken basement window. They had a key, he surmised.

In one comment, he described his stepmother as "flashy" and guessed that the killer might be someone close to her.

John Andrew also buttressed the comments of the housekeeper's husband, Mervin Pugh, and former nanny Suzanne Savage about the house being difficult to navigate. "You don't know your way around real easy right off the bat. . . . You have to open lots of doors. It has lots of ups and downs," and the basement entrance was hard to find. It was becoming very clear to the police just how difficult it would have been for any stranger to get to that distant basement storage room.

On the afternoon of December 28 Commander Eller again urged Pete Hofstrom from the DA's office to try to secure interviews with John and Patsy Ramsey. "We need to talk to those parents," he said.

Hofstrom replied that the family was leaving Boulder the next day, as if that made a difference, and once again brought up the issue of releasing the body for burial. Eller told him nothing had changed, it was still evidence. Take it up with Chief Koby, he said.

That evening, however, Eller spoke to Bob Keatley, our legal adviser, who saw that the issue was heading into a morass. The possibility of finding further evidence beyond what had come from the autopsy might not be enough to convince a court to hold the body further. He advised that it would be best to release it for burial. Eller did so.

———

As dusk closed over the mountains, Detective Gosage and I made an unannounced visit to the home of Barbara and John Fernie, who had rushed to comfort the Ramseys on December 26 and then gave them refuge.

We learned that our questions were a bit late, even though the investigation was only beginning. The Fernies told us that a private investigator working for the Ramseys had been there earlier, making his own inquiries.

That rocked us. Clearly a separate and well-organized investigation about which we knew nothing was already under way.

As any experienced officer knows, it is important to lock someone to a story as soon as possible after a crime has been committed. As I saw it, for a defense team to employ that tactic was tantamount to an attack on police investigators, for our own inquiries would be subject to comparison with what the PIs had gotten in the first interviews.

We realized how quickly they had moved only when we later learned that the Whites had also been visited by the private investigators the day after the murder. The two couples that had rushed to aid their friends gave statements to Ramsey representatives even before the child was buried, and the private investigators had not shared a shred of their findings with the police.

There was no sign of the Ramseys at the Fernie residence, but we did pick up one bit of interesting information. Some friends of Patsy's were concerned about how JonBenét was being groomed for pageants with the heavy makeup, the elaborate costumes, and the recent addition of platinum-dyed hair. It was creating a "mega-JonBenét thing," and some friends had planned to have a talk about it with Patsy after Christmas.

———————

As the second full day of the investigation came to a close, the parents still would not give interviews to police and had hired lawyers and private investigators who were tying down the testimony of witnesses before police got to them.

"Why won't they help us?" I wondered. "What are they afraid of?"

———————

The next day, Patsy Ramsey's fortieth birthday, St. John's Episcopal Church at Fourteenth and Pine was packed for the memorial service, and the congregation included four Boulder detectives. It was a cold, cloudy Sunday afternoon. I sat in the last row, Detective Gosage worked a hidden camera to film every face, and Sergeant Mason and Detective Arndt were at strategic points. It is not unusual for a killer to attend such services, so we were watchful.

Outside the church the media waited for a glimpse of the family, and I began to understand how far this case had moved beyond normal press coverage. JonBenét was going to be a superstar in death.

The press also had been in a stand-down mode during the holidays, when newspapers run canned feature stories, and football games and reruns are the normal television fare. So when the murder of a child beauty queen surfaced, the media pounced to fill the idle Christmas air time and headlines. It meant ratings and advertising dollars during a traditionally slack time, and the unexpected combination of a horrible murder, kiddie beauty pageants, puzzling parents, and tranquil Boulder promised fascinating stories.

When pictures and videos were found of a singing, dancing Jon-Benét, it became the biggest story in the United States.

With the aggressive media buying information and photographs, the police were soon conducting an investigation in a goldfish bowl, our every move watched and dissected. And although we didn't yet understand how the media worked, everything we did seemed to be in print or on the air within hours, tarnishing witnesses and exposing evidence.

While the media lurked outside, Father Rol Hoverstock conducted a brief but moving memorial service for the slain child. Sunlight brightened the stained glass windows and washed across his face.

In prayer Patsy's sisters, Pam and Polly, waved their arms over their heads and loudly called for heavenly help. As an Arkansas native, I had often seen such performances in southern churches, but their actions were so unusual in Boulder that a little girl in the pew beside me was swept up by their spirit and joined in, twirling her arms and shouting.

A surprise speaker was Bill McReynolds, an eccentric old guy with a snow-white beard who looked like and played Santa Claus at the Ramseys' Christmas parties. He offered a heartfelt tribute to the little girl who once gave him some "stardust" to sprinkle in his beard. Patsy, in a black veil, stepped into the aisle to give Santa Bill a big hug. He would soon be on the suspect list.

John Ramsey rose to say a few words, his arms across his chest and his voice tight. He said he had grown spiritually from the death of Jon-Benét, then shared a secret. He said he once missed the talent portion of a pageant in which his daughter had won a medal. She had given him the medal, and today he wore it outside his shirt. It was one of the items taken from the house by Pam Paugh that police failed to inventory.

I wondered how I could distinguish between a genuinely grieving parent and one whose grief might be masking some possible involvement in a crime.

After the service, Patsy hugged her housekeeper, Linda Hoffmann-Pugh, who did not know that Patsy had named her as the first suspect.

A scuffle broke out between men of the church and photographers, and John Andrew Ramsey was suddenly in my face, shouting for me to "get rid of them!" I resented being treated like hired help, and when I asked a photographer to move, he taunted me for protecting a killer. I was disgusted with both of them.

John Ramsey approached me. After such an emotional service, I thought he might be ready to tell me to find the bastard who killed his little girl. Instead he offered a mild "Thank you" and a weak handshake, not making eye contact. I didn't let go of his hand until he looked up, and I said, "Good luck."

He walked quickly to a waiting motorcade of luxury cars, and, escorted by a Boulder Police black-and-white, the family headed off to meet a private jet for the flight to Atlanta. Ramsey never looked back.

They carried along Sister Socks, a gray-and-white stuffed animal that had been left behind during Pam Paugh's sweep through the house. Sister Socks was retrieved for them by Detective Arndt.

———

Rumors were flying that the Ramseys were reluctant to deal with police because Commander Eller had heartlessly tried to force interviews by holding the corpse of JonBenét hostage until he got what he wanted.

To me it was a play for sympathy as part of a well-conceived strategy to shift attention away from their refusal to cooperate. Instead they would blame their silence on the Boulder Police.

But the excuse that we had attempted to "ransom the body" left me wondering why the exact words Pete Hofstrom had used in his meeting with Commander Eller were now coming from the mouths of the Ramseys' lawyers.

Detective Arndt made one final try at persuading the lawyers to grant interviews but was told that the family would be out of state for an unknown time. She responded that she had a single page of questions the police would like to have answered, and the attorney said, "Fax them."

7

The body of JonBenét Ramsey was embalmed in Boulder, then put aboard Delta Air Lines flight 584 for Atlanta, where the Mayes Ward-Dobbins Funeral Home in the suburb of Marietta prepared her for a private viewing, with burial the following day, December 31.

Cosmetics and a pageant gown concealed the deep furrow around her neck. She wore a tiara, and Sister Socks was at her side. One person who was there told us that John and Patsy were in a receiving line to greet the several hundred people who came to pay their respects. Patsy's mother, Nedra Paugh, "flitted about," taking people by the arm and leading them to the open casket to see her beautiful granddaughter in her crown and gown.

———

Detective Sergeant Tom Wickman arrived back in Boulder after learning about the murder while visiting in-laws in Chicago. He was immediately put in charge of the crime scene, and Larry Mason was shifted to supervise the investigative work. I was glad to see Wickman on the job, for he was sharp, technically competent, and knowledgeable about the latest technology. In his forties, he was competitive and mercurial, and it was best to catch him at just the right moment if you had bad news. With Eller in the office and Wickman on the ground, a bit of order was being restored, although I thought it was much too late for anyone to rescue this crime scene.

———

Father Rol Hoverstock came by the police department to give hair and handwriting samples—we were even checking out the family minister—and we asked his opinion about Psalms 35 and 36, without revealing why. That started him thinking about that book of the Bible, and when Detective Gosage and I met him later in the day at his home, Father Rol suggested that we take a look at Psalm 118. He thought it might be the origin of the $118,000 ransom figure. And in his sonorous voice, he read aloud one of the verses, which contained the phrase "bind the sacrifice with cords."

Before long, the media, fed by the Ramsey forces, were promoting Psalm 118 as a key to the case. As incredible as it was, the verse was only an odd coincidence, for the Bible on John Ramsey's desk was both a different edition, with different wording of even that verse, and open to a different place.

————

Defense lawyers love Pete Hofstrom, chief of the felony division in the office of District Attorney Alex Hunter and a consummate deal-maker who seldom sends a case to trial. That Hofstrom was working so closely and so quickly with the Ramsey lawyers scared the hell out of us. We felt things were being done behind our backs.

Originally from Brooklyn, Hofstrom moved to California, where he went to college and worked as a guard at San Quentin prison, then came to Colorado, graduated from law school in 1973, and went to work for Hunter. A short, five feet, four inches tall fireplug guy with a shiny bald crown that he tends to rub when nervous and a gravel voice from years of smoking cigars, Hofstrom's preferred mode of dress is not a suit and tie but khaki pants and tennis shoes. He has nurtured a tough-guy persona and massages a San Quentin story into almost every conversation.

As Hofstrom rose in rank through the DA's office, so did his eccentric philosophy that the law is not "simply a set of rules that people are supposed to observe." In his opinion, as stated in a newspaper interview, the law allows him room to "advance society's interest," and he is the one to define those interests.

One thing his vision did not require was spending a lot of time in the courtroom trying cases, when gentlemanly attorneys could agree to avoid such nastiness with plea bargains that traded a watered-down sentence for a conviction on lesser charges. Pete Hofstrom was dealing down more than 90 percent of the felony cases in Boulder County, including some of the most heinous crimes one could imagine— murders, rapes, and cocaine dealing.

In just one example, a man sliced the throat of another man from ear to ear outside a Pearl Street bar in 1981, then fled. Somehow the victim survived. The suspect was found on the Caribbean island of St. Croix eleven years later and extradited back to Boulder to face attempted murder charges. The sentence after the plea bargain was three years' probation, which he was allowed to serve in St. Croix.

In the 1990s Hofstrom dominated the district attorney's office. Being "fair" to defendants was preferred to trials, and the result was a lack of courtroom confidence and grand jury experience among a staff of prosecutors that earned the questionable reputation of not being able to bring home the big ones. Police called it the "3-D Shop," where everything was dismissed, deferred, or dispositioned.

During Alex Hunter's first campaign for district attorney in 1972, he was highly critical of the incumbent for plea-bargaining some 65 percent of his cases. By the mid-1990s, Hunter admitted the figure for his office was about 93 percent, although one newspaper put it nearer 97 percent of the felony cases. At the start of the year 2000, one of his own deputies, Mary Keenan, was campaigning to become district attorney herself and claimed that only seven-tenths of 1 percent of the cases filed in Boulder go to trial. That meant an astounding 99.3 percent of the cases were being plea-bargained!

We had long been aware of the close relationship between Hofstrom and one of the new Ramsey attorneys, Bryan Morgan of Boulder. Proof of just how close their links were came when Commander John Eller went out to the Colorado Bureau of Investigation on December 30.

Eller wanted to discuss some possible evidence that would soon be coming to the CBI for testing, but he was interrupted by one of the examiners, who said they had already been contacted by the office of the district attorney and told not to begin any such tests.

Before Eller could even ask why, Hofstrom walked in, almost as if on cue, to deliver a letter ordering the CBI not to test certain types of evidence, particularly very small samples. The instructions came not from the DA's office or the police department but from Bryan Morgan.

No one had been arrested or charged with anything, so by law, until a suspect became a defendant, they had no right to observe the testing, much less dictate how it was to be done. The fact that the DA's top prosecutor was hand-delivering mail for a defense attorney instead of fighting the unreasonable demand was outrageous.

Morgan wrote a letter of thanks that day to Hofstrom for disclosing the major findings made by the coroner. The Ramseys had the autopsy results almost as soon as we did.

Such instances would broaden the gap of distrust that existed between the police department and the DA's office. At times, I didn't know whose side they were really on.

———

Even before my first visit to the Ramseys' home at 755 Fifteenth Street, I realized that the house itself was a player in this drama. At 6,500 square feet, it had been chopped and added to over the years until it was a maze of rooms. Witnesses who said a stranger could not easily find his way around were telling the truth.

Just finding the light switch to the basement stairwell was a challenge, for it was not on the wall just inside the door where switches are usually placed. Instead I had to reach behind me to another wall. It would be impossible for someone unfamiliar with the house to know that.

Downstairs I checked the little room where the body was found, again a difficult journey just to get there. *Had to know where they were going*. Police had started calling it the "wine cellar" to differentiate it from the overall basement area, although no wine was stored in it. Four concrete walls, no windows, a fluorescent lighting fixture laid sideways on a shelf, with two switches near the outward-opening white door. Cold and claustrophobic.

I tried to imagine what her last thoughts may have been as she sustained the devastating blow to her head. I hoped she was unconscious after that, unable to experience the panic and fear of having the garrote tighten around her neck. I hoped the vaginal trauma happened after death.

From another basement storage closet, a crime scene tech pulled a plaque denoting that John Ramsey had served in the navy at Subic Bay in the Philippines. The media erroneously added the words *Training Center* to Subic Bay and obtained an explanation for the SBTC acronym, although Subic Bay was a massive naval installation, not a training base. Everybody had a theory.

Back upstairs, I walked through each room and was struck by the paradox that although the home seemed planned for a *House & Garden* photo shoot, the clean lines, antiques, rich wood, and designer colors seemed to have gone too far and crossed into overdecorated gaudiness. The farther I moved from the front door and showcase living and dining rooms, the messier it got. Dirty clothes on the upstairs floors, toys scattered everywhere, clutter in the corners, various items seemingly pushed out of the way rather than neatly stored, cobwebs in some corners.

I wondered just how many people had been through this house: home tours, social guests, church events, parties, construction workers, domestic help, friends, family, crowds of visitors during an open house tour the previous Christmas. Thousands. Fingerprints galore. How would we possibly identify them all?

Although some of the house was a frilly showplace, the alcove containing John Ramsey's study was strictly masculine. Dark walls, dark patterned drapes, furniture of heavy wood. Arched bay windows framed a classic view of the Flatiron Mountains. I sat at his big L-shaped desk, which stood solid on emerald carpet and bespoke power and control. In here he kicked off shoes and worked in private. A model airplane rose from one corner, and a multibutton black telephone connected him with his business world. A brass-hinged cigar humidor sat near the small sculpture of a sturdy lion. A drawer was filled with family photographs.

A handwritten ledger reflected his increasing wealth over the years. Later I would find records showing that as of May 1, 1996, Ramsey had assets of $7,348,628, and a total net worth of $6,230,628. Total liabilities were an even $1,118,000, and the similarity of that figure to the ransom demand of $118,000 jumped out at me. I noted it as a possible source.

In the bedroom of JonBenét, I stood looking at the formal portrait in the ornate gold frame above her dresser, gripped by a haunting feeling that she wanted me to look harder. Later, strips of black duct tape similar to what had been taped over her mouth were discovered on the back of that picture. She was a beautiful child, but the pageant videos were disturbing. Trained, rehearsed, and packaged at six years old.

I would spend many hours at that house over the next year and a half, and I always left with more questions than answers. What kidnapper would come to steal a child in the night without first having written a ransom demand, then be so brazen as to take the time to begin one or two, discard them, and compose a complicated three-page letter on a pad conveniently found in the house, with a pen found there too, and fashion a handy paintbrush into part of a murder weapon? Would an intruder take the trouble to fake an elaborate kidnapping to disguise a murder? Why tuck a blanket around the corpse, almost as if to protect her from the basement chill? In a locked room like the wine cellar, why cover the body at all? This would have taken even more time, which again pointed to the murderer being in no hurry and unafraid of being caught while lugging the child through the dark house. And the ransom note was suspicious to everyone who read it. What kidnapper would insert a commercial plug—"We respect your bussiness"—in a ransom demand? Or advise sleeping people to "be rested." Did the kidnapping stop for a while to let the victim eat some pineapple? There was no apparent forced entry, so how could someone come through that little broken window without disturbing spiderwebs and the dust on the sill? Would it have made any difference if someone had a key?

And how did the intruder know intimate family details such as John Ramsey's bonus or that he had "good southern common sense"?

There were so many questions, so few answers.

I felt certain about only one thing: Anyone who had ever known JonBenét would do anything they could to help us find her killer.

I had never been so wrong in my life.

While I was still in Boulder going through the house on the last day of 1996, the funeral services were held in Atlanta's Peachtree Presbyterian Church. The Reverend Dr. W. Frank Harrington told the mourners, "I can tell you that the heart of God is broken by the tragic death of JonBenét."

In the front row, Patsy Ramsey wept and John Ramsey rubbed her back as the organist played "In Christ Alone." There was a Bible reading from Thessalonians 4:13 ("We want to know the truth") and the congregation sang the children's hymn "Jesus Loves Me." Harrington raised his arms and said, "The mind cannot grasp and the heart refuses to accept the death of one so young, who is suddenly taken from us by cruelty and malice by some unworthy person."

The small coffin was taken from the church to the St. James Episcopal Cemetery, which was carpeted with floral tributes. A hole had been dug in lot 352 beside the grave of Beth Ramsey, and JonBenét was laid to rest in a Wilbert Continental burial container beside her stepsister.

Later a friend, who had come out from Boulder for the services, recalled that she was asked by Patsy to retrieve the black jeans Patsy had worn on the morning of December 26. Although the friend said Patsy really liked those jeans, I could only think of another reason why she would want those particular jeans from fifteen hundred miles away, since she had plenty of money and credit cards with her: fiber evidence.

———

After the funeral Ramsey's friend and financial adviser, Rod Westmoreland, took him aside for a private moment and expressed concern that the public was viewing John and Patsy more as uncooperative suspects than as grieving parents. People couldn't understand why parents whose daughter had been killed would not talk to the cops.

The message would be repeated more strongly later that day by Fleet White in a tense meeting that became one of the most curious incidents of the case.

Fleet and Priscilla White were trusted friends of the Ramseys and had been the first people Patsy Ramsey called on the day of the murder after she called the police. The Whites had rallied behind the Ramseys in that time of crisis, but as the days passed, they grew troubled that John and Patsy seemed to be dodging the police, and decided to talk to them about it.

The Whites flew to Atlanta for the funeral with other friends and stayed at the home of John's brother, Jeff. When Jeff learned of the Whites' plans, he called the home of Patsy's parents, where the clan had gathered. Emotions were running high, and the family overreacted.

I was later able to piece the story together from interviews with many of those present. Some of them grew afraid, and one of Patsy's sisters thought the Whites were coming over to kill them all. The situation, no more than a possibly unpleasant conversation between two old friends, was clearly pushed into a danger zone, although there was no evidence that the Whites were even angry.

Nevertheless, Patsy's father, Don Paugh, loaded two pistols and tucked them beneath a couch cushion so that he could be ready to protect his family. John Ramsey calmed everyone down before the Whites arrived, saying that Fleet was his friend and would not harm anyone. Rod Westmoreland told Paugh to put away the guns, and Don said he did so, although his wife continued to believe her husband was sitting on a pistol that night.

Fleet White is a large, intense man who does not hide his opinions, and although his voice was muted, the extended Ramsey family characterized him as waving his big hands about, speaking excitedly, and following Ramsey around the room in what they considered to be a confrontational manner. Fleet wanted John to know how chagrined his friends and supporters were that he seemed to be avoiding the cops.

Don't hide behind your attorneys, he said. They're giving you bad advice.

White later told me that he did not understand the reports about his meeting with John Ramsey being some sort of battle. Nothing extraordinary happened at all, he said, and the only truly emotional moments came when everyone watched a television broadcast about the funeral.

Fleet and Priscilla White were both soon named by the Ramseys as possible murder suspects. Before the case was done, many other friends the Ramseys had in Boulder would join the Whites on the suspect list.

In Boulder the investigation had turned into an uphill fight. The parents were gone, the crime scene was trashed, and I considered our own prosecutors to be in bed with the Ramsey attorneys, leaving the police to chase their tails.

Eller had his detectives and technicians on jobs ranging from checking the lint trap in the dryer to investigating the significance of the $118,000 ransom demand. Patsy Ramsey's handwriting samples were being gathered, videotapes and the family computer were seized for review, and the duct tape was being researched.

I wanted to collect banking and telephone records, one of the most elementary and important steps in the investigative process. It has been proved time and again that crimes can sometimes be solved simply by finding a purchase receipt that leads to incriminating evidence. The right piece of paper will put a suspect at a certain place, at an exact time, doing a specific thing. Whom did they call? What did they buy? When did they do it? Where? Such records can be almost as good as a photograph, and the warrants to get them are so routine that they are considered boilerplate.

When I resigned from the Boulder Police Department eighteen months later, the district attorney's office was still preventing our access to the Ramseys' complete toll records and credit card receipts. We didn't have them the first week, and we didn't have them a year and a half later, because the DA's office stonewalled us, never really explaining why. My guess was that they had either made a quiet deal with the Ramsey attorneys or were afraid of them or were simply overwhelmed by the legal firepower of the Ramsey attorneys or a combination of the above. I considered their lack of action to be obstructing our investigation.

Jeff Merrick, who had known John Ramsey for twenty years, was the second person they had named as a possible murder suspect. He was not surprised when we contacted him, for that friendship had ended in bitterness when Merrick was pushed out of Ramsey's company, Access Graphics, in April 1996.

The firing was done in a particularly Machiavellian manner; Merrick was promoted, then his new executive position was abolished. John Ramsey refused to intervene, or even to see his old friend, and Merrick appealed to corporate owner Lockheed-Martin, which offered a cash settlement. When we contacted him, he thought the animosity that led to his firing was still at work. "I'm the only guy who ever pulled on the Ramsey halo," he said.

For months to come we crawled all over Merrick, who finally walked into the police department one Saturday morning to answer still more questions, against the advice of his attorney but wanting to settle things once and for all.

"I'm here, on a murder case, without a lawyer, talking to two detectives, having been pointed out by John Ramsey as a suspect," Merrick said to me. "Now, where is John Ramsey?"

He was eventually cleared. I was curious about the depth of John Ramsey's friendships.

———

I returned to the Ramsey house briefly, taking care to stay out of the way of the crime scene investigators. Inside, it seemed like Grand Central Station. Detective Linda Arndt and women from the department of social services leafed through Patsy's picture albums, exclaiming about the decor.

———

Joe and Betty Barnhill, the elderly neighbors so trusted by the Ramseys that JonBenét's silver Christmas bicycle had been hidden with them, would also eventually be pointed at as possible murder suspects by the Ramseys. From the moment I saw them, I knew it was ridiculous that they should be considered and that we should be spending time investigating them.

Joe, a silver-haired man in his seventies, was taking care of his wife, who had Alzheimer's disease, and Joe was crippled so badly with palsy himself that he needed both hands to sign a shaky signature allowing us to obtain their personal and medical records. He never asked for a lawyer, and shook our hands as we left, saying, "I'm confident that you will solve it." That sort of cooperation was rare, and we certainly weren't getting it from the Ramseys. We soon cleared the Barnhills.

The Barnhills rented out a basement room to Glenn Meyer, who would be pointed out by Ramsey investigators as a possible suspect because he carried a heavy load of debt. Meyer was an even more unlikely suspect than the Barnhills, since his own son had been murdered in Boston. He could not have been more cooperative with us. After an interview, giving writing and hair samples, and passing a polygraph, he was also cleared.

Meyer and the Barnhills also alibied each other, having watched television together on Christmas night and all going to bed early, Meyer with a case of the flu.

Another reason to interview the Barnhills, however, was that Joe had told the police he had seen JonBenét's older half-brother, John Andrew, in Boulder on the evening of December 25. John Andrew claimed to have been in Atlanta at the time. During the interview Barnhill sheepishly told us he had made a mistake and apologized, saying that he probably would not even recognize the young man in a crowd. That went a long way toward firming up John Andrew's alibi.

The Barnhills also had a key to the Ramsey home, something we had not known. The Ramseys initially said that the only outsiders with keys were two relatives and the housekeeper. Since then we had turned up one with the former nanny Suzanne Savage and now another with the Barnhills. We didn't know how many keys existed, and the number would continue to grow.

Jacques, the white bichon frise dog that belonged to JonBenét and was temporarily in the care of the Barnhills, jumped into my lap while we all watched the five o'clock news about the funeral in Atlanta.

In a few days another neighbor, Melody Stanton, who lived at 738 Fifteenth Street, diagonally across from the Ramsey home, also changed her original story, which was that she had not noticed anything unusual on the night JonBenét died. When a detective interviewed her a second time, Stanton admitted that she had not told the truth earlier because she did not want to be involved in the case. She now claimed to have heard the piercing scream of a child between midnight and two o'clock on the morning of December 26.

If that cry came from JonBenét, it would help determine the time of death. If a neighbor clear across the street heard the scream, I wondered how anyone in the house could not have heard it.

Her story, which seemed to be a clear piece of evidence, contained its own seed of destruction, however. More than a year later we would discover that Stanton also told the detective, "It may not have been an audible scream but rather the negative energy radiating from Jon-Benét."

The detective returned to that odd point several times during the interview, but Stanton never again mentioned the "negative energy." She insisted that she heard an audible scream, so the detective did not include the "negative energy" comment in his report.

A year later he was ordered to write an amended report. Changing a report is a huge issue for police since it brings the validity of the entire statement into question. His revised report was not the first, and it would not be the last, that would enter the Ramsey case file.

I knew nothing about child beauty pageants, had never even heard of them until this case, and was baffled about why parents would parade their little girls in such contests. My image had been of some kids wearing starched sundresses. Since JonBenét had been a star on these tiny tot beauty runways, I had to learn about that peculiar world.

My education began with a visit to the home of a pageant mother whose house was filled to bursting with sashes, tiaras, trophies, pageant pictures, magazines, and other accoutrements of the trade, a gaudy showcase of kids in costume. It seemed to me that the overweight woman was having a second try at being young and beautiful by living through her prepubescent daughter, who pranced about while we spoke. What is all this? I wondered, as the mother launched into a diatribe of petty, scathing comments about other pageant moms. In no time at all they would be offering each other up as possible suspects. I found that somewhat scary and awfully sad. But I would learn that there were thousands of women across the nation like her, all wanting their girls to be Miss America. The pageant world of JonBenét was not for the faint of heart.

FBI statistics show twelve-to-one odds that in child homicides, a family member or insider is involved, so there was no way we could just give the Ramseys a pass.

Anyway, they were avoiding us, and we needed to find out why.

Late on New Year's Eve at the city fuel yard in Boulder, Sergeant Wickman rolled up just as Ron Gosage and I were putting gas in our cars. It gave me a chance to campaign for getting some detectives to Atlanta right away. The funeral was there, the family was there, answers to some of our questions were there, while in Boulder all we had was an abandoned house that had crime scene techs crawling all over it.

Sergeant Larry Mason had asked me, "Why do we need to go to Georgia?" Sergeant Wickman, who had now returned and was the crime scene superviser, realized the urgency and said, "Go."

It wasn't that we would ignore other leads. We would continue to investigate the Linda Hoffmann-Pughs, the Jeff Merricks, the Suzanne Savages, and all the others whose names were popping up. But who *were* John and Patsy Ramsey?

———

Not much time was left in 1996, and a bitter wind swept the rooftop of the empty parking structure at Foley's department store where Police Chief Tom Koby, Commander John Eller, Sergeant Tom Wickman, and Detective Tom Trujillo, in charge of the evidence, had gathered for an urgent talk about new information from the Colorado Bureau of Investigation.

I was told later that the isolated spot was deliberately chosen to avoid the reporters, cameras, and microphones that had turned Boulder into a media center. Only after the police officials had made very sure they were alone did Wickman and Trujillo bring the commander and the chief up to date.

Chet Ubowski at the CBI had pulled startling information from the tablet belonging to Patsy Ramsey. By comparing tear patterns, Ubowski had determined that the first twelve pages were missing and the next four—pages 13 through 16—contained doodles and lists and some miscellaneous writing.

But the next group of pages, 17 through 25, were also missing from the tablet. The following page, 26, was the practice ransom note (Mr. and Mrs. I), and that page showed evidence of ink bleedthrough from the missing page 25.

Comparisons of the ragged tops of the ransom note pages with the remnants left in the tablet proved that it had come from pages 27, 28, and 29.

To me, being able to prove that the ransom note came from her tablet was an incredible piece of evidence.

Furthermore, the ink bleedthrough discovered on page 26 indicated that perhaps still *another* practice note could have been written on page 25 and been discarded. Two possible practice notes and one real one covering three pages led me to believe that the killer had spent more time in the house composing the ransom note than we originally thought.

But even more significant, it seemed clear that whoever wrote it was unafraid of being caught in the house. We never found the missing pages.

Then Eller and Koby were told that Ubowski had moved from examining the tablet to looking at the ransom note itself, comparing its writing with known samples the detectives had gathered from various sources.

What the CBI examiner told them, very privately, was astounding: Twenty-four of the alphabet's twenty-six letters looked as if they had been written by Patsy.

When taken together, the tablet, the Sharpie pen, and the writing formed a powerful base of evidence. And that evidence pointed directly at Patsy Ramsey.

8

To further understand the personalities of Patsy and John Ramsey, we compiled detailed biographies.

From a very young age, Patsy appeared determined to rise above her West Virginia upbringing to succeed, and showed that she appreciated the value of a good appearance. You could almost plot her progression from high school sweetheart to glamorous beauty queen to well-to-do hostess in the pretty front rooms of an expensive home. Her history showed she understood the value of drama and staging. The FBI would tell us that the disposal of the body of JonBenét had the classic elements of a staged crime, complete with a Hollywoodized ransom note.

Her husband was just as much a product of his environment, a solid Midwestern man who appeared quiet and thoughtful but who seemed as determined as his wife to take charge of his destiny.

Eventually, I would drive with Detective Gosage across a bridge and into Parkersburg, West Virginia, Patsy's hometown, and stand in the neighborhood where her parents, Don and Nedra Paugh, had bought four consecutive homes rather than move away. Many years later they moved to an upscale home in Charleston, South Carolina, but even then held on to the property at 2006 Thirty-fifth Street.

Patricia Ann Paugh, a right-handed baby girl with brown hair and green eyes, was born on December 29, 1956, at St. Joseph's Hospital and was brought home to Thirty-fifth Street. She was soon followed by two sisters, Pam and Polly. They knew everyone on Thirty-fifth Street and everyone knew them. It was that kind of America for a hardworking, God-fearing Methodist family like the Paughs.

Don Paugh began his working life at the B&O Railroad as a relief telegraph operator. When he was laid off, he passed through a series of menial jobs in dairies and marble quarries until he went off to West Virginia University. He and Nedra, who dated for seven years, were married in 1955, and Don earned his engineering degree the year Patsy was born.

The education brought a better job at Bendix Westinghouse. Then the army scooped him up for the Corps of Engineers. Active duty ended with Paugh holding captain's rank, and he drove up the Ohio River knocking on corporate doors until he found a job with the Bakelite Company, which would become Union Carbide, and he and Nedra settled down with their growing family.

Patsy had an uneventful childhood and developed a drive to succeed that was coupled with physical beauty and popularity. Her teachers at Emerson Elementary and Vandevender Junior High remembered her as a quiet, well-behaved student who made good grades. On the playground she was a leader, surrounded by friends.

When she was thirteen she attended a Miss West Virginia contest and fell under the pageant spell, confiding to her sister Pam, "I want to do that someday." Popular, slim, and smart, Patsy had set her course.

She was named a fraternity sweetheart and participated in her first pageant at a county fair, a title that both she and Pam eventually won. The third sister, Polly, chose not to follow them on the pageant runways. In her sophomore year in high school, Patsy was first runner-up for Miss Teen-Age West Virginia. As a kid she had liked to dance and play the flute, but in the talent competition she performed dramatic readings. Linda McLean, her drama coach at Parkersburg High, became her coach, while Patsy's father had her stand behind a kitchen chair as if it were a lectern and practice enunciating clearly so as to be heard by a room filled with people. The high school had competitions with other schools in public speaking and dramatic interpretation, and Patsy excelled. Her senior entry in the 1975 Parchisian took up more space than almost anyone else in her class of about seven hundred students.

PAUGH, PATSY—Elks leadership contest, Field House office assistant, Junior Orchesis, Junior West winner, Little Red cheerleader, Masque and Gavel, Mummers, Pep Club, Red Wing Drill Team, Revue, Senior West winner, Sports Carnival, Student-Faculty Forum, teenager of the month nominee, Thespians, Voice of Democracy School Winner, WEO, National Forensics League, state drama festival winner.

I traced her from Parkersburg to journalism school at West Virginia University in the fall of 1975, where she joined Alpha Xi Delta. One sorority sister, Theresa Lucas, was also involved in the pageant world. Patsy continued gathering experience in the evening gown, interview, talent, and swimsuit categories and won more titles: second runner-up for Miss Morgantown, then first runner-up for Miss Wood County and Last Person Standing in an at-large competition. Theresa was named Miss West Virginia of 1976 and the following year relinquished her crown to her sorority sister, Patsy Paugh, who would represent her home state in the Miss America pageant.

Her talent performance for Miss West Virginia had been a moving soliloquy from *The Prime of Miss Jean Brodie*, but there was a problem in getting copyright clearance to use it on a national stage. Linda McLean told us that she and Patsy wrote an original three-minute speech, entitled *Deadline*, about censorship, and it won a nonfinalist talent award in Atlantic City and a $2,000 scholarship.

The celebrity of being a Miss America contestant and winning the Miss West Virginia crown gave Patsy a Cinderella kind of year, and she grew more popular and confident, always appearing in public in coordinated outfits, heels, and with her hair perfectly done. She dated few boys, usually older and from the best families.

She graduated from the university in 1979 with a magna cum laude degree in journalism and a minor in advertising. Her father bought her a new car, and just as he had as a young man, she drove away looking for a job. Atlanta, the big city, was calling, and together with her college friend Stephanie McCutcheon, Patsy headed to Georgia over the July Fourth weekend.

They stayed for a while with Stephanie's brother, Dan, at his apartment on Powers Ferry Road and partied in Underground Atlanta and other hot spots. The welcome mat was always out for someone who had walked the Miss America runway. Dan, however, was of a more serious nature, and one evening his upstairs neighbor called wanting to talk about some computer business. Dan told the girls they had to be quiet and behave because "Mister Ramsey's coming down."

———

Putting together the background of John Bennett Ramsey, I found that flying was part of his life. He was born on December 7, 1943, exactly two years after Japanese aircraft laid waste to Pearl Harbor. His father went off to war. James "Jay" Ramsey was a pilot, flying cargo into China over the "Hump" of the Himalayas, while his wife, Mary Jane, stayed in Nebraska to look after their only child. When the war ended, James came home wearing the Distinguished Flying Cross, the Air Medal, and three battle stars and became director of the Nebraska Department of Aeronautics in Lincoln. John entered Randolph Elementary School the same year that his brother, Jeff, was born.

The boys grew up in a home ruled by midwestern principles and military correctness and inherited the fervent belief that hard work led to success. By the time he started Lefler Junior High in Lincoln, John Ramsey was known for being optimistic yet quiet.

When his father was appointed director of the Michigan Aeronautics Commission, the family moved again, and John went to high school in the small town of Okemos. He held summer jobs with an engineering company and the state highway department and also worked for his father at the aeronautics commission while attending Michigan State University. Surrounding himself with friends at school, he was involved in activities but remained in the background while he studied engineering.

He married dark-haired Lucinda Lou Pasch a month after earning his degree in electrical engineering in 1966. Commissioned as a navy ensign, he and Lucinda were posted to the huge Subic Bay naval base in the Philippines, but Ramsey did not follow his father into military aviation.

Subic Bay served the Seventh Fleet during the Vietnam years, and Ramsey, a civil engineer, stayed busy with public works projects and received excellent performance reviews. Lucinda gave birth to their first child, Beth, in the Philippines. After active duty, John moved back to Michigan and took a master's degree at the Michigan State University Business School. Shortly thereafter, his second daughter, Melinda, was born.

He ran into problems while working with AT&T in Columbus, Ohio, where his quiet manner was apparently viewed as a sign that he had difficulty communicating. He lost that job but took a technical sales position in Huntsville, Alabama, and a year and a half later moved to Atlanta in another sales job.

In 1976 his son was born, but John Ramsey's marriage soured after he had an affair with a woman he would later say seduced and stalked him. Tracking her down would become a difficult part of my investigation because he gave us few details. His wife filed for divorce in 1977, which he would call his "year in hell." She got three children, he moved into an apartment by himself, and his mother died of cancer.

But John's career was about to take off. He joined the computer revolution as manager of Southern Peripherals and Instruments in Atlanta. The company didn't do well, and his bosses were unhappy because they said Ramsey tried to expense about $5,000 worth of repair work on his Porsche and personal flying costs. Despite their differences, the owner described him as a quiet gentleman.

Friends told me he was a flop as a bachelor, too introverted to be very good with women, although he exercised the power of his American Express card. "John knew how to close the sale," a friend said. Even in the heat of the chase, however, John would unfailingly find a telephone each night and call his children.

He leaned over his apartment balcony in Atlanta one afternoon and saw a beautiful young woman visiting his downstairs neighbor. On the pretext of having to discuss a computer problem, Ramsey went down to talk to Dan McCutcheon. Once seated, he kept peering at her, smitten even before being introduced. John soon left his shyness behind and gave the AmEx card a workout, squiring his beauty queen to the best places in Atlanta in his little brown Porsche. "Patsy was his Jackie O," recalled one friend.

Patsy's parents detested divorce, but their misgivings evaporated when Ramsey flew up to meet them in West Virginia, holding hands with his three well-behaved kids as they crossed the airport tarmac. John and Patsy were married on November 5, 1980, at the Peachtree Presbyterian Church in Atlanta, where he became a deacon, and they settled into their first home. He was thirty-six years old, and she was twenty-three.

Borrowing money from Don Paugh, John and Patsy moved to the Atlanta subdivision of Dunwoody and in their basement launched a company they called Technical Equipment Specialists, Inc., known as TecSpec, which sold computer equipment for other businesses. Patsy handled the office, and her mother helped in sales. When neighbors complained about the delivery trucks, Ramsey rented office space at the airport so that he could fly in his spare time.

John Ramsey then joined with two other entrepreneurs to create MicroSouth, a distributor of computer instrumentation in the Southeast, and he was named president. When they hit the $500,000 mark in sales, MicroSouth held a big party, unaware of the fortunes on the horizon.

MicroSouth linked with a California firm, Calcomp. They also created the Advanced Products Group in 1986. Don Paugh, Ramsey's father-in-law, was hired to run the new company.

The next step was to go national, and APG merged with CAD Distributors in Boulder and CAD Sources from New Jersey to form another company that would primarily sell Sun Microsystems components. The partners hunted through a dictionary for an appropriate name, and *Access* jumped out. Not only did it represent entry to information, but it began with the letter *A,* which meant prime placement in the Yellow Pages. Access Graphics was born, with headquarters in Boulder and John Ramsey in charge of sales. He was soon named president and commuted from Atlanta to Boulder, where Patsy rented an apartment for him near the Access offices.

In 1991 the little garage start-up caught the attention of huge Lockheed-Martin, which bought it and kept Ramsey in place as president. He and Patsy decided to leave Atlanta, and she oversaw a massive remodeling of a brick home on Fifteenth Street, not far from the University of Colorado and Chautauqua Park at the foot of the Rocky Mountains. Things could not have been any better.

But on January 8, 1992, a tragedy occurred that shook John to his very core when his eldest child, Beth, was killed in an automobile accident near Chicago. Later that year his father died. John Ramsey fell apart on the death of Beth. The strong, silent executive collapsed inward, and nothing could soothe him. He would be heard in the middle of the night, crying and wailing in the attic, wrapped in pain. I would often consider the visible agony he endured on the death of Beth in comparison with his almost businesslike response to the murder of Jon-Benét.

Some questioned if John Ramsey ever really got over Beth's death, for he surrounded himself with her photographs and reminders of their relationship. He read the Bible daily and immersed himself in readings about the afterlife. When he bought a plane, he had Beth's name stenciled on the cabin.

Access Graphics was extraordinarily successful, with several hundred employees and offices in Mexico, Canada, and Europe, and Ramsey had enough money to indulge his family and his own passions of flying and sailing. He raced his sloop *Miss America,* using his children and friends as crew, and designed a new boat from scratch, with traditional lines, and named it the *Grand Season.* Ramsey had two airplanes, and when cataracts diminished his vision, he hired pilots to help him fly.

John Ramsey had become a millionaire, and his wife would sometimes awaken and find him sitting on the side of the bed, calculator in hand, crunching numbers to make his investments grow even larger. He had two more children, a son, Burke, and a third daughter, JonBenét.

Through it all, he remained a "mystery man" to many, allowing only his closest friends to see his wry humor. He was reserved and modest in all things, from conservative suits to Republican beliefs. He drank only socially. The family regularly attended the Episcopal church. Their little white dog, who peed all over the house, served as a reminder that nothing is perfect.

Access Graphics celebrated its $1 billion sales mark as 1996 neared an end. John Ramsey had lived the American dream, coming from modest beginnings, doing well in school, serving his country, working hard and prospering, marrying one beauty queen and fathering another. His future seemed bright and limitless.

———

Patsy had spent only three days partying in Atlanta before John Ramsey stepped into her life. The evening they met was tentative, and when he left for a moment to go call his children, she thought it was just an excuse and that would be the last she would see of him. But he came back, and by the end of a game of charades, Patsy and John were an item.

When they married, Patsy joked that at the age of only twenty-two, she had inherited three kids, two dogs, and a station wagon. That same year, her sister Pam won the Miss West Virginia crown, the first time in state history that sisters had done that, and only the second time in the Miss America competition.

Patsy landed an advertising job with McCann-Erickson but soon joined her husband in running their home-grown business, TecSpec, out of the remodeled basement. Later Patsy joined a friend's company, Hayes Computers, as head of the creative department.

People had begun noticing a marked change in the fresh-faced Patsy as her husband's accumulating fortune offered a lifestyle that she fully embraced. She drove a Mercedes and wore a mink coat to work, diamonds sparkling on her fingers as she produced technical manuals. She had a breast augmentation. She stayed with Hayes Computers until she became pregnant six years after she was married. Her first child, Burke, was born on January 27, 1987. JonBenét came along three years later.

Patsy stayed busy with a huge social calendar that touched all the right bases in Atlanta—Twigs, the Junior League, hostess for the symphony's Black-and-White ball, head of a million-dollar fund-raiser for the Egleston Children's Hospital, and patron of the Miss America scholarship program. It was reported that Patsy spent $30,000 on a single *Gone With the Wind* luncheon party in Atlanta. Her home was a showplace, and every Christmas she hired a Santa Claus for her parties.

John denied her nothing. With money no object, he bought a vacation home, a 110-year-old Victorian house on Belvedere Avenue in Charlevoix, Michigan, on a bluff overlooking Round Lake Harbor and the yacht basin, and Patsy set about a three-year renovation that almost reduced the place to its foundations before rebuilding. Landscaping alone cost more than $100,000. With its peaked roofline, a mast for flags on the lawn, and gingerbread gables, the place needed a grand name, so she christened it Summerhill. When Patsy took her morning coffee on the broad open porch, one could almost hear the old pump organ being played by Olive Eckinger, the opera singer who had married tycoon Roy MacArthur in that very house in 1917. Olive had planted showy, fragrant peonies. So did Patsy.

She plunged into community events there, too, because she wanted Charlevoix to consider the Ramseys more than mere summer people. As soon as the home was finished, Patsy put it on the town's historic tour to benefit a local hospital and personally greeted each visitor.

In Boulder Patsy also poured money into a makeover of their new home on Fifteenth Street. But her fairy-tale life slammed into reality in 1993, when she was thirty-six years old. She had endured steady discomfort in her shoulders and elsewhere for about six months and was taking sixteen aspirin every day. While judging a Miss West Virginia pageant in July, she felt a lump in her stomach. Atlanta doctors found an advanced case of ovarian cancer. Her head was still spinning with the news when they performed a hysterectomy. "A nightmare," she told an interviewer.

In a life-or-death gamble, John and an Atlanta doctor friend pulled strings and arranged for Patsy to become part of an experimental cancer-fighting protocol at the National Institutes of Health in Bethesda, Maryland, where she would receive high experimental doses of drugs and therapy. In the coming months she traveled to NIH every three weeks and spent four days undergoing the risky treatments, then flew back to Boulder and within a few days entered the Boulder Community Hospital to recuperate. Then a few weeks later, it was back to NIH to do it all over again. Her hair fell out, and for days she was only able to lie in bed exhausted. But she had an immense drive to recover, partly, one friend would later say, to keep an unnamed "blond bitch" down the street from getting her husband.

The steel in that comment showed the West Virginia girl who had apparently discovered that a pretty face in public could cover up private problems. The family spaces in their house were a mess, but the front room was showplace clean. Her little daughter's bed-wetting was private; the pretty gowns and a winning smile were what the public saw. Life inside the family was not the perfect image portrayed for the outside world.

Patsy Ramsey conquered cancer, receiving a good report from NIH after Thanksgiving 1995, and Christmas, her favorite season, was coming. The Boulder house was on the Tour of Homes for that year. Starting in September, a procession of fourteen maids scrubbed the huge house, and decorators were given a free hand and an open checkbook. A sash wrapped every doorway. The basement was converted into a bustling headquarters for the guides and servers as some two thousand people visited. Ten volunteers manned the house every hour. Patsy's pageant gown was carefully arranged on her bed with the tiara displayed on black velvet in the huge closet amid feathers and ball gowns and hats. It took four days to remove, wrap, and store all the decorations and left a maze of finger- and footprints for our crime scene technicians to examine after the murder.

Patsy's social life recovered apace with her health. Soon people saw the black Jeep Grand Cherokee or the white Jaguar once again cruising between appointments in Boulder as Patsy plunged into social activities that included the Colorado Dance Festival, the Boulder Philharmonic, the hospital auxiliary, and the university's women's club, and she played on a women's softball team called Mom's Gone Bad. She helped create the Good Fairy Project and chaired the science fair at High Peaks Elementary, where Burke and JonBenét were students.

Throughout it all, she steered her daughter through the world of child beauty pageants, a time-consuming effort that fueled the shared dream of Patsy and her mother and sister that JonBenét might some day grab the gold ring that Patsy and Pam had missed and become Miss America. My profile of Patsy led me to believe that she had gone beyond living vicariously through her daughter. She was enhancing JonBenét's pageant résumés with such things as violin and French lessons, and was even attributing highly improbable quotes to the child, such as how the world would be a better place if we planted daffodils. Just to have JonBenét win titles didn't seem to be enough for Patsy. It seemed to me that she sought perfection.

———

It looked as if 1996 would be another fortune-blessed year for Patsy, as if time wanted to make up for her illness. In January she and John went to the Cotton Bowl, and in the spring, a patio party with musicians helped celebrate the running of the Bolder Boulder 10-kilometer road race. Patsy took an art class at the university, where her expensive clothes, flashy jewels, big hair, and makeup did not fit in with the other students, who wore Birkenstock shoes and smocks. "One of those rich Atlanta-Dallas women," said an instructor.

The lake house was the scene of a family reunion of about thirty people. Space was so tight that guests slept on floors and even in the family boat. They dined on smoked trout and grilled whitefish. Patsy organized and Police Chief Dennis Halverson helped judge a bicycle decorating contest at the Charlevoix Venetian Festival. It was won by JonBenét, who turned six that summer.

The holiday season of 1996 was a long series of parties, including an early surprise fortieth birthday celebration at the Brown Palace Hotel in Denver, attended by Patsy's friends. None of her Atlanta women friends responded to their invitations. A comic dressed up like the girl who beat Patsy out for the Miss America crown did a three-minute spoof from material supplied by Nedra.

The Boulder house looked splendid, the front walkway bordered by candy canes and theme-decorated Christmas trees in every major room. On December 23, Patsy held a glittering Christmas party. About two dozen adults and children decorated gingerbread houses on the big dining room table. JonBenét looked happy and beautiful in a black velvet dress. The only odd moment was when a policeman arrived to say he was answering an emergency 911 call. He did not enter the festive house but was told through a speaker that all was well, and he went away. Santa Bill McReynolds entertained the guests, and housekeeper Linda Hoffmann-Pugh helped serve.

Within three days, a ransom note, a murder, and the focus of a horrified nation brought the dream to an abrupt end.

PART TWO

A GATHERING STORM

9

John and Patsy Ramsey broke their silence on New Year's Day with an interview on the Cable News Network instead of talking to us. Arranging an interview with a news organization was a tactic they would use repeatedly in coming years, and in my opinion it was always sheer propaganda, allowing them to spin a public relations story while avoiding the police. Most of the time the reporters involved agreed in advance not to ask them anything about the murder of their daughter. And the reporters, however well informed, knew only a fraction of the real case. Cops wanted to ask tougher, deeper questions—and on the first day of 1997 our topics would have included a long ransom note written in a familiar hand, JonBenét's bed-wetting, a broken paintbrush used to make a garrote, pineapple found in a bowl and in the victim's stomach, and what looked like traces of semen on the victim. The only danger to Patsy and John Ramsey when they put on their dog and pony shows did not come from the interviewers but from themselves. Even a carefully controlled statement still might give us something we could use.

Patsy did exactly that when she declared on CNN, "You know America has just been hurt so deeply with the tragic things that have happened. The young woman who drove her children into the water, and we don't know what happened with O. J. Simpson. And I mean, America is suffering because of lost faith in the American family. We are a Christian, God-fearing family. We love our children."

I had taught many police classes about deceptive responses, and it was always a red flag when someone proclaimed innocence by repeated religious affirmations. And why was she bringing up Susan Smith's lies about murdering her own children?

The Ramseys also told the national television audience that they were "not angry" about the murder of their daughter and wanted to move on with their lives. That left an opening, which the reporter didn't grasp, to ask how anyone could *not* be angry about such a thing. Anger, particularly only days after a person's child is violently slain, is a natural emotion.

John said that the murder of his daughter "makes no sense" and announced a $50,000 reward.

Patsy, apparently still feeling the effects of her tranquilizers, gave several reasons why she felt JonBenét was better off dead, then issued a warning. "There's someone out there," she declared. "There is a killer on the loose. I don't know who it is. I don't know if it's a he or a she. But if I were a resident of Boulder, I would tell my friends to keep your babies close to you."

The subject came around to whether they would be talking to the Boulder police. "Whatever anyone wants, we will cooperate," Patsy Ramsey told CNN.

That came as good news to us because we were on the way to Atlanta, where they were sitting in a television studio. Maybe we were reading them all wrong. It sounded as if all we had to do in Georgia was knock on their door and get those interviews.

And it certainly was no secret when Detectives Ron Gosage, Tom Trujillo, and Jane Harmer, Sergeant Larry Mason, and I arrived. We were met on the tarmac in Atlanta by a convoy of police cars that escorted us into the city. The Ramseys knew we were coming, and Commander John Eller was pushing the DA's office to arrange a meeting.

Gosage and I stayed up all night reviewing the case, readying questions, but our quarry fled without warning. The Ramseys were on their private plane again, headed for points unknown. We never saw them. So much for their promised "cooperation."

———

Trujillo and I went over to the Peachtree Presbyterian Church to talk with the Reverend Dr. Frank Harrington the next morning. He knew the family well, had married John and Patsy, buried Beth, baptized Jon-Benét, and had just buried her, too. If anyone could provide us with some insight, it should be the Reverend Harrington.

The minister met us with a frosty demeanor and a curt, "I'm not sure I want to talk to you. I will tell you I will share no privileged information."

That set me thinking about the rules of privilege, in which information can legally be kept in confidence, such as between doctor and patient or lawyer and client. Also privileged would be a confession by a parishioner to a clergyman. "*Is* there privileged information?" I asked.

"I won't answer that," Harrington said. "Do I need an attorney?"

"We're not here as adversaries, and you're not a suspect," I said, hoping to smooth things out. But we had to wait around for ten minutes until both a witness and a lawyer arrived, and our brief exchange yielded little information.

Why would a man of God reach for a lawyer rather than voluntarily give police everything he could to try to solve the terrible murder of a child, particularly if he wasn't violating the sanctity of confession? But Harrington wasn't alone in that peculiar behavior. I would repeatedly run into that same wall of silence, and more lawyers than I can remember, in the coming months. I wanted to scream at these people, "Don't you even care?"

If people were not going to help, I had to start considering other options, including the possibility of a grand jury that would have subpoena power and could demand answers.

———

From the church we went to the funeral home, where an assistant director told us that there were no suspicious visitors during the viewing, no one seemed out of place. Just hundreds of people paying their respects to a dead child. We asked if the parents were curious about the injuries that had been skillfully hidden by clothing and cosmetics. No, he said, "They never asked."

The St. James Episcopal Cemetery is an old burial ground filled with weathered nineteenth-century tombstones. Live oaks and magnolias tower over a black wrought iron fence around the perimeter. A six-foot-tall old rugged cross, erected in 1862, stands along the path to a slight rise in a rear corner, a place I would come to know well. JonBenét's grave was blanketed with flowers. It was sunset, and in the failing light I sat on a stone bench beside the plot and frustration churned within me. I felt such a responsibility—we had to find her murderer.

———

Back in Boulder Commander John Eller was unhappy that Deputy DA Pete Hofstrom had failed to get the interviews, and he was particularly incensed about how the "ransom the body" phrase that had originated with Hofstrom had ended up in the press, which then criticized the police for something that never happened.

It seemed to me that the prosecutor was working in tandem with the Ramsey lawyers and that the automatic distance that separates prosecutors and defense attorneys elsewhere in the nation had evaporated in Boulder. It hurt the investigation when details about the case showed up in headlines and on television.

Eller lit into Hofstrom in his office that evening, telling him that the police were in charge of the investigation. The DA's staff could be legal advisers for the cops but would no longer be privy to our confidential material, he said. Taking an extraordinary step, Eller removed the DA's office from the investigation, a move endorsed by Chief Koby.

Hofstrom huffed, "Don't ask us back, because we're not coming," then bolted from Eller's office so quickly that he forgot his pager. Within ten minutes it buzzed, and Eller read the telephone number of Ramsey lawyer Bryan Morgan. Eller sighed. To the cops, this was like having KGB agents in the Pentagon.

———

One room in the large brick home of Patsy's parents, Don and Nedra Paugh, in the Atlanta suburb of Roswell is a shrine to beauty pageants, filled with pictures and articles and with trophies and crowns won by Patsy and Pam. Nedra seemed obsessed by pageants. Only a few minutes into a homicide interview and she wouldn't stop talking about beauty contests. She told us that JonBenét had started on the runways at the age of four for exactly the same reason children begin training for the Olympics at an early age. If you don't start them young, she said, "They fall miserably behind."

Since John and Patsy were dodging us, we were attempting to build a historical file the hard way, through talking to their friends and family members. We were hunting for a name from the past, someone with a grudge, perhaps an enemy capable of negotiating that big confusing house in Boulder and killing JonBenét.

Nedra gave us some two dozen suspects off the top of her head, and when we asked if the initials SBTC meant anything to her, she snapped, "Yes. Son of a bitch Tom Carson." Years before, Carson, the current chief financial officer at Access Graphics, had been involved in Nedra's dismissal from the company. She also pointed to Fleet and Priscilla White, Jeff Merrick and his "vicious" wife, housekeeper Linda Hoffmann-Pugh, a handyman, a painter, the gardener, the nanny, and a couple of neighborhood kids. While thinking about other possible suspects, she accused one worker of theft, called a black man "boy," and described a little girl the same age as JonBenét as homely. But she had not one negative word to say about John Ramsey, which I thought was unique for a mother-in-law.

Nedra was a sad sight, with her head tilted listlessly to the side, her bathrobe hanging open, and both hands gnarled by arthritis, but she spoke almost without pause, giving us a mass of information that we would dig through for months.

She was swift to defend John Ramsey for assembling his own team of lawyers and investigators. "It's not that you folks in Boulder aren't doing a good job and can't resolve this," she said. "But it's my understanding that . . . there's never been a kidnapping in Boulder, so if you've never been on a kidnapping before, you need great minds who have done this before."

She agreed with Mervin Pugh, Suzanne Savage, and John Andrew Ramsey in thinking that no stranger could have navigated that maze of a house. "You couldn't find the basement in that house if you didn't know where it was. You know it was down, but which door would you go through to find it? There's a lot of doors that look like a basement door in that house."

Such identical statements coming from a number of independent witnesses who were all well acquainted with the house were painting a good picture that no stranger was involved in this crime. Whoever did it knew the layout. Nedra said Patsy would never return to that house and had told her husband: "Torch it."

Nedra was chatty about almost everything else but became evasive when asked about the bed-wetting history of JonBenét. During the interview questions kept coming to my mind. I was very curious about the bag of diapers that police had found hanging out of the cabinet just outside JonBenét's room and about why Patsy had told police that the child went to sleep in a red turtleneck although the body was found in a white top and the turtleneck had been discovered rolled up on the bathroom sink. Could there have been a bed-soiling accident that night? Patsy was the only person who could tell us, and she wouldn't.

It is not unusual for a parent to lash out in unreasoning anger after becoming extremely frustrated with a child over toileting issues. It is also not unheard of for children to dirty themselves as a defense against sexual abuse and incest, intentionally making themselves unattractive to the offender. We let Nedra's evasiveness go for now but would later become convinced that bed-wetting played a significant role in whatever happened to the child.

Detectives don't like to jump to conclusions, and we did not yet know what had happened. We try to let the evidence lead where it will, and we were too early in the process of interviewing those who best knew JonBenét to make a definite decision.

I wanted to know what JonBenét would do if awakened suddenly. "She didn't like you pulling her out of bed," her grandmother replied. "She would scream bloody murder." From my perspective, Nedra apparently saw where this line of questioning might lead. "Unless they chloroformed her or taped her mouth, she would have screamed like you wouldn't believe." So in the view of one family member, it seemed unlikely that a stranger could have slipped the girl quietly out of the bedroom. I liked the idea that JonBenét was a fighter.

———

The press was ready to pounce as soon as we walked out of the Paughs' home. When we had entered, only a lone media sentinel was staking out the place, but when we left, there must have been a hundred newspeople waiting for us.

It was like stepping onto a stage and took me so much by surprise that I made the brief extemporaneous comment that we were in Atlanta merely as part of conducting a full investigation, not to serve warrants or make arrests. Off camera, I naively told the reporters to relax, they weren't going to miss anything. My short, nondescript comment became a sound bite for the nation. *Ramsey detective speaks!*

The insatiable news beast stalked us relentlessly. We would make last-second turns and run red lights only to discover more media waiting when we arrived at our destination. They laid siege to the Roswell Police Department, which had lent us a private room, and constantly telephoned our unlisted numbers.

Reporters booked every other room around ours on the entire floor of the Holiday Inn, forcing us to speak in whispers for fear of some high-tech eavesdropping. As the cliché goes, it's not paranoia if they really are after you.

After the holidays, with regular reporters back on duty, the JonBenét case had become even bigger than before. National television shows were dedicating whole chunks of time to it, flashing the pageant pictures, and newspapers from major big-city dailies to ragtag supermarket tabloids ran stories in every edition. Freelancers fought to dredge up crumbs of information to sell.

And whatever they were doing was working, for case information that should have been confidential was winding up in the media almost daily, and Chief Tom Koby and Commander John Eller of the Boulder Police Department were concerned. Not only were the cops being heavily criticized, but the investigation was being placed in jeopardy by whoever was leaking our findings to the press.

When a story hit later in the week that "Reports out of Denver indicate the ransom note was from a pad found inside the home," Koby and Eller became so angry that they actually considered a deal offered by one media outlet, who were willing to give up their source in exchange for an exclusive interview.

On Turtle Lake Drive in Marietta is a pleasant two-story pale brick house with gray shutters and a stand of slender trees shading its neat sloping lawn. It is the residence of Lucinda Lou Johnson, the first wife of John Ramsey and the mother of Beth, Melinda, and John Andrew. She engaged in a cat-and-mouse game with us from the very start, and I wasn't really sure who was the cat and who was the mouse.

Our interview, of course, could not begin until a friend of hers arrived to be a witness. Again we wanted background, or historical, information. Somewhere in the past might lie the answer to the murder.

John and Lucinda were married on July 16, 1966, in Kalamazoo, Michigan. During twelve years together they moved often as Ramsey served in the navy and then began his business career. They had three children, but after her husband had an affair with another woman, they "went their separate ways" during the last years of their marriage.

"Who was she?" I asked.

"I don't recall her name," she replied.

It was difficult for me to believe that any scorned ex-wife could ever forget the name of the "other woman" who broke up her marriage.

They divorced on February 24, 1978, and the judge granted Lucinda custody of all three kids, with generous visitation rights for John Ramsey, who paid $200 per child and $200 in alimony each month plus the college expenses for all three, and the package became more generous as the years passed and John Ramsey prospered. The property settlement was simple: Each spouse got half interest in their home in Lilburn, Georgia, where she continued to live until it was sold. She kept the 1977 Cutlass station wagon, and the court gave John the '69 Olds, an eight-track tape deck, and his tools.

Lucinda soon met a man ten years younger than she during a skiing trip and married him. Her new husband never replaced John Ramsey as the father of the three children. They moved to Turtle Lake Drive, where she continued to live following her second divorce in May 1991. He kept a 1987 Honda and paid for the termite inspection, and this time she kept the tools.

She remained on good terms with John Ramsey and even visited the family in Boulder, for although divorced, they were still related because after John's mother died, his father married Lucinda's widowed mother. From being John's wife for a dozen years, Lucinda became his stepsister. She and Patsy coexisted, even working together on the social scene when Beth became a debutante.

Although not too illuminating, our interview was cordial enough, and I thought I saw some room for a bit of future bargaining. Lucinda wanted a public declaration that her children, John Andrew and Melinda, were innocent of any involvement in the murder of their stepsister, something stronger than the recent official statement from the City of Boulder. And we needed to find and talk to the mistress. As I left, I thought something might be worked out.

———

Sergeant Larry Mason and I go way back. When I was involved in my first shooting, Mason gave me a bear hug and later nominated me for a decoration of valor. But that was a long time ago, and things had changed between us.

I had seen him talking with reporters inside the private room set aside for our use at the Roswell PD, and at dinner one night, when Detective Trujillo and I agreed that whoever was talking to the press should get smoked, Mason said he was worried that someone might "get set up" over the leaks. At that moment Art Harris, a CNN reporter, sat down at our dinner table and popped open his laptop computer. Mason, who had invited him, told him to leave, then explained that the only reason Harris was there was because of negotiations to get the transcript of the Ramsey interview on CNN. I didn't believe him.

When the Roswell police public relations officer suggested that we issue a brief news release, Mason drafted a statement. Shortly after 3 A.M. the next morning, Commander Eller sent a fax to the Holiday Inn ordering Mason not to address the media and gave instructions for the hotel staff to slip the fax beneath Mason's door. If the hotel carried out that routine instruction, Mason must have stepped over the envelope to open his door the next day. He would deny seeing Eller's fax, and later that day he stepped before the cameras and read his statement. No one could have imagined that such a small event would turn into such a demoralizing and important sideshow to the Ramsey investigation.

Every morning I asked Mason over breakfast, Do you have the FBI team on surveillance? Did you find a particular witness? Did you run the computer queries? No. No. Always no. He was like a kid on vacation and babbled on about how much he enjoyed the grits.

One day I picked up a ringing phone at the Roswell Police Department, and Art Harris of CNN was on the other end, looking for Mason. The sergeant growled, "Fuck CNN," then disappeared with a cell phone, only to return a moment later to say he had to go back to the hotel and turn in his key. I pointed out that the key was a plastic throwaway. He left anyway.

In the midst of one interview during a twenty-hour workday, my pager went off and I found a telephone.

"What are you doing?" Larry Mason wanted to know.

"Conducting interviews. What are you doing?"

"I'm in Alpharetta having a piece of pie and coffee."

One of my last jobs in Atlanta was running down a tip that Mason said he received from Alli Krupski, a reporter from the Boulder *Daily Camera* newspaper who was on assignment in Georgia. Krupski claimed to have sources who knew about sexual molestations involving John Ramsey but refused to name them, citing press shield laws. The episode chewed up a lot of detective time over the coming months until we concluded the allegations were groundless.

Watching his growing relationship with the press made me lose confidence in the sergeant who was managing the Atlanta end of the investigation.

———

The Boulder detectives were not the first ones to knock on the doors along Northridge Drive in Atlanta, where John and Patsy Ramsey had lived before moving to Boulder. The networks, the tabloids, magazines, and newspapers had already interviewed many of these people and would do so again right after we left.

I was disgusted to be pounding the pavement in a place the Ramseys had lived a decade earlier, trying to question former neighbors and nannies, when John and Patsy were the ones with the information.

But police follow tips from one source to another, and Nedra Paugh had given us the name of Vesta Taylor, who had lived across the street from John and Patsy for ten years. Nedra described her as "the crier of the neighborhood" because nothing happened on that street that she didn't know about, so she seemed to be a good place to start. Sure enough, Mrs. Taylor, with a charming southern drawl, steered us toward the "Lunch Bunch," ten influential couples who were among John and Patsy Ramsey's oldest and closest friends.

That sent us back to the moneyed side of Atlanta, where the Lunch Bunch lived in impressive homes that bespoke Old South money—doctors, lawyers, accountants, and their exquisite wives, who had gone to church and on weekend getaways with the Ramseys. It required months to speak to them all.

Not surprisingly, they folded protectively around their absent friends, remaining courteous to us but wary. "Don't waste your time investigating John and Patsy," was the common refrain. There was unanimous and unquestioning support, but none could explain why the Ramseys were not talking to the police. If Patsy or John was ever shown to be the killer, I knew these people would be shaken to the core, for as one said, "It would be a Jekyll and Hyde ten thousand times over."

Colorado Bureau of Investigation technicians gave us some bad news when they determined that the substance found on JonBenét's leg during the ultraviolet light examination at the autopsy, initially thought to be semen, was just a smear of blood. Without a semen sample to match, our hopes for a quick breakthrough vanished and the universe of potential suspects grew astronomically. A woman could as easily have been the killer as a man.

Despite rumors in the press, I began to doubt that John Ramsey had been involved in some sort of incestuous attack on his daughter that ended in murder. Nothing I had seen or learned during the investigation thus far indicated such a thing. Other detectives, however, clung to that possibility for many months.

As our time in Atlanta neared an end, Sergeant Tom Wickman in Boulder officially released 755 Fifteenth Street as a crime scene after ten days of searching that had given us hundreds of items to examine but not the silver bullet that would prove who killed JonBenét. We were well aware that the trashed crime scene would haunt the case forever.

An unusual "swipe" was discovered on the white door of the small basement room where JonBenét had been found, so the victim's hands were traced and measured by Georgia police before the funeral. It would not be the last time that the premature release of the body would hamper the investigation. To many of us, the original decision to hold it pending evidence testing was correct.

Wickman had an argument at the Ramsey house with Detective Greg Idler, who had carefully lifted the metal grate above the broken window and found that the spiderweb between the window well bricks and the grate wasn't necessarily attached. Wickman challenged Idler's findings. The original web had never been photographed or committed to a report, a huge error that would become extraordinarily controversial in months to come. "I have detectives who will testify to it," Wickman barked at Idler about the web being attached.

———

On the long flight home, I weighed the results of the Atlanta trip and felt that at best we were coming back with a mixed bag. Our interviews with relatives, neighbors, and friends had added some valuable material to the biographical records but did not come close to breaking the case. What we *didn't* get, however, was important. The Ramseys had gone out of their way to avoid us, and the lack of cooperation we found in Atlanta had taken us by surprise. We had expected an outpouring of assistance from ministers and friends and relatives. We didn't get it.

———

Time was working against us, for the murder was ten days old and cooling fast. We needed a task force of forty investigators, not just a handful of detectives, and I could not understand why Chief Koby had recently turned down offers of help from the Denver police and other agencies.

Three years later, when two student gunmen massacred eleven other pupils at Columbine High School in neighboring Jefferson County, Colorado, a multiagency task force of some 150 investigators was assigned to the case. When I told one of them that our department sure would have welcomed that sort of response in the Ramsey case, he replied, "All they ever had to do was ask for help. Nobody asked."

10

John Ramsey was keeping his mouth shut, but his money was talking loudly.

Certainly everyone has the right to hire a lawyer and the right to remain silent, and I could not blame someone with a lot of money for hiring an attorney with impeccable credentials. But Ramsey had gone far beyond protecting his interests. What he had done would be unheard of in most big cities, even in the largest police investigations, and he simply overwhelmed a little town like Boulder.

Starting only a few hours after he found the body of his daughter, he retreated into a legal stronghold that could not be cracked. At least, not by us.

Hal Haddon of Denver had been the chief trial deputy in the state public defender's office before going into partnership with two other attorneys, Bryan Morgan (the friend and occasional breakfast partner of Pete Hofstrom in the DA's office) and Lee Foreman, in 1976. Eight years later, when Colorado Senator Gary Hart failed spectacularly in his presidential bid, Haddon was his campaign manager. His candidate crashed, but Haddon was left plugged into the Democratic Party political network, particularly in Colorado. In the nineties, as the attorney for Rockwell International, he engineered a plea bargain as a grand jury investigated the company for alleged environmental crimes at the Rocky Flats nuclear weapons plant just outside Boulder. The deal so enraged the grand jurors that they leaked their secret report to the press. Ramsey hired Haddon.

Bryan Morgan of Boulder was no stranger to law enforcement, partially from his representation of a woman named Lee Lindsley in a case several years before. Police responding to her early morning 911 call had found the snow around the house undisturbed and her physician husband shot to death. She was charged with murder, but Morgan successfully argued that two intruders did it, and Lindsley was acquitted. She moved to Atlanta and taught at the elementary school attended by the older children of John Ramsey. The Lindsley and Ramsey cases had a lot of similarities, including a claim of an intruder and the same defense attorney, but Deputy DA Trip DeMuth, in an extraordinary decision, forbade my pursuing that line. "The case is sealed," he said. We had never intended to razor-blade open the file but thought to interview some of the major participants. "Don't go near it." Ramsey hired Morgan.

John Ramsey hired Patrick Burke of Denver to represent Patsy. Burke had once worked with Pat Furman, a professor of law at the University of Colorado, to gain acquittal for a man allegedly involved in the white supremacist slaying of Denver talk-show host Alan Berg. Ramsey hired Furman, too. The police found it particularly interesting that John and Patsy would be represented by separate attorneys, a move that can indicate a possible conflict of interest between the parties.

A lawyer was needed in Atlanta for the family members back there, and someone suggested Jim Jenkins, one of the top lawyers in Georgia. Ramsey hired Jenkins.

The private investigative firm of Ellis Armistead in Denver was brought aboard. Pat Korten, a public relations specialist in Washington, D.C., was hired to deal with the press. Handwriting experts were hired. And John Douglas, a former FBI profiler who had spent a career getting into the minds of killers, was hired.

We referred to the whole pack as Team Ramsey, and although the attorneys resented being called "defense lawyers," that's precisely what they were, as one would later openly declare.

One of the first bitter tastes of their new media-spinning strategy came on the first Sunday of January, when Pat Korten, their PR man, used the dignified surroundings of St. John's Church in Boulder for a photo op. After the solemn service, John and Patsy did not leave through the usual eastside exit but instead walked out through the front doors and straight into waiting press cameras. The church had been used to help create an image of a grieving father and mother.

Boulder County District Attorney Alex Hunter had been on vacation in Hawaii over Christmas, and his subordinates chose not to ruin his holiday. Staying somewhat distant from an unpopular event was a tactic favored by Hunter, a Teflon politician who was always at least one step removed from any carnage left behind by his office. Hunter would blame an unfavorable development on a judge, a cop, a subordinate, the press, the statutes, grand jury secrecy, or some other surrogate and would seldom accept personal responsibility if a case went bad. So it would be in the Ramsey case, when he would surround himself with other lawyers and experts to present whatever happened as a team decision. He would refer to them as his "trusted advisers" and thus dodge personal responsibility for directing the case.

Hunter was a millionaire land developer before he ran for office on a vow to protect the environment. His other two major promises were to go easy on marijuana, which got the student vote, and to abolish plea bargaining. "Alex will be in the courtroom," promised a campaign flyer. He narrowly won the DA's office in 1972, one of the few Democrats to win anything that November as President Richard Nixon led a nationwide Republican sweep. U.S. bombers attacked Hanoi, the big movie was *Cabaret,* astronaut Gene Cernan became the last man to walk on the moon, and personal computers didn't exist.

The world had changed many times since then, but in Boulder there was one constant—at the end of the century, Alex Hunter, at the age of sixty-three, was still in office and thinking about running for reelection once again.

The seat of power in Boulder was Hunter's office inside the Criminal Justice Center at Sixth and Canyon Streets. The DA had seen scandals, outrages, murders, fads, riots, and other elected officials come and go and survived them all. In the White House the presidents change, and new administrations almost totally replace old ones. Previous philosophies and the way things are done change as the new broom of elections sweeps the place clean. That did not happen in the Boulder County District Attorney's office. Alex Hunter and his people settled in as permanent staff, set in their ways, and in the process he became the most powerful figure in the small political pond that is Boulder. Hunter was so untouchable that few—especially the local newspaper—would say a word against him, much less point out that the emperor of Boulder County wasn't wearing any clothes.

Hunter's first act after taking office in 1972 was to hire his business partner, Bill Wise, as his first assistant district attorney. Wise had been Alex Hunter's best buddy since they attended law school together, and they later became law partners and business associates, even owning real estate with one of the many Ramsey attorneys. After a couple of decades of administrative work, Wise was still at his friend's elbow and drawing a $108,000 public paycheck but rarely setting foot in a courtroom. Wise was a favorite source for reporters, even going to ball games with them. Police believed that he was a source of many of the press leaks.

After Hunter's first year in office, he had to suspend or fire seven people in his office for attending a party at which a platter of cocaine was shared. Three were prosecutors.

And his pledge of no plea bargaining evolved into what is now called "precharging negotiations." Prosecutors and defense lawyers make the deals *before* a defendant is charged, a practice that has resulted in some truly awful agreements. Questionable results stacked up like cordwood before a cold winter. Despite overseeing more than 200,000 cases for prosecution and handling a number of horrible murder cases, DA Alex Hunter had never sent a killer to death row.

In 1981 Christopher Courtney shot two people dead in a public building and was charged with murder. The district attorney blamed the mistrial that followed on a flaw in the law. Courtney pled guilty to criminally negligent homicide and took a two-year prison sentence.

The next year, hired killer "Tattoo Bob" Landry kidnapped a woman and, when his gun didn't work, crushed her head with a rock. The DA accepted a confession in exchange for life imprisonment, saying that it was the same as the death penalty because Tattoo Bob was very sick. County Undersheriff Kirk Long resigned in disgust over that case, writing that "The only adversarial relationship that exists in the Boulder criminal justice community is between the district attorney's office and law enforcement." One police chief called the DA "gutless."

If Christopher Courtney and Tattoo Bob were strikes one and two, Thayne Smika should have been a big strike three. In 1983 Sidney Wells, the boyfriend of Robert Redford's daughter, was murdered by a shotgun blast, and detectives arrested Smika and recovered a shotgun and matching shells. Hunter entered into a secret agreement with the defense lawyer that the grand jury would not return a true bill against Smika "for *any* criminal conduct." Members of the victim's family, the arresting detectives, and the grand jurors were unaware of Hunter's written pledge, and Smika vanished. He hasn't been seen since, and police are seeking still another warrant for his arrest.

Despite his electioneering boast, Hunter's courtroom skills were modest. In 1979 he decided to make an example of a woman who smoked marijuana with some underage boys and took her to court on a charge that could net her fourteen years in prison. After Hunter's opening statement, the defense lawyer said the charge against his client was incorrect, the judge agreed, and the woman paid a $100 fine and walked away, leaving Hunter standing there with a law book, trying to find the amended statute.

His last major case came when he was named special prosecutor in neighboring Adams County, where the sheriff faced a range of serious charges. Hunter offered to drop the felony counts if the sheriff would resign and plead guilty to minor charges, but a judge rejected the deal. Hunter lost at trial and retreated from the courtroom.

He had not personally tried a case in more than a decade.

Any other prosecutor turning in such performances would have been run out of town on a rail, but Hunter was a deft politician who stayed closely attuned to voter sentiments. For example, in one recent year, thirteen rape cases were filed, but there were no trials, and half the rapists didn't spend a day in jail. The DA did not pursue a hard line on sex crimes until the Boulder County Rape Crisis Team released a damning report pointing out among other things that out of sixty cases of sexual assault on children, only *one* offender went to prison. Thereafter, his office took a hard line on sexual assaults. But in 1996, a university student at her twenty-first birthday party had too much to drink. The innocent virgin was horribly raped by the disc jockey and was impregnated by the attack. The detective was able to collect DNA, irrefutably linking the suspect to the crime. In most any other prosecutor's office, this assault on a blameless victim would ordinarily bring a lengthy prison sentence. Our DA's office declared, "It's too early to give up on him" and allowed the rapist to forfeit only his weekends for two years in the local jail.

Overall, little changed. Boulder was doing fine economically, life was good in the shadow of the Flatirons. Alex Hunter kept getting re-elected, given a free ride by the local paper, which seemed to me to have abrogated its watchdog role. Republicans chided Hunter for being the Monty Hall of district attorneys, likening him to the host of the TV show *Let's Make a Deal*. But the GOP was such a minority in liberal Boulder that they could not beat him and eventually quit trying. There would be no new broom sweeping through the DA's office.

Public defenders and defense attorneys had free access to Hunter's office and were allowed to wander the halls, retrieve case files, and use the office copier while the drumbeat of plea bargaining continued. In many other cities they would have gotten that far only by appointment, and then only for a specific piece of business.

The death penalty continued to elude the DA's office. Randy La-Farge was stabbed fifty times, and Hunter would not seek the death penalty against the murderer. Scott Mutchler fatally stabbed a man and his ten-year-old son, and Alex Hunter chose not to go after the death penalty. Michael Grainger killed his sleeping wife and got three years.

Michael Bell murdered a convenience store clerk, then shot to death a man sleeping in his car, then went into the mountains and killed two more people and wounded three others. The mass murderer was captured after the biggest manhunt in Boulder County history. Despite facing multiple counts of first-degree murder and having witnesses to testify, Bell dodged the death penalty by accepting a life sentence. Anywhere else, the only question would have been in which arm to stick the needle, but Hunter and Pete Hofstrom, his chief trial deputy, won over the families of the four people Bell murdered by explaining the difficulties of a death prosecution.

Brittany Gomez, only six months old, was left blind and retarded after being brutally shaken by her baby-sitter, who drew only probation and ninety days in a halfway house after pleading to felony child abuse. Then Brittany died, the case was ruled a homicide, and murder charges were filed. The baby-sitter again pled guilty in exchange for no prison time. She killed a child and never spent a day behind bars.

———

Accordingly, the strain between the police and Hunter's office existed long before JonBenét was even born. We were all too familiar with the prosecutors' familiar bleat that there was "insufficient evidence" to go to trial, or that "a jury won't convict." I believed they had been so weakened in trial experience after decades of plea bargaining that they were afraid to take their chances in court.

Of the twenty-three murder cases filed between 1992 and 1996 in Boulder County, none went to trial. All were plea bargained. Pete Hofstrom told a reporter in 1996, "I haven't tried a case this year, and I don't intend to unless absolutely necessary."

So what was happening early in the Ramsey case did not shock any cops. It wasn't just that the Ramseys had money, it was that the Boulder DA's office did not embrace assertive and aggressive prosecution. The Ramsey case exploited weak points that had been in place for years, and the more the prosecutors tried to "build trust" with this defense team, the deeper they dug the hole. Several decades of their unorthodox thinking fell on us all like a ton of bricks.

Therefore, based upon years of experience with the DA's ivory-tower office, where justice seemed to be an abstract concept, I thought it unlikely that the killer of JonBenét Ramsey would ever see the inside of a courtroom. Elsewhere, a tough DA would have told the defense lawyers nothing more than was absolutely required by law and would have applied pressure at every turn to bring a killer to justice. But to do so in Boulder would violate the culture of cowardice and tradition of timidity that were the hallmarks of the DA's office. None of them were suddenly going to start looking like a gutsy prosecutor and adopt a "go-to-hell" attitude toward defense attorneys.

The coziness between the DA's office and Team Ramsey was illustrated once again in early January when the Colorado Bureau of Investigation wanted to see more of Patsy's handwriting. Pete Hofstrom brokered an unbelievable deal that she would not have to enter any law enforcement building, and she gave the sample not in the police department but at the kitchen table in Hofstrom's home.

The chief trial deputy bantered easily with both Ramseys, showed off some of his memorabilia, and turned on the basketball game in his living room so that John would have something to do while his wife was writing. Hofstrom took a walk while the sample was being given.

It was so bizarre that even Chief Tom Koby, who rarely got upset, almost shouted at Hofstrom in disbelief when he learned of it. "You took a handwriting exemplar from a *murder* suspect in your *home*?"

———

The third member of the troika of prosecutors was Senior Trial Deputy Laurence W. "Trip" DeMuth III ("Trip"), a lanky third-generation Colorado lawyer and a firm disciple of the plea-bargain philosophy of Hunter and Hofstrom. DeMuth, who favors bomber jackets and whom I often saw with his dress pants tucked into cowboy boots, was appointed to be the liaison man between the district attorney's office and the police department and became the bane of our existence. He piloted a separate investigation, fostered the Intruder Theory of the murder, refused to sign search warrants, and in general drove us nuts. In my opinion, DeMuth had no idea how to prosecute this monster.

———

Boulder never wanted a tough police force. One of the most politically correct places in America, Boulder viewed cops with an arrogance bordering on contempt. Tom Koby fit the place like a tailor-made glove. Instead of being a strong police chief to balance the defense-friendly DA's office, Koby became their quiet accomplice and counted Alex Hunter as a close friend.

Tom Kobalinsky (the name was later shortened to Koby) started his police career as a nineteen-year-old Houston patrolman in 1969 and rose to assistant chief there. When Chief Lee Brown left Houston to become the police commissioner in New York City, Koby was a leading candidate to replace him, but Houston wanted tougher policing, and his star waned as fast as it had risen. He looked for work elsewhere.

A month after I joined the Boulder Police Department in 1991, Koby was chosen from among 170 candidates to be Boulder's top cop because the city manager wanted someone with "sensitivity." From that moment, the department began sliding into little more than a social service agency as Koby spread his message of love and understanding. Before he even arrived, he sent each top police official a framed, hand-embroidered motto: *Police Unto Others As You Would Have Them Police Unto You.* What did that mean? Don't arrest anybody because you wouldn't like to be arrested?

Koby launched a sweeping reorganization that eliminated the military-style command structure of lieutenants and division chiefs. The next rank above sergeant was the new position of commander, which was just below the chief himself. It confused the chain of command and was a key reason that in the early hours of the JonBenét investigation nobody higher in rank than sergeant was in charge.

Koby abolished inspections, scrapped the rules and regulations book, and replaced the standard field training manual with a Value-Based Directive System that was more philosophical than practical. One principle declared, "We encourage creative problem-solving celebrating our accomplishments and acknowledging that there will be mistakes from which we can learn." Partnership! Celebration! Individuality! It was blue-sky psychobabble. We called it "Koby's Ten Commandments." Internal Affairs investigators would go after a cop who was perceived as being rude to a citizen, even if the citizen was a bad guy.

Koby oversaw his social engineering experiment while sporting a rat-tail haircut, beard, and collarless shirt, and he brought in eccentrics more suited for a touchy-feely encounter group than life in a blue uniform. The street skills of patrol officers eroded. Experienced cops went elsewhere rather than be a part of the new culture. The system and the organization had worked because of discipline, standards, and accountability. Koby did away with it all.

Early in the Ramsey investigation, I was tracked down by Kris Gibson, the victim's advocate coordinator, who held the equivalent rank and position of a police commander such as John Eller. She was nervous, which was not unusual when she got involved in a serious crime, since she had no law enforcement background. With long brown hair, beads, and ankle-length dresses, she was more flower child than cop and was known around the department as "Granola."

The Ramsey attorneys were saying that their clients, as *victims,* were entitled to see all police reports under the Colorado Victims' Rights Bill. The Ramseys would not talk to detectives, but they met willingly with Gibson. Afterward she told me that she "did not get the intuition that they are involved." I thanked her for that valuable observation.

Among Koby's other hires was a woman he convinced to join the force, and although she could not meet training standards and hated being a police officer, he wouldn't let her quit. Still another was a gang member who had fought with cops and had an outstanding warrant against him. The chief quashed the charge and allowed his new intern access to confidential files, including the identities of undercover officers.

Equally strange were Koby's tactical choices, such as when he would order the SWAT team *away* from violent confrontations because he felt its presence would only "escalate the situation." The chief once removed confidential surveillance videotapes of drug dealers from a detective's desk and gave them to a community activist just before arrests were planned. The suspects mysteriously vanished. The detective resigned.

Koby could be charming over lunch, then bedevil you with some off-the-wall philosophy, such as why some police departments should be disbanded. It was amazing that so many good cops actually stayed around, because Koby did not like hard-chargers, and stood by while discipline, standards, and accountability walked out the door in the persons of a Who's Who of the BPD's finest.

So the department was totally unprepared when JonBenét Ramsey was murdered. There was no plan to handle a homicide of such magnitude. In fact, there were no plans at all—just Koby's Ten Commandments.

Combined with the lackluster record of the DA's office, we had a textbook example of how a justice system can rot from within to the point of being virtually ineffective.

When I returned from Atlanta and had an opportunity to look objectively at the matchup, Us vs. Them, I recognized that Team Ramsey was not only richer but much better organized than we were.

11

The only three ways to solve a crime are through a confession, witnesses, or evidence. We did not have, nor were we likely to get, the first, there were none of the second, and the material that we had pulled from the compromised crime scene, although powerful, could not stand alone in a Boulder court of law. We needed more.

That did not mean we were completely stymied, for we did have a growing amount of significant evidence that was pointing inside the house. Then we found some nuggets of useful information in the written replies to the sixteen questions that Detective Arndt had faxed to the Ramseys.

It was obvious that lawyers wrote the answers, which were crafted in stilted legalese—"best recollection," "it is believed," "the custom is"—so that there was plenty of wiggle room on every question. But there were definite inconsistencies in their stories.

We knew Patsy had mentioned during the 911 call both the SBTC initials and the word *Victory,* which were at the bottom of the ransom note's third page. But the new answers said, "Patsy read only the first part of the note, not the entire note, and immediately checked Jon-Benét's room, confirming that JonBenét was not in her bed." Those were contradictions not only of the emergency call but of the sequence of events Patsy first related to the first officer, in which she found the bed empty before finding the note.

Another important point was the answer to what JonBenét had to eat that night: "JonBenét may have eaten some seafood, such as cracked crab and/or shrimp" at the Whites' party. Neither the question nor the answer mentioned pineapple, which indicated that she ate what was found in her stomach at the autopsy *after* coming home, and we had found a ceramic bowl on the breakfast table containing pineapple. Patsy's prints were on the bowl.

The question "What was JonBenét wearing when she went to bed on Christmas Day night?" was obliquely answered: "The best recollection is that she was wearing long underwear pants and a polo shirt when she went to bed." It did not mention what color the shirt was—the white one on the body or red, as Patsy had said on December 26. It did not mention the word *turtleneck,* which she had told police on the morning the body was found. It was an extremely evasive answer to a simple question.

There is a downside to such probing questions, however, for they can educate a suspect about what investigators know, and I thought too much was being given away here. Also, written questions give no chance for a trained police interviewer to follow up on inconsistencies and bore in deep for information or to observe the body language of a nervous suspect.

Both John and Patsy went to bed "around 10" and were asleep "around 10:40." Patsy awoke the next morning "at approximately 5:30 a.m. John woke up a little earlier and was already in the bathroom when Patsy awoke."

To the question of which interior house lights were on when everyone went to bed, the peculiar reply was "The custom is (and it is believed custom was followed that night), that JonBenét's bathroom light would have been on, with the door open a crack to allow a little light into her bedroom from her bathroom."

Asked if either of them got up during the night, which I considered to be a yes or no question, the answer came back, "Neither has a memory of doing so." I thought this conveniently allowed the possibility that some witness may have seen one of the parents up and about.

Asked who checked to see if the doors and windows were secure, the innocuous reply was "Patsy did not check the doors and windows. John does not believe that he did." He had told several policemen that the house was locked.

The Ramseys' public relations man soon put a media spin on the nonanswers, which did not come close to being a true interview. "John and Patsy Ramsey have cooperated extensively with the police and other law enforcement authorities from the very beginning of their investigation, and this cooperation will continue. Written answers to all of the written questions submitted by the Boulder Police Department have been delivered to them this afternoon." The statement was outrageous. What extensive cooperation was he talking about? We had hardly seen these people since the day of the murder and, except for this minimal communication, had heard nothing from them.

———

We got very little from an interview with nine-year-old Burke Ramsey, for whom Team Ramsey had dictated stringent terms to an agreeable district attorney's office: No police could be in the room, the questioning would be by child psychologist Suzanne Bernhard, and the session would not be held in a police building. Any possible police leverage was bargained away before the session began. We all felt sorry for Burke, but damn, he might actually know something! And while Bernhard's professional credentials were fine, some prosecutors in surrounding jurisdictions refused to use her because of a perceived pro-defense bias.

Detectives Jane Harmer and Ron Gosage, a group of social workers, and Burke's lawyer, Patrick Burke, watched from behind a two-way mirror. The detectives were able to make suggestions to Bernhard, but the psychologist asked shrink questions, and the interview became an entirely different sort than one to solicit evidentiary information.

The boy remembered his sister as being "nice" but added, "Sometimes she bugged me." JonBenét would tickle him and rummage through his desk to find candy and baseball cards. Bernhard asked how he was dealing with his sister's death, and Burke replied, "I kind of forget about it. I just kind of go . . ." and he lapsed into sounds similar to Nintendo beeps.

What do you think happened to your sister?

I know what happened to my sister. She was killed.

But what happened?

I know what happened.

How was she killed? Have you talked to your parents about it?

I asked my dad, Where did you find her body? He said, In the basement. I think someone took her down in the basement . . . took a knife out [losing words, he made a slashing gesture] or hit her on the head.

He said the house was usually always locked.

His descriptions were flat and indifferent. Bernhard detected no fear that the killer might come back for him or that Burke thought the family was in danger. The psychologist said it was very unusual for a child to feel safe when a sibling had been violently killed.

It was the only time that authorities had been allowed to speak to

Burke since December 26, when a detective managed to ask him a few questions before the boy left the home of Fleet White. More than a year and a half would pass before Burke was allowed to be interviewed again.

————

The most incredible thing about the interview had nothing at all to do with the boy. It was, in my view, a step by Team Ramsey to build a bridge to a specific detective they apparently believed to be sympathetic.

Attorney Patrick Burke, his client Patsy Ramsey, and her son were escorted to the interview by Detective Linda Arndt. While the boy settled in to talk with Bernhard, Patsy and the detective waited in a nearby kitchen, alone. They stayed together during the full hour of the interview. Arndt submitted a report.

Patsy was coughing with bronchitis, which led to a discussion of her ovarian cancer, her difficult recovery, and how she had been saddened that her chemotherapy ordeal vied for the family's attention with her younger sister's pregnancy. She told Arndt about moving from West Virginia to Atlanta and laughed that she was the black sheep of the family. The conversation rambled from Patsy's being invited to join the board of the Boulder Philharmonic to how being a mother was so important to her.

Then, Arndt recalled, Patsy bowed her head and cried, confessing that she could have no more children because of a hysterectomy following the cancer. The conversation drifted to her relationship with Jon-Benét and how she had taken her daughter to New York and they had seen five Broadway shows in four days. Patsy said Burke was going back to school, John was going back to work, but she had nothing to return to. She loved Burke, but really missed JonBenét, and Burke did not like to wear makeup and bake cookies.

Then she said it was good that Detective Arndt was on the case and urged her to find the killer.

Team Ramsey had gone out of its way to put Patsy and John off-limits to police, but an experienced defense attorney like Patrick Burke had allowed Arndt and Patsy to be alone for an hour. I felt that was no accident.

A few hours after the interview, Arndt reported that the lawyer called her at the police department, asking if there was a second ransom note and what results had been received from the Colorado Bureau of Investigation. Arndt reported she told him there had been but the single ransom note and that we hadn't received anything from the CBI.

Although we pursued these logical avenues of investigation, we did not focus just on the Ramseys, although they complained that we did. Patsy told one friend, "They're trying to frame us." We were much too busy to do that. Our mailboxes, telephone voice mail, and desks in the Situation Room were littered with unsolicited theories, possible suspects, and hate mail. Sketch artists offered everything from a Michael Jackson look-alike to "the Fly" as the culprit, a Beverly Hills psychic left multiple hours-long voice mail messages for me, and Internet groupies passed along their ideas. Letters flooded in, sick, twisted stuff from the underbelly of society, which were read when we had a chance.

Not only was Team Ramsey throwing us suspects to check out, but names were coming in from everywhere. A woman tipped us that her ex-husband had sexually assaulted their daughter, tied her up, and covered her mouth with duct tape, so we ordered him in. He turned out to be a spit-and-polish graduate of the Naval Academy and a successful businessman. We had asked only a few questions when he responded, "Have you been talking to my ex-wife?" We wouldn't tell him, but he explained the poisonous relationship that had followed their breakup. We checked his story, and the alleged assaults on the child never happened. Angry and rejected lovers were a prime source of potential suspects, and for every person we cleared, two more appeared.

We invested huge amounts of time over the coming months chasing these phantom leads while the public wondered why it was taking us so long to solve the case. Nothing illustrated these futile efforts better than our investigation of Santa Claus.

"Santa Bill" McReynolds was trapped, and his life ruined, by his fondness for appearing on television. Once he and his family emerged as suspects, they would be hounded for years, although nothing more than innuendo ever connected them to the death of JonBenét.

The retired professor of journalism at the University of Colorado had played Santa at previous Ramsey Christmas parties and in 1996 had been included in a Santa special produced by folksy CBS-TV correspondent Charles Kuralt, who finished filming McReynolds just before he went to the Ramsey home. Such a colorful character became an overnight celebrity.

McReynolds, who hugged Patsy in church during the memorial service, was anything but a roly-poly Jolly Old Elf. Instead he was a frail sixty-seven-year-old man with a flowing white beard who was still recovering from heart and lung surgery performed in August 1996, only four months before the murder.

Sick or not, we weren't going to cut him any slack in our first interview. The Ramseys had put him on their early list of suspects, and a witness had told police that JonBenét said a "Secret Santa" was going to visit her. McReynolds knew nothing about that.

In our interview McReynolds suggested incest as a possible motive for the murder, but he later retracted that and told the *Today* show that the Ramseys were a terrific family.

We took hair, handwriting, blood, and prints, then had a long talk. Santa Bill told us how special JonBenét was, never asking for gifts for herself, just wanting "joy and peace" for everyone. "There are angels everywhere," she told him. "Every day is Christmas."

JonBenét had led McReynolds by the hand on a tour of the house during the 1995 Christmas party, including her bedroom and the basement to see where the Christmas trees were kept, and had given him a vial of glittery "stardust" to sprinkle in his beard. He carried it to the hospital as a lucky charm during the surgery.

He confirmed being at the 1996 party but said he was at home in Rollinsville, a little mountain town about an hour from Boulder, with his wife and friends on Christmas night. After their guests left that evening, both husband and wife climbed into bed and slept all night. He was on postsurgical medication and needed his rest.

McReynolds said what was truly terrible was that this wasn't the first child to die during his Santa years. A little boy who was "a special friend" had been murdered several years previously.

Detective Gosage and I felt there were a lot of loose ends with Santa Bill. Anything else you want to tell us? Anything else we're going to find out? He floored us. When his own daughter was ten years old, she and another girl were kidnapped, and the friend was molested before both girls were released. When did that happen? He didn't remember, it was so long ago, about twenty-five years.

When I got up to thank him for coming in, McReynolds grabbed me around the shoulders. "Santa doesn't shake hands," he said. "Santa hugs."

Gosage called McReynolds's daughter, who corroborated his alibi and confirmed the kidnapping episode when she was a child. Gosage got a police report on the abduction, read it, and slammed the papers down on the desk. The kids had been snatched on December 26, 1974—*exactly* twenty-two years before the murder of JonBenét. McReynolds had not told us that!

Then when a couple of reporters discovered that Santa's wife, Janet McReynolds, had written a play about a girl who was tortured and murdered in the basement of her home, my jaw hit the floor. All the other coincidences, and now this. This wasn't a hiccup of a lead, it was an atomic bomb.

Janet McReynolds was quiet and impressive, her grandmotherly appearance existing comfortably with a considerable intellect. With degrees from three universities, including a Ph.D., she had worked as a teacher and a writer and had won a grant from the National Endowment for the Arts for her play, *Hey, Rube*, which was produced in New York and Los Angeles. It was based on a true story about the horrible murder of a teenage girl in Indianapolis.

Despite the subject matter, there was nothing to link the play or its author to the murder of JonBenét. We asked if there was anything else we should know. She said there wasn't.

We still had to check out her two sons, Tristan and Jesse. Tristan had a tight alibi, having been in Michigan with his girlfriend over the Christmas holidays. Jesse was a different story. He had done two and a half years in an Arizona prison for conspiracy, aggravated robbery . . . and kidnapping.

Then came the final undoing of Santa Bill. McReynolds loved appearing on television, and someone recognized him as a regular customer at a local adult bookstore. He came in again for an interview that cleared him of suspicion, but at a personal price.

McReynolds was distraught by the discovery of something he thought was buried so deep in his private life that his wife of thirty-five years was unaware of it until we called him. He emphasized that his sexual fantasies never involved children or child pornography.

Analysis proved that Santa Bill didn't write the ransom note, and he was much too frail to have made a midnight run from Rollinsville, done a Spiderman entry of the Ramsey home, awakened his victim, fed her pineapple, and then killed her, all the while fearless of being discovered and without leaving behind a shred of evidence.

Additional information he shared with us at the interview, which we were later able to confirm, further eliminated him. We investigated the hell out of this old man. He didn't do it.

Bill McReynolds retired from the Santa Claus business that day, but although I no longer considered him a suspect, I couldn't say the same about his son Jesse, who had no corroborated alibi. He had come home from the Christmas party at his parents' home, had a drink of scotch, swallowed some powerful prescription drugs he took for depression, and gone to bed alone, not awakening until late the next morning.

Jesse McReynolds, now thirty-eight, had botched a $113 gas station robbery in Arizona during which he forced the clerk to move from Point A to Point B. Thus the kidnapping charge. And while living in Nederland, near Boulder, he had some other scrapes with the law.

An ex-con knows what's going on in an interrogation room with two detectives, and Jesse McReynolds knew he looked good to Gosage and me as a suspect in the Ramsey case. His best chance was to work with us, so he became a picture of cooperation. Blood sample? OK. Lengthy interview? OK. Whatever we wanted, he gave, and Jesse's handwriting eliminated him as the author of the ransom note.

Seldom has one family given so many different leads to investigators, but in the end, after following the trail for months, there was nothing to link any of them with this crime. Nevertheless, the DA's office repeatedly resurrected them as suspects.

12

The investigative team, now narrowed to four primary detectives with Sergeant Tom Wickman in charge, received new assignments after Atlanta. For the next phase of the investigation, Ron Gosage and I took Access Graphics, business associates, St. John's Church, and all the Atlanta assignments. Detectives Jane Harmer and Linda Arndt got the friends, the domestic help, and the pageants. Wickman would assist Detective Tom Trujillo with the forensics and evidence, while other detectives helped on peripheral assignments.

Eller made a couple of smart moves in the realignment, as he rounded the team into its final form. The thoroughly professional Harmer would offset the sympathetic Arndt, who we worried might be getting too emotionally involved to remain objective. Although putting Trujillo on evidence would remove him from fieldwork, he seemed to have a problem with priorities, and I was concerned that his slowness in accomplishing tasks might hinder the testing of evidence. For instance, a full *year* passed before he completed his report on the initial Atlanta trip. Trujillo and Arndt still were not speaking, and the sergeant who reported the undisturbed snow now filed an amended report. The first officer was having difficulty in recollecting certain events. Then Arndt began amending her reports, too. I saw big trouble ahead.

The best business address in Boulder is the Pearl Street Mall, a shady pedestrian thoroughfare bordered on both sides by restaurants, government buildings, boutiques, and bookstores. Thousands of people, from musicians to corporate executives to tourists, flock there daily. A tasteful sign above one doorway reads Access Graphics. The staff was unexpectedly arrogant, defiant, and unhelpful when asked to help police pursue the murderer of their CEO's daughter. In fact, eventually they threw us out of the building.

At first Detective Gosage and I worked out of the quiet fourth-floor office of Don Paugh, Patsy's father and an Access vice president. We had to consider the possibility that it might be bugged. We learned later that John Ramsey was in daily contact with his top officers.

We had one list of current employees and another of those who had left or been dismissed by the company—hundreds of names. So we started at the top of the Access hierarchy and best-guessed which others to interview. Vice presidents and other key employees filed in to see us, and we took their hair and handwriting samples and recorded their alibis. They agreed to take polygraphs if necessary. Our questions were standard. Know of any enemies or zealots? Lawsuits? Ever been in the Ramsey home? What about hostile takeover attempts? Trouble in other countries? We learned about petty corporate politics, who didn't like whom, who was on the fast track, and occasionally someone vindictively tried to get a rival investigated. A lot of agendas were at work in the Pearl Street Mall. When we asked why the Ramseys would not talk to us, the answer was always a shaking head and "I don't know."

On our second day, Denise Wolf, the fiercely loyal assistant to President and CEO John Ramsey, handed me a slip of paper containing the 1995 bonus her boss was paid in 1996 under a deferred compensation plan. I did a double take as I read the numbers. John Ramsey received a net bonus of $118,117.50, almost the exact amount asked for in the ransom note. To me, that was too precise to be a coincidence, and it was known to very few people.

Finally Gary Merriman, the head of human resources, let us know that our questions were interfering with the running of a billion-dollar business, and they kicked us out, citing concerns over "trade secrets" and "liability." Our further requests were met with stony replies, although they professed continued cooperation. But in reality we were told to get a search warrant or a court order.

We posted a sign-up sheet for them to come down to police headquarters and talk to us in an interrogation room. The interviews with Access employees continued throughout January, sometimes helpful, sometimes hostile, and turned up nothing.

They weren't the only ones not cooperating. Detective Jane Harmer advised us that the High Peaks Elementary School, which had been attended by the Ramsey children, found that having detectives around was "disruptive." Burke Ramsey had returned to classes, without police escort, a few weeks after a "small foreign faction" killed his sister. When Detective Gosage called a therapist who we were told had seen Jon-Benét, he was told to "talk to the parents' attorneys." The pediatrician, Dr. Beuf, would not talk to us. Team Ramsey claimed, contrary to legal opinion the cops had received, that the doctor-patient privilege between Beuf and JonBenét extended past the grave. Patsy's sister Pam Paugh suggested that the Ramseys "might be available by fax." I thought the conspiracy of silence was growing stronger by the day, and felt we were now past the point where a grand jury *might* be helpful. Now I thought one was absolutely necessary.

But when we broached the subject with the DA's office, as early as January 1997, we were stopped cold. Elsewhere grand juries are kept in session or on call year-round to handle just these sort of situations, but Boulder County seldom used them. Instead of immediately convening a grand jury to help the police investigate this murder, District Attorney Alex Hunter suggested that we "ask permission" from the Ramseys to speak to the pediatrician and others. His deputies, Pete Hofstrom and Trip DeMuth, were advocating a soft, hand-holding approach to "build trust" with the Ramseys as the best way to get information instead of being aggressive. To me it appeared that Team Ramsey was playing them like puppets. If these people wanted to act like suspects, it was time to treat them as such.

———

At seven o'clock on January 9, Chief Koby was at the Boulder Public Library for his first press briefing, and as our spokesman, he was a disaster.

First, he had limited the session to the locals and left the major newspaper and television reporters cooling their heels outside, their bad mood growing by the minute. Excluding the national media was a huge mistake since the case was the focus of worldwide attention. Anytime you turned on the TV, in Miami or Anchorage, Bangor or San Diego, there was JonBenét parading on stage in provocative clothing and poses. Every newspaper in the land carried stories almost daily, and commentators filled the airwaves with opinions. Our chief of police, with his long hair and beard, consistently failed to understand the media.

He stepped into trouble immediately when he attempted to defend the botched handling of the crime scene. "Most legal experts will tell you, police officials and legal experts will tell you, we've done it just right," he said. Astounded reporters scribbled in their notebooks.

Equally surprised were his detectives as we watched the broadcast in the Situation Room. The chief said it would have been "totally unreasonable" to interview the Ramseys on that first day. I couldn't have disagreed more, and probably so did most of America. That had been *exactly* the right time to interview them, while events were fresh and before they created Team Ramsey.

Then, instead of *using* the press, Koby attacked it! "I have never, in the twenty-eight years I have been in this business, seen such media focus on an event. It is intrusive, and making it much more difficult to work through this situation. . . . The less you know, the easier it is to give advice."

After that, we could almost hear the sound of the hunting horns. Angry at him, the indignant media came after us harder than ever.

————

The police department had split into factions because Commander John Eller had taken Sergeant Larry Mason's credentials and suspended him, accusing Mason of leaking confidential information to the media during the trip to Atlanta. "We got him," Eller had whispered to me as Mason got off the plane, carrying a *Daily Camera*. "We set him up." That decision eventually would bury John Eller.

The commander had chosen the wrong incident, and Mason fought back. Just when the department needed unity, Commander Mark Beckner launched an Internal Affairs investigation, and Mason sued Eller. Cops questioning cops played out over the coming weeks until Mason was officially cleared of leaking information. Chief Koby, who had sanctioned Eller's original decision to suspend Mason, would issue an apology and write a $10,000 check to the sergeant to settle the case. A review board finally ruled that Eller did nothing wrong and had been duty-bound to pursue Mason in the first place.

Several years later my wife and I had dinner with Lawrence Schiller, the author of *Perfect Murder, Perfect Town,* also about this case. He told us that when he was conducting interviews, Mason surprised him with the comment "You knew I was [*Daily Camera* reporter] Alli Krupski's source, didn't you?"

The fighting within the department became sharp, bitter, and divisive and interfered with our investigation into who killed JonBenét. It also created an unofficial gag order that would be strictly adhered to thereafter by cops. There was never a general order posted on the board, but it became an iron rule—the chief would be the police spokesman. Nobody else would say anything, no matter how we were attacked. That left the field open for the DA's office, which was a leaking sieve to the press, to blame the cops for every problem in the case.

The detectives wanted the chief to stand up and denounce the bullshit propaganda, but Koby thought it best to "ride out the storm." His strategy, apparently, was no strategy at all. He ventured out only periodically, and then only to self-destruct before the press.

————

The SitRoom was littered with to-do lists, Polaroids of people interviewed, memos, and diagrams, all pieces of a giant puzzle we were trying to assemble, and I was still running into DA-imposed roadblocks. They still didn't support warrants to obtain the credit card and telephone records from the Ramseys.

————

McGuckin's Hardware is a Boulder landmark built around the idea that if you can't find what you need at McGuckin's, you probably don't need it. Office Manager Joann Hanks had a puzzling telephone conversation with a brusque caller who identified himself only as "John." He wanted to know about a couple of December charges on his American Express bill. He read the dates and amounts of the purchases. When told the information had been purged from the store computer and would require a hand search of receipts, the man said he would call back on Monday, January 20.

Hanks found the receipts and was startled to see the signature of Patricia Ramsey. A $46.31 purchase on December 2, 1996, at 7:40 P.M. and a $99.88 receipt on December 9 at 11:14 A.M. Hanks notified John Christie, the head of security, who called the police. We wondered why John Ramsey, so soon after the murder of his child, was hunting up old credit card purchases.

Gosage and I were at the store to await the call. The McGuckin's people put us in the president's office and had Joann Hanks's calls transferred to his telephone. We managed to record three conversations with "John Ramsey." It was not John Ramsey at all, but an impersonator. Through the most circuitous routes, we found that the number had been washed several times to disguise its point of origin, which was a Denver boiler room operation known as Touch Tone, Inc. I began the legal paperwork needed to take a closer look.

But while still in McGuckin's, it dawned upon me that the huge store had an elaborate video surveillance system that keeps watch over every square inch of corridor and bin of merchandise. The receipts did not itemize what Patsy had bought, but if luck was on our side, there was a possibility we might be able to *see* whatever she bought. If she bought duct tape or white cord, it would be powerful evidence.

The security manager cut short that investigative avenue. The recorded security tapes were recycled every thirty days. The ones we wanted from December 2 and 9 had already been reused. We had missed by only a couple of weeks, but it might as well have been a lifetime. If the DA's office had let us aggressively pursue the Ramsey credit card receipts early on, those videotapes could have been in evidence by now. It was a missed opportunity to get evidence, whatever it might have shown.

The manager showed us where black duct tape was sold in the paint department and explained that purchases were not listed as specific items on receipts. Instead the computers logged them according to the sections from which they came, and during rush times like holidays, harried cashiers sometimes hit the wrong computer key and credited an item by mistake to an adjacent department. The paint department was next to the builder's hardware department. Among the items on Patsy's December 9 receipt was an item from builder's hardware. The price was $1.99. On the December 2 slip, there was an item from the garden department. It was $1.99. Duct tape also sold for $1.99. We had no way of knowing what she had bought.

———

Although still too distraught to meet with us, John and Patsy Ramsey spoke for several hours with their newest trophy hire, John Douglas, formerly with the FBI's behavioral sciences unit.

John Ramsey's lawyer Bryan Morgan was at the profiler's side and permitted no direct questions about the Ramseys during a long interview.

Douglas, wearing a silk tie and an expensive suit, talked with machine-gun rapidity. He said the killer was someone who knew the house well, because it was a high-risk situation, and he pronounced the murder to be a crime of anger directed toward John Ramsey.

His former colleagues in the FBI disagreed and would tell us they were unaware of anyone killing a child as revenge against the parents. To my mind, a revenge killer would probably have left the lifeless body splayed beside the Christmas tree for maximum shock value.

I asked if Douglas knew of *any* kidnapping for ransom in which the victim was killed and left on the premises. He recalled a case involving a family member.

They also had recited a list of suspects for us—Jeff Merrick, Mike Glynn, and Jim Marino, all former Access employees who had been seen at a mysterious dinner with Tom Carson, currently the company's chief financial officer. Then he shocked us by also offering the name of Fleet White. The Ramsey camp had turned on one of its best friends.

Among the books Sergeant Wickman said were on John Ramsey's night stand was *Mindhunter,* by John Douglas. In the book he wrote that when loved ones or family members are the killers, careful attention is given to "staging" and diverting suspicion elsewhere. In the Ramsey case, the amateurish ransom note diverted the authorities for several hours.

Douglas also wrote that holidays were particularly stressful times and could trigger violent behavior. JonBenét was killed over Christmas.

Douglas stated that in parental murders, great care is usually shown in the disposal of the body. JonBenét had been carefully tucked into a blanket in a cellar room, and not discarded outside in the freezing cold.

John Douglas was almost denying his own writings in order to give the Ramseys a pass. The dust jacket of his next book identified him as a consultant on the JonBenét Ramsey case. It did not say for which side.

That same day, John Ramsey doubled the reward he was offering, to $100,000.

Gosage and I returned to Access Graphics for an appointment with CFO Tom Carson, who had been so negatively portrayed by Patsy's mother and who was now linked by John Douglas to a suspicious dinner with Merrick, Marino, and another friend, Mike Glynn. Unlike most of the others at Access, Carson was open and helpful and had a rock-solid alibi. At the time JonBenét was killed, he was in France with his girlfriend, Natalie, and her parents.

He dismissed the controversial dinner as just a get-together with old friends, not a conspiracy to commit murder across a table in a public restaurant in which John Ramsey was a part-owner. I would devote many hours to running down the stories of the others named, and the result was always the same. It was an innocent gathering that meant nothing to our case.

Carson had no idea the Ramseys had given us a copy of the gently worded handwritten sympathy note he sent them after the murder. Team Ramsey asked us to see if there was any link to the ransom note.

————

Another of those at the dinner, Jim Marino, had known John Ramsey since the 1970s in Atlanta and said he was a good guy with no enemies. When Marino had an accident in 1978 and was temporarily confined to a wheelchair, Ramsey offered him a sales job, which turned into long-term employment. Marino was making $51,600 a year when he left Access Graphics and considered himself a loyal friend of John Ramsey.

Detective Gosage started to take hair samples before Marino could warn him that some were hair plugs that cost ten dollars apiece. He would be cleared as a suspect but remained an ongoing character in the case. Even while he defended his pal John Ramsey on national television, Marino would repeatedly be pointed out by Ramsey and his lawyer as a murder suspect.

13

To make headway with the case, we needed to get the district attorney's office on board, so as January neared an end, we gave them a six-hour presentation in an attempt to repair our frayed relationship. It had been difficult to work together before the presentation. Afterward it was almost impossible.

Bob Keatley, the police department's legal adviser, practically ordered us to the table. An ethical and scholarly man who keeps books about Lincoln in his office, Keatley insisted that the breach between the two law enforcement arms charged with making the case had to be repaired. Let's get everybody on the same page, he said.

The DA's office had complained they were not being kept up to date, which was true, since Eller had kicked them off the case. Now we were inviting them back as full partners. They would hear it all, as we demonstrated the breadth and depth of the investigation to date—and showed that, after a month of hard work, we had found nothing that persuaded us that anyone broke into the house and murdered JonBenét Ramsey. That was a backward way of telling them the department's position that Patsy and John Ramsey should be named the chief suspects in the death of their daughter.

So on a cold and snowy day, we all filed into the SitRoom, where Keatley, Eller, Koby, and Hunter took places at the front of a square of tables. Seven detectives were around the edges, along with the DA's top two men on the case, Pete Hofstrom and Trip DeMuth.

Eller began, saying we wanted the weak points of our case highlighted and their legal opinion of the best future strategy. Detective Melissa Hickman gave the detailed timeline, and Sergeant Bob Whitson reviewed the events of December 26.

Detective Mike Everett went through an exhaustive review of the crime scene, including finding pineapple in the victim's intestinal tract as well as in a bowl that bore the fingerprints of Patsy and Burke. I considered that to be an extraordinary piece of evidence. We knew JonBenét did not eat the fruit during the White's party, yet it was in her stomach.

One by one, the detectives gave the DA and his lieutenants everything, including the trauma to the vagina, the still unknown murder weapon, the conclusion of several doctors that the strangulation followed the blow to the head, and that DNA had been found in the panties and beneath the fingernails. We pointed out that the DNA could be totally unrelated to the case, since no skin or blood was found beneath the nails to indicate that JonBenét had scratched her killer.

And we brought them in on the secret that the lab had discovered what was believed to be a pubic hair on the blanket. So far we had been unable to identify it. That single hair would become one of the most lingering and controversial questions of the entire case, for Team Ramsey and those within the DA's office who believed an intruder killed the child would insist that it had to have come from the murderer. As we would discover, there was almost an unlimited number of possible sources for the mysterious hair.

Sergeant Wickman concentrated on the ransom note, and when he disclosed that our handwriting expert thought Patsy was the possible author, the room went pin-drop silent. Hunter pushed back his chair and groaned, "Awwww, Jesus."

We reported on the preliminary FBI determinations. The FBI had been given a chance to look at the note and determined that it was written in the comfort of the home and probably after the killing, not before. The crime scene reflected careful staging, they said, a criminally unsophisticated killer attempting to cover up what had happened.

I recapped the memorial service, Atlanta, Access Graphics, our scores of interviews with an incredible range of suspects, and pointed to all the false trails we had followed, the fact that we had had hundreds of telephone tips and letters and that the Crimestoppers' number was jammed. And still no outsider had surfaced that legitimately looked like the killer.

We wanted to know from the DA: Based on everything you've heard, are the Ramseys suspects or not?

It was a rhetorical question, because obviously in our eyes they were.

But the Ramseys were not going to be labeled as such. We couldn't call the suspects "suspects."

Hunter, Hofstrom, and DeMuth accused us of not knowing how the system worked and reminded us again that while our job was to make an arrest based on probable cause, the threshold they would face in court would be proof "beyond a reasonable doubt." They pointed out that we had no silver bullet, no slam dunk for a jury. We understood that, but we argued in return that they were interpreting beyond a reasonable doubt (BARD) as meaning an Absolutely No-Doubt Confession.

Since I doubted that they ever wanted to see this case in front of a jury, I felt their argument was an excuse. We accused them of being played like fish on a hook. We wanted some prosecutorial backbone, some definite guidance—get this-and-this, call so-and-so, wrap up such-and-such a detail. We told them we needed a grand jury to use when people slammed doors in our faces. We had shown them a hell of a lot of circumstantial evidence, and we felt we could get them to that higher legal level they demanded if they would only back us to the hilt and stop lying down for Team Ramsey.

Hofstrom, scribbling on a big tablet with a black Magic Marker held like a crayon, thought we were being too tough on the Ramseys. "So you've got a guy that acts a little weird and won't talk to you," he said. "So what? Doesn't mean he's a killer."

That was the defining moment that drove the final spike between the DA's office and the police department. They still were not going to intervene aggressively and get that grand jury going for us. In other jurisdictions, we would probably have been handing out subpoenas already and hauling reluctant witnesses into a room where they had to talk. I could not comprehend why this laid-back Boulder attitude was still the rule for the DA's shop while the world's media were accurately reflecting the mood of the people to Do Something!

Our chief of police sat there quietly uninvolved as the meeting collapsed. Tom Koby observed that when it came time to question the Ramseys, he should probably do it himself because he was "more on their intellectual level."

———

That we had made little headway in resolving our problems was repeatedly illustrated during the coming weeks. Deputy DA Trip DeMuth told us that we should back off from the Ramseys and let Hofstrom get in there and "work his magic." Hofstrom called Commander Eller to

ask what he could tell Team Ramsey, and the commander curtly replied, "Nothing."

———

Even the Colorado Attorney General's office was against letting the
defense lawyers learn anything more than what was absolutely required
by law. In a briefing with us, Assistant Attorney General Mary Malatesta, head of a special unit that deals only with capital cases, likened
it to an all-out war. Don't share anything at all with the defense, she
told District Attorney Alex Hunter. Tell them nothing. Instead, after
the AG's representative left the room, Hunter requested police blessing
for Hofstrom to speak with the Ramsey lawyers—without informing
us—"in order to maintain and build their trust." Had he even heard
what Malatesta had just said? *Don't share anything at all with the defense—
tell them nothing.* As much as we would have liked to have Malatesta's
gunslingers in our corner, we never saw them again.

———

The situation reached an apex of lunacy when the DA told Chief Koby
and Commander Eller a few days later that he was thinking about offering a deal to the unknown killer of JonBenét.

Hunter was planning a press conference to unveil his latest weapons,
criminalist Dr. Henry Lee and DNA specialist Barry Scheck, both of
whom had been tainted with the dubious fame of helping O. J. Simpson
beat a murder rap. By hiring them, Hunter made sure Team Ramsey
did not.

The DA figured that while he was talking to the press anyway, he
could announce a "mercy window" to the murderer, and if the killer
surrendered during that time, then Hunter would "plead for his soul"
and ask the court to be lenient. To me, that was not unexpected. It
would be the easy way out, the quick fix, business as usual in Boulder.

But by the time Hunter appeared before the cameras on February
13, he had performed a complete flip-flop and played the part of the
fire-hardened district attorney, vowing "no mercy" for the killer
and promising "you will pay." Alex Hunter was all over the map on
the JonBenét Ramsey case and would continue to be so throughout the
long investigation. One day he would say one thing to one person, the
next day the exact opposite to someone else. He drove us all to distrac-
tion because you trusted his word at your peril.

The reporters were kept waiting before the news conference while
the principals deliberated backstage in a direct reversal of roles. Koby

and Eller had gotten a glimpse of Hunter's intention of playing the hard-line prosecutor and wanted him to tone it down because they didn't want him to bluff with cards he didn't hold. Hunter agreed with them and kept his promise until he stepped into the bright lights.

"We're going to solve this case," the DA pledged, as Koby and Eller stood by bewildered. "I want to say something to the person or persons that committed this crime, the person or persons that took this baby from us," he continued, gazing directly into the cameras. "I mentioned the list of suspects narrows. Soon there will be no one left on the list but you. You have stripped us of any mercy we may have had in the beginning of this case. We will see that justice is served and that you pay for what you've done to this beautiful little girl."

Bespectacled, mustached, and looking like comedian Martin Mull, the district attorney promised, "You will not get away with what you have done."

He disclosed the Scheck and Lee hirings and said he was being advised by four other area district attorneys, whom he called his Expert Prosecution Task Force.

I wondered what the hell he was doing up there. That tough talk was coming from a man who had not even read the Ramsey case file. Our district attorney was never the law-and-order sort, but most people didn't know that this rhetoric didn't match his track record. Around the police department, we likened Hunter's fierce words that day to the sort of loud blather that comes before a match in the World Wrestling Federation, and it became known as Hunter's WWF speech. I remembered President Reagan's Cold War jabs at Soviet Premier Gorbachev, "Deeds, not words," and realized the district attorney was playing politics. Hunter would later explain that he was just trying to "smoke out the killer."

Koby was so shaken by the DA's broken agreement that by the time he took the podium, he could hardly say much more than "We are in this for the long haul."

Then once again he alienated journalists by belittling a reporter with the memorable remark "I don't answer stupid questions."

––––––––

While the press conference was making news in one building, more headlines were being generated in another one nearby by First Assistant District Attorney Bill Wise, who was telling the Boulder County Commission that Alex Hunter needed extra appropriations because "one of the suspects has money." We weren't allowed to call them suspects, but the number two man in the DA's office had carelessly done just that.

Then he knifed us by saying that the district attorney needed a good, experienced homicide investigator of his own, someone who would do "a real live investigation." It was a direct insult to the police.

"Doesn't Pete [Hofstrom] do some of that?" asked one commissioner.

"That's part of the problem," Wise responded. "He'd like to do a lot of that, and the Boulder Police Department says, 'Get out of our business.' They don't like lawyers sticking their noses into their investigation.

"I'm not going to criticize the Boulder Police Department, but I'd sure like to," Wise added.

When his comments were published, Wise was removed from the case and the district attorney spewed apologies. "Mister Wise regrets any statement that would indicate displeasure with the Boulder Police Department's investigation," said Hunter.

While we were in disarray, Team Ramsey was running like the proverbial well-oiled machine, and they were kicking our butts. John Ramsey had gotten his money's worth. His people were absolutely relentless, and no matter what they were given, they always asked for more.

Pat Korten, Ramsey's PR man, peddled the spin that the Ramseys had never been asked to take a polygraph and were in daily contact with the "authorities." Those "authorities" to whom he referred did not mean the police.

The Ramseys had not been asked to take a polygraph because Hofstrom never made the request. He and DeMuth said they "didn't believe in" lie detector tests.

On top of that, we learned that it had been disclosed to Patsy's lawyer, Patrick Burke, that our experts were saying Patsy's handwriting looked very much like that on the ransom note. It was a huge concession. Team Ramsey immediately started rounding up specialists of their own to dispute the damaging findings.

One day Burke rushed up to me in the police department lobby, and after I grabbed Detective Trujillo to be a witness, I listened to his demands. Always referring to his client as "my lady," he wanted (1) a first-generation copy of the ransom note and to know (2) whether semen had indeed been discovered, (3) whether there was in fact a practice note, (4) how many detectives were working the case, and (5) if we had accounted for a couple of "prime suspects" they had named.

We stared hard at each other. I was insulted that he thought I would hand over confidential case information just because he demanded it. I told him that if the parents had worked with us, they might have been cleared by now. "Tell your lady to come by any day or every day," I said.

He simply went around me and got the information elsewhere. Few secrets were held for very long.

Another Team Ramsey lawyer, Bryan Morgan, had me meet him at the police department on a Saturday to tell me of a major development. They had just learned of Father Rol's theory about Psalm 118 and wanted us to check it out. I said we had already done that. Soon they would be wanting to know why the detectives were asking about Psalms 35 and 36.

Their main successes in January, however, were stalling the requested interviews and blocking the testing of evidence. That underscored my belief that they had moved away from any pretense of finding a killer and were deep into trial defense preparation. I feared they would hinder the investigation whenever possible.

I hand-delivered a letter to Commander Eller from attorney Patrick Burke that laid out their conditions for us to interview the Ramseys. The points, which were plainly unacceptable, included having the session take place the very next day in the office of another Ramsey lawyer. Patsy would have both a doctor and a lawyer at her side, probably be available for only one hour, and be questioned only by Detective Arndt. They wanted Peter Hofstrom of the DA's office present.

Hofstrom and Trip DeMuth told us that we were being pigheaded by rejecting the offer. They said we should be willing to meet the Ramseys anytime, anywhere, and under any conditions.

Negotiations to arrange interviews of suspects are commonplace between prosecutors and defense attorneys, for under the Constitution, a person cannot be compelled to speak. Police officers know and accept that fact. The difference in this case was the wide gap between what the cops and the DA's office viewed as acceptable conditions for the interviews. They did not seem to understand that police do not like it when suspects dictate when, where, how, and with which detective they meet.

Eller wasn't about to let them stack the deck. The short lead time of less than twenty-four hours would give us no time to prepare, and we refused to walk in unprepared. He countered with an alternative suggestion—simultaneous interviews the following week at police head-quarters, with Eller assigning any detectives he wanted to do the questioning. The interview would continue until police were satisfied, would be videotaped, and Hofstrom was not welcome.

Team Ramsey came right back with a diatribe. How dare we turn down their guidelines? This was another example of the "cruel and insensitive treatment" of their clients by police. Anyone could see that the anguished Ramseys had nothing to do with the death of their daughter, and it was inexplicable why police continued to treat them as suspects.

These exchanges were only the opening shots, and the interview issue remained unresolved. As far as the detectives were concerned, the Ramseys were being treated like suspects because they had done noth-ing to convince us they weren't.

———

Father Rol came by on his way to lunch with the Ramseys and asked if I had any "good news." The minister described Patsy as devastated that the proposed interview had been canceled. She was seeing a thera-pist and "wanted to come out of hiding." John was "very down." Hov-erstock said they *wanted* to talk, but their attorneys were forcing them to remain quiet. I felt sorry for this well-meaning man, so I didn't tell him that both parents were silent by choice, not edict.

———

Team Ramsey also made a full assault on the testing of forensic evidence but suffered one of their rare setbacks.

The lawyers argued that they be notified in advance of any testing so that they might *approve* or *participate* in such examinations, and they raised concerns about specific and technical points and the testing meth-ods themselves. Team Ramsey wanted their experts present for any DNA testing, serology, and swab splitting, among other things.

I was surprised Hofstrom was even entertaining these demands, but he was doing more than that. He disclosed to Team Ramsey that testing had begun without their being notified. He should not have done so, because we were under no obligation to provide that information. The DA's chief trial deputy then suggested that an officially designated "sus-pect" would have the right to observe the CBI lab work. With Hof-strom's interpretation of the law in hand, the defense attorneys agreed to allow their clients to be called "suspects" for that one specific pur-pose. It looked as if they were going to get inside the labs.

By tracking every test, their own experts would make careful note of every single step of the process. Armed with such knowledge, a good defense attorney could impeach the lab's findings in court by challenging the methods used, all of the results, and even the qualifications of the scientists doing the tests.

Finally, the no-nonsense director of the Colorado Bureau of Investigation, Carl Whiteside, stomped on them. He pointed out that there were no charged defendants in the Ramsey homicide, and until someone was charged, no defense representatives would be allowed in his CBI lab for evidence testing.

Attorney Patrick Burke soon replied that "if my earlier comments have delayed the testing in any way, they are withdrawn." All it took was for someone in authority, instead of interpreting the law to benefit Team Ramsey, to just say no.

14

The ransom note had been very specific in telling John Ramsey that the "gentlemen watching over your daughter do not particularly like you." We wanted to find out who these gentlemen were, but as Detective Ron Gosage and I launched into another road trip, we learned that no matter where we went, we were still one step behind Team Ramsey.

Weeks before our plane took off from Denver in mid-February, I had contacted Lucinda Ramsey Johnson, the first wife of John Ramsey, to offer an exchange of information. I would help clear their son, John Andrew, if she would give me the name of the woman with whom John Ramsey had an affair. She was clearly uncomfortable speaking with me, and the day before the interview she canceled it.

"I've got an attorney," she told me by telephone.

"Why? You aren't suspected of anything."

"It seems like the thing to do."

I offered her a sweetheart deal and dropped my condition to get the name of the mistress: If she would help us clear their children John Andrew and Melinda, I would go public to say they were not involved. I didn't like it, but moving them off the table would let us get on with more promising leads.

The next day in Atlanta I called her new lawyer, Jim Jenkins. Yes, he said, my proposal was quite attractive. No, there could be no interviews of Lucinda Ramsey Johnson or her daughter, Melinda Ramsey, because the scheduling had come too fast. I reminded him we had made the appointments well in advance, but he countered that since he had just come aboard, he would need to see "all prior statements" before his client spoke to us.

Giving witnesses a chance to review previous statements to police is one of the worst things that can happen before an interview. It totally removes the element of surprise from future questions, telegraphs what you're looking for, and gives witnesses and their lawyers time to study the documents carefully and plan strategy. Unless legally required to do so, as in the discovery process before a trial, a cop would rather eat glass than hand over previous statements. The tactic would be used time and again by Team Ramsey, often successfully and with terrible results for us.

Two months would pass before we finally got to interview Lucinda Ramsey Johnson. In the meantime, we learned that John Ramsey was paying both for his first wife's lawyer and for the mortgage on her house. There was no doubt about her loyalty.

Gosage and I had been in Georgia less than twenty-four hours before the telephone started ringing on the desk of our boss in Boulder, Commander Eller. The Ramsey attorneys were seething that we were asking about infidelities and personal details. To hell with them, I replied. If they don't want us searching all over God's green earth for former lovers and mysterious enemies, all they have to do is give us the information firsthand.

In the following days, we documented the whereabouts of John Andrew Ramsey on the night his little stepsister was killed. Although the family had been of minimal help, Gosage and I backtracked through interviews, records, friends, and associates to put him officially in the Atlanta-Marietta area, except for about six hours when he was presumably asleep at his mother's home. Unless there was a far-reaching conspiracy or a Harrier jet in the backyard, he didn't do it.

The strangest moment of the trip came when we emerged from interviewing one of Lucinda Johnson's neighbors on Turtle Lake Drive and found her and her son, John Andrew, standing directly across the street in their own driveway, looking at us. Fifteen hundred miles from Boulder, and two of the people we most wanted to talk to about the murder of JonBenét stood right in front of us, and wouldn't even say hello. It was surreal.

On the last day of the month, I wrote in an exhaustive report that "one can conclude John Andrew Ramsey's whereabouts have been reasonably accounted for." A few days later the city spokesperson announced that both John Andrew and his sister Melinda had been cleared of suspicion.

That was a huge gift to the Ramseys. Once the older kids were cleared we had no more leverage in Atlanta, and it was a milepost in the sham of cooperation.

To me, it seemed that their priorities were seriously out of order.

One morning I listened to the radio as the father of another murdered girl called for the Ramseys to take lie detector tests. Marc Klass, the father of Polly Klass, had a special perspective on our case since he had gone through a similar hell when his daughter was slain and he was considered a suspect. Despite negative publicity, the man had almost lived at the police station during his ordeal, baring his soul to detectives, helping in any possible way. He urged the Ramseys to do as he had done and *ask* to be polygraphed so that police would not have to waste any more time investigating them. That was the sort of response I had always expected but never got from John and Patsy Ramsey, their relatives, and their defenders.

Detectives are professionally insulted by suspects who commit atrocious crimes. We are driven to apprehend them, and usually we have the methods, tools, and resources with which to do that. The victim's family and the detectives have a common bond and goal. Who better to turn to than the cop who will do anything possible to catch the killer of a loved one?

We returned to Atlanta's finest neighborhoods to interview more of the Lunch Bunch, who seemed terribly inconvenienced by it all. Private investigators had made the rounds the day before, spreading the word that we only wanted to "interrogate the Ramseys," thus painting us as the bad guys in a murder investigation.

One couple was typical. The wife said, "John and Patsy just want to move on" with their lives, so we should leave them alone. I wondered what that meant, since we weren't standing on her front porch with questions about a stolen bicycle but about the murder of their friends' daughter. The husband, who was an attorney, barely contained his contempt for us and demanded that we talk to the Ramseys "like in a living room, on a couch and stuff." Not how we do business, we said, and the door slammed shut behind us.

Another assignment for the trip had been to research the death of John Ramsey's first child, Beth. Because of the vaginal trauma inflicted on JonBenét, we had to determine if there had ever been any sexual abuse involving Beth. There had not.

We traveled to Arizona, Georgia, Ohio, and Illinois and felt like cold-calling encyclopedia salesmen showing up on a doorstep. Some people demanded to have their lawyers present, some wanted to see the questions in advance, and others would not talk at all.

All the information we gathered said the same thing: Beth was a sweet girl with a bright future, and there was nothing untoward in her relationship with her father, who was utterly devastated when she was killed in an automobile accident.

Elizabeth Pasch Ramsey was born in the Philippines while her father was in the navy but was brought to the United States while still a baby. She was her daddy's girl, always at his right hand, always on his mind. John Ramsey adored his firstborn child and thrilled in her accomplishments as she captained the Wheeler High cheerleading squad in Marietta, took a degree in finance at Miami University in Ohio, spent a summer studying in London, and got a job at Delta Air Lines as a flight attendant in 1991. Some time after her first boyfriend died of cystic fibrosis, she resumed a relationship with former classmate Matt Derrington, and friends said they were considering marriage. On January 8, 1992, she was a passenger in Derrington's BMW when it slid on a patch of ice at I-55 and North County Line Road outside of Chicago, into the path of a bakery truck. Both were killed. She was only twenty-two years old.

What interested me as an investigator were the totally opposite reactions that John Ramsey showed to the deaths of his eldest and youngest daughters. When Beth died, in an *accident,* he was inconsolable, and relatives spoke of how he could be heard late at night almost howling in grief. Years later her presence was still large in his life. Pictures of her filled a desk drawer, her name was on his plane. But when JonBenét was *murdered,* we saw little open grief.

I wondered where was all of that emotion this time? Where was the anger? Why wasn't he acting more like Marc Klass than a cool CEO hiding some minor transgression behind a buffer of lawyers?

———

We were all concerned about that unidentified pubic hair the lab found on the white blanket that was wrapped around JonBenét, for it opened the possibility that a sexual attack had taken place and the hair was left behind by the killer. Despite Team Ramsey's claim that the hair belonged to the unknown intruder, in reality it may have come from a huge number of sources.

However, it could be meaningless and of innocent origin. A former FBI profiler explained that there are always "artifacts" at a crime scene and that not every cigarette butt or beer can is related to the murder.

Nevertheless, it became the subject of a thorough investigation all its own. Detective Trujillo reported that the Colorado Bureau of Investigation concluded it did not come from John or Patsy Ramsey.

Later the CBI lab suggested that it might not be a pubic hair at all but an "ancillary" hair that could have come from someone's arm, chest, or other area of the body. FBI testing was delayed because Team Ramsey wanted their own people to watch any such examination, which the FBI would not allow.

When I thought of the pubic hair, I vividly remembered the shock of discovering that a number of visitors to the Ramsey home had stayed as overnight guests, and some had slept in the bed of JonBenét. Any of them could have been the source of the mysterious hair.

I first came across that line of investigation in an interview with Brad Millard, a college friend of John Andrew Ramsey. We routinely asked if he had ever been in the Ramsey home in Boulder. Not only had he been there, but he even spent a night in JonBenét's bed, he said.

I felt like breaking my pen. With a simple fluke question, a young man volunteered that he had slept in the victim's bed! How many other guests had slept there?

Patsy's mother, Nedra Paugh, and her daughters Pam and Polly came in to see us at the Roswell PD but didn't bring much new information. To dodge the press, Pam drove in with Nedra lying flat in the backseat. One of the first things the grandmother told us was that she too had slept in JonBenét's bed.

Now we knew that two people—Millard and Nedra—had slept there, and as time passed, so many more names would surface that JonBenét's room started to remind me of a Motel 6.

In my opinion, there was no reason to assume the pubic hair had come from an attacker who actually crawled into bed with JonBenét during a sexual assault. The hair displayed microscopic consistencies with Melinda Ramsey. But there were also a number of other hairs and fibers collected from the blanket—many of which were consistent with JonBenét and Patsy Ramsey. Others were never sourced.

We would find that a number of visitors had used the bed while the child was elsewhere. The hair could have come from any of them, or it could have been transferred through some other contact, such as in a washing machine or dryer. We also found that obtaining pubic hair samples was even more difficult than trying to interview people.

————

Despite my explaining how a Q-and-A worked, Nedra talked nonstop. But if you could stay with her long enough, reality might drop into the conversation.

She revealed a bit more about JonBenét messing her pants and bed, a subject she had minimized in our previous interview. Now, however, she said that the child did not wipe properly after a bowel movement, and quite often an adult would have to wash her bottom and change her undies. They called it "dirtying." The grandmother also mentioned two occasions when the little girl had gone to play with her best friend, Daphne White, and had come home with Fleet White carrying her soiled underwear, saying that JonBenét had had an accident and was wearing a pair of Daphne's panties. That made me think of another alternative to the foreign DNA found in her clothing.

We tried to get information about bedtime snacks and managed to learn that the girl loved grapes, sliced apples, and fruit of all kinds, especially pineapple. Give her a whole can and she'd eat it. We knew she ate pineapple the night she died, and now her grandmother told us how much the child loved it. While she was talking, I weighed some alternatives. That she was given a bedtime snack from the bowl that had Patsy's fingerprints made more sense to me than the possibility of an intruder feeding the child pineapple, keeping her alive long enough for it to reach her digestive tract, then killing her.

Nedra was also obviously aware of the current evidence. When she talked about "an old booger of a dog" that JonBenét liked to wrestle, she pointed out that the dog did not scratch the girl's vagina.

Pam Paugh answered some pageant questions. JonBenét was the driving force behind the pageants, she said, and loved the femininity and girlishness of the contests. Pam denied that the child's hair had been dyed. It had only been "highlighted" because JonBenét wanted to be even more blond. And the child "played hard" and always had dirt beneath her fingernails. "Wouldn't let you trim them," she said. Bingo, I thought. More DNA possibilities. But Pam stubbornly insisted there was no bed-wetting problem.

The younger sister, Polly, added the name of Barb Fernie, the friend who was so close to the Ramseys that Patsy called her on the morning of December 26, to the list of people considered suspects. The other woman who rushed to Patsy's side that morning, Priscilla White, was also suspicious, said Polly. Priscilla had been seen copying Patsy's Daytimer calendar, and Polly said that might explain how someone's handwriting might be duplicated, perhaps on a ransom note. Finally, she also pointed to Lori Wagner, a top Access Graphics vice president and staunch defender of John Ramsey. Polly denied that JonBenét had a bed-wetting problem and claimed that she had never seen her sister Patsy get angry, not once in her entire life. Never.

It bothered me that we were having to get all of this secondhand from aunts and a grandmother. John and Patsy Ramsey were in Atlanta. Gosage and I were in Atlanta. We had a lot of questions about their murdered daughter, and they stonewalled us.

Pam wanted to know why we couldn't just write out our questions and let John and Patsy respond that way. "If John and Patsy remain suspects, you may never talk to them," she said. But Nedra said she thought Patsy should talk to us, and Polly remarked that she did not see why John and Patsy couldn't come in and talk to us, just as she was doing. "I don't even see a problem with coming to the Boulder Police Department. You just want to know the facts," she said. That's how we felt too.

––––––––

Unexpectedly, a witness stepped forward and broke both his silence and John Ramsey's story about the timing of the discovery of JonBenét's body.

In a telephone interview, Stewart Long, the boyfriend of John Ramsey's daughter Melinda, recounted for me the sudden rush to reach Colorado that he, Melinda, and her brother, John Andrew, had made on the morning of December 26. When they arrived at the Ramsey home about 1 P.M., they were unaware of anything more than that JonBenét had been kidnapped.

Long said that John Ramsey climbed into a van with him and John Andrew and told them that JonBenét "was with Beth now." The father and son broke down in tears as John Ramsey described how he had discovered the body around eleven o'clock that morning.

I almost dropped the telephone as I reached to make sure the "record" button was pressed on my tape recorder. "When you say eleven o'clock that morning, are you assuming that was Mountain time or Eastern time?"

"I'm assuming that was Mountain time. He said eleven o'clock, so I'm assuming he was speaking of his own time reference."

I was blown away. We had just found a credible witness who heard John Ramsey say he'd discovered the body *two hours* earlier than we previously believed. That punched a big hole in the generally accepted timeline. Eleven o'clock would have been just about the time John Ramsey temporarily vanished from the sight of Detective Arndt, when she thought he had gone out to get the mail. I recalled how Arndt described the marked change in his behavior after he came back, silent, brooding, and nervous.

Under those circumstances, any investigator would have to consider the possibility that Ramsey might have found the body on his private walk through his home and not when he and Fleet White went to the basement a few hours later.

————

The detectives were concerned about one of their own. Linda Arndt, who had been a good cop, now seemed unhappy, withdrawn, or out-right hostile. It looked as if the problems she had encountered as the first detective at the Ramsey home were eating her up inside.

In early March Arndt had a private meeting with Patsy. She drove to the home of a Ramsey friend, where Patsy greeted her with a hug. Arndt reported that she took off her blazer and even lifted her sweater to prove to lawyer Patrick Burke that she wore no recording device and carried no police equipment whatsoever, not even a gun. We were enraged about the unauthorized visit, which Arndt termed "personal."

Since we had been trying for so long without success to get formal interviews, any information would have been welcome, but when I asked what they talked about during the hour-long chat, she looked me in the eye: "I told Patsy our conversation would be in confidence. I can't tell you."

"You're a detective, Arndt!" I protested. "You have a duty to give us that information."

"I can't tell you," she repeated, and she never did.

Only four days later I drove Arndt to a repair shop to pick up her car and used the private moment to ask where her head was at. Tears welled in her eyes as she confided her concern that she was about to be kicked off the team. I suggested that she become more of a team player and got the cold reply that she preferred to work alone.

She raised a finger to her forehead, thumb back like a cocked pistol, and told me, "If I get kicked off this thing, I'm going to take out myself and everyone else."

15

Evidence was accumulating to indicate the involvement of a parent, but we could not ignore other leads, and there were dozens of them. That we kept clearing the other potential suspects, one after another, from Massachusetts to California, didn't impress the DA's office.

- As Gosage whistled the theme from *Deliverance,* we tracked down a computer whiz who was said to have been acting weird. He and his barefoot girlfriend lived in a mobile home amid a landscape of rusting cars, junk heaps, and hound dogs in northwest Georgia. The man had visited Boulder several times on business and might have met John Ramsey, but that was it. Ironclad alibi of Christmas dinner in Georgia with his girlfriend's family.
- In a dirty interview cubicle at the Denver County Jail, we interrogated Sandra Henderson. She and her ex-husband, Bud, had run their own technology business, and Sandra once embezzled from Access Graphics. They were each $18,000 in debt to Access—a 1 away from the ransom amount and close enough for a look. She was in a Department of Corrections halfway house the night Jon-Benét was killed, and Bud Henderson was at home, alone and asleep.
- One of Father Rol's parishioners claimed he came across a crazed-looking man standing beside a truck behind the Ramsey house, holding some white cord and a stick and grunting, "You can't have her. She's mine." He embellished his story periodically with new

140

clues from "visions." He said the mysterious stranger was also at St. John's Church during the Christmas pageant just before the murder and whispered to him, "Don't you just want to strangle her?" We checked out everyone he named, then even searched his apartment to make sure *he* wasn't the murderer. Gosage and I probably spent about two hundred man-hours chasing the alleyway boogie-man, and it came to nothing.

- Detectives tracked every known pedophile in Boulder County and came up dry. Chief Koby passed along a name suggested by a friend of the wife of the district attorney. Other detectives gave us that "I'm glad it's not us" look.

The worst of the bunch, and the most likely suspect we came across other than the Ramseys, was John Brewer Eustace III, in custody in Charlotte, North Carolina, for kidnapping a two-year-old girl. Police found the name of JonBenét Ramsey atop a bizarre list of the pedophile's favorite sexual fantasies, and he kept a scrapbook filled with photographs of JonBenét alongside a Barbie doll on a makeshift altar. The guy sounded real.

Even in his orange jail overalls, the gaunt Eustace looked like a predator. When he found out who we were, he waived his Miranda rights because he wanted to talk about the "good-looking little girl."

No matter what his other crimes, we needed information from him, so we offered some fresh air and took him from the jail to the Charlotte PD a few blocks away.

Gosage, with a baby at home, could barely contain his disgust as Eustace recounted, "hypothetically, of course," how he would molest little girls and the importance of wiping fingerprints from bodies. In the North Carolina incident, he confessed to entering the apartment through a garden-level window while an adult was awake in the living room, shushing the little blond child, and taking her away through a window, leaving behind a flashlight. He later tied her, put tape over her mouth, and wrapped electrical cord around her head to control her. The similarities to our case convinced us that we had to investigate this suspect upside-down.

He smoked three packs of Marlboros while recounting dozens of molestations, watching our reactions through half-closed eyes, carefully avoiding dates or places. But he feigned forgetfulness when we tried to account for his whereabouts on December 25.

When we sought samples of pubic hair, he shrugged that he couldn't provide any because he shaved his crotch so as not to leave telltale DNA evidence. But in a fourth-floor detective bureau bathroom, Eustace pinched folds of pubic skin and we plucked stubs of hair with tweezers. Finally we returned him to his county jail cell. Back at the hotel I stood beneath a steaming shower scrubbing hard with soap to rid myself of the stench of John Eustace.

We found that he'd had a temporary job with a film processing lab during Christmas week, and a computer-generated time sheet showed that he was at work on December 26. Coworkers remembered he had tried to kiss an unwilling woman employee that night. It was impossible to be in North Carolina and Colorado at the same time. We cleared Eustace but hoped the Charlotte cops would put him away for a couple of forevers.

———

It was extremely frustrating to chase the nonsense leads, and we seemed to be constantly heading down roads that led nowhere. Information evaporated before our eyes, suspects were cleared, tips were not what they seemed. The effort spent on such things was chewing up detective hours and not getting us close to the people on whom we should be concentrating.

Evidence at hand pointed to the Ramseys. But instead of the focus narrowing, as in normal investigations, this one widened like an inverted funnel. At some point we hoped common sense would take over; we wanted to stop chasing phantoms. There was no shortage of suspects, just a shortage of detectives.

One day I asked Trip DeMuth, our primary contact with Alex Hunter's office, why they didn't see what we saw. Everyone we had interviewed had resulted in a dead end, the evidence was piling up, and of all of the handwriting examples, only one person—Patsy Ramsey—came back as the likely author. We saw nothing that pointed to anyone outside the home being involved. Locked house. Dead child. Two parents. Hello?

"We need to follow the evidence, but we're headed off in every direction but that one," I told him.

He responded, "What if it isn't the Ramseys?" That was the bottom line for the district attorney's people. To me, they weren't following the evidence. They seemed to be bending over backward for the prime suspects.

———

Our police chief, Tom Koby, pledged, "Even if solving the case costs a million dollars, we will do it." A few months later, he took a look at the overtime and expenses and announced, "We may need to scale back the investigation." Within weeks, he reassigned Detective Linda Arndt, whom I didn't mind losing, but also the indefatigable Detective Melissa Hickman, whom we hated to see go.

Sergeant Wickman remained in command, and Detective Tom Trujillo would continue at his desk, handling the evidence. That left Ron Gosage, Jane Harmer, and myself to face the Ramsey juggernaut. At the same time, the Denver police had thirty-five detectives working a January homicide.

While the chief would not even hire extra clerical help for us, he spared no expense on the frivolous. Command staff received massage certificates. A retreat was planned for his departmental leaders, although this was hardly the proper time to be taking time off. Then he announced that his role in the case would change, and he would back away from the day-to-day operations so "the detectives can do their jobs." His timing was remarkable. The ship was sinking and the captain was heading for a lifeboat.

We were handed over to a psychologist in the banquet room at the Marriott Courtyard. We hated being there. When asked to speak, we did, although our body language belied our comments. Arms crossed chests, eyes roamed the ceiling, and smiles were nonexistent. Who could talk about "feelings" when a to-do list ten miles long waited back at the office?

I wondered how many murder investigations around America were run this way.

———

Chief Koby surprised me one day when he found me working late, alone in the SitRoom, and took a chair. He ventured his opinion that the Ramseys' not being constantly on our doorstep offering help was indicative of guilty people.

———

The story was still huge news and showed no sign of waning. JonBenét stared out from newspapers, panels of "expert" talking heads filled the airwaves, and the Australian edition of *People* featured her on its cover. Santa Bill McReynolds popped up everywhere, housekeeper Linda Hoffmann-Pugh was riding around in a limousine paid for by the tabloids, and *USA Today* predicted we were close to an arrest.

Out of the pack of hundreds of journalists, Jeff Shapiro of the sensationalist *Globe* tabloid would stand out from the others. He was deceitful but dug deeper than any of them, caused a crisis in journalistic ethics with secret tape recordings, and damn near brought down the district attorney.

He surfaced in the middle of March, stalking John Andrew Ramsey. A high school friend of John Andrew's was approached by someone who identified himself both as Matt Hayworth and Jeffrey Scott and was talking about the case. When I checked him out with an early morning telephone call, a young man's sleepy voice confirmed I was talking to Jeffrey Scott.

He came awake in a hurry when I told him I was a cop. The guy was obviously a reporter and was lying. A short time later, an editor from the *Globe* telephoned to apologize. Jeffrey Scott was one of theirs, and his real name was Jeff Shapiro. Before long, I would recruit him to be a confidential informant.

The Colorado Bureau of Investigation lab discovered a semen stain after all on a blanket inside the suitcase that had been retrieved from the basement. DNA tests matched the specimen to John Andrew, and since we had cleared him, another trail ended where it started. Intruder theorists in the DA's office would try to weave the semen stain, the blanket, and a Doctor Seuss book also found in the suitcase into a convoluted scenario in which JonBenét was lured from her bed with the book. The plan was then to stuff her in the suitcase and take it out through the window. When it was argued that the suitcase didn't fit through the basement window, the theory simply changed to having her taken out through a door while the suitcase was used as a stairstep to the window. It was a convenient arrangement of these facts.

We kept sending the CBI evidence to test, and they were moving us to the head of the line and doing solid work. The DA's office decided that future DNA tests would be conducted by CellMark Diagnostic in Maryland, the largest independent testing lab in the country. In my opinion, the main reason was to placate Team Ramsey.

The reason was painfully obvious. CBI director Carl Whiteside had banned Ramsey experts from observing the testing procedures, so they simply opened a new line of attack, and Trip DeMuth cleared the way for them. DeMuth gave CellMark orders not to begin testing without prior authorization from the Boulder County District Attorney's office. "The reason for this restriction is that arrangements must be made to allow a representative from the Ramsey family to be present," he wrote.

To me, we had squandered a huge advantage. We should have done the testing as we wished and let the defense conduct their tests only if and when someone was charged. Their complaint that all the evidence would be destroyed in the tests was a tactic, not a fact.

They never stopped pushing, and when they pushed on the DA's office, it seemed to me that they usually got what they wanted.

––––––––

As often happens when detectives start kicking around seemingly unrelated items, we figured out that Patsy's fur boots might be a possible source for a beaver hair the FBI lab had identified on the sticky side of the tape that had been across JonBenét's mouth. It could even have been a case-breaking discovery, and we should have been off and running with search warrants in hand to get those boots. But the DA's office once again stopped us in our tracks by shrugging their shoulders and declining to proceed with a warrant.

When Detective Trujillo mentioned that Patsy had worn a pair of fur boots at her latest handwriting appearance, he sparked my recollection that Melinda Ramsey's boyfriend, Stewart Long, had told me that when he arrived at the house on December 26, Patsy was standing out in front, wearing a fur coat.

Despite our repeated explanations during the rest of my association with the case, the DA's office never pursued a search warrant for the fur coat or boots. To me, it was inexplicable.

––––––––

The Ramsey house was also through giving up information. Gosage and I drove by 755 Fifteenth Street late one afternoon, and it looked as busy as a bus station. Detectives weren't allowed beyond the sidewalk without a warrant, but a small army of carpenters, painters, construction workers, and cleanup crews were rushing about, performing a massive overhaul. Any trace evidence that might still exist vanished beneath new coats of paint or was vacuumed up or tossed out with the trash. I called out to a painter in the garage. He looked at me, reached up, punched a button, and the door rumbled closed in my face.

––––––––

We hoped that Dr. Henry Lee might be able to put some of this puzzle together, but at the conclusion of our first briefing for him, the nation's most celebrated criminalist was shocked almost to silence by how badly the crime scene had been botched.

While about three dozen men and women from Boulder County

law enforcement, including Koby and Hunter, waited in a big conference room at police headquarters, Lee hung out downstairs, bantering with the detectives.

He told us that he was not a magician, and pretending to look through an imaginary magnifying glass, he said, "I see the same things you see."

At the time, Lee was director of the Connecticut State Police Crime Laboratory, and when the official session got under way, he gave us all a primer in the basics, from crime scene to laboratory to courtroom. The man was a walking textbook.

Then we showed him photos of the crime scene. "Wait," Lee said. "The pillow in the kitchen in this picture doesn't show up in that one. Why?" His eyebrows rose in wonder when he learned how things had been moved and how many people had trampled through the place before the photographers took their pictures. What he was viewing was not necessarily how things looked on the day of the murder. Lee said nothing but made a note.

We went through numerous pieces of evidence—the body, the clothing, the first officers' observations, no forced entry, the ransom note, ink and pen.

Lee suggested that the cellar room in which the body was found was not necessarily the location of the primary attack. He also wondered about the presence of the pink nightgown discovered near the victim. A kidnapper, he ventured, probably would not bring a victim's favorite piece of clothing along with a dead body.

John Meyer, the Boulder County coroner, had barely begun his autopsy findings before Lee questioned the urine stains found on the crotch of the long-john pants and the panties beneath them. Were there corresponding stains on the bed sheets? We didn't know, although when the crime became a murder instead of a kidnapping, those sheets should have been promptly collected for testing.

Meyer said he found a lot of redness, some small flecks of blood, and dark-colored fibers in the vaginal area, but no old scarring. There was some abrasion and hemorrhaging in the vagina. Also present was irritation and chronic inflammation in the vaginal vault, which he said was evident for some period. He was unsure whether the cause was infection, digital manipulation, lying in urine, or even the very unlikely event of self-manipulation. It was inconsistent with penile penetration, but chronic vaginal abuse was a possibility, Meyer said.

I was struck by the word *chronic,* which would indicate prior abuse. The coroner also said there was acute vaginal injury that had happened around the time of death. He could not pinpoint the time of death closer than six to twelve hours before she was brought upstairs, stiff in full rigor mortis, by her father at 1 P.M.

That would put the time of death very roughly about 1 A.M. and no later than 7 A.M. Since the 911 call had come in shortly before 6 o'clock in the morning, and the murder, staging, and the ransom note would all have required a substantial amount of time to accomplish, the earlier time was the most logical—which would put the time of death between the time the family arrived home that night about 10 P.M. and 1 A.M.

After the large group broke up, Lee stayed on with Koby, Hunter, the coroner, and the detectives. He questioned why a six-year-old girl, who could easily have been manually strangled, had been choked with a garrote. Such complicated violence did not fit the crime. Lee suggested the possibility that death had been accidental, with a cover-up, and noted distinctive elements of "staging." He suggested that we look at the family members or someone very close to the family as suspects.

Hunter obviously wasn't buying our conclusion that Santa Bill was innocent, and he asked Lee for some thoughts on Bill McReynolds. Lee suggested vacuuming the McReynolds's car for fibers that might match something from the crime scene. Why, I wondered, would the DA's office entertain the idea of searching McReynolds's automobile yet not give us a search warrant for Patsy's fur boots and coat?

Lee told us the case was going to be very difficult. The house had been compromised. We had to figure out what happened that night without relying on what had been found.

"Rice already cooked," said Lee. "Crime scene gone."

———

The man who probably did more than any other person to sink our Ramsey investigation was someone I admire a great deal, Lou Smit. Before he came aboard, we had been punching holes in Team Ramsey's single cry of "The Ramseys didn't do it." Smit, with impeccable police credentials, brought the Intruder Theory to life.

Alex Hunter had launched his own investigation, allegedly to identify holes in the case that might be exploited by a defense attorney. He brought over Steve Ainsworth, an investigator from the sheriff's department, then hired Smit, a slight, balding sixty-one-year-old former lawman from Colorado Springs.

Lou Smit is a gentle man and a gentleman. He has a gregarious personality, never has a bad word to say about anyone, and unfailingly shook my hand each time we met, no matter how upset we might be with each other. That unassuming manner and soft voice puts people off guard, and his easy smile, with a country boy toothpick at the side of his mouth, gets their trust. He is a family man and a devout Christian but can turn confrontational sometimes. Then the smile vanishes and a sharp retort replaces politeness. A term was coined for such moments: "You've just been Smit on."

Smit had a terrific record as a homicide investigator but seemed out of place in Boulder, with his three-piece pinstripe suits, a little over-and-under .22 caliber Derringer tucked into a Velcro belt holster, and a wallet filled with family-style photographs of some of the 150 homicide victims whose cases he had worked.

His legend was based upon the 1991 murder of a little girl named Heather Dawn Church. When everything pointed to the family as the killers of their child, Lou refused to give up, complaining that the police would not look elsewhere for a suspect. Smit matched an overlooked print on a screen that led to the real killer and emerged an absolute hero.

His sole job in Boulder, we were told by the DA's office, would be to implement his particularly successful system of indexing, organizing, and cross-referencing the case file. We had urged the police department to lease either the Overwatch or the ZY Index computer programs to do exactly that, but our request had been denied as being cost prohibitive.

Soon after Smit was hired we went out for a cup of coffee, and he told me one of his personal commandments: "Murders are usually what they seem. Rarely are they perfectly planned," he said.

He was cautious and noncommittal, which I considered prudent, since he had not yet had a chance to read the thousands of pages in the file. He spoke at length about Heather Dawn Church, as if the murder of that little girl might be the blueprint for this case too.

Three days later at a detective briefing, Smit made his first appearance, greeting us all and taking a seat along the west wall. We went around the table to update our findings. Finally it was his turn. He had been around only about seventy-two hours, not anywhere near long enough to devour the case material, but we hoped he might have some initial insights. He did.

Lou shifted the toothpick to a corner of his mouth, and his eyes twinkled with the excitement of a good bird dog on point. He said, "I don't think it was the Ramseys."

He never budged from that position.

16

The Ramsey case was taking an enormous toll on the investigating officers. We were worn out, and there was no relief in sight. When my father was rushed to the emergency room with heart failure in Denver, I was in Atlanta again and, in one of the worst decisions of my life, chose not to come home. I no longer worked out, socialized, or went to movies, investing all my time in the case.

It absorbed all our energy, and we were running ourselves into trouble, taking our families along. There was no way for them to understand something we couldn't even talk about. I seldom saw my wife of only eight months, who watched with a frustration equal to my own as I was consumed by this unmerciful mystery. This case would wreck marriages and careers.

Among the most distraught was Patrol Officer Rick French, a decorated army officer, a respected SWAT team member, and a gold-medal–winning athlete, for he had been branded "the first officer on the scene." He believed John and Patsy Ramsey had misled him and said he had the "gut feeling" early on the morning of December 26 that the parents were somehow involved in the little girl's disappearance.

"Why couldn't I have found her?" he asked me in one private moment. "If only I had looked in there, you would have had a pristine crime scene and could solve this."

He was inconsolable. "I'm the fucking cop! I should have found her!"

Trip DeMuth, the deputy DA, gave me the parallel universe theory of the case. He claimed he had been given the job of "defensing" the case, or trying to look at it for holes the defense lawyers could exploit, but DeMuth seemed to truly *believe* that someone broke into the house and killed this little girl. "Why don't you come to our side?" he once asked me. His allegiance to the intruder idea was apparently so strong that he was eventually removed from the investigation.

DeMuth, who has young daughters, told me, "Steve, you're not a parent. I hold my daughters every night. It's unfathomable that a parent could do such a thing to their child."

"Trip, I may not be a parent, but I am a cop," I replied. "Believe me. It happens all the time." In fact, according to Department of Justice statistics, it has happened 11,000 times since 1976.

He looked at me blankly and said that if either John or Patsy Ramsey were involved, "one of them will have a bout of conscience" and would step forward. I told him not to bet on that when the result of the decision could be the death penalty. Trip DeMuth and his boss Pete Hofstrom might as well have been twins, for Hofstrom later told me, "When good people do bad things, they can't live with their consciences and eventually come forward and admit their guilt."

They were naive to a fault and suggested a plan to tell Team Ramsey, "Every DA from now to eternity will look at this case file, all prepped and ready to go, and they may pull the trigger. That's why you might want to deal with us now, before the next DA comes in." In other words, as I heard it, somebody else—years from now—may have the guts to do what we don't. The Ramsey lawyers didn't accept that strange challenge. They had every reason to celebrate their good fortune instead.

Actually, the detectives would have loved to have found some stranger whom we could wrap in a tight cloak of evidence, for there is no joy in looking at a parent for murder. We found no such person out there, although a recent letter from the Ramsey private investigator supplied a multitude of new "suspects" who had had "frequent and recent access" to the house—hundreds of *unnamed* guests at Christmas parties, nannies, friends, neighbors, people from the Historic Boulder tour, a battalion of cleaning women, street musicians, caterers, florists, friends, contractors, window cleaners, plumbers, and videotaping crews. When the case began, police were told that the only outsiders with keys were John Andrew Ramsey and the housekeeper, Linda Hoffmann-Pugh. Now a couple of dozen keys were said to be missing.

Who were all these people, where were those keys, and how the hell was a handful of detectives supposed to track them down? I felt their strategy, if not clear before, was crystal now. Team Ramsey was overwhelming us with useless leads while keeping Patsy and John safely beyond our reach.

We needed more help, but that was one of the core problems in Boulder. The determination to protect the small town's image overrode common sense, and outsiders were not welcome. Boulder became xenophobic as Chief Koby turned down offers of help, District Attorney Hunter's office kept the case close to home, and the little local newspaper criticized other media for covering the story. City leaders believed that if the outsiders would just go away, so would the problem. Their real fear, I believe, was that outsiders might peek beneath the curtain and see what the problems really were.

———

As if I weren't already up to my ears in work, Sergeant Wickman assigned me to be what is known as the "Affiant" on all future warrants and to put together the document that would be the basis for any arrest. Everything had to be grounded in precise language, and just because the Ramseys were prime suspects did not mean I could or would ignore any evidence that might point away from them. For more than a year I carried the ever-changing Master Affidavit everywhere I went, carefully locked in a silver aluminum suitcase. If there was to be an arrest, I wanted it up-to-date and at my fingertips. I also became the case file curator, in charge of updating what was to become some eighty-plus notebooks.

———

Detective Gosage and I checked into the Holiday Inn in Atlanta on April 8, at the start of an eleven-day road trip, and the desk clerk recognized us as Boulder detectives. "Please get them," she said.

The Ramsey strategy to gain public sympathy wasn't working. Although they were under no obligation to talk to the police, they were casting suspicion on themselves by dodging us, and people were not buying the declarations of cooperation.

Ellis Armistead, Ramsey's private snoop, let me know that my work had not been welcomed by the Ramseys and their friends. I could have cared less. Later I would see his comment as a veiled alert that the Ramseys had developed a personal animus toward me. "Why is it always Steve Thomas digging into our affairs?" Patsy asked someone.

We made a surprise visit to the home of Patsy's parents, and Nedra launched into us like a cruise missile, unshakable in her belief that we were only out to persecute her daughter and son-in-law. We also got another installment of pageant news.

While I steered Don Paugh into a conversation about taxes, Gosage sought some unrehearsed writings by Patsy and struck gold. "If Patsy didn't write the [ransom] note, why not offer some handwriting to prove it?" he asked Nedra. She defiantly thrust a piece of paper at him and declared, "Patsy wrote that just this morning."

As we drove away, Ron examined the list of addresses and telephone numbers Patsy had written. It included the name of her friend Barbara Fernie with an important, telltale correction.

In the 376-word ransom note, the small letter "a" was printed in manuscript style 109 times and written in cursive lowercase style only 5 times. The entry on Fernie contained just such a printed manuscript "a" as the second letter of the word *Barbara,* but it had been boldly written over with a black felt-tip pen and made into the cursive-style "a."

We had noticed earlier that in prehomicide writings, Patsy consistently used the manuscript "a," but posthomicide, it disappeared from her samples of writing. This was a major find, for it looked as if she was consciously changing her lettering. She had more handwriting styles than a class of sixth graders and was seemingly able to change as easily as turning on and off different computer fonts.

I thought about how big a mistake it had been to provide the defense lawyers with a copy of the note. A suspect could study it prior to giving writing samples and consciously avoid certain characteristics, such as the style of writing the first letter of the alphabet.

The Colorado Bureau of Investigation, after studying several of Patsy's handwriting exemplars, noted "evidence which indicates the questioned handwritten note may have been written by [Patricia Ramsey], but the evidence falls short of that necessary to support a definite conclusion." Chet Ubowski of the CBI, who was being asked to make the call of a lifetime, couldn't do it with courtroom certainty. Privately, however, Ubowski, who had made the early discovery that Patsy's handwriting was consistent with the ransom note on twenty-four of the twenty-six alphabet letters, had recently told one detective, "I believe she wrote it."

Ubowski also pointed out that the tablet contained only seven fingerprints in all: five belonging to Patsy, one from the police sergeant who handled the pad, and one from a laboratory examiner.

To me, the evidence was mounting. There was only one person who looked good as the author of the note, whose pen and pad were used to write it, and whom we could place in the home at the time of the murder—Patsy Ramsey—and the DA's office still would not call her a suspect.

The problem was demonstrated once again when I called Trip De-Muth about our handwriting find from Nedra Paugh and found the prosecutor unimpressed. "She probably doesn't want to make her 'a' like that anymore because she knows we are looking at her handwriting and the ransom note," he said.

"Yes, Trip," I agreed. "You're probably right." I hung up the phone very gently to keep from throwing it against the wall. How could someone simultaneously understand and misunderstand that important point?

Detective Gosage and I went out for dinner in Atlanta and sought solace in a few beers while surrounded by a crowd of normal people with normal lives. We wondered whether our own lives would ever be normal again. This case changed everyone it touched.

Rain slammed down in sheets as we drove to the Ramsey's old home in Northridge, where the baby footprints of newborn JonBenét were imbedded in a cement patio. I got out of the car and stood in the pouring rain, feeling crushed by the futility of chasing the killer of this little girl. "God," I asked silently, "Please help us."

We finally got to speak with Lucinda Ramsey Johnson and her daughter, Melinda, but the interviews were in the twenty-fifth-floor office of attorney Jim Jenkins and turned out to be a farce. We made a previous agreement on conditions for the interview, but now Jenkins informed us that there were "ground rules." We were not allowed to ask anything about John Ramsey, and our time would be limited.

We spoke first to Melinda, who added the names of multiple friends who had stayed in the Boulder house overnight, including some who had slept in JonBenét's room. I wanted to shout, "Why didn't you tell us this months ago?" Anyone who had slept in the very bed of the victim could potentially be the source of the unidentified pubic hair.

The interview with Lucinda was almost useless. We managed to pin down that the suitcase found in the basement had been with the family for some time, which meant it wasn't hauled in by an intruder. She, too, added more names to the mushrooming roster of overnight guests in the Boulder house, some of whom had stayed in JonBenét's bedroom. Their whereabouts were unknown, she said.

But anytime we mentioned her first ex-husband, she would glance over at her lawyer, then reply, "I'm not going to answer any questions about John Ramsey." The interview lasted only twenty minutes, when we had enough questions for twenty hours. Gosage closed his notebook in disgust.

On our way out, Lucinda tried to hand us a large stuffed rabbit and a bag of other items that people had left at JonBenét's grave because they might be "clues." "Mail it," I told her. They wanted us to look at garbage but wouldn't answer vital questions. More wasted time, more wasted effort. The killer of JonBenét remained at large.

I went outside the office tower in downtown Atlanta and stood in the sunshine as angry as I had ever been. These people seemed to have something higher on their value scale than the life of a child.

———

The DA's investigators, Lou Smit and Steve Ainsworth, claimed that they could now place a stun gun in the hands of their unknown intruder. We would spend months proving to our satisfaction that it simply did not exist, but they wouldn't give up on the idea.

Smit and Ainsworth concluded from studying photographs of the body that some of the abrasions were marks left by the prongs of a stun gun. When they asked the coroner about it, the answer was "Sure, anything is possible." With that, they began to consider whether the child's body should be disinterred so the skin around the marks could be tested.

Experts engaged by the police concluded there was no stun gun involved at all, but the DA's team never relinquished their claim that such an exotic weapon was used to subdue JonBenét.

———

Back in Boulder, Linda Arndt was a happy detective. She had won a victim's assistance award in April and came into the SitRoom to show off a vase of beautiful flowers, which she said were from "John and Patsy." She turned and left immediately, and Detective Jane Harmer looked at me in disbelief. "What the fuck was that all about?" she asked. Detectives normally do not receive flowers from suspects.

———

The weekly meetings of the leadership in the police department and the DA's office became so acrimonious that Commander Eller said they were nothing but occasions to see "who could bring the most guns to the table and outshout each other."

We felt the DA would never aggressively pursue the Ramseys, and they resented us not buying into the "trust-building" strategy that would enable Pete Hofstrom to "work his magic." In my opinion, all his magic had done was to help the Ramseys disappear.

PART THREE

ROCKY ROAD TO NOWHERE

17

Negotiations to arrange police interviews with the Ramseys continued through March and April, and when agreement was reached, in my opinion the DA's office had given away the store.

It was not that we were without leverage, because the Ramseys were being hammered by an international press corps for not cooperating with us. One of the first things prosecutors can do when a subject refuses to talk is to compel them to appear before a grand jury. But under the Fifth Amendment a suspect cannot be forced to testify. So sometimes prosecutors will try to negotiate an interview.

While it was totally appropriate for Deputy DA Pete Hofstrom to be working with the Ramsey attorneys to arrange a meeting between the detectives and their clients, I felt that his "trust building" strategy and evidence sharing in this clearly adversarial situation were steering the case right off the cliff.

Sergeant Wickman outlined the specific conditions to us at a breakfast meeting, giving us instant indigestion. Each parent would be interviewed for two hours only, with a two-hour break between, during which they could talk to their lawyers. The interview would be held at the office of one of their attorneys and take place in only two days. The attorneys would be present, the questioning would be limited, it would not be videotaped, and they would be supplied with all their prior statements. And I was not to be one of the questioners.

"Well, what do you guys think?" Wickman asked.

"What the fuck should we think? This is totally absurd," I said.

"Hofstrom thought he negotiated a pretty good deal," Wickman stated.

If the goal was to stay friendly with Team Ramsey, then it was a great deal. For the police, it was a disaster. We would never allow such luxuries to the parents of a poor kid killed in the projects, so why should we coddle these people?

No, we told Wickman. Absolutely not.

We might as well have said nothing. At the afternoon briefing we learned that the police documents had been released early that morning, before we were informed. Not only did the prior statements go over, but so did the official reports of Officer Rick French, Sergeant Bob Whitson, and Detectives Fred Patterson, Linda Arndt, and myself. Those documents specified what we had said, done, and observed and were utterly priceless, far above and beyond what we had been told had been requested.

It gave the defense lawyers an incredible windfall of information and did irreparable damage to the case.

The entire Q-and-A had been undermined. We would now be questioning a couple of intelligent, well-coached people who could study as if preparing for a high school test.

We were in free fall, and the ground was coming up fast.

———

Then they dropped the other shoe. Team Ramsey would also get to examine the actual ransom note, receive exact one-to-one copies of both the ransom note and the practice note, and get photographic negatives of important evidence pictures.

When we protested to Deputy DA DeMuth about the treasure trove being given away, he responded, "They'll get it anyway if they are ever charged." So wait until someone is charged, I said.

I considered it an act of treason and refused to participate in handing it over. I just couldn't do it. My defiance would be duly noted, and I didn't care. While Detective Trujillo was in the lobby giving the material to defense lawyer Patrick Burke, Detective Arndt came up and gave Burke a hug.

Then the defense attorneys were allowed inside the Boulder Police Department to examine the actual ligature and garrote that killed Jon-Benét. I watched, sick inside, and Sergeant Wickman bellowed in protest, "You're giving the fucking murder weapon to the suspects!" In my opinion, Team Ramsey was being allowed to loot our Property and Evidence Room.

There was one last terrible surprise in store.

Deputy DA Pete Hofstrom told the Ramseys with great sorrow that they had been treated "unfairly" and then added, "We have nothing to indicate you are involved in this crime." Then he suggested that the Ramseys propose the interview conditions.

John Ramsey casually waved his hand and said, "We'll cooperate."

Easy decision.

Detective Melissa Hickman plopped into a SitRoom chair and flipped her tablet onto her desk with weary resignation. She had just been at the office of the district attorney and seen one of the Ramsey attorneys in the conference room, the depository of the most sensitive and confidential information in our case. The defense lawyer should not have been allowed anywhere near an area that was supposedly so off-limits that the DA was calling it his "War Room."

Hickman reported that Lou Smit had handed the defense lawyer a card of condolence and asked that it be forwarded to "John and Patsy."

Chief Koby, just back from a vacation mountain biking and skiing in Taos, New Mexico, popped his head into the SitRoom. "Got it cracked?" he asked.

Three FBI agents from the Child Abduction and Serial Killer Unit who came to Boulder to advise us on the interviews termed the conditions "ridiculous." All control had been lost, and the proposed interviews would be useless, they said. Had the same thing happened within an FBI bureau, they said, there would be "thunder rolling down the halls."

The Ramseys could stall for two hours, then walk away and tell the media they had cooperated, the CASKU guys said. Like most of America, the FBI wondered what the hell was going on in Boulder.

"The case is not being handled well," said the CASKU agents.

The Intruder Theory? Absurd.

Hofstrom? Needs to act like a prosecutor, not a public defender.

Tomorrow's interview? Don't do it.

Grand jury? As soon as possible.

We canceled the interviews, backed by an FBI news release stating that the conditions "were inconsistent with sound investigative practices."

When Team Ramsey protested, as expected, DA Alex Hunter and

Chief Koby crawled back with a letter blaming an "unfortunate miscommunication."

They sent along an alternate set of conditions, which was not too far from the Ramseys' original list. There would be separate interviews but within a single day. Talks would be recorded by audio but not video, and detectives designated by the police department would conduct the interviews. Pete Hofstrom would be in the room. To get them to the table, the deal was accepted, which meant I would get a shot at questioning them, and even under the dubious conditions, I looked forward to the opportunity. Maybe I might be able to pry something loose.

Sergeant Wickman took the CASKU team over to the DA's office for a courtesy call, and when they returned, one said, "I have a new appreciation of what you are up against."

One FBI agent said that CASKU offered their expertise and made grand jury suggestions, but "they didn't even listen to us." Trip De-Muth telephoned me at home that night to say he thought the FBI agents were "a presumptuous bunch."

I knew the interviews would be a one-shot chance. Once the Ramseys walked out, we wouldn't be seeing them again.

Pete Hofstrom urged me to be "soft and comfortable" with John and Patsy, for "they might want to work with us."

I guess he wanted me to ask tough questions like "What's it like living in Atlanta? Hot and humid, I bet, huh?"

But I had conducted many interrogations, and I knew this one was going to be the hardest of them all. The most difficult thing in police work is to obtain a murder confession, and I damned well knew one was not going to come during this silly fishbowl interview. One-on-one in an interview room the day the body was found, I might have had a chance to have gotten an acknowledgment of some involvement, but not here and now, with a bunch of lawyers hanging on every word.

I spent hours examining every piece of evidence, every photograph, every officer's report.

A picture taken at the Whites' dinner party on Christmas night caught my eye, and something nagged at my memory. Then it came to me—Patsy was wearing a red turtleneck sweater and black pants in the picture. I found in an interview with Rick French that he said the morning of December 26 she was wearing a red turtleneck and black pants. She was wearing the same damned clothes! Had she been up all night in them? I wondered.

This woman, to whom looking good appeared always so important that she had a closet filled with designer clothes, had attended a party, come home late, put her children to bed, gone to sleep herself, arose early to fly across the country, put on fresh makeup and fixed her hair, and then put on the same clothes she had worn the previous night? Not likely, in my opinion. When I mentioned it the next day to Trip De-Muth, he remarked, "So she wore the same clothes two days in a row. Big deal."

Maybe it wasn't for him, but to a former Miss America contestant?

18

The interviews with Patsy and John Ramsey produced no earthshaking revelations. Having had the opportunity to study police reports, and with their lawyers and experts crawling all over evidence that should never have been shared, I felt the parents were about as well rehearsed as actors taking the stage. But at the end of the day, I concluded that as investigators, we had reached our goal—we had established probable cause. And when Patsy Ramsey left that room, I believe she could have been in handcuffs and charged with involvement in the death of Jon-Benét.

Patsy was magna cum laude smart and Miss America pretty, cancer survivor strong and drama queen talented, tenacious, and determined. John was the condescending and cool CEO, who displayed confidence that he would have little trouble handling the interview. Each was accompanied by a lawyer, and more of them lurked in the halls. Pete Hofstrom from the DA's office, whom I considered a Team Ramsey ally, sat behind me. I had conducted hundreds of interviews, but never under such adverse conditions.

Detective Tom Trujillo and I watched as Patsy was solicitously helped to a chair by her attorney. As soon as she sat down and adjusted herself, any hint of weakness vanished, those green eyes flashed, and a nervous smile played at her lips.

It was the first time I had seen her since the nontestimonial evidence session on December 28, and she hardly seemed to be the same woman. No longer distraught and disheveled, she was immaculate in a blue suit with white trim over a white sweater, a silver angel pin on her lapel, and gold earrings, watch, and wedding ring, and her perfume reached across the table. She placed a small cup of tea to mark her territory.

It is rare for a woman to go eye-to-eye with a detective, but Patsy Ramsey was a savvy sophisticate who knew how to work a man, even one with a badge. When I had a question, she would lean so close across that narrow pine table that we were almost in kissing distance, invading my personal space before answering.

We started at 9:05 A.M. and went for six hours.

She confirmed that the last thing JonBenét had to eat was some cracked crab at the Whites' dinner party on December 25. I knew the Whites served no pineapple that night, but pineapple was found in the victim's stomach, and a bowl of pineapple bearing Patsy's fingerprints was on her kitchen table. Inconsistent.

JonBenét had fallen asleep in the car on the way home, and John Ramsey carried her upstairs, where Patsy replaced the child's pants with the long-john bottoms. The white shirt with the sequin star stayed on, she said. That was the first we had heard that she was asleep and carried to bed and clothes were changed. On December 26 Patsy had told police that JonBenét went to sleep wearing the red turtleneck top, which was later found balled up on the bathroom sink. Now it was the white one in which the body was found. Inconsistent.

The door to the child's bedroom was left open a little bit, she said, which corroborated her January 1 statement on CNN that she pushed the door open that morning. It seemed unlikely that an intruder abducting a child from her bed would take time to close the door behind him.

She got up just after her husband, about five-thirty the next morning, only an hour before their plane was to leave for Michigan. This didn't seem like much time to pack, get two kids ready, and drive to the airport. In their separate bathrooms, John showered as she did her makeup and hair.

Early in the interview I moved to lock her into a statement that she had worn the same clothes on the night of December 25 and the morning of December 26. Those questions revealed that Patsy and JonBenét had "a little rift" about what to wear to the Whites'. We knew they often wore matched sets of clothing, and Patsy said that on Christmas night she put on a red-and-black outfit, but her daughter demanded to wear her new crewneck shirt with the star on it from The Gap. That was interesting because it showed that Patsy was upset with JonBenét early that evening.

When I returned to the clothing issue a little later by asking what Patsy had put on the next morning, her attorney came to attention. When she replied, "I put on the same black velvet pants and the red turtleneck sweater," her lawyer actually began to sweat, perhaps making the same link we did—wondering why Patsy would take time to fix her hair and makeup but ignore a closet full of fresh clothing in favor of clothes she had worn to a party twelve hours earlier.

Back on the time line, we established that she went downstairs, stopping briefly in the laundry room outside JonBenét's room to examine some stains on her daughter's red jumpsuit. I recalled that there was the big bag of diapers that was hanging out of the cabinet, which wasn't mentioned.

She descended the spiral staircase, saw the three pieces of paper laid out side by side on the third rung, stepped over them, turned around, and read the note. "The first couple of lines . . . I didn't know what it was. It dawned on me that it said something about 'we have your daughter' or something, and I ran back up the stairs and pushed open the door to her room, and she wasn't in bed." It was another inconsistent statement, for if she "only glanced" at the first few lines, how could she have known to tell the 911 dispatcher about the SBTC acronym and the word *Victory,* both of which were at the bottom of the third page? And how did the intruder know to place the ransom note on the rear staircase that would be used by Patsy?

Throughout the interview, I was constantly reminded of just how well prepared she appeared. Her answers reeked of lawyerly advice, avoiding specifics and hedging with open-ended answers instead of yes or no. Trying to get a straight answer from her was maddening.

"Who moved the note?" I asked.

"I think he [John] did," she replied. "I don't think I did."

"Did you touch the note?"

"I don't recall doing that, but I may have."

"Did you take the note upstairs with you?"

"I don't remember exactly."

"Do you recall moving the note from the stairs?"

"I don't recall."

"Did you read the note?"

"I think I glanced at it."

"Do you remember touching the note?"

"Not specifically, but I may have."

"Did you check on JonBenét that night?"

"I don't believe I did."

Later she was asked if JonBenét would have been paralyzed by fear or screamed and fought if grabbed by an intruder. Patsy Ramsey said, "I just don't know."

"Have you talked to Burke about that night?"

"I haven't really talked to him much about it."

Because we had the enhancement of the 911 tape to prove that their son, Burke, was awake when the call was made, I wanted Patsy to confirm her earlier statement that he had been asleep, and she did so several times.

She said she asked John, "Oh my God, what about Burke? He [John] told me he [Burke] was OK."

Later she was asked again, "Did all the commotion wake Burke up at all?" She said it did not.

In an hour I returned to the same point. "Obviously Burke was OK, he was still asleep through this until he was later awakened, is that right?"

"Right."

When we asked John Ramsey the same question, we got the same answer. "When you checked on Burke . . . did he wake up at all?" Ramsey answered, "No, he was asleep still."

It was as close to a lock as we got on anything all day.

––––––

Throughout the day, Patsy's manner would change abruptly depending on the question. Inquiries about Access Graphics and John's bonus were met with "I really just don't know much about what goes on at work. . . . I wasn't aware he got a bonus." Soft words, big doe eyes. All America knew that $118,000 figure, and she didn't? Asked about the ransom note being written on a pad from her home, the little-girl persona emerged. "It was? I didn't know that." She denied knowing anything about the "small foreign faction" mentioned in the note and said she "didn't have a clue" about the sign-off acronym, S.B.T.C. The woman was a chameleon.

––––––

The only time her composure broke was when she was asked to describe the discovery of her daughter's body. She dissolved into weeping, and although it was touching, it was also her weakest point of the session and the time for me to press harder, to really exploit the opportunity. But just as I was about to allow an opening by suggesting, "It was an accident, wasn't it? You didn't mean for this to happen, did you?" Pat Burke and Pete Hofstrom ruined the moment, consolingly saying, "Let's take a break." Our own DA's chief trial deputy helped destroy what in my opinion was the best opportunity of the day. By the time the interview resumed, Patsy Ramsey had gotten her wind back. I felt she knew she had dodged a bullet.

During our brief breaks, I went to Alex Hunter's office, which had been set aside for the detectives. The first time I walked in, the district attorney asked, "Got a confession?"

Patsy and her team did not have to cool their heels in the hallway. Team Ramsey had been given Pete Hofstrom's private office, which violated the basic police procedure of keeping the parties being interviewed from contacting each other. I figured they were briefing John Ramsey, who would come in later.

The agreement not to allow any audio or video feed from the interview room hurt us since my fellow detectives could not watch and jot down follow-up questions, and we had no opportunity to allow specialists to examine Patsy's body language. Sergeant Wickman and Detectives Gosage and Harmer huddled in rapid-fire discussions with Trujillo and me during the breaks.

Patsy was evasive to the point of disbelief on a number of questions. When asked about the mystery woman who broke up her husband's first marriage, she replied, "I'm not aware of anything like that."

Her mother, both sisters, and half Atlanta knew about the affair, and Lucinda Ramsey Johnson was one of Patsy's friends. The subject of the affair had never even been mentioned?

On the pageants, she offered, "It was a Sunday afternoon kind of thing."

Thousands of dollars spent, hundreds of miles traveled, and every member of the family involved. It was the strangest comment of the day.

About the broken basement window, Patsy said she personally vacuumed up the errant pieces of glass after John kicked in the window last year and was certain she got them all.

Five times this woman, whose own housekeeper described her as slovenly, and who hired legions of cleaning people, would claim to have gone downstairs to a place used basically as a storeroom to clean up glass. It seemed like a prepared answer, and I didn't believe it.

Before leaving questions about the basement, we locked her into saying that the housekeeper had moved the painting and art supplies down there before the holidays. That made me think how odd it would be for a total stranger, presumably working in the dark, to know where to find the paintbrush that became part of the garrote.

Patsy provided plenty of possibilities for the unidentified pubic hair when I asked if anyone else ever slept in her daughter's bedroom. She reeled off the names of family members, then added people she knew only as Erin, Brian, and Brad, among others. The list grew steadily longer. It would be impossible to track down all these emerging names and take samples for testing. But it also showed that there were plenty of potential sources other than an intruder.

————————

At one point she interrupted with a statement: "I hope that you are trying to find out who killed my daughter. That is the bottom line, you know, we've got to find out who did this, so I'm praying that your department is doing all they know how to do."

I stared at her. "Well, Patsy, I can tell you this. Since December 28 when I was asked to participate in this case, this has been my entire life, seven days a week, every waking thought. . . . We are committed to finding the person who did this. That is the truth, and that's entirely what we're working toward, regardless of what you read in the tabloids or the newspaper."

She seemed not to expect such a strong response. "I don't read it, I don't read any of it."

"Do you think this was a premeditated act, or something that got out of hand?"

"I don't have any idea."

"Patsy, did you write the note?"

"No, I did not write the note."

"Did you participate in any way in the death of JonBenét?"

"No, absolutely not."

"Patsy, do you have any knowledge of John participating in this in any way?"

"No."

"This is not a case where something terribly wrong happened in that house and that you're covering up for a spouse?"

"No."

I told her that handwriting experts thought she might have written the ransom note, and we wondered why experts would think that.

"I've given handwriting after handwriting after handwriting," she replied. "You know maybe it's a female that wrote the note, I don't know. . . . I don't know what else to tell you. I write like I write."

It was of interest that she of all people suggested that a woman might be the author.

We ran out of time before we ran out of questions, and I felt we had only scratched the surface. We could have used four days for this interview and still not have gotten everything we needed, but it was a lousy one-day deal, and we still had to interview the husband. Patsy Ramsey walked out.

We had John Ramsey for just ninety minutes. As he crossed his legs, folded his hands, and nodded permission for us to begin, his cool confidence grated on me. He was just as imprecise as she had been, using the guarded answers that prevented them from being pinned down.

"Did you ever leave the bed at any time during the night?"

"Not that I recall."

"Were you in the room when Patsy changed JonBenét's clothes?"

"I don't think so. Not that I remember."

"Was JonBenét's door open or closed?"

"I don't remember."

He confirmed his wife's account that JonBenét had fallen asleep in the car and that he had carried her upstairs still asleep, but that was contrary to the December 26 statements in which he said he read to the kids. He confirmed Patsy changed JonBenét into bedclothes. He said he helped Burke assemble a Christmas toy before getting him into his pajamas.

Then he said that Patsy was already in bed when he got there, the only indication we had that she had gotten out of her clothes and gone to bed. "Did Patsy stay up reading that night?" he was asked, but he gave only another vague "Not that I recall."

John Ramsey said he read for a bit and took an over-the-counter melatonin to help him fall asleep about 10:30. He heard no suspicious sounds that night.

Did Patsy shower and dress that next morning [December 26]? we asked. "Well, she got up, I mean she was downstairs, I don't remember if she took a shower or not, she was, I think she was dressed when I saw her first."

––––––––

His recall of the ransom note was infuriatingly imprecise. "Did she show you the note on the landing?"

"I don't remember."

He said he grabbed it and laid it on the floor to better read it "really fast without having to sit and read it." The visual image was disturbing to me. Why spread such an important document on the floor, which meant he would have had to get down on his hands and knees to read it? And if he grabbed it, as he said, why weren't his fingerprints on the note? His answers only reinforced the mystery.

––––––––

We walked him through events after the police arrived. Ramsey said that Detective Linda Arndt had suggested he and Fleet White look through the house. Then, when I asked about the trip to the basement, he revealed the biggest piece of new information of the day.

Ramsey said he checked Burke's train room, where he and Fleet discussed the broken window. He then added, "I'd actually gone down there earlier that morning, and the window was broken, but I didn't see any glass around, so I assumed it was broken last summer. I used that window to get in the house one time when I didn't have a key, but the window was open, I don't know, maybe an inch, and I just kind of latched it."

What? I had to work to keep my face neutral, for while he was describing the broken window, he had also admitted going down to the basement alone and unseen *before* he went down with Fleet White and found the body.

I pushed on that. "Fleet had talked about earlier being down there alone and discovering that window. When you say that you found it earlier that day and latched it, at what time?"

"I don't know, probably before ten."

Just about when Detective Arndt lost track of him and thought he had left to get the mail. Now he admits being in the basement!

————

He then described going to the little cellar room on the subsequent trip downstairs with Fleet White, unlatching and opening the white door. He snapped his fingers and said, "It was instant, I mean, as soon as I opened the door I saw the white blanket . . . and I knew what was up." She was on her back on the floor with the white blanket folded around her, her arms were tied, and there was a piece of black tape over her lips, he said, and her head was cocked to one side.

The door opens outward, so he would have had to step back or aside before moving through. He did not say he saw the blanket after turning on the light but "instantly." Fleet White had stood in that same doorway that morning and could see nothing in the windowless darkness. I had always considered that Ramsey might have known something before he entered, and with this new admission of going to the basement earlier, I was sure of it. By the time he went back downstairs with Fleet White, I thought he knew exactly where the body was.

————

Nevertheless, his theory was that "someone came in through the basement window, because there was a blue Samsonite suitcase sitting right under the window and he . . . could have gotten in the house without that, but you couldn't have gotten out that window without something to step on. Even to have known those windows were there wouldn't have been obvious to anybody just walking by." The grate, he added, could be pulled off, and the window was not painted shut.

This was the DA's Intruder Theory, although it contradicted the events of December 26, when Fleet White said Ramsey shrugged off the open window. Now it had become very important, for the open window pointed toward their intruder. And we knew that Fleet White said he had moved the suitcase, so the intruder had not done that.

Ramsey added that during the morning of December 26, "I went around and I looked around the house that morning and . . . all the doors were locked and I had checked every door on the first floor . . . and they appeared to be locked." To me, if all the doors on the first floor were locked, that meant an intruder would have had to either have a key or enter and exit at some other point, which made the basement window even more important. And the undisturbed dirt and debris on the sill of the basement window, along with the unbroken spiderweb between the metal grate and the wall, demonstrated to me that no one came through that window. In my opinion, there was no intruder.

Both the Ramseys' answers when asked whether they had reviewed the police reports were astonishing. Patsy said, "We got them, but I didn't read them, I don't think." John Ramsey said he only "scanned them." I turned that over in my mind: Your child is murdered, you hire a top-dollar legal team and believe the police are trying to frame you, but you are not interested enough to do more than "scan" police reports? Most unlikely.

But even with that cursory reading, John Ramsey said he found "errors or misunderstandings." He said that not only did he not check *every* door in the house the night before but he did not believe he checked *any* door. Also incorrect was the police notation that Ramsey said he read to the kids before going to bed. "That did not happen. I mean what happened was that the kids went to bed and then I read."

I asked, "Do you attribute that simply to an officer's error in recollection, or might you have said that?"

"No, I wouldn't have said that. I think that maybe the way I said it was misinterpreted. I clearly did not read to the kids that night. Jon-Benét was asleep, we wanted Burke to get to sleep. We were going to get up early the next morning."

To believe him now, one would have to believe that three police officers—Officer French, Detective Arndt, and Sergeant Reichenbach—were all mistaken about what Ramsey had told them.

I asked about the infidelity in his first marriage. He identified the woman as Jodi Roberts, who worked for him as a secretary in the late seventies. "I haven't seen her since then," he said. "It was certainly one of those things you regret in life. When I heard of the movie *Fatal Attraction,* we didn't go see it because I think I could have written it." I considered that to be a very peculiar answer because if Roberts was such a menace, why was he only now supplying her name, when he had given up so many other people, including close friends, as murder suspects? We asked about any other suspects. He mentioned business associates from the eighties, former Access employees, the cleaning lady.

He also put a dent in part of the latest Intruder Theory, in which the DA's investigator Lou Smit claimed the killer left a scarf behind. Ramsey identified the scarf as a gift from one of his kids. Patsy had said the same thing.

———————

As we neared the end of the interview, Ramsey said, "I've seen a lot of effort and time and money being spent trying to categorize Patsy and I as child abusers, and that couldn't be further from the truth."

I told him a lot of effort had been made to make the crime look like something it wasn't. "One theory is that something happened in that house that may have been accidental, that turned to panic, that turned to cover-up."

"That's a false theory," he almost snarled. "Anyone who knows Patsy and I can tell you that is total bullshit."

"John," I asked, "are you involved in any way in the death of your daughter?"

"No."

"John, are you involved in any way in the preparation of that note?"

"No . . . I will spend every dime I have, every minute of time I have, if that's what it takes to find who killed her."

———————

Before concluding each interview, I asked if they would take lie detector tests, and the responses were decisive and totally opposite.

Patsy became the forthright, wrongly blamed victim and snapped, "I don't know how those work, but if they tell the truth, I'm telling the truth. I've never given anybody a reason to think otherwise."

Does that mean yes, you'd pass it?

"Yes, I would pass it. . . . I'll take ten of them. Do whatever you want."

Now a detective never refuses a suspect who offers to take a polygraph, and we had been using an FBI polygrapher on other suspects. He should have been set up and waiting in the next room for just such an eventuality. But Pete Hofstrom, who didn't believe in lie detector tests, had told me that if we asked, the Ramseys would "just say no."

But Patsy Ramsey had just said yes. It was a golden opportunity, and we weren't allowed to capitalize on it.

John Ramsey appeared ready for the question. "What I've been told is that I felt tremendous guilt after we lost JonBenét because I hadn't protected her. You know, I'd failed as a parent. I was told that with that kind of an emotion, you shouldn't take a lie detector test because you do have that guilt feeling. So I don't know anything about the test, but

I did not kill my daughter, if that's what you want to ask me. She was the most precious thing to me in the world. So if the lie detector test is correct and it's done correctly, I would pass it one hundred percent."

I told him that others had already been polygraphed and then asked point-blank if he would take one. He grew angry, a remarkable attitude change in just one question. "I would be insulted if you asked me to take a polygraph test. Frankly, I mean if you haven't talked to enough people to tell you what kind of people we are . . . I will do whatever these guys [indicating his attorneys] recommend me to do, but we are not the kind of people you're trying to make us out to be. It's a tragic misdirection I think that you're on, and the sooner we get off of that, the sooner we'll find who killed JonBenét."

In later months, Team Ramsey would insist that the Ramseys had never been asked to take a polygraph. I had asked both of them, and neither ever did.

———

And that was it. They had marched into the DA's office with their army and marched right back out again, victorious.

19

The *Colorado Peace Officer's Handbook*, written by our departmental attorney, Bob Keatley, says that "probable cause" for an arrest exists "When you have sufficient reliable information to believe that under the totality of the circumstances there is a fair probability that the suspect has committed . . . a crime." To make the decision, the officer relies upon, among other things, personal observations, past experience, a suspect's presence at the scene, information from other officers, attempts to avoid detection, and incriminating, contradictory, or evasive answers from the suspect.

We had all of that and a lot more.

If there was one certainty in this entire investigation, it was the nearly unanimous consensus within the law enforcement community that probable cause existed to arrest Patsy Ramsey. I believed that, as did every detective on the investigating squad and our boss Sergeant Tom Wickman, who one day suggested, "The probable cause is there. Maybe the five of us should just go make the arrest." Commander John Eller believed it, as did Police Chief Tom Koby and his successor, Mark Beckner, who personally told me so.

Chief Koby would also tell me later that District Attorney Alex Hunter thought "from day one that Patsy did it" and that probable cause existed.

There was no doubt at all that we had the elements of probable cause.

But it wasn't enough, because the DA's office—which would eventually admit that the Ramseys were "prime suspects" and that enough evidence existed to get a grand jury indictment—changed the rules. When Deputy DA Mary Keenan announced several years later that she was a candidate to succeed Alex Hunter, she mentioned that the history of plea bargaining by his office had eroded the courtroom skills of Hunter's prosecutors.

That was the catch. There was no prosecutor in Boulder who could take the Ramseys into court, fight off their defense team, and bring the pieces of the puzzle together for a jury. Years of plea bargaining had made them paper tigers. In one case, a woman bought a pistol the day after being separated from her husband, practiced at a firing range, then wrote a will and farewell letters to her children. When her husband came to remove his belongings from the house, she shot him in cold blood, then surrendered to a cop. Detective Kim Stewart and I interviewed the woman, a criminology professor, arrested for the first-degree murder of her husband. Compared with the Ramsey fiasco, this was easy, as she waived her Miranda rights and confessed the premeditated act to Detective Stewart and me. Only four hours after the shots were fired, we had the confession on tape. But Deputy DA Pete Hofstrom began negotiating with the public defender that day, and the killer, instead of facing a death penalty trial, quickly accepted a reduced charge and twenty years.

Now in the Ramsey case they told us there would be no arrest, because we couldn't yet prove the case "beyond a reasonable doubt." Therefore their interpretation of BARD became the new standard for the investigation. I felt that the DA's office was asking on the one hand for a slam-dunk certainty of conviction while on the other hand seemed to be doing everything possible to prevent us from getting it.

But was there any case that they would take? They had an abysmal record in murder trials, had not taken one to court in years, and sure as hell didn't want this one. Their prayer was for a confession, so they could make a deal and not have to face a jury.

———

Team Ramsey counterattacked at noon on the day after the interviews, when John and Patsy Ramsey met with seven handpicked reporters from Boulder and Denver. Lawyers stood nearby to make sure that certain topics, such as the death of JonBenét, were not discussed. I wondered why any legitimate journalist would attend such a prearranged performance. The only issue was murder, and they had agreed not to ask about it.

John Ramsey immediately overstepped their own guideline and said,

"I did not kill my daughter JonBenét." Patsy added, "Let me assure you that I did not kill JonBenét and did not have anything to do with this."

No new ground was likely to be broken in such an orchestrated meeting. Patsy wagged a finger at the camera and said two knew who killed her daughter, the killer and someone the killer had told. She warned, "We will find you." Her husband looked sternly into the camera and echoed the threat: "We will find you. I have that as the sole mission for the rest of my life."

I didn't have to listen to their words, for the real message was visual. As soon as I saw Patsy, it made sense why this time had been set up for television so quickly. The day before, I had surprised them with our knowledge that the clothes she was wearing on the morning of December 26 were the same she had worn to the Christmas party the previous night. This indicated that she had not changed clothes, and possibly had not even gone to bed that night. My guess was that she had been up all night, dealing with the death of JonBenét.

Today, on television, she wore the identical ensemble she had on during the interview—blue suit with white trim, white sweater, even the silver angel pin on her lapel. I could almost hear a defense attorney's question at trial: *Detective Thomas, what was Mrs. Ramsey wearing. . . . ?*

What little morale was left in the Boulder Police Department was crushed on the first weekend of May, when the area around the University of Colorado erupted in three nights of rioting. Firefighters and police officers were assaulted by more than a thousand rioters with a blizzard of debris and Molotov cocktails, and although SWAT teams said they could end it in thirty minutes, Chief Koby would not allow a response, even as he watched his officers fall. After that, he was useless as a leader.

Koby walked into the crowd on the second night, waving his hands like a messiah, and they ridiculed and spat on him. By the third night, there was no law on University Hill, as city leaders surrendered to mob rule.

I was not on the line but watched in disbelief as the police department took on the look of a hospital emergency room. Scores of cops were injured, and the skull of a friend of mine was crushed by a thrown cinder block. Another angry, bandaged cop told me, "We're getting goddamn murdered out there."

In the midst of the furor, John Andrew Ramsey stumbled out of an alley, appearing intoxicated. Spotting a familiar face among the SWAT team officers, he called out, "Ron!" An astonished Detective Ron Gosage shook the kid's hand and told him to leave the area. John Andrew agreed and sauntered away, saying, "I got enough problems of my own."

At the end of the month, our union gave Chief Koby a no-confidence vote, and he distanced himself even further from the additional controversy of the Ramsey case.

At the end of May we hit the boiler room operation in Denver that was the source of the calls made by the phony "John Ramsey" to McGuckin's Hardware back in January. It was launched by my search warrant handled by Deputy DA Trip DeMuth, who apparently had no problem authorizing warrants that were not directed at the Ramseys.

Touch Tone Information Acquisition, Inc., sold private information on people, including cops, to anyone who would buy it, such as the supermarket tabloids. Home addresses, names of wives and kids, credit bureau reports, bank statements, and unlisted telephone and pager numbers were all for sale. Touch Tone was pulling in more than $1.5 million a year for their information, and a prisoner had tipped us that a Boulder cop was among those selling data and that there had been an attempt to purchase the ransom note. We could not ignore such serious allegations.

Among the dossiers we found on celebrities, cops, and business executives in several cities—including Boulder detectives—were the very things the DA had been blocking us from obtaining: the Ramseys' long-distance telephone and itemized credit card records. But our legal adviser Bob Keatley jerked them from our hands, saying the credit cards had been specified only as a target of the Touch Tone warrant, and we could not use them in another investigation.

He was right, but you can't unring a bell. I walked around for days thinking of what I had seen on those records from hardware stores and marine supply outlets in various states. Such places sell duct tape and cord like that used in the murder. But the Touch Tone material went into the Boulder Police Department's evidence storage, where it sat useless right under our noses, and we couldn't touch it. It might as well have been stored on the moon.

Our DA's office did nothing further with Touch Tone, and DeMuth waved it off with another "So what?" But selling private data on detectives and undercover cops was extremely dangerous, and we later learned that undercover cops with the Los Angeles Police Department had been compromised by Touch Tone. Two years later, prosecutors from neighboring Jefferson County, the Colorado Bureau of Investigation, and the Federal Trade Commission built on my original warrant and grabbed Touch Tone's owners, James and Regana Rapp, on felony racketeering charges.

———

On the final night of May, I got a taste of the damage that could result from selling personal information on Boulder detectives and was angry that our DA didn't care.

I live in a small neighborhood at the edge of farming country, a place where people are caring and things are quiet, but when I stepped outside my house about eleven o'clock, I tripped over a cat that had been killed, mutilated, and thrown onto my lawn. The garden hose was sliced, my wife's flower garden shredded.

Ten days earlier, Sergeant Bob Whitson, who retrieved the ransom note tablet on December 26, was in his home when two shots from a high-powered rifle shattered his bedroom window and narrowly missed him. A third shot drilled through a wall, then a fourth struck the house as Whitson dove to a closet floor, grabbed his weapon and a phone, and dialed 911. Whoever had fired the shots vanished.

Detective Linda Arndt, who rarely carried her gun, telephoned me several times during the investigation, plainly frightened. On one occasion blood was splashed on her front door, and another time she was concerned about a prowler.

There was no follow-up by the police department, which apparently regarded bullets, blood, and dead cats as minor. No stakeouts, no investigation. It was damned difficult to ignore attacks on three detectives deeply involved in the Ramsey investigation as being coincidental and unrelated.

———

Chief Tom Koby and District Attorney Alex Hunter came up with a very Boulder solution to resolving the differences between our offices. We would sit down with a mediator and reason together. It didn't have a prayer of success.

We gathered in a fourth-floor conference room at the University of Colorado for what were termed the SALT talks, as if nuclear proliferation, and not cooperation to catch a killer, was the topic. "We're married and can't get divorced," Hunter told the group, reminding us that soon we would all be moving into the Criminal Justice Center, working side by side in what he called his War Room. The only war would be among the people in there.

The detectives complained about the constant drumbeat of damaging media leaks, the lack of prosecutorial vigor, and the rupture of trust. The DA's office charged that we were concentrating too narrowly on the Ramseys. When Trip DeMuth said he wanted "an enthusiastic investigation of the intruder," Alex Hunter said DeMuth was "making too much" of that subject. DeMuth rolled his eyes and turned away.

The district attorney then declared, "I have no confidence in my people on issues surrounding the media." It was my opinion that the "law enforcement" sources always quoted by the press were in the DA's office, not the police department. Hofstrom challenged Hunter about leaking news to reporters himself. It was not a good day for the DA in terms of respect from his subordinates.

The mediation accomplished absolutely nothing.

On June 3 the detectives were transferred to the War Room, on the ground floor of the Justice Center, about two miles from the police department. It was as if we were stepping into a blindside ambush, and we all knew it was a sham. But since $36,000 was spent to create the working space and the DA wanted to show a unified front—*We're working the case!*—there we were.

The DA's investigators, Steve Ainsworth and Lou Smit, were at desks on one side of the room. Detectives Gosage, Harmer, Trujillo, and I stayed on the other, while Sergeant Tom Wickman took a desk in a private office beside Deputy DA DeMuth.

Only authorized personnel were allowed inside, or so we thought. To enter, you pressed an identification card flat against a scanning device that unlocked the only door and recorded your personal code. But since the room was in the same building as the offices of the district attorney, we were concerned about the security of the files, notes, and computers, which had been moved from the police department Situation Room.

I found a couple of red binders on the shelves among our white case notebooks. I pulled one down, started to read, and couldn't believe my eyes. They were the compiled reports of Ainsworth and Smit and documented that more evidence had been released to Team Ramsey without our knowledge, that the two DA investigators were conducting an independent investigation without telling us, and that they were filing reports about what was said by the detectives behind closed doors during strategy sessions. Lou Smit was talking privately with Patsy Ramsey. He was writing about stun guns, sex offenders, flashlights, and exhumation. They had shown photo lineups of ex-cons and drifters to the Ramseys. What the hell was all this?

Although neither Smit nor Ainsworth was a handwriting expert, one report noted that a suspect's handwriting contained "similarities . . . to the ransom note." It appeared to me that anything that would bolster the Intruder Theory was logged. Once logged, it was part of the case file and would eventually be open to discovery by a defense attorney. Wild and independent speculation should never be in a case file.

When we complained to Alex Hunter, he claimed that he was "kept in the dark on a lot of this."

The tension in the War Room was so high that Sergeant Wickman lost his temper and kicked over a chair when a fax arrived that showed DeMuth had not consulted him before giving further orders about testing the ransom note.

It was just a sign of things to come.

Only a few days into the new working space, the police computer containing preliminary DNA results and other case information was broken into, and we accused the district attorney's people of being behind it. A separate investigation then began that ended in what I considered a political cover-up close to an obstruction of justice.

When the preliminary DNA results came back from the CellMark labs, we logged them away in Detective Tom Trujillo's computer in the high-security War Room. That early report was very ambiguous. We would get a more thorough briefing in five months and would hold this early material as confidential.

Since we did not trust the DA's office with sensitive information, we kept it from them, and Pete Hofstrom began to gripe that he *had to have* the DNA results. "Little fucker pouts when I don't tell him," Wickman said.

When a newspaper reported that the district attorney's office had not been provided with the data, Alex Hunter called Commander John Eller, who questioned why Hunter had to respond to the media at all.

"I can't dodge it," Hunter replied. "I'd like to sanitize this thing."

"Just tell them the BPD investigators are in possession of the results."

"But why aren't we [the DA's office] in possession?" He paused, maybe remembering all that had leaked from his office. He changed the subject. "I hope [the War Room] will be productive. I'm optimistic. My people are ready to go."

"I'd like to think so," said Eller. "My cops have never lost focus."

"Our goal is to get this case solved," said Hunter, and Eller couldn't resist the opening.

"Really? Have you been down there? DeMuth is going behind our backs to CBI, and the reports your investigators are putting in the case file are insane."

Hunter predicted that if the people in the War Room could not get along, "We are going to get eaten A-fucking-live."

In a second call that day, the district attorney bemoaned the DNA incident as the "first major crack in the public impression that we are not working together." He asked Eller to at least confide the DNA results to Pete Hofstrom, who "keeps things from me and has done so for years." Then he could tell the press in truth that the DA's office had the results.

"I don't trust Pete, and it's not appropriate," Eller replied, remembering Hofstrom's involvement in the "ransom the body" episode that caused so much trouble at the start of the case.

Hunter played a political card. "The city council will now have a reason to take Koby to task. Councilman [Bob] Greenlee and those birdbrains will do this."

"Koby was part of this decision," Eller said, and the second conversation ended. Two more calls followed on that Friday afternoon, the final one a shouting, cursing demand by the district attorney. Eller still refused.

On Monday morning I found a furious Ron Gosage and Al Alvarado, our computer expert, in the War Room. Someone had breached the computer over the weekend. Alvarado said Trujillo's password had been overridden, and the documents on the hard drive were compromised. The hacker could not restore it to the original state, so he just put it back together and left. Our entire evidence file, including the new DNA results, was in jeopardy.

Eller was advised that the card scanner had denied an attempt to enter the room over the weekend and that the denied card belonged to Deputy DA Mary Keenan. It is possible someone else used her key. It was also possible that someone who had been escorted into the War Room on Friday had stayed behind, because the card scanner only recorded entries, not exits. Among those people was a computer expert from the DA's office.

A few days later, a Colorado Bureau of Investigation expert said the problem was not due to a lapsed battery, power surge, or lightning strike and that a computer chip had been bypassed. Commander Eller called Chief Koby, who was vacationing in Texas, to inform him that we wanted an investigation. Koby approved but asked that Alex Hunter be given an opportunity to respond. The chief later denied sanctioning the investigation.

The following day John Eller advised the city manager and the head of the CBI of what he was going to do, then asked Hunter for a private meeting. As the two men walked along Boulder Creek, Eller told the district attorney that information might have been stolen from the breached computer and that the cops thought Hunter's office was responsible. Eller told me later that the district attorney offered no denial, only a "Hmmm, do what you have to do."

———————

Then Detective Trujillo brought us some good news and some bad news. He had never entered the DNA results into his computer, so that was safe, and he had electronically hidden my Master Affidavit, which also contained the information. But now his ZIP drive, which contained the backup of the case file, had also gone missing. This was turning into a *Spy vs. Spy* episode.

CBI agents investigated Computergate, and we underwent videotaped questioning. I responded with "Absolutely" when asked to take a polygraph. Investigators even searched Trip DeMuth's home computer.

Several days later, it all started going south on us when Detective Trujillo found the missing ZIP drive. He had simply misplaced it.

Chief Koby then voluntarily handed Hunter the DNA secrets that we had so zealously guarded and told Commander Eller to apologize to the district attorney. Eller refused. Koby, who had originally backed the investigation, now abandoned the commander. "How could you do this?" Koby asked.

The chief and the DA then sought to have all the CBI interview tapes made during the computer breach investigation destroyed because "people let their hair down." That was tantamount to destroying evidence in an official investigation, and Eller protested, "I can't believe this is even being considered." A press release went out that announced the Colorado Bureau of Investigation determined there was an equipment problem and absolved the DA's office of any involvement.

Eller had been on borrowed time because of his dogged insistence on treating the case like a serious murder investigation, but after accusing the DA of a burglary that couldn't be proved, the commander became the fall guy for the entire investigation.

The internal Computergate probe died in that final conference. The CBI agent eventually suggested that the problem was merely a malfunction, perhaps just "a microscopic bump."

But our computer guy, Al Alvarado, never wavered in his conclusion and said a CBI agent confirmed to him that there had been an unauthorized breach but that instructions had come down to issue a formal statement that said otherwise.

It was a cover-up.

———

Meanwhile, our Twilight Zone existence continued in the War Room.

- Pete Hofstrom, wearing a Do Not Disturb sweatband around his bald head, asked if the labs had made a call on the handwriting and said he needed the information because Team Ramsey wanted to respond to an East Coast newspaper.
- I found the shelves of the steel cabinets in the War Room almost empty. "Where the hell are our notebooks?" I yelled, throwing up my hands in total shock. We found the notebooks containing all the details of our case, many of them open, strewn across the DA's conference table before Alex Hunter and Lou Smit, who were having their pictures taken for a magazine. Our case files had become props for a Hunter photo shoot.
- Lou Smit, whom I considered thoroughly compromised because of his unwavering commitment to the Ramseys, met privately with the Ramseys at 755 Fifteenth Street and prayed with them inside his van. He later announced that he would never participate in their indictment or arrest.

———

I drove to the nearby War Room for a scheduled briefing. Lou Smit was the only one there, and he confronted me with a tone I had never heard from him before. "Do you got a problem with me?"

I stood up, and we were nose to nose and arguing hard. I insisted he was damaging the case with so many unproved theories about what might have happened.

"There is nothing to indicate their involvement, and I'll write my reports that way," he stormed.

"It's outright sabotage," I responded.

He said the DA's office was lining up experts to counter our experts and prove that a stun gun was used. Talk about a united front. "So, you got a problem?" he shouted.

"Yeah," I shouted back. "You!" I blasted him for polluting the file. "If we had the same evidence against anyone else that we have against Patsy Ramsey *right now,* their ass would be in jail."

For the only time in our months together, I felt that if Lou were twenty years younger, we would have come to blows. I was closer to this man than to anyone in the DA's unit, but we were miles apart philosophically. As tempers quieted, Lou returned to his desk but couldn't resist one last punch, whispering over his shoulder, "Wickman's on our side."

Despite our differences, I still respected Smit. On many nights we sat alone in the War Room debating our conflicting theories. We argued without letup, but neither of us wavered. He did not care for the picture of convicted child-slayer Susan Smith that a detective had tacked on a wall, and detested the screen-saver on one computer that continuously scrolled the brightly lettered sentence THE RAMSEYS ARE THE KILLAS . . . THE RAMSEYS ARE THE KILLAS . . .

———

A month and a half after moving into the War Room, we could take it no longer. I bought thirty heavy-duty four-inch-wide binders, picked up Detective Ron Gosage, and set off to the War Room on a Saturday night to "borrow" the case file for a few hours. Through a pager code, Detective Jane Harmer let us know the coast was clear. We were in and out of there just as fast as we could load the folders into my Mustang.

I had hatched a deal with the manager of Kinko's copy shop so we could duplicate about twenty thousand pages late that night. We would put the copies in the police department and return the originals to the DA's office. In very careful words, Sergeant Wickman had obliquely told me that we would need a copy of the case file in the police department if we ever pulled out of the War Room. So while okaying the project, he avoided knowing the details.

Working like fiends on high-speed machines, Gosage and I copied thousands and thousands of pages, tore open reams of paper, punched tens of thousands of holes, and slowly assembled a duplicate file, looking over our shoulders and wondering what our excuse could be if someone from the DA's office walked in. "Screw 'em," Gosage said. "This is our case."

It was hard not to stop and read, for we kept finding material we had never seen before, such as potential "points of entry" for an intruder and diagrams suggesting "open" doors. I kept wondering why was this shit in the official files? Didn't the DA's investigators realize the potential damage? Don't think, just copy, copy, copy.

After midnight Bob Keatley marched in and put the entire charge on his personal credit card. "Might look better this way," he said. Keatley explained that we had the legal right to copy our own files, but I still felt as if I was involved with the likes of G. Gordon Liddy and Bob Haldeman. We finished at 2 A.M., and in the dark of night we returned the originals to the steel cabinet, then locked our new file up tight in the police department. Except for periodic briefings, I never went back to the War Room.

20

The Ramseys vanished right before our eyes. After their interviews and the following press conference, they ducked behind their shield of attorneys and public relations spinners. To me, they were almost taunting the police. Since their lawyers had been given nearly all our evidence by the DA's office, they knew what they were facing and had reason to be confident that any future discoveries would also be passed along. And when we didn't move on probable cause, Team Ramsey had to know we wouldn't move at all.

John and Patsy Ramsey spent the summer at their lakeside house in Michigan, where Patsy cooked a batch of warm cupcakes for the Charlevoix cops. We were left behind to fight among ourselves.

And we did. An airport meeting with Dr. Henry Lee, the forensics specialist working for the DA's office, fell into shambles. Instead of getting further insight into the evidence, Lee was exasperated at the ill will between us and the DA's office. To our chagrin, he likened our bickering to the backroom fights he watched while working on the O. J. Simpson case. Lee said he did not know what his role was in Boulder, did not like what his friends were saying about his involvement in the Ramsey case, did not know what District Attorney Alex Hunter wanted from him, did not have a crystal ball with which to solve the crime, and would not be made to look like a fool in court. Lee snapped at Hunter, "Captain this ship."

The ship truly was without a captain. Boulder city manager Tim Honey was fired, Mayor Leslie Durgin was leaving at the end of her

term, and several top bureaucrats were dismissed or quit. The leaderless
city was in turmoil as Councilman Bob Greenlee, enjoying minifame as
a frequent talking head on Ramsey panel shows, became mayor.

———————

I still felt that the house on Fifteenth Street was a central character in
the mystery of JonBenét Ramsey's death. Both the DA's office and the
police wanted to go back into it, but for different reasons. I wanted to
re-create and document John Ramsey's improbable description of how
he found the body, while Deputy DA Trip DeMuth wanted to look
for "new evidence" that would substantiate his Intruder Theory. Why
DeMuth expected there would be anything left to find was beyond me.
Team Ramsey private investigators, defense lawyers, painters, carpenters, and cleaners had scoured the place for four months, and you can't
pull old evidence from new paint. Police wanted entry through a search
warrant, but the DA's office and the Ramseys agreed to a consent-to-
search. That was promptly heralded in the next day's paper as the Ramseys' continued cooperation with authorities.

The house occupied a prime half-acre on University Hill and had
undergone considerable additions and remodeling since it was built in
1927. It sprawled over most of the lot, and the classy red brick Tudor
front masked an ugly California stucco rear. In all there were almost
7,000 square feet of living space in the three-story, million-dollar house
that Patsy's mother, Nedra, called "a hell-hole."

The smell of fresh paint was strong when I returned for another look
on July 2, 1997, and with most of the furniture removed the place
seemed much less gaudy than I remembered.

I ascended the main staircase near the front door, passed a second-
floor landing, and emerged on the top floor, a converted 1,500-square-
foot attic that was the master bedroom suite of John and Patsy Ramsey.
The stairs ended just opposite the bed. High ceilings, expensive curtains
over large arched windows, a photograph of Patsy and Burke on one
wall, a painting of flowers over the fireplace mantel. Detective Gosage
was toying with the electronic control that lowered an eight-foot movie
screen from the ceiling. There were no personal effects or clothing, and
the drawers were empty. It looked like a furniture showroom.

Half the top floor was taken up by the parents' individual dressing
rooms and bathrooms. I took Lou Smit into the cavernous closet that
Patsy Ramsey had once filled with designer clothing and argued how
unlikely it was for such a woman to wear the same outfit on two consecutive days. He shrugged.

The second staircase, the one Patsy said she descended on the morning of December 26, started nearby, and I went down to the second floor. From that landing the stairway changed to the spiral staircase that led to the first floor.

The middle level was called the children's floor and was divided by a large playroom. Burke Ramsey's room was dominated by a big wooden propeller from one of his grandfather's aircraft hanging on the east wall. Next door was the room of his stepsister, Melinda. It contained a wicker rocking chair that had been in the family for four generations.

At the other end of the floor was John Andrew's room, to which Patsy had retreated during her cancer therapy.

The common landing that separated John Andrew's room from the spacious bedroom of JonBenét was bordered by a counter, sink, and cabinets. It was one of those overhead cabinets that had been open, with a package of pull-up diapers hanging halfway out of it, on the night JonBenét was killed. A washer-dryer combination was stacked next to the spiral staircase. Housekeeper Linda Hoffmann-Pugh said she would often find JonBenét's bed stripped of sheets that were already in the washer when she arrived.

JonBenét's room had once been the fanciful canvas of a professional designer but now was only empty space. The antique English burl walnut beds were gone, as was the corner cabinet that had been hand-carved on the theme of the cat and the fiddle and a cow jumping over the moon. A mural showing the child's love of hats had vanished beneath a new coat of cream-colored paint. The closets were empty, the trophies removed, the carpeting was replaced. At the rear were two doors, one into her bathroom and the other out to a small balcony.

I leaned against a wall and visualized it as it was last Christmas. The dresser in the corner, the beautiful tree with angel ornaments, the portrait with the innocent smile, kid stuff all over the floor. What a life she would have had.

In her bathroom I examined every item—the faucets, the side of the tub, the countertop where the rolled-up red turtleneck was found, everything—trying to imagine what surface could have crushed her skull. I walked to where her bed had been and pretended, as the intruder, to scoop her into my arms. It was difficult to close the door behind me, but the intruder would have done so, because Patsy said she had to push it open that morning. I descended the spiral stairs to the first floor with my eyes closed, imagining the trek in darkness while carrying a child either unconscious or fighting, knowing the parents were asleep upstairs and her brother was just down the hall. Each footstep had to be taken so carefully that I thought the whole scenario impossible.

I repeated the experiment by going down the main staircase, but that would have meant passing Burke's bedroom and coming closer to the parents asleep upstairs. Not a likely path. In either event I would have ended up at the head of the basement staircase, trying to find the odd light switch that was on the wall behind me, not inside the door where one would expect it to be.

The spiral staircase ended at the rear of a small hardwood hallway on the main floor. Patsy said she stepped over the ransom note, which was spread out on the third step from the bottom, then turned around to read it. It was extremely hard to miss any of those steps without falling, and I was doing it in daylight. Patsy's account wasn't ringing true to me.

On my right was the garage and the entry through a small mudroom, which the family called the cubby room. Beyond that was a bay-windowed study that matched the shape of JonBenét's balcony directly above it. Wide windows faced the patio overlooking the garden.

To my left were the hallway table, sink, and countertop. This was where the ransom note tablet had been retrieved. Below the counter was a drawer that had contained rolls of tape: Scotch tape, packaging tape, but not black duct tape. Beyond the counter was a "butler's kitchen," out of sight but complete with everything necessary for caterers during a party.

Down the short hall was the main kitchen. The telephone from which the 911 call was made was located in a small recessed nook on the southwest wall. Beneath the phone had been the cup that held the Sharpie pen. How would any stranger know the writing implements were so handy, and why take the time to put it in the cup when he wanted to flee from a murder scene? Why not just leave them on the table when finished writing? Why not bring a completed ransom note with him?

The kitchen, with a restaurant-sized walk-in refrigerator, gas stove-top, convection and microwave ovens, was arranged in an efficient work-flow pattern. Lou Smit wanted to examine a place where photographs indicated an unexplained spot of blood, but Detective Gosage pointed out, "It wasn't blood, Lou, just some spilled juice."

A big black flashlight found in the kitchen remained unexplained.

The kitchen was the demarcation line between backstage and the front of the curtain, and I moved through to the formal areas and the main rooms.

Down the main hall was the front door, with a mahogany grandfather clock in the foyer. To the south was the living room, dominated by a Steinway grand piano. French and English oil paintings had complemented a 1781 spinning wheel beside a big fireplace with a limestone mantel. We had sifted the ash box below to be sure no evidence had been burned, although we thought it highly unlikely that an intruder would light a fire in an occupied home to destroy evidence.

Through the living room was the small solarium with brick walls and leaded glass windows. In there, Patsy, seated in an overstuffed chintz chair, had "eyeballed" Officer Rick French while the lifeless body of her daughter lay in the basement ten feet below her.

I moved west, into the formal dining room, which had been converted from a sunporch. The mahogany dining table, banded with an inlay of ebony and rosewood, was ten feet long and surrounded by Chippendale chairs. A sideboard topped with marble was along one wall, a hand-carved china cabinet was in a corner, and a crystal chandelier hung overhead. An antique mirror and an original oil painting dominated walls that were hand-painted by a Denver artist named Shoshone in what Patsy had referred to as a green malachite faux finish.

Connecting the dining room back to the kitchen was the family's breakfast room, in which a table had been surrounded by hand-painted cabinets, a collection of dainty figurines, and an antique cupboard from Wales. To one side had been a Singer sewing machine that Patsy's grandmother received as a wedding present in 1918.

It was on that table that police had found the porcelain bowl containing fresh pineapple and bearing the fingerprints of Patsy and Burke. To me, that connected Patsy to pineapple, and pineapple was found in JonBenét's stomach, and one plus one equals two. I came to believe Patsy had given JonBenét pineapple that night.

Our experts studied the pineapple in the stomach and reported that it was fresh-cut pineapple, consistent down to the rind with what had been found in the bowl. It was solid proof that it wasn't canned pineapple, and what were the chances that an intruder would have brought in a fresh pineapple to cut up for his victim?

At lunch we had our sandwiches at that table while trying to convince Lou Smit of the connection between the mother's fingerprints on the bowl and the pineapple remains found in the child's body. He countered that a crime scene photo showed a Tupperware container in a paper sack in JonBenét's bedroom, and he believed the contents of that plastic bowl might have been pineapple.

Maybe she got up during the night and ate the pineapple in her room, he said, giving us an unlikely alternative. The Tupperware container, never seized, was long gone, and the grainy photo on which he relied was totally inconclusive. I thought the material could have been popcorn, maybe beads, certainly not unrefrigerated pineapple. Perhaps, Smit argued, if she knew the intruder, he might have fed her. "Maybe Santa," he ventured.

For an entire week we prowled the property, sitting on the Ramseys' chairs, lying on their bed, walking in their footsteps. The entire team went up to the master suite one midnight. We turned on no lights, and the stillness was total, further convincing me of the implausibility of an intruder.

———

One night we tried to figure out if the parents could have heard Jon-Benét scream. While some of us stayed in the master suite, Detective Gosage tiptoed through the dark house, then shouted. His shout was clearly audible to me, but Trip DeMuth said it was difficult to hear. We could even hear a shout from the basement, although our intruder theorists could not.

But we all agreed that Melody Stanton, the neighbor who claimed to have heard a scream, "obviously that of a child," on Christmas night, could have done so. I wanted to go over and talk to her right then and dig deeper into her story, but Deputy DA DeMuth refused, putting a blockade between police and Melody Stanton. He said he planned to "prep her" before trial. DeMuth didn't explain his reasons to mere police officers and detectives. I could not fathom why a prosecutor would intentionally stop us from talking to her. Such a thing had never happened before in any investigation I was involved in, but with a wave of his hand—*poof!*—DeMuth sealed off an important avenue of investigation from the investigators. I knew that in other cities, not only would the prosecutor have okayed the interview but he probably would have helped conduct it on the spot. The difference of opinion between the DA's office and the police had thrown into question whether or not there was a scream at all. It would be up to a jury to make the ultimate decision.

Detective Gosage wrote in his official report that he could hear movement and noise, even when people were trying to be quiet, no matter where he stood in the house. Sergeant Wickman told him that Deputy DA DeMuth wanted that report changed. Gosage refused. I found it incomprehensible that any prosecutor would make such a demand, for defense lawyers would pounce on the alteration to paint the cop as unsure of what he saw or heard. DeMuth was putting us on dangerous ground.

————

Lou Smit and I stayed into the wee hours on several nights, since the Ramsey case really had its hooks into both of us, and our discussions frequently turned to debate and then to flat-out argument. We went to the basement, to the bedrooms, to the stairwell. What happened, Lou? How did an intruder slip in on the quietest night of the year, commit a violent murder, stage the scene, spend considerable time writing at least two ransom notes with Patsy's pad and pen, and depart undetected while three people in the house slept through it all? He offered that the intruder could have broken in while the Ramseys were at the Whites' party, learned the layout of the house, researched the family's history, prepared the ransom note, and hidden while waiting to strike.

"Lou," I said, "we're here at two o'clock in the morning in a house that is so old we can hear it creak every time we take a step, and nobody heard anything that night. No intruder snuck in and murdered that child."

"Yes, they did."

"No, they didn't."

All night long.

DeMuth now wanted the locks removed to be reexamined six months after the crime, although our lock guy and the Colorado Bureau of Investigation had examined them earlier and found no signs of tampering. Repeating the tests at this point only invited another legal challenge. Investigator Steve Ainsworth was down on his knees with pieces of adhesive tape, picking up fibers from the closet. Useless busywork. Six months after the murder, the integrity of any hair and fiber evidence was questionable at best after an army of people had been through the house.

The media camped outside, while continually criticizing the police for being inept, had no idea what was really going on inside the investigation nor did they know of the distance between the two sets of investigators.

In the basement, Detective Gosage and I got filthy while snaking through three connecting crawl spaces that got smaller and tighter as we went. We found only dirt and some newspapers from the 1920s, probably left behind by the original carpenters. The basement that had been so cluttered and messy at the time of the murder was now pristine.

One of the two possible basement-level points of entry was a north-east corner foot-square window into a bathroom. Smit, examining a photograph with his magnifying glass, thought he had seen a thumb-print in the thick layer of dust on the exterior sill. We argued that it wasn't a print at all. "Then he wore gloves," Smit concluded. Sergeant Wickman retorted that someone needed a "magic X-ray wand" to un-lock that window from the outside. The carpet of pine needles and the dirt around the window were intact, and photos from December 27 showed the window secured and undamaged. A vanity shelf just inside was undisturbed.

As the press watched and cameras clicked, we tested it for possible entry. Wickman wiggled through headfirst on his stomach and had to use his hands to grab overhead pipes and lever himself in. Smit managed to slither in on his back. Both dragged significant amounts of debris in with them, and no such debris was found during the original search. The techs had found no unknown prints when they dusted the pipes that Wickman grasped to make his entry. Even Lou Smit eventually admitted that the small window wasn't a possible point of entry for an intruder. He just moved on to another theory that in my opinion was equally farfetched.

He and DeMuth walked the premises deep in conversation, discuss-ing how the intruder committed the crime. Not *if* there was an intruder, just *how* he did it. Gosage and I tagged along, rudely countering their suppositions with cold evidence. "Just because something is humanly possible, or that an acrobatic circus monkey could get through a win-dow, doesn't mean it happened," we protested. It made no difference.

Two new padlocks had been placed on the grate that covered the well leading to the broken basement window. We unlocked them and continued our review. A thick tangle of foliage bordered the heavy metal grate, and although crime scene investigators in December said the growth was intact and showed no impressions, Smit challenged both points.

He deduced from the photographs that foliage growth beneath the edges proved the grate had been removed and replaced. We showed that it was simply not a flush fit and that space gave the foliage plenty of room to grow, just as weeds come up through sidewalk cracks. Smit then suggested the foliage appeared crushed under the grate. We learned a detective had lifted the grate during the initial investigation, checked the window well, and then replaced it, so there were several explana-tions for why the ground cover was beneath the rim.

Lou Smit was certain that another photo showed a footprint at the bottom of the window well. We would later clear away the leaves and debris and take new, detailed photographs. The "footprint" was a blemish in the concrete.

Their theories were built on an improbable series of what-ifs. If *this* happened, then it just might be possible for *that* to happen, and therefore something else *might* have occurred that could *possibly* explain away some incriminating evidence, and there you had it!—an intruder creeping around with murder on his mind. They were supposed to be playing the role of devil's advocate to look for holes in our case, but I thought this was ridiculous.

They made the pictures and the facts show anything they imagined. Every time we knocked down one point, they took refuge in another, forcing us to demonstrate how something didn't happen rather than what actually took place, and apparently ignoring any evidence that might lead to John or Patsy Ramsey.

Just below the metal grate was the window broken by John Ramsey after forgetting his key the previous summer. The scuff mark on the interior basement wall beneath the broken window was now viewed by Smit and DeMuth as having been made by the intruder, not Ramsey. If it was a shoe scuff at all! That vital point was never proved, and in a cluttered basement, many things could have left such a scrape on a wall.

In December both Sergeant Wickman and Detective Mike Everett had seen at least three strands of a spiderweb reaching from the brick window well upward to the covering grate. No one had photographed it. The sill had a complete coating of undisturbed dust. Now spiders had woven another palm-sized web into the same general area. When we moved the end of the grate, several strands broke.

Smit, however, had managed to ease it open in an elaborately cautious way without breaking strands, and that was enough for him. This was how the intruder oozed into the window like an amoeba, knowing in the darkness not to disturb the web. Or, DeMuth argued, "The sticky spiderweb may have reconnected itself after the intruder came in." How could we dispute such a deduction?

I pointed out that the murder happened on a frigid December night, when Colorado spiders are dormant. Experts would be found to say that it got warm enough the next afternoon for a spider to wake up and spin another web exactly at the point where the other was broken. Possible? Maybe. Probable? No.

We conducted tedious re-creations in the small room where the body was found, duplicating lighting conditions with the help of a photographic expert with sensitive meters and placing a white cotton blanket where JonBenét had lain.

John Ramsey had said he spotted the blanket instantly when he opened the door. It was as dark as a coal mine at midnight in there, and to open the door, he would have had to step back to a point where a blind corner would have blocked his view. I stood where Ramsey had been and saw only a wall of impenetrable blackness.

Lou Smit: "I can see in there."

Even with the light on, Detective Gosage said, "I had to step completely into the cellar and look around the corner to my left to see the blanket on the floor."

When I finally left the house, it was with a sense of keen disappointment, for I felt we had all betrayed JonBenét by being unable to resolve our differences.

21

I rounded a corner in the police department and literally bumped into Chief Koby. Back from Texas, he looked fit, tanned, and rested and asked how the case was going. I told him we had probable cause to make an arrest but were stymied by the DA's office. Koby was carrying a pair of grannie glasses and a book, *Care of the Soul*, and observed that the Ramsey matter was "an encounter between good and evil" and I was a "warrior of the light." He promised that "the light will prevail." The chief would have been a terrific monk on a mountaintop, but he was too Zen for me.

———

We thought we had successfully knocked down the preposterous stun gun scenario but underestimated the tenacity of DA investigator Lou Smit. The idea, although demonstrably wrong, stuck to the case like glue, no matter how many times we thought we had proved it couldn't have happened that way.

Smit told us that he had located the type of stun gun used in the attack, and I listened in amazement one afternoon as Trip DeMuth emphatically described to his boss Pete Hofstrom just how the intruder had used it to immobilize JonBenét.

"We have a killer out there who may kill again," Smit told me, almost with tears in his eyes. Forensic scientist Dr. Werner Spitz in Michigan definitively discounted the stun gun, but that also made no difference. When Pete Hofstrom arranged a private interview between

Smit and the Ramseys, the stun gun moved to center stage, helped by the opinion of a county coroner Smit found who said that it could not be totally discounted.

The police detectives were neither informed in advance nor invited to the interview, and it was held at a Team Ramsey law office. The main subject of their chat was the nonexistent stun gun, "something which only the killer and we know about, which can lead us to the killer," Smit told them.

"Do you know what a stun gun is?" he asked John Ramsey.

"It's an electrical thing," Ramsey answered.

"Patsy, do you know what a stun gun is?"

"No."

He pressed to learn if any of their friends or acquaintances owned, had access to, or had ever mentioned a stun gun. "This case could be as easy as that," said Smit.

JOHN: Can you buy those?
PATSY: What's a stun gun?

John Ramsey decided, for no apparent reason, that a woman would be more likely to use a stun gun than a man, and turned once again on his old friends Fleet and Priscilla White. He suggested that if he had to pick between the two, then Priscilla would be more likely to use such a tool. His reasoning was that "She came from California."

Smit wrapped up their twenty-five-minute meeting with the flat statement "Look, the killer made a mistake if he took that device in with him. He made a very big mistake. . . . It could be his undoing."

Unmentioned was that police had taken from John Ramsey's desk a sales videotape from an I Spy store in Florida that contained information about stun guns. I believed that if Smit really wanted to pursue the stun gun issue, he would have to cross-examine Ramsey hard on that point since the videotape indicated a logical source. They couldn't ignore the possibility that their favored assault weapon might belong to someone other than an intruder. Many months would pass before Ramsey was questioned about the tape, and he would say he never watched it.

––––––––

The killer did leave something behind, but not as exotic as a make-believe weapon. The person who killed JonBenét left that three-page ransom note, and we were able to use it to clear a number of suspects. Unless there was a conspiracy, if they didn't write the note, they did not kill the child. And while outside experts stopped short of saying Patsy Ramsey was the author, mostly because of rigid standards for expert court testimony, none could eliminate her either.

But in still another unwarranted "trust-building" deal, the DA's office allowed Ramsey-hired handwriting experts full access to our best piece of evidence. They made a lot of "Aha!" sounds as they pored over the 376-word note inside the Boulder Police Department Evidence Room and a few hours later gave us a complicated presentation that concluded Patsy Ramsey could not be identified as the author. I expected nothing less from people paid for by the defense team but was pleased that, when pressed, even they had to admit that they could not *eliminate* her as the writer either.

One thing we managed to keep from them for a while was that the lab analysts had a partial print from the ransom note. However, it didn't belong to the killer but to Chet Ubowski of the Colorado Bureau of Investigation, who handled the note during his examination. The *only* print identified on that note belonged to the document examiner. There was no indication that an intruder had ever touched the ransom note. And it seemed odd to us that no prints were on the note from either of the parents, who presumably would have handled it and even gripped it tightly.

But lab analysts *did* identify seven latent fingerprints on the tablet from which the ransom note came. None of them belonged to an intruder. One belonged to Sergeant Whitson, who handled the tablet on the morning of December 26. A second belonged to CBI's Ubowski. The remaining five fingerprints were Patricia Ramsey's.

In October I would make a ten-day trip to Michigan, Maryland, and Washington, D.C., carrying the ransom note and folders filled with Patsy Ramsey's handwriting samples. No one ever took the possibility of car-jacking as seriously as I did in those cities, and I made certain that I always had quick access to my pistol. The two boxes I carried were more valuable than gold.

The Speckin Forensic Laboratories in Okemos, Michigan, a retired Secret Service document examiner, and a current Secret Service analyst all took a crack at the ransom note. Their conclusions were of varying strengths, but they did agree on one thing—just like the people hired by Team Ramsey, they could not eliminate Patsy as the possible author.

That made five independent sources that would not rule her out, plus Chet Ubowski at the Colorado Bureau of Investigation, who thought she wrote it but could not say so under oath in a courtroom. And the Speckin Lab was ready to testify that there was only an infinitesimal chance that some random intruder would have handwriting characteristics so remarkably similar to those of a parent sleeping upstairs.

Taken together, the six opinions formed a strong body of evidence, but I wanted more—I wanted someone willing to stand in a court of law and decisively declare who wrote the note.

I had no idea where to find such a person.

————

Two new encounters with the DA's office finally led me to the personal decision that they wouldn't lift a finger against the Ramseys, no matter who we interviewed or what we discovered. Short of a confession, they weren't going to move.

Pete Hofstrom and I got into it in a parking lot one evening. Frustrated by the lack of cooperation we were getting from the DA's office, I demanded to know exactly where he, the chief trial deputy, stood on the case.

"I'm middle-of-the-road on this," Hofstrom barked, using his favorite line, which indicated that it did not matter to him whether the Ramseys were guilty or innocent. He rationalized that there was nothing to indicate they were involved, which I challenged, and nothing to indicate they were not.

"You're not in a vacuum," I replied, wondering why he thought his job was to sit on the sidelines as the investigation foundered around him. "You're the prosecutor. You have to have some sort of opinion by now, or we're in worse shape than I thought."

"Thomas, I'm right down the fucking middle!" he shouted, waving his arms. The bantam prison guard was mad.

"That's nothing but a cop-out," I said. Hofstrom shot back, "If you're so mistaken about me and my motivations, the same could be true in you being mistaken about the Ramseys."

"No." I shook my head. "Look at the case."

"So what good is an arrest if we won't prosecute the case? It will just ruin their lives," Hofstrom bellowed. "Just because she wrote the note doesn't mean we can prove a murder."

"It's not much of a stretch," I replied.

As we parted, he got in the last shot, telling me that he would "continue to have breakfast with Bryan Morgan."

I was left standing there, wondering why a chief prosecutor had already declared, "This is not a prosecutable case."

Only a few days later, I discovered that the DA's office had sat on potentially incriminating evidence.

Frank Coffman, a local writer, had told me that Pam Griffin, a friend of Patsy Ramsey's from kiddie pageant circles, claimed Patsy had told her about writing the so-called practice note for some innocent reason. I jumped at the possibility that a suspect had admitted to a third party that she had written it. It was a huge development, and I brought it up promptly.

DA investigator Lou Smit coughed, then acknowledged that he had received the same information some time earlier. "I was going to write a report on that," he said. I was appalled that he had not placed it before us immediately. It seemed to me that if something pointed against the Ramseys, it might never reach the detectives. If that had surfaced, what else could there be? Why were they putting material that might help the Ramsey cause into the case file when legitimate leads such as this were stashed in a desk drawer somewhere? Burying leads from fellow investigators is one of the worst things a detective can do because it destroys trust.

Nothing came from several attempts to get Pam Griffin to repeat her statement to police, and the DA's office wasn't impressed enough to force her immediate testimony.

With the latest incidents involving Hofstrom and Smit fresh in my mind, I felt that we desperately needed some outside help. To get it I took a gamble that could have cost me my badge, although that no longer seemed like such a terrible price to pay if it would move this impossible case forward. The result was better than I had dared imagine.

Dan Caplis, a well-respected Denver lawyer whose father was a cop in Chicago, was also a talk-show host to whom I often listened, and I set up a meeting to ask—beg—for his help. Caplis revealed his longtime relationships with some of the prosecutors in Alex Hunter's office but offered his assistance. "I've got some ideas," he said. "Let's stay in touch."

Within a few weeks Caplis had recruited Rich Baer, a powerful Denver attorney who happened to have been a take-no-shit homicide prosecutor in New York. That alone was a coup, but he also lined up Dan Hoffman, a former dean of the Denver University Law School and a former state public safety commissioner, and Bob Miller, who once served as a Reagan-appointed U.S. Attorney.

I was way out of bounds by scheming to bring in outsiders while

Alex Hunter was officially the lead prosecutor, but now that these top private attorneys were willing to help, I wasn't about to let them go. With them aboard, I felt the DA's office would no longer be able to push us around.

When I met Rich Baer, a partner in one of the best law firms in Colorado, he confirmed that other colleagues, including former judges and federal prosecutors, also wanted to help. "We will have only one shot to make this case successful in prosecution," Baer said. "If it takes thirty days or three hundred, we are willing to commit our time and resources." The price tag: nothing. All I had to do now was get them in the game. I felt like a high school football coach bringing out the Dallas Cowboys to face a rival. We called them our "Dream Team."

A week later Rich Baer, Dan Hoffman, and Bob Miller walked into Chief Koby's conference room, the dollar value of their Rolex watches alone probably more than a cop's salary. Awaiting them around the cherry-wood conference table were Chief Koby, Commander Eller, Sergeant Wickman, and the four detectives.

Disclosing their links to the other side, they admitted knowing and working with some of the Ramsey lawyers and officials in the district attorney's office, dating all the way back to law school. But they pledged to represent only the Boulder Police Department and our interests. Commander Eller noted that two of them had done work for Lockheed, which owned Access Graphics, and asked, "What if Lockheed doesn't let you do this?" Hoffman replied, "Lockheed doesn't tell me what to do."

Hoffman said all three wanted to work for something truly worthwhile, such as finding the killer of a child. "I'm in it through thick or thin, limited only by my life's duration," he promised.

Baer said they could review the case, pare it down to its essence, and help plug any loopholes. I edged the discussion into how the district attorney's office seemed reluctant to prosecute this case and revealed some of the problems we were having because they seemed afraid to tangle with Team Ramsey in a courtroom.

And I listened with growing confidence as our new Dream Team, veteran trial lawyers all, said that many of the issues the DA's office viewed as insurmountable weren't so tough after all. Bob Miller commented, "Sometimes you gotta pull the trigger and go for it, even if you lose."

———

Chief Koby cordially escorted our new attorneys out while the rest of us remained in his office, trying to imagine the thunderclap when the news reached Team Ramsey and DA Alex Hunter. Our euphoria vanished when Koby returned, his face clouded with anger, and jumped me for suggesting "to outsiders" that the DA's office wasn't 100 percent supportive of our investigation.

Apparently Koby was less interested in telling the truth to the Dream Team than in maintaining the public charade of cooperation. He actually used the War Room as an example of how we were all getting along, and asked how things were going over there. "Fine," Sergeant Wickman responded.

Since I had pulled out of the War Room, I gave Koby the truth about how serious the problems actually were. "We're not a team at all," I said. Detective Jane Harmer agreed that the atmosphere was "terribly oppressive" and asked, "How many times are we going to get fucked by them?" Detective Ron Gosage said he did not trust Deputy DA Trip DeMuth and felt that investigator Lou Smit was undermining the case. "Things are a mess," observed Detective Tom Trujillo. Sergeant Wickman did a quick about-face and lined up with us.

Chief Koby had to choose between the district attorney and his cops, and came down on our side. He told Wickman to assign investigator Steve Ainsworth back to the sheriff's office and tie Lou Smit down to organizing reports. "Get rid of them if necessary," the chief said, "and tell DeMuth, 'This is the way the ship's going, with or without you.' " Then he deflated the moment by saying he wanted to "talk to Alex."

I learned later that when the district attorney was informed of our Dream Team, he blanched as white as a kid in the principal's office before muttering, "Glad to have them aboard."

I could no longer read Sergeant Tom Wickman, who followed neither of Koby's suggestions. Abandoned by Chief Koby and with Commander Eller well on his way to being fired, he seemed to be falling under the spell of Pete Hofstrom, the DA's persuasive deal-making Svengali.

Wickman told me that he was keeping things from both Koby and Eller because he didn't trust either of them, and he encouraged me to do the same. I couldn't keep track of his shifting alliances, which became a game of who-knows-what.

To unlock that damned S.B.T.C. acronym at the bottom of the ransom note, I called the U.S. Treasury Department's Financial Crimes Enforcement Network, a governmental unit straight out of a Tom Clancy novel. These people are summoned when the White House wants something yesterday, and I wasn't sure they would help a couple of outgunned detectives in Colorado. "I've been waiting for this call for six months," said Linda Percy, a deputy director at Treasury.

Percy tasked her Rapid Start Team to do a computer search that would look at every piece of public paper ever issued regarding the Ramseys. If SBTC was out there, FinCEN would find it. "We'll put together a package," Percy promised. "We're all behind you." But even FinCEN was blocked by our lack of a search warrant to get the Ramseys' credit card and telephone records.

Since John Ramsey had no faith in the Boulder police, I thought perhaps he had sought help from the security experts of Access Graphics' parent company. "I've never spoken to him," Bernie Lamoreaux, the director of security for Lockheed-Martin, told me. "I'm not aware of any threats by foreign terrorists of any kind." His elite team of professionals, who protected one of the world's largest defense contractors, had never heard of SBTC, either.

Team Ramsey launched a long-running campaign of newspaper advertisements, announcing a $100,000 reward "for information leading to the arrest and indictment of the murderer of JonBenét Ramsey." The detectives asked if we could put in for it.

The ad urged "Anyone with information concerning an adult male approaching young children in Boulder in late 1996" to call a telephone number unrelated to the police department.

We soon learned that the advertisement was developed with information provided by Trip DeMuth. Alex Hunter acknowledged the error and scolded DeMuth, while Ramsey attorney Bryan Morgan crowed that he was "deeply grateful" for the assistance.

What surprised me even more, however, were the similarities between the advertisement and a letter I had received a few weeks earlier from an inmate at the federal penitentiary in Atlanta. The prisoner, serving a long sentence for the kidnap and sexual molestation of an eight-year-old girl, likened himself to the genius madman Doctor Hannibal Lecter in the Thomas Harris novel *Silence of the Lambs*.

This pedophile wrote that he knew exactly how the killer of Jon-Benét thought, and offered this advice. "Run adds [*sic*] with pleas for assistance, regarding any leads, concerning any young (especially blonde, blue-eyed) girls who have been approached by a well dressed, seemingly normal looking man." The pervert being sought, this Doctor Lecter impersonator advised, was "an adult male." The latest Ramsey move seemed to have been spawned from our not-so-secret case file.

Ten days later newspapers reported that another deputy district attorney wrote in a court motion that there was a "real possibility" that JonBenét was killed by an intruder.

Then came an "Open Letter from John and Patsy Ramsey" that was faxed to every major news organization, complaining that police had not worked "past us" to find the real killer. They released a profile of their version of the suspected murderer, and another Ramsey-paid advertisement in the Boulder *Daily Camera* soon expanded that theme. The new ad contained movie lines from *Ransom* and *Dirty Harry*, which were compared with language in the ransom note. As I read it, I could almost hear the voice of Lou Smit, who had only recently told me the same thing.

––––––––––

Consumed by the case, I lived with a headache, survived on tuna sandwiches and Cokes, and lost an alarming twenty-eight pounds. When Commander Eller ordered me to take a weekend off, I looked at the calendar. My one-year wedding anniversary was coming up. Throughout the case my wife had given me understanding and support, and I had pretty much ignored her. I owed her a lot, although I doubted if I could ever make up for all the arguments brought on by this unending nightmare. We boarded a train bound for the resort of Glenwood Springs, but even as it crawled west over the Continental Divide, I was thinking about the Ramsey case.

22

On August 6, 1997, which would have been JonBenét's seventh birth-day, Detective Ron Gosage and I and a team of agents from the Georgia Bureau of Investigation kept covert watch on her grave site from a command post set up in Marietta High School room 212, directly across the street from the St. James Episcopal Cemetery. We had the latest technology and a dozen GBI agents who didn't understand why Boulder was pussyfooting around with the Ramseys. There were no sugges-tions for "trust-building" from them. Instead, GBI Special Agent John Lang asked, "Why don't we just put a bumper lock on these people and show them we are all over their asses? Why isn't any pressure being applied to these suspects?"

We were grasping at straws, reduced to listening for a graveside con-fession. I knew it was a long shot at best, but we were about out of options. In my opinion, unless our DA's office actually *heard* the killer admit the murder, the case was going nowhere.

Special Agent Lang, a former Vietnam Marine and a veteran of years of undercover work with the GBI, had gone to JonBenét's funeral on his own time in December and wondered why no Boulder cops were there. He became our link to the highly professional GBI, which re-peatedly helped us in the coming months of the investigation, although they never came to understand Boulder-style justice.

The warrants for the covert vigil came from the DA in Cobb County, Georgia, because we were afraid to let our own DA's office know what we were doing. Once again I saw an example of how different the

Boulder DA's office was from the more traditional law-and-order prosecutors' shops around the nation. In Georgia the deputy district attorneys were eager to help the police. Boulder would have stopped us in our tracks on a grave-site surveillance.

Sergeant Wickman was no help, putting himself at arm's length from the controversial operation. He didn't want to know the details, and his single instruction was "Don't get caught."

The surveillance began on a curious note the morning before JonBenét's birthday, when we found all three wrought iron gates to the cemetery, which had stood open for the past seven months, chained and padlocked. Lang picked one of the locks, then left the gate ajar for visitors. The FBI had told us of other cases in which confessions were made on significant anniversaries at the victim's grave, so we sat back to wait and watch and hope.

Narrow windows behind the shiny green leaves of a pair of huge magnolia trees provided a straight view across the street, beyond the tall fence, all the way to the grave, which still had no headstone. It had the look of a calm park. A microphone was beneath the stone bench beside the plot, and a camera was hidden in a BellSouth box, feeding information back to our command center, where three television monitors, recorders, a microwave feed, laptop computers, and cell phones blinked ready. The press swarm arrived early.

Curious gawkers, well-wishers, and ordinary people paid their respects to JonBenét throughout the day, and a woman who looked very much like Patsy startled us when she sat on the bench and read from a Bible. A salesman signed up an elderly couple for a nearby plot. No Ramseys came by.

On the birthday itself, a black Mazda pulled up to a gate. The driver opened the padlock with a key and drove through to the grave. Melinda Ramsey and her mother, Lucinda Ramsey Johnson, got out and placed some flowers but left quickly when the media lunged to the cemetery fences with microphones and telephoto cameras.

Pam Paugh, Patsy's sister, showed up that evening in a sleek black Infiniti. The press flooded to the fence again, and we crowded around our TV monitors and windows about fifty yards away. I watched through a pair of binoculars as the heavy woman in shorts, sunglasses, and a headband approached the grave. The former Miss America contestant, never married, had put on a lot of weight since her pageant days, and I felt sorry for her as she tried to create a private moment amid the media chaos. She placed a bouquet, emptied her pockets onto the bench, then plopped down right on top of the JonBenét plot, looking so despondent that someone at my elbow whispered, "Suicide?"

Pam then softly read from a Bible, and at the conclusion of the Twenty-third Psalm, she said, "JonBenét, whoever did this to you . . ." Her whispering became unintelligible over our microphone as we strained to hear. Then she quietly sang a song to JonBenét, knelt and whispered a prayer at Beth's headstone, and drove away. It was a melancholy moment.

John and Patsy Ramsey didn't visit the grave on their daughter's birthday, but we hoped they might come late, after the media pulled out. The GBI had borrowed a $55,000 Panasonic night vision camera from the Las Vegas Police Department, so we had eyes after the sun went down, but there were no more visitors.

After midnight, several of us ventured into the dark cemetery and examined the flowers, stuffed bunnies, and trinkets that had been left that day. I read the cards. Pam's was simply, "Good-bye. You'll be missed."

Gosage and I stopped by the Georgia State Penitentiary. While there I paid a visit to death row, and we were given a tour of the "last mile" walked by condemned men. Guards said the most frequent request made by those heading for the cinder block death house was to be allowed to step off the concrete sidewalk and walk barefoot through the grass one last time. I sat in the electric chair, a massive monstrosity of polished pine bolted to the floor, in a room kept immaculately clean by trustees. Thick leather straps and steel buckles. I pulled the stiff mask over my face and wondered what those last few seconds were like before one entered the abyss, awaiting that surge. Maybe just a sense of hearing the train coming as a hundred thousand volts barreled down the line. It was an indescribable feeling. Many men had left this world from this very spot. With the mask covering my face, I thought of the way money perverts our justice system.

Although the grave-site surveillance had failed, we weren't ready to give up trying to overhear a confession. "This ain't the time for Marquis of Queensbury rules," snorted Bob Miller of our Dream Team. "A child has been murdered. We've got to play hardball." He suggested electronically bugging the Ramsey house in Atlanta.

It wasn't just some wild idea: when Miller was a U.S. Attorney, he hid a microphone in an outlaw bikers' clubhouse and recorded conversations that led to racketeering indictments.

In layman's terms, a "Title-3" operation meant that we would plant some listening devices. Then we'd drop grand jury subpoenas on all the Ramseys, including young Burke. "That will fire up some conversations in that house," Miller said, and our bugs would catch every word. Electronic eavesdropping has long been used by police agencies, but the Boulder Police Department had never done a "T-3." We thought it was a terrific idea, and the GBI, just as enthusiastic, started making plans to launch the operation.

The DA's office seethed about our collaborating with the Dream Team, which the media viewed as a direct slam against the way Alex Hunter ran his office. The DA himself admitted, "There is no question that outside lawyers providing assistance to a police department is unusual in a criminal investigation." Hunter's people struck back immediately.

Our new attorneys told us to draw up warrants to get the Ramseys' phone records and cellular phone logs and Patsy's boots to match against the puzzling beaver hair found on the duct tape. They couldn't believe similar requests had been denied for months.

Sergeant Tom Wickman and I took my affidavit for the Ramsey records from US West and AirTouch over to Deputy DA Trip DeMuth for review. He was arrogant and aloof, read the two-page warrant, then abruptly said he had to "run it by" someone else in the office. He was back in a few minutes and proclaimed that the warrant lacked probable cause. Bob Keatley, our in-house lawyer, tried in vain to explain that it contained more than enough sufficient facts and information.

DeMuth then left to confer with his immediate superior, Deputy DA Pete Hofstrom, and returned with a litany of other problems, alleging vague sources and material omissions.

Wickman was dumbfounded, and I almost lost my temper. "For Christ's sake. This is a simple affidavit for telephone records. Do you want the pineapple, the duct tape, and the kitchen sink in there too?" I thought I was being rhetorical.

"Yes," he said. "You need all of that. This is a death penalty case, and we have to be careful."

I said that an eighty-page affidavit was not needed for telephone records and cited other cases, but DeMuth dug in his heels and asked, "What are you hoping to find?"

"Who knows? Did a kidnapper call? Did the Ramseys call anyone before they called 911? If I knew what I would find, I wouldn't be getting a friggin' search warrant!"

DeMuth specifically noted an item that he said "inferred" the Ramseys were not cooperating. "Maybe we should just ask them—"

"No fucking way!" Sergeant Wickman broke in.

What began as a request for a simple warrant I felt became payback for bringing the Dream Team aboard.

As we walked out, DeMuth said that although we had the legal right to take the warrant directly to a judge, "Make sure you tell him it does not have the support of the district attorney's office." It was a cold threat.

———————

Not long thereafter, a list of "prioritized tasks" for us to tackle followed from Hofstrom and DeMuth. After a single reading we started referring to it as the Five-Year Plan. Among the things demanded:

- Make a list of potential suspects culled from all friends, neighbors, business associates and individuals associated with the Ramseys and obtain biological samples from *each* of them for DNA testing. (Clearly impossible.)
- Interview *every* neighbor, person, stranger, or visitor in the Ramsey neighborhood, investigate all their alibis, and question each on whether they owned duct tape, cord, or stun guns. (Clearly impossible, and it would bring up those damned stun guns again.)
- Interview and get DNA samples from *all* Ramsey associates and schoolmates and all sex offenders. (Clearly impossible.)
- Identify *every* person present at *all* of JonBenét's beauty pageants, interview each of them, investigate their alibis, and find out whether they possessed duct tape, cord, or stun guns. (Preposterous.)
- Summarize *every* sexual assault or burglary that ever occurred in Boulder, before and after the murder. (Ridiculous.)
- Establish a "closer rapport" with the Ramseys. (That one in particular was a slap in the face.)

It seemed to me that the DA's office had lost touch with reality. Their wish list—*all, each, every*—involved thousands of unknown people and was beyond accomplishing. If that was their standard, then failure was knocking at the door. By raising the bar so high, they knew we would never be able to hand the case off to them for prosecution.

At the end of August Chief Koby turned down a city council offer of $150,000 to hire and train six new police officers. Koby declined. His department was strained to the breaking point, but the chief was in his leadership mode. Within a week orders came down for us to knock off the overtime and work strict forty-hour weeks. Most of us continued our grueling schedule, unpaid.

We could have used twenty more detectives. I recruited an intern to help with the filing in the SitRoom. The detective bureau's two secretaries had fallen far behind in transcribing the overflowing box of taped interviews, and we had about three billion leads still pouring in from kooks, clairvoyants, and con artists. Interpol passed along the services of a seer in Holland.

Among the best leads of the month was still another that we could not touch. The Ramsey credit card purchases showed up again, this time through the mail anonymously from a tabloid newspaper to Sergeant Wickman. There were copies of purchase records from marine supply depots, hardware stores, and boating retailers in Charlevoix, Atlanta, and Boulder during 1996. Any of these places could have sold duct tape and cord. An investigator's dream come true—the paper trail.

Sergeant Tom Wickman and I took it in to Bob Keatley for a legal opinion, and he almost had a heart attack. His exact words were most un-Keatley-like—"Shit, shit, shit!"—and he snatched the documents away. "Put it out of your mind," he ordered, imagining how a defense lawyer would do an O.J.-style "Police Planted the Glove" tap dance on us.

It was a struggle to let those Visa documents vanish into the Evidence Room, where the Touch Tone records were already gathering dust.

23

Then came *Vanity Fair.* In this unlikely magazine venue, reporter Ann Bardach tipped the JonBenét investigation right over the precipice by exposing how the hunt for the killer had become lost to internecine battles between law enforcement agencies in an unforgivable breach of public trust. Bardach stopped just short of accusing the Boulder County District Attorney of obstructing justice.

The DA, who should have stayed above the media fray, had instead long been a leading participant. In June he welcomed Bardach into his office for a three-and-a-half-hour interview, asked her what she thought he should do, and was allegedly horrified to discover that she planned to quote him. It was difficult to believe that someone who had been in public office for almost three decades could be so naive about the press, but Alex Hunter was used to getting his way with the local media. Bardach said she told him up front that everything was on the record.

She pillaged the city, and by the time she contacted me she had already talked to about fifty people, including other cops, and had a pile of information. I agreed to meet her, without making any commitment. The police were tired of being tarred and feathered in the media though unable to respond. If the DA could talk to her for more than three hours, why couldn't I speak to her? A couple of cops approached me about "setting the record straight."

As the publication date drew near, Hunter was worried about Bardach's portrayal of him in the magazine. In a tape-recorded interview later, my confidential informant, Jeff Shapiro of the *Globe,* recalled what happened. He said the district attorney told him, "Let me know if you come across it. That would be very interesting."

"It was pretty apparent [what Hunter was suggesting by way of an advance copy]," said Shapiro, who was talking with Hunter daily. "But he's the fucking DA. . . . He's not so stupid as to say, 'Go commit a crime for me.' "

But Shapiro said he took the oblique comment to be tantamount to an order, and not long after that the *Globe* went out of its way to snag a prepublication copy of *Vanity Fair.*

As another *Globe* reporter drove them over to the Criminal Justice Center, Shapiro called Hunter on a cell phone to ask if the article should be dropped off at the front counter. According to Shapiro, the DA replied with a laugh, "No. I think something like that can get you in here for a few minutes."

Hunter's first assistant district attorney and longtime pal Bill Wise ushered them to a reserved parking space, then personally escorted them into the district attorney's private chambers, where they all spent an hour reading the story.

"No matter what mistakes the police made, they have been exponentially compounded by blunders and improprieties in the DA's office," Bardach wrote. She published a list of the DA's actions that ranged from asking advice from Hal Haddon, head of the defense team, to giving away confidential information. Former FBI profiler Gregg McCrary was quoted as saying that the sharing of vital evidence was "unprecedented and unprofessional and an obstruction of justice. It's criminal. . . . It's possible you could make a case for prosecutorial malfeasance. It completely undermines the investigation."

The article was the equivalent of an explosion and for the first time posed serious questions to a nationwide audience about the way Hunter's office was handling the JonBenét murder investigation. Although some of us in the police department were delighted to see the truth finally come to light, the story could not have been published at a worse time.

We had been invited to Quantico, Virginia, to give a full presentation to the Child Abduction and Serial Killer Unit of the FBI, and we

jumped at the opportunity. Having the CASKU experts hear and analyze your case was not an everyday thing for local cops.

To our pleasant surprise, District Attorney Hunter had agreed to attend the presentation instead of hiding behind his "trusted advisers."
Maybe he would listen to the FBI. He told CASKU's Bill Hagmaier
that he would like to "see what you can do for us." I considered Hunter's presence at the meeting a big step forward.

Prior to leaving for Virginia, we gave the DA's office a preview of
what we planned to show CASKU, unaware that Hunter and his staff
had read the Bardach article and were stewing with anger.

We withheld the 911 tape and grave-site surveillance from the preliminary discussion but went through the physical evidence, its analysis,
and current status. After a few questions, Hunter and his people filed
out in silence.

A few hours later the district attorney abruptly canceled his plans to
go to Virginia, claiming that the police had only "half a loaf. It's not
enough for me to go." I concluded that after reading the Bardach article, Alex Hunter was not about to leave his little Boulder County kingdom and risk having to explain his actions to the FBI. Once again he
sidestepped personal responsibility.

We flew to Virginia by ourselves. In Quantico Sergeant Tom Wickman dealt photocopies of the *Vanity Fair* article to us like a deck of
cards. The room went silent, the only sound the turning of pages and
someone whispering, "Jesus H. Christ." I braced for the shit storm that
was bound to come, but I wasn't sorry that I had spoken as a background source. The information I gave wasn't about evidence in a murder investigation but about possible malfeasance in government.

On Monday morning an FBI van with tinted windows picked us up at
our hotel, then swung by another hotel for the DA's contingent. The
long ride to the FBI Training Academy at Quantico was made in total
silence.

A huge conference table dominated a large windowless room, with
the American flag in one corner and the FBI shield on the far wall.
About two dozen people were waiting for us—some of the nation's
foremost pathologists, behavioral science specialists, CASKU team
members, hair and fiber experts, the Critical Incidence Response
Group, and other veteran agents.

Bob Miller and Dan Hoffman of our Dream Team took chairs beside
Detectives Gosage, Harmer, and Trujillo, Sergeant Wickman, and me.

The DA's group—Deputy DAs Pete Hofstrom and Trip DeMuth and investigator Lou Smit—were scattered around the table, and when Hofstrom introduced himself, he mentioned having been a guard at San Quentin.

As I presented the overview of our case and Detective Trujillo reviewed the evidence, DeMuth heckled: "Can't hear you!" and "Is that all you have indicating Ramsey involvement?" The FBI agents were openly surprised by his effrontery.

Sergeant Wickman told the group how forensic specialist Dr. Werner Spitz had discounted the stun gun, and we discussed the issue of whether or not the little girl had sustained previous vaginal trauma, which the FBI considered extremely important.

We reviewed the autopsy results and crime scene photos, and I mentioned how the duct tape seemed to be part of the staging. There was a perfect lip impression on the tape and no tongue indentation to indicate that JonBenét had been alive and fought to remove it. Pictures showed that bloody mucus in the mouth area had been covered by the tape, indicating that it was applied after the injuries. To me, the inescapable conclusion was that the tape was applied after she was dead.

In turn, the CASKU agents noted that of the more than seventeen hundred murdered children they had studied since the 1960s, there was only one case in which the victim was a female under the age of twelve, who had been murdered in her home by strangulation, with sexual assault and a ransom note present—and that was JonBenét Ramsey.

They told us that while it might be possible that someone broke into the house that night, it wasn't very probable. The staging, evidence, and totality of the case pointed in one direction—that this was not the act of an intruder.

The crime, they said, did not fit an act of sex or revenge or one in which money was the motivation. Taken alone, they said, each piece of evidence might be argued, but together, enough pebbles become a block of evidentiary granite.

These conclusions by the FBI's highly respected profilers were exactly what I hoped would provide a breakthrough in the case, but Hofstrom, DeMuth, and Smit seemed unimpressed. They ignored CASKU, just as they ignored us. It felt like we were on a train to nowhere.

The CASKU meeting had been derailed before it even started. That was the pattern in this entire case. Any spark for optimism was soon doused by reality.

CASKU observed that they had never seen anything like the Ramsey ransom note. Kidnapping demands are usually terse, such as "We have your kid. A million dollars. Will call you." From a kidnapper's point of view, the fewer words, the less police have to go on.

Based on their studies of the evidence we provided, they believed the note was written in the home, after the murder, and indicated panic. Ransom notes are normally written prior to the crime, usually proof-read, and not written by hand, in order to disguise the authorship.

The FBI deemed the entire crime "criminally unsophisticated," citing the child being left on the premises, the disingenuous $118,000 demand in relation to the net worth of the family, the description of the accomplices as "gentlemen," and the concept of a ransom delivery where one would be "scanned for electronic devices." Kidnappers prefer isolated drops for the ransom delivery, not a face-to-face meeting.

There was also an absence of strong language and anger, and the victim was never referred to by name, thus depersonalizing her to the offender. The intelligent wording suggested an educated writer who had some exposure to the South, as shown by the reference to "southern common sense."

The crime was an incredibly risky one for an outsider to undertake, the profilers said, and was committed by someone who had a high degree of comfort inside the home. The note was created to misdirect law enforcement and focus attention elsewhere and was a cathartic act that allowed the offender to "undo" the murder in one's own mind.

Their bottom line was that there had never been a kidnapping attempt.

CASKU further said that placing JonBenét in the basement was consistent with a parent not wanting to put the body outside in the winter elements. The familiarity with and relocking of the peg on the white cellar door were noted. The ligatures, they said, indicated staging rather than control, and the garrote was used from behind so the killer could avoid eye contact, typical of someone who cares for the victim. They had the gut feeling that "no one intended to kill this child."

The following day the profilers had some pointed questions for the DA's staff.

Why hadn't phone records been gathered? *Damn good question,* I thought. *Why did everyone but the DA's office understand the importance of those documents?* Only fifteen days before, Deputy DA DeMuth had rejected our affidavit to do just that, and now he said the police warrant "was shit."

Hofstrom chimed in, "Let's just ask the Ramseys" for permission, a response that left the FBI agents incredulous. Many months would pass before we discovered that the DA's office had not overridden the Ramsey attorneys' request to maintain an "island of privacy." Our prosecutors should have handed them a grand jury subpoena on the spot, demanding the records, and they never explained to us why they would not do so.

The FBI also wondered, since the police had not been offensive or confrontational in December 1996, why had the parents lawyered up so fast? Hofstrom answered that the attorneys only came aboard after "a police supervisor" had tried to "ransom the body" to get an interview. That was false, since Mike Bynum was giving advice and more lawyers and private investigators were being brought aboard long before the body became an issue.

An agent wanted to know why Patsy, who had volunteered to take ten polygraphs, had not been given the opportunity to do so. No one had an answer.

Did "anyone look good on the handwriting?" Detective Gosage said that of the dozens of people examined so far, Patsy Ramsey could not be eliminated as the author of the note. Deputy DA Hofstrom said handwriting analysis was an art, not a science, and had the gall to describe to disbelieving agents how "John and Patsy" had been invited into his own home to give a handwriting example. They just stared at him.

I thought we all must look like total amateurs to these professional law enforcement officers. This case had become a black eye and an embarrassment to cops everywhere.

Hofstrom then took the offensive, saying that if the police would bring the DA's office a case, they would look at it. It was Catch-22, and everyone there knew it, because how could we deliver a case while the same DA's office hindered our investigation?

The FBI encouraged the district attorney's representatives to convene a grand jury immediately and assist the police department. Get the Ramseys in there to testify under the hammer of perjury. Don't "ask the Ramseys" for anything, just issue the warrants and subpoenas and take the evidence. It should have been done long ago. The world is watching, and the right thing needs to be done. You have a responsibility, CASKU said. The language was blunt.

Despite the animosity, apparently Pete Hofstrom heard at least some of what was said and privately ventured an acceptable goal. If experts could determine prior vaginal abuse, and we could get an expert to identify the author of the note, then the investigation would have reached "a turning point" toward prosecution. Given his track record, however, I took his promise with a grain of salt.

————

Throughout the FBI sessions, Lou Smit said not a word about his Intruder Theory. But he ducked out early on the final day to fly secretly to Tennessee and fetch back to Boulder, in manacles, an itinerant worker named Kevin Raburn, whom he and investigator Steve Ainsworth had decided was an intruder candidate. Raburn was held for a while on an unrelated charge, then released when his alibi checked out. He had nothing to do with the death of JonBenét.

————

The open contact that the district attorney was having with the media had been known to us for some time, but the claims of *Globe* reporter Jeff Shapiro went beyond cozy press relations and into possible criminal wrongdoing. Chief Koby did not believe Alex Hunter would do anything unprofessional, so we were authorized to get Shapiro's candid comments on tape. I was reluctant to burn my confidential informant, but there was no other way to shake Koby awake. When the chief heard what was recorded during our "sting," he stepped into the realm of questionable activity himself by ordering the evidence destroyed.

On a rainy September evening at Chautauqua Park, only five blocks from the Ramsey house, Detective Gosage and I bought some beer and invited Shapiro to join us in my undercover car. A cordless microphone in Gosage's baseball cap connected us with the wireless receiver and recorder in a nearby van.

Shapiro, only twenty-four years old, told us he and the district attorney spoke at least every other day, sometimes in Hunter's office, and for up to three hours. Shapiro said he would occasionally answer his cell phone and hear a familiar voice say, "Hey, buddy, it's Alex," then launch into a discussion involving anything from investigative strategy and theories to what other reporters were doing.

"He'd bounce ideas off of me," Shapiro said, opening his loose-leaf binder. "I've got notes." What did Shapiro think of Patsy being the killer? What about Fleet White? How would the public react to a certain position? And Hunter wanted to be sure Shapiro kept their contact secret, telling him, "Just keep this between us boys."

Shapiro said the DA fed him confidential evidentiary information. Once when Shapiro complained about a problem with an editor, the DA said, "Here's something you might want to look at"—if the Ramseys woke up at 5:30 A.M., as they said, and were scheduled to leave at 6:15, they would never have made their flight. This was deep inside stuff, the police conclusion on the time line, and it became a story of the week for a tabloid newspaper, apparently courtesy of the DA himself.

"This is a good story," Shapiro said he told the DA.

"That's why I gave it to you," replied Hunter. Shapiro said the DA also told him about the paintbrush fracture match and information about the garrote, long before those subjects became public. He quoted the district attorney as saying the detectives "ain't got shit" for evidence.

The DA had held closed-door sessions with Patsy's friend Pam Griffin, and she had described the meetings to Shapiro. According to Jeff, Griffin said, "Alex has told me that it is not John's DNA beneath her fingernails. It is not any of the Ramseys' DNA, and he didn't think the Ramseys did it."

In return for tips, Shapiro performed secret assignments for the DA. "He'd tell me it would be interesting to check this out, like the next time you talk to Pam Griffin, ask about JonBenét's bed-wetting. Things like that." Then Hunter dangled Fleet White as a possible story, adding, "You ought to fly to California for that." Even Shapiro balked. "Alex, I don't think it's a good idea to treat your main witness as a suspect. Are you serious?"

"I just want to know about this guy," Hunter was quoted as replying. "He's strange. I want to know about his past."

Following another Hunter suggestion, Shapiro flew to Michigan to thoroughly background John Ramsey.

The very mention of John Eller's name would work Hunter into a rage. "He's a fucking prick," Shapiro quoted Hunter as ranting. "He's an overweight storm trooper Nazi guy. I hate the guy! I don't know what his fucking problem is." He insulted Eller's hobby of painting. "Half art but half fuckin' lunatic. What kind of guy is this? That paints?"

When Shapiro suggested that the *Globe* do a story on Eller, the DA smiled and declared, "I think it's *his time*. . . . Everybody gets their turn at being torn apart." Hunter volunteered to hand over Eller's confidential personnel file and mentioned charges of incompetence and sexual harassment. However, Shapiro and other journalists who had been given the same information found no basis for those accusations.

Long before the text of the ransom note became public, Shapiro's boss, Craig Lewis, had gone to see Hunter's top aide, Bill Wise, wanting something to publish. A following issue of the *Globe* contained a previously unseen phrase from the note.

Shapiro said that Hunter called him, frantic to discover the source. Where did they get it? the DA had asked.

You remember when Lewis went in to see Wise a few days ago?

No.

Well, he did.

Are you saying that Bill Wise was the one who . . . ?

Yes, Shapiro replied.

Shapiro said that Hunter, Bill Wise, and another Ramsey attorney, William Gray, owned a building together. "This is a serious Boys' Club," the reporter commented, then read from his notes a list of the DA's political and financial relationships. In Colorado, a district attorney should recuse himself at the mere *appearance* of conflict of interest. In my opinion, Hunter had gone far beyond the mere appearance.

One day when Shapiro telephoned Hunter, he said, the DA whispered, "I'm in the middle of something right now. Why don't you call me back a little later?" Shapiro did, and the district attorney said he had been unable to talk because "I had that fucking Koby in my office."

The reporter quoted Hunter as saying that the chief of police was a nice guy but "He told me when this is all over, he wants to open a bicycle repair shop." The district attorney had laughed in derision, Shapiro recalled. "Is that who you want running a murder investigation?"

Shapiro later said Hunter had such a tight relationship with the *Globe* that he and the tabloid's editor, Tony Frost, giggled like boys as they paged through a *Playboy* magazine together in the DA's office. The name of the magazine was unimportant. It was the presence of the editor of a tabloid inside the DA's office that was a breach of Hunter's official responsibilities, particularly since he had prosecuted several fringe players in the Ramsey investigation for peddling pictures and information to those same journals. Hardly any district attorney in the country would have placed himself in such a situation.

I still had a hard time believing this kid had compromised the district attorney so thoroughly. But when I challenged Shapiro to confirm his close contact by telephoning Hunter, he punched in a number on my mobile speaker phone without hesitation. After five rings we heard some chimes, then a voice say, "This is the Hunter residence."

We had enough. I told Shapiro we had to get home, but before getting out, he gave us a final story. Shapiro had been busted by the sheriff's office for pestering a lady he was trying to question. The DA's office would prosecute the case, and Shapiro wanted guidance straight from the top guy, his "buddy," Alex Hunter.

"Whatever you do," advised the district attorney, famous for his plea bargains, "don't plead guilty."

———

I was out of town when Commander Eller and Detective Gosage played the Shapiro tapes for Chief Koby, who paled when he heard Hunter ridicule that "fucking Koby" for wanting to own a bike repair shop. He knew the tapes were real and documented a range of questionable and possibly illegal acts, from giving up confidential personnel files to assigning secret investigations to funneling confidential case information to a tabloid.

But instead of being angry at the district attorney, Chief Koby chastised Eller and Gosage. He asked if any copies had been made of the tape. Eller said just one and pulled it from his pocket. Koby ordered the commander to destroy the tape in his presence, and Eller reluctantly unspooled it into a trash can. Police preserve backups of important tapes specifically to prevent vital evidence from disappearing if something happens to the original. But the chief could not be certain that all copies of the tapes had been destroyed, and he had to assume that the information might someday become public or be put before a judge or a bar committee.

Koby said that Hunter's acts might not actually be illegal but were certainly unethical. He took possession of the original tape and once again told the detectives, "I need to talk to Alex." Exactly the wrong thing to do. A better conversation would have been with a U.S. Attorney or the state attorney general or someone else with oversight capability.

Chief Koby later chewed me out for recording the informant. I believed the chief's conduct was unprofessional and absurd. We had eyewitness corroboration of an elected official's misconduct, in addition to the serious ethical questions that begged answers, and Koby went after his own cops instead of squaring off against the district attorney. It was such bullshit. I was told to get on the team, quit rocking the boat, be a good little detective, and don't sniff around the political landscape of the district attorney.

Once again a feeling of impotent rage engulfed me. Nothing, absolutely nothing, ever seemed to go right in this investigation. At lunch I read an article in a weekly newspaper about a city council candidate who had wanted a recall vote on the district attorney until Alex Hunter called him in and "laid the blame right where it belonged, at the feet of the Boulder Police Department."

Other than burning two detectives and a confidential informant, the sting operation that documented multiple violations of the public trust by the district attorney was quietly buried. But I realized that Koby was in a delicate position, for how could he censure me, a whistleblower, without risking that I would blow the whistle even louder? He admitted that I had created "a real problem."

Part Four

NOT SO GRAND JURY

24

In mid-September, a panel of pediatric experts from around the country reached one of the major conclusions of the investigation—that Jon-Benét had suffered vaginal trauma prior to the day she was killed.

There were no dissenting opinions among them on the issue, and they firmly rejected any possibility that the trauma to the hymen and chronic vaginal inflammation were caused by urination issues or masturbation. We gathered affidavits stating in clear language that there were injuries "consistent with prior trauma and sexual abuse" . . . "There was chronic abuse" . . . "Past violation of the vagina" . . . "Evidence of both acute injury and chronic sexual abuse." In other words, the doctors were saying it had happened before. One expert summed it up well when he said the injuries were not consistent with sexual assault but with a child who was being physically abused.

Such findings would lead an investigator to conclude that the person who inflicted that abuse was someone with frequent or unquestioned access to the child, and that limited the number of suspects. Every statistic in the book pointed to someone inside the family.

The detectives could not imagine a scenario in which some mysterious intruder broke into the house, not only on the night JonBenét was killed but also on previous occasions, in order to abuse her.

A much more likely cause of the injuries to my thinking was some sort of corporal punishment being meted out as discipline if JonBenét wet or soiled the bed. That possibility was buttressed by the absence of semen on the body and an expert's opinion that the vaginal and hymenal damage was not due to an act of sexual gratification.

The results, however, were not what is known in the legal world as "conclusive"—which means that there can be no other interpretation—and I would fully expect defense lawyers to argue something different. Nevertheless, our highly qualified doctors had brought in a remarkable finding.

We had reached one of the two levels that Deputy DA Pete Hofstrom had said would mark the turning point toward prosecution—all of the experts we consulted agreed on prior vaginal abuse. We still needed the second point, an expert opinion that Patsy Ramsey wrote the ransom note.

———

Then we had the experts assess why a tiny splinter had been found in JonBenét's vagina.

The cellulose splinter was believed to have come from the same paintbrush that had been used to make the garrote. Although the source of the splinter was never definitively proved, I considered it highly unlikely that it originated anywhere else. And that brush belonged to Patsy Ramsey.

———

In a three-page report, forensics expert Dr. Werner Spitz furnished a logical sequence of events on the night JonBenét was killed.

- First there had been a manual strangulation, by twisting the collar of the shirt, with the perpetrator's knuckles causing the neck abrasion. That was consistent with a rage-type attack.
- Then came the devastating blow to the head, followed by the garrote strangulation. The detectives felt this could have been done either to ensure death or as part of a staging. Another doctor said that the head was hit with great force and that the cracking skull would have made a tremendous noise. It was agreed that the cord around the throat was applied to a victim who offered little or no resistance, probably as she lay grievously wounded by the head injury.
- By examining the condition of the pineapple in the stomach and the rate of digestion, Spitz put the time of death "about or before 1 A.M."

To my mind, what Spitz described was consistent with someone being out of control. It was not consistent with someone trying to kidnap a child for ransom.

———

We reached a crucial turning point in aggressively pursuing the murder investigation when Commander John Eller was dismissed from the case in October. His replacement was Commander Mark Beckner, a company man. The change, which was for political rather than practical reasons, inexorably shifted the centerpoint of the investigation from the police SitRoom to the office of the district attorney.

Our New Age chief, Tom Koby, who preached sunshine and good feelings, ruled that John Eller—the last ranking cop who had not risen to command through Koby's touchy-feely administration—wasn't really suited for police work. While temporarily leaving Eller in charge of the detective bureau, the chief would soon fire him.

Only days before his appointment, Mark Beckner had been leading a new Internal Affairs witch-hunt to track down the anonymous police sources in the *Vanity Fair* article, planning polygraphs and suggesting possible criminal charges against whoever had talked to the reporter. Apparently it was a mortal sin for anyone in the police department to speak to a reporter.

And this was going to be our new leader? I couldn't believe it.

I remembered Beckner from back when he succeeded Eller as head of Tom Koby's nonviolent SWAT team. With Eller in charge, the team was motivated and highly trained. He bonded with us, and parties at his house featured John on his electric guitar, lots of beer, and doing stupid things like holding Roman candles in our teeth. We would go through a door for John Eller any day. Beckner was remembered for refusing to bring his boat to a SWAT team party at the reservoir, explaining that "I don't want you guys messing it up." Our attitude became "OK, Mark, be sure to call us the next time you need someone to risk his life." That was one reason I left the team and went into undercover narcotics.

Chief Koby had authorized a series of actions—such as holding the body of JonBenét for further testing, going after Sergeant Mason for talking to the media, and the sting linking the *Globe*'s Jeff Shapiro with the district attorney—only to roll back on his decisions and leave Commander Eller to take the heat. Koby made Eller the scapegoat for the entire mess.

Losing Commander Eller meant we were losing our chief defender at a critical time in the investigation. Eller had neither needed, wanted, respected, nor feared the DA's people. They in turn hated him. With his removal, we felt terribly exposed. The only people we had left to prevent the DA's intrusive power and political positioning from taking over were the department's legal adviser, Bob Keatley, and our Dream Team of outside attorneys, all of whom were soon to be brushed aside and their input ignored.

―――――――

Chief Koby gave another disastrous news conference, this time speaking to a full house of journalists with plenty of national network cameras present. He read a prepared statement about the Eller-Beckner change of command, then announced that the police were officially leaving the DA's War Room.

The chief seemed determined not to antagonize the media this time, but like a lemming running off a cliff, he just couldn't avoid self-destructing. He pulled a copy of the United States Constitution from his pocket and lectured the savvy press corps about their First Amendment responsibilities. His moralizing was silly because as he chastised the media for lacking leadership, accountability, and standards, his cops were saying the same thing about him.

―――――――

Commander Mark Beckner rode in on a charger of personal optimism. Things were going to change, he promised. We were getting three new detectives and new support staffing! We were going to get those warrants! We were no longer going to waste our time chasing every wagging-tail suspect that was thrown at us! Unless something met a "reasonable standard" for follow-up investigation, we wouldn't do it! We were going to make our case! That lasted only until he read the DA's Five-Year Plan. He then commented, "This is not going to be easy."

His initial attitude was fire and brimstone. Ours was wait and see. And as the weeks passed, examples stacked up to show that he was unwilling to fight the district attorney's office. On paper Commander Beckner looked pretty good, but many of us felt he was just a paper-chasing administrator who desperately wanted to be chief. In my opinion, he wasn't about to go to bat for the detectives on the Ramsey case if such actions put his career plans at risk.

After he had been in command for only a month, the detectives were almost in open mutiny.

It began at a briefing in which our new boss unveiled a to-do list that he thought would carry the case to a conclusion. We pointed out that we already had plenty of lists and he was just shuffling what was already on the table. His list was not some crystal ball in which the face of the killer would suddenly appear.

Then Commander Beckner ordered us to be "more objective" in our reports and not skew them to theories that a Ramsey was involved in the death of JonBenét. It was an insult.

He appeared to be already in the DA's camp, because those accusatory words were all too familiar. We challenged him, demanding that he show us even one report in which we had slanted our views. He could not.

Tell the same thing to the DA's investigators, Lou Smit and Steve Ainsworth, we argued. Read their red notebooks and see how the case is being polluted with their nonsense.

Beckner plunged ahead and suggested that since Smit was "just sitting over there in the DA's office," we should use him to run down possible intruder leads. Oh, really? What about flying off to pick up Kevin Raburn in Tennessee? What about their stun guns and exhumation plans? Beckner stammered. Sergeant Tom Wickman, who believed he was being cut out of his leadership position by Beckner, rolled his eyes in exasperation.

The commander warned that we should be prepared for Smit to make an arrest without us if the DA's office developed a "good suspect." I asked why we couldn't do the same thing and arrest a suspect whom we could put at the crime scene and for whom we already had probable cause. Detective Gosage said he wasn't worried about Smit, Ainsworth, and Trip DeMuth turning up some unknown intruder. "Let 'em fucking look. They're never going to find him," he said.

Nevertheless, it irked us that the DA's office seemed to be trying to solve the case without us. It would be the ultimate political ploy. They would crow about how the police had screwed up the investigation but the DA saved it.

We believed Beckner had been seduced by the DA's team, and without much of a struggle. When he sought to become chief of police, he would need the political clout of DA Alex Hunter. In my opinion, as events unfolded, it would not come without a price.

———

Trying to mend fences after the briefing fiasco, Beckner came by for a talk but did nothing to ameliorate my concern.

If a grand jury is called, he said, the DA's office will handle it and not bring in outside help.

"Why?" I asked. They did not have experience with grand juries and didn't even *like* them. Beckner said there was no choice, since Alex Hunter was the only game in town. "We still have to work with them when this is over," he explained. "That's the reality. We can't burn that bridge down."

I asked Beckner point-blank if he thought the Ramseys did it, and he took a big breath. Yes, he said, one or both were involved. He did not think it was an intruder and agreed there was probable cause for an arrest but thought we didn't have it "beyond a reasonable doubt."

"That's what a trial is for, Mark. If we have the right defendant in the courtroom, a prosecutor can bring the pieces of the puzzle together," I replied. There was a whole mountain of circumstantial evidence, and in my opinion a tough prosecutor could do it.

Commander Beckner shook his head. "We may never file a case, Steve. You need to prepare for the eventuality that this case might not be prosecuted." That was language straight out of the DA's office, and it sounded to me as if he were already throwing in the towel.

————

We achieved a Pyrrhic victory on November 5 when Beckner burst into the SitRoom and proudly handed me a "Consent to Release of Telephone Records" signed by both John Ramsey and Pete Hofstrom. It allowed us to obtain the Ramseys' cellular and home telephone records between December 1 and 27, 1996. We had had to wait almost a year to see them, which had given the Ramsey lawyers months to work through the limited documents. The woefully incomplete permission slip did not give up Ramsey's company phones, calls made with a telephone card, or records about calls before or after December. We found nothing worthwhile. Just another exhausting trip to nowhere.

I sent a fax to AirTouch in Washington state and personally served the paper on US West in downtown Denver.

"I've been waiting for a phone call from you guys since last December," a telephone company security official said as he handed me the packet. "Usually cops come and get these things right away."

I winced, so tired of being embarrassed by this case.

"Yeah, I get subpoenas and warrants every day," he repeated. "Surprised you took so long."

"I'll have to explain it to you someday," I replied and headed for the elevator.

The AirTouch cell phone records were useless. Ramsey started the service in January 1994. AirTouch said that 91 minutes of use were logged during the August–September billing period of 1996, and 108 minutes were used in September–October. October–November was just as busy.

December, however, the only period we were allowed to see, was empty. No calls at all. I asked if someone could have removed billing records from the computer? "No way," the AirTouch source told me.

"All these months preceding December are busy, and not one call was logged for that entire month?"

The representative was firm: "There ain't no way anybody altered these records." It wasn't logical. A search warrant might have answered the question eleven months ago, but we had only this thin new "consent."

Checking the records, I found a repeat caller to John Ramsey's private office line. Three calls the day after the murder and two more a few days later came from the home phone of the lieutenant governor of the State of Colorado, Gail Schoettler.

Treating her like any other witness simply didn't work. The lieutenant governor strutted her political power and stonewalled me until she was damned good and ready to answer questions. Her husband, Don Stevens, a friend of John Ramsey for thirty-five years, had made the calls merely to convey sympathy, Schoettler told me. The experience demonstrated how deeply John Ramsey was now plugged into the Democratic Party power structure. Colorado Governor Roy Romer was chairman of the Democratic National Committee and advised by the politically astute Hal Haddon, one of John Ramsey's attorneys. Haddon's firm prepared President Clinton's taxes. When Schoettler left office, she was appointed head of the U.S. delegation to an international commission by President Clinton.

––––––––

Detective Tom Trujillo, who was steadily falling further behind in getting the evidence tested, fumbled a major opportunity concerning the cord used in the murder. He was adamant that the cord was polypropylene, citing the findings of a lab analyst. Another opportunity would soon be lost.

Following a tip six months earlier, I had found what seemed to be identical cord, packaged as "nylon," in both the Boulder Army Store and McGuckin's Hardware, and collected more than fifty samples. Everyone agreed that it seemed a visual match for the neck ligature, but

Trujillo insisted that the ligatures in the Ramsey case were not nylon and that we needed to find a polypropylene rope. I told him to have it tested anyway.

In the middle of November, John Van Tassell of the Royal Canadian Mounted Police, one of the world's foremost experts on knots and cords, reviewed the neck ligature, the length of white cord that had been twisted around the broken paintbrush handle to create a terrible killing tool. Van Tassell commented that it was "a soft nylon cord." Sergeant Wickman and I immediately caught the term.

We asked if he was certain, and the Mountie studied it some more. Sure looks like soft nylon, he said, as he examined what looked like a soft flat white shoelace. Not stiff and rigid like polypropylene.

I retrieved one sample package, a fifty-foot length of white Stansport 32-strand, $3/16$-inch woven cord that I had bought. Van Tassell pulled the cord out, frayed an end, held it against the end of the neck ligature, and said, "Look." The soft white braid and inner weave appeared identical. "I think this is the same cord," he said.

If a hole had appeared in the earth, Trujillo would have let it swallow him. He had not submitted any of my evidence for comparison. Beckner ordered him to get it to the lab immediately.

My file for May 21, 1997, detailed my purchase of white nylon cord from the sporting goods section of McGuckin's, some of which was identical in brand and model to the cord I bought at the army store. The price was $2.29. On December 2, 1996, Patsy Ramsey purchased an item from the McGuckin's sporting goods section. The price was $2.29.

I didn't know whether to laugh or cry, it was so frustrating. Because Trujillo had not submitted the evidence for testing and remained firm that we had the wrong type of cord, I had held back from searching the army surplus store records. Now so much time had elapsed, the records were unavailable. I had seldom felt such a level of defeat since the investigation began.

Internal politics within the police department detonated in a staccato of actions that further sidetracked the Ramsey investigation. We couldn't concentrate on catching a killer while all hell was breaking loose inside our own house.

Chief Koby forced Commander Eller out totally in November by giving him the choice of handing in his papers voluntarily or getting fired and losing all his benefits. I had always thought truth would prevail and that doing the right thing would pay off in the end, but the political lynching of John Eller proved that was not true in Boulder. He was allowed to stay around until the first of the year.

I felt sorry for my friend and boss. This case was gobbling up cops like candy.

The Internal Affairs Citizen Review Panel investigating the allegations against John Eller found that he was neither untruthful nor negligent in pursuing Sergeant Larry Mason and complimented him for following through on that action. They said he had been obligated to act. What they didn't understand was why Chief Koby, who had known of the event from the start, first backed Eller and then reversed himself when things began to unravel and wrote Mason a $10,000 check to settle the matter. Not that it made any difference now, but the bottom line was that Commander Eller had done the right thing.

The timing of his firing was no accident, for Chief Koby was cleaning up loose ends. A few days after John Eller was axed, I was copying some papers when another detective came by wearing a huge grin. "Koby's quitting," he said. I looked up, and he repeated it: "Koby's quitting." Another cop arrived who had gotten a similar report from a sergeant who got it from a commander. Good news travels fast around a police department. *Yes!* I thought, wanting to shout in triumph.

But although Koby was resigning, he planned to stay on for another six months and proclaimed that he would be the one to decide the future of the Ramsey case. That Koby, who had never checked out a single file, held the future in his hands scared us. I doubted if he would ever send it over to the district attorney.

––––––––

The final scene in this installment of the department's soap opera occurred when the police union handed the chief still another vote of "no confidence." Only his retirement announcement saved him from the disgrace of our demanding his immediate resignation.

Normally only a few officers attend police union meetings, but this was not a normal night. About seventy-five traffic, patrol, SWAT, narcotics, and special units officers and sergeants and detectives were packed together into a conference room at the Boulder Holiday Inn. Every chair was taken, and cops stood along the walls.

The chief faced an openly hostile audience, and as he started to speak in his low voice, many cops continued to eat chicken wings from plates in their laps and carried on whispered conversations. There was utter disrespect as Koby went through a political tap dance about how much had been accomplished on the issues raised in the last no-confidence vote after the May riots.

The chief said he was sorry that the department had divided into factions just because people disliked him personally. He promised to use a new tax increase to hire thirty-three more officers and went on about what he hoped to accomplish during his lame-duck tenure, as if he really thought he could survive without the support of his troops.

When he was done, an Internal Affairs sergeant read a prepared statement about how the chief was the victim of a few narrow-minded people in the department. There was open laughter. Koby's only support had come from the despised IA.

A series of officers stood and took the chief to task, and if he tried to interrupt, they would say, "Sir, will you allow me to finish?" After being pummeled for a while, Koby finally left, taking the commanders along with him, and the open discussion began.

For twenty minutes, heated accusations flew like poison arrows. When the IA sergeant again tried to defend Koby, he was told to shut up. When a rookie spoke up for the chief, veteran cops yelled, "Fuck off!"

As tempers, voices, and rhetoric rose, I was shocked to see Commander Mark Beckner seated in the back of the room. It was improper and unwarranted for command staff to attend the meeting because rank-and-file union members needed to be free to speak without fear of future punishment. But Beckner had come in just after the chief and stayed behind, a mole in place. He scurried out as soon as the no-confidence vote passed.

After the meeting, bets were placed about who would succeed Koby in the chief's chair. Detective Gosage put his money on Commander Beckner because the odds against that happening were so huge.

With our Dream Team, we tallied the points supporting probable cause and found more than fifty items. Viewed in a macro-perspective, the case was compelling and imposing.

But our lawyers cautioned that the district attorney's office held quite the opposite view. Deputy DA Pete Hofstrom had told them the police "had no case" at all.

We spent a long day going over every possible weak point. A Hi-Tec boot print found on the wine cellar floor where the body was discovered had not been identified. Neither had one of the palm prints on the cellar door. The DA's office still refused to allow testing of the confusing pubic hair found on the white blanket wrapped around Jon-Benét. The FBI had been asked to do those tests but would not allow Team Ramsey to watch. Therefore it remained in limbo. We felt the DNA could be argued either way, but without resolving other core problems, it was unlikely the case would ever see the inside of a court-room.

Bob Miller of the Dream Team said the time had come to be more aggressive and launch the Title-3 eavesdropping of the Ramsey home. I agreed that was our best bet for hearing incriminating statements.

Commander Beckner, however, was pessimistic that Chief Koby would approve something as aggressive as a Title-3. Dan Hoffman of the Dream Team remarked, "Koby's going to be gone soon." Whoever was the next chief might do the right thing.

———

The unidentified palm print on the door was more of a riddle than a mystery. There were actually three palm prints on that door, which the killer had to close in order to lock. We had already determined that two of those prints belonged to Patsy Ramsey. Arguing that the third could only be that of an intruder was a stretch.

We needed to identify the print to eliminate it but discovered that even some law enforcement officers were reluctant to cooperate with us. Detective Jane Harmer was unable to get sheriff's investigators who had been in the Ramsey house during the crime scene search to even return her calls when she sought their palm prints. Complicating mat-ters was the problem of Detective Trujillo not having submitted numer-ous prints, including those of some police, for comparison.

Even if and when we got all the cops' prints out of the way, we still had to deal with the other two or three thousand people who had passed through the house.

———

The Hi-Tec boot print became one of the biggest questions of the in-vestigation. Since Hi-Tecs are popular among cops, a year after the murder I became convinced that a sight-seeing law enforcement officer stepped somewhere he or she shouldn't have on December 26 and didn't want to admit it.

Detective Ron Gosage had the impossible job of trying to identify the origin of the boot print, a nightmare assignment if there ever was one. He contacted more than four hundred people, even construction workers who had been in the house five years ago, but did not find the matching print.

I doubted that any member of the Ramsey family would admit to owning a pair of Hi-Tecs, whether they did or not, but Detective Gosage had to ask them. That alerted Team Ramsey, and the defense lawyers and our DA's office soon began insisting that the unknown boot print was left behind by the intruder.

What they didn't know was that lab technicians had found not just one but three different unidentified shoe prints in that little room—the main print and two less pronounced impressions that overlapped each other. We considered that a positive development, for how likely would it be that three intruders carried the body into the room? And the possibilities were great that the print was totally unrelated to the murder. Just because something is found at the site of a murder doesn't mean it is part of the crime.

On a below-freezing winter day, I went with Gosage and another detective to Vail on a tip that a clerk recalled seeing Patsy and JonBenét try on hiking boots at Pepi Sports in that ski resort town. They might have been Hi-Tecs.

A bookkeeper carried in boxes crammed with thousands of receipts for everything from skis to bike rentals, and we hand-searched every one of them. It wasn't the first or the last hand search we made of receipts. In a Home Depot outside of Atlanta, Gosage and I had to check some twenty-five thousand individual records and journal rolls in a vain search for the possible purchase of cord and duct tape. A clerk said she had waited on Patsy Ramsey during such a transaction. We found nothing, and now we were doing it again in Vail.

"Why don't you just subpoena all the credit card records of the Ramseys?" asked the bookkeeper.

"Long story." I was so tired of that question.

"Is the case as fucked up as it sounds? I mean, they've already finished TWA Flight 800, sentenced McVeigh to death for Oklahoma City, convicted Nichols, and are doing their thing with the Unabomber. Why are you guys taking so long?"

"Long story."

We found no receipts for the Ramseys, but a cash or check transaction would not have listed a name, unlike a credit card sale.

As with the palm print, the most frustrating part of the Hi-Tec hunt was the inexplicable lack of cooperation from other cops.

Two pairs of boots that were among the most difficult to retrieve belonged to Detective Sergeant Larry Mason and Detective Linda

Arndt, both of whom had been in the house during the first hours. Arndt's clothing had been collected at the crime scene but not her footwear. It took a direct order from Commander Beckner before Arndt and Mason gave up their boots for testing, about a year after the murder, and it took still longer to get their fingerprints. Mason, the on-scene detective supervisor on December 26, had still not submitted a written report of his actions that day when I left after eighteen months.

A reserve sheriff's deputy who wore Hi-Tecs at the crime scene retained a lawyer before talking to Detective Gosage. Then we got the name of another patrol sergeant who had been in the basement that day. That was also a year late. At fourteen months, Gosage found that an FBI agent from Denver had been in the basement and owned Hi-Tecs.

The final embarrassment in the Hi-Tec hunt came when Detective Gosage compared the radio log for December 26 with other reports and discovered that a number of boot-wearing law enforcement types had also been at the house but had never "aired out," or given their location, on the radio.

That meant we never really knew which cops, firefighters, paramedics, and sheriff's deputies were there. It seemed that everybody and their damned brother went wandering through the crime scene that day, and running them down was a virtual impossibility.

What staggered me, however, was the realization that we could no longer count on cooperation from even our fellow Boulder police officers. If that was so, then it was probably time to fold our tents and go home.

———

Another strange part of the puzzle was the big black flashlight that had been found standing on its lens end on the kitchen counter. Some perceived it as a possible murder weapon, although that was never proved.

Dr. Werner Spitz, the forensic scientist, even ran macabre tests to see if the heavy flashlight could have inflicted the kind of massive skull fracture that was found on JonBenét. To do so, a child's cadaver was obtained so he could strike the skull with a similar flashlight and examine the resulting injury pattern. He said the results were consistent, that the damage could have been caused by the flashlight—but it could also have been caused by other things.

There were three theories about the origin of the flashlight.

First, that it belonged to the family. John Andrew Ramsey had given to his father as a gift a flashlight that was consistent in color, make, and model to the one found in the house. The Ramseys could not account for it but hedged away from saying that the one discovered by police belonged to them.

The second possibility was that the flashlight was brought in by the intruder, used in the crime, then left behind in his haste to escape. To me, this was not consistent, for he had not hurried about anything else and, according to the intruder theorists, had carefully taken away other pieces of evidence such as the duct tape and cord. Since the flashlight held no fingerprints, did the intruder carefully wipe it down, inside and out, even the batteries, then just forget it? It didn't fit.

Besides its being the Ramseys', what also made sense was the third option, that some cop brought the heavy flashlight inside (they arrived before dawn) and left it on the counter by mistake. It was the Mag-Lite type preferred by policemen. That it bore no fingerprints was consistent with a piece of equipment being handled in cold weather by a cop wearing gloves. But we were unable to trace the serial number. And, like the palm print and Hi-Tec boot print, once the case blew up, no one wanted to claim ownership.

The internal resistance reached a pinnacle of absurdity when Detective Linda Arndt and Detective Sergeant Larry Mason claimed they had been stricken with amnesia about the Ramsey case. That introduced an unbelievable element of chaos and left us unsure about what our own people would say in sworn testimony.

I couldn't understand how they could break faith with their responsibilities like that. I wanted to yell at them, "This is a murder investigation. Cooperate, for God's sake, and be done with it."

Arndt told Commander Beckner that she "couldn't remember anything about December 26th. The 26th and the next several months are a total loss." The only detective inside the home when the body was found went silent, and her threat of a lawsuit froze the department brass into immobility, so they declined to pressure her. When I asked her directly, she repeated her memory loss: "You know, I don't remember a lot of stuff from last year. Whatever is in my reports, just go with that."

That was just the point. She had submitted reports that contained amended words and phrases that left me with no idea how she would testify about the ransom note, comments by the parents, and finding the body.

A few months later, Detective Jane Harmer came into the SitRoom with a strange, disbelieving look on her face and announced in an empty voice, "We have another Linda Arndt."

Following a line of inquiry about who did what on that first morning, she had gone to see Sergeant Larry Mason. The detective said the sergeant told her, "I don't remember a thing about the Ramsey case."

I never knew amnesia was contagious.

25

The detectives hoped a news conference in early December would be an opportunity to exert pressure on the Ramseys and force new interviews. Commander Beckner, who as the Internal Affairs boss had wanted to root out any cops who talked to *Vanity Fair,* was now advocating a campaign of "strategic press leaks." But even such a routine tactic as spinning the press seemed beyond our grasp. Commander Beckner apparently had another agenda, and I thought he wanted to appear before the media as the savior of the case, which would give him an edge in his bid to become chief of police. It drove another wedge between him and us, just when we needed to present a unified front.

Beckner proposed that he alone should address the media, and we were told it would be "awkward" for us to share the stage with him, although we were welcome to stand along the walls of the auditorium. After much bickering, the investigative team was instructed to line up behind the commander, who would handle the formal message and the questions.

We critiqued Beckner's proposed statement line by line because we wanted the primary message to be very clear—that we were asking for new interviews with the Ramseys. Secondly, we wanted to show police solidarity and indicate that Alex Hunter's people had an advisory status only.

The biggest internal debate was about whether the Ramseys should finally be called suspects. A year into the investigation and still nobody would utter "The S-Word." Sergeant Wickman pointed out they had done nothing to remove themselves from beneath the "umbrella of suspicion" and that using such a phrase would avoid the forbidden word while making it clear that they were our primary focus.

At nine o'clock sharp on the morning of December 5, we filed into the city council chambers, and the lights of the television cameras hit us. We took our places on stage, shoulder to shoulder, and Mark Beckner stepped to the podium and introduced us individually.

Beckner handled his script smoothly, announcing that seventy-two tasks had needed to be done when he took over nine weeks ago and that the list had been pared by twenty-eight, with another dozen items nearing completion. We were making progress, he said. The detectives knew his statistics were worthless, for our actual workload was as heavy as ever, and the to-do list was constantly being revised as new information came in.

"I can tell you that we are going to be focused and aggressive in moving this investigation forward," Beckner said, and called for the Ramseys to grant new interviews.

I looked away when the commander complimented the DA's office for its support and "positive and professional" assistance. That was brown-nosing bullshit, and I would have no part of it.

Then he skirted the truth by stating that no arrest warrant had ever been prepared, although he had read the Master Affidavit I carried everywhere. I recall his words, "But it's not *really* a warrant," and I replied that that was *exactly* what it was. Today he did not return my questioning look.

"I am confident we will solve this case," Beckner told the press and added that the Ramseys remained beneath "an umbrella of suspicion." Everybody left the room happy. The press had its sound bite, we had tightened the screws a bit, and Mark Beckner had become a media darling.

———

Only a few hours later a letter arrived from Patsy Ramsey, written in flowing script, dated almost two weeks before, and delivered to the police department by a Team Ramsey lawyer. The contents would have been startling had we not been so familiar with her empty promises.

They were ready to work closely with Beckner "in *any* way," the letter said, and meet anytime "in the spirit of cooperation to achieve a common goal." But the letter contained the large caveat that they would speak with the "capable professionals" in the district attorney's office. It was bogus. How could they pledge to help a police commander in any way while simultaneously refusing to meet with his detectives? We warned Beckner to be wary.

"Don't let Patsy fool you with that letter," Wickman said. Detective Harmer added, "Patsy is in total denial. She's rationalized this in her mind and can probably even visualize an intruder."

————

Team Ramsey followed up a few days later to let us know they weren't happy that we had stirred up the coals. They moaned to Beckner that the media were again bothering their clients, then added the usual double-talk, putting Patsy's letter promising open cooperation in a more familiar light. The Ramseys would now help if they were allowed to first "assess our intentions" by reviewing any new evidence and questions. They didn't trust the police, the lawyers wrote, but had been meeting with DA investigator Lou Smit. That was the first we had heard about it.

We got Beckner to respond in the same harsh tone. We would no longer share investigative information with potential suspects or witnesses. We wanted open access to the Ramseys at any time and would not participate in prolonged negotiations every time we needed a question answered.

Again, what looked pretty good on paper wasn't even close to the truth. Evidence and information continued to flow to Team Ramsey, and we never had access to John and Patsy. And instead of living up to his refusal to enter into prolonged negotiations, Commander Beckner himself ended up making deals with the Ramsey lawyers.

————

A group of our Dream Team attorneys and detectives walked into an ambush during a visit to the Fifteenth Street Ramsey home, after receiving permission and being let in by a Realtor. As they spent two hours going from room to room, discussing how the case facts fit with the geographic layout of the house, Team Ramsey was secretly videotaping our moves.

Police discovered four tiny cameras hidden inside motion detectors and followed the wires to a videotape recorder and monitor locked in a basement closet. The cameras covered the basement, JonBenét's bedroom, and part of the main floor—precisely the areas where our team had stopped and talked about the case. A tape was retrieved showing our team on the site.

The videotape recorder did not record continuously but required a physical act to switch it on. Someone had activated it only an hour and fifteen minutes before our people arrived.

The covert surveillance could have been a crime if a listening device had also been found. I was willing to bet there was a miniaturized bug planted in there somewhere, but FBI technicians said they would be unable to find it without tearing the house apart. Beckner declared it a crime scene, had the locks changed, and seized all the video equipment as evidence.

The Ramsey lawyers and private investigators later admitted that the video equipment belonged to them and claimed it was installed because of concerns about trespassing. If that were true, why didn't they tell us before, and why did they have the cameras running? I didn't believe them, but although the incident screamed for a thorough investigation, it went away, just like Computergate.

———

I returned to Atlanta for one more grave-site surveillance try with the Georgia Bureau of Investigation at Christmas 1997 and again came up short in the quest to eavesdrop on a confession.

Chief Koby didn't think the trip was a good idea, and Sergeant Wickman told me he was worried about the operation, but GBI Agent John Lang supported going ahead with the hundred-to-one shot anyway. Pray for a break, for without a confession, this case was going nowhere. "You guys, in the end, may simply look back and agree it was a hell of a ride," he said. "But you were home-cooked from the beginning. This was a no-win."

With a warrant from the Cobb County District Attorney, we once again set up a command post in Marietta High School. This time our recording equipment was hidden in a fake but realistic tombstone constructed by a movie special effects company. It appeared to be made of granite but was actually a converted decorative mantelpiece from Home Depot. The family name THOMAS was inscribed in large letters over "John Thomas 1936–1992." It was a combination of my name and that of Agent John Lang.

The gates of St. James Episcopal Cemetery were open on the night of December 20 as our little convoy of undercover cars entered to plant our fake tombstone. When our headlights swept across JonBenét's grave, we were surprised to find a marble headstone:

JONBENÉT PATRICIA RAMSEY
AUGUST 6, 1990–DECEMBER 25, 1996

It was a clue from nowhere.

I knew that the Ramseys had returned from the Whites' Christmas party at 10 P.M., and the day ended two hours later. The dates on the grave marker were another argument for establishing a time of death. For some reason, the parents were stating that JonBenét had died before midnight.

Fresh flowers were on the graves of both JonBenét and Beth Ramsey, Christmas ornaments hung in a nearby tree, there was a photo in a little framed heart, and a six-foot-long strip of Astroturf covered the ground. A stuffed bunny and a ceramic angel, a box with a Nativity scene, and other mementos surrounded the grave.

"We missed them," I told Lang dejectedly. "That headstone didn't get here by itself. They came early and held some sort of memorial service." As I kicked myself, Lang said it didn't matter because our warrant didn't begin for another three days anyway. Even had we been here, we would only have been able to watch from a distance without any recording equipment.

We installed our high-tech headstone on a plot forty-five feet west of the child's grave, feeling like ghouls, then departed the cemetery as inconspicuously as one can at two o'clock in the morning while carrying a shovel, flashlight, and sledgehammer.

For the surveillance, the GBI gave us everything we had before and more, and we began at dawn on December 24, as a slashing rain stopped and the sun rose on the drenched cemetery. Over the next eighty-eight hours, tourists looked at the grave, the press looked at the tourists, and we looked at them all.

Burgers and Cokes fueled us while we recorded the gamut of people—women with babies in strollers, self-appointed experts explaining the case, families, kids, dog walkers, and Rollerbladers. It was a tourist mecca.

A white Corvette pulled in, and a blonde with an inch of dark roots emerged, wearing a Mickey Mouse sweatshirt, stirrup stretch pants, and dark glasses. Detective Gosage and I thought we recognized her. "That looks like Pam Paugh," he said. She sat on the little bench and wept as the merciless photographers stalked nearer. She knelt for a moment on the grave and whispered a few words we couldn't hear through all the media noise. *Speak louder!* we urged from the command post. She gave the headstone a kiss and escaped after only four minutes. We never figured out who she really was.

A middle-aged couple and their son stopped by, and the boy wandered away to look at our John Thomas headstone. Our hearts almost stopped when he rocked it back and forth and loudly called, "This is made of wood!" After a few minutes of tut-tutting about how anyone could possibly buy such a cheap marker for the dearly departed, the family moved away.

The reporters and photographers kept a discreet distance at first but soon abandoned any restraint and became jackals. One photographer set her camera tripod right on the grave and rearranged the items at the headstone to suit her picture. Anything she didn't want was callously tossed. A poem in a glass frame shattered. For an hour she refused to relinquish the site. We cursed everything about her.

She wasn't much worse than the rest, however. The women reporters stayed in their vehicles preening in the mirrors until some unsuspecting visitor came to the grave. Then they rushed up in tight skirts, microphones extended like elephant snouts, shouting, "Do you know the family? Why are you here?"

The swarm eventually camped out at the grave itself, smoking cigarettes and flipping the butts on the grass, standing around telling dirty jokes, setting up camera tripods on other graves, and pissing in the bushes. They were disgusting and had no respect whatsoever for the little girl in a coffin six feet below them.

With the press sprawled all over the place, there was no hope of anybody saying anything worthwhile.

————

After midnight on Christmas—the first anniversary of JonBenét's murder—I drove to the nearby suburb of Vinings and parked across the street from the Ramsey house. Security lights flooded the grounds, a single white rose was in the mailbox, and two great Christmas wreaths hung on the doors. I wanted to go ring the bell and say, "Let's talk." But I had been forbidden from doing so.

Instead I went back to my hotel room and called home. My wife was crying. She had been with me through thick and thin, but our arguments had become fierce over the past few months. I would spend all day at work and nights on the telephone with witnesses or writing reports, working through the weekends. The Ramseys had become part of our marriage, and she had cursed both them and me when I told her that I would be away over Christmas.

She was lonely and depressed and had every right to be. After hanging up, I took a couple of aspirin for the headache that never left me and lay back on the hotel pillow. Christmas dinner was room service, and I watched a movie. Soon, I promised myself, it would get better.

But deep down I was coming to realize that there might never be a resolution to this case that dominated my existence.

————

Back at the grave site, our only real opportunity came on the day after Christmas, when a clean-cut white male about forty years old, wearing dark glasses and looking nervous, sidled into the cemetery, careful to keep his back to the press. He pulled out a little camera, snapped a few shots, and put it away as the press started to film him. Lang and I dashed for our car as he got into a truck and headed east on Polk Street, and I couldn't believe my eyes. "That's a Colorado plate," I said, pulling close behind him. Lang replied, "We gotta take this guy down and ID him."

We followed him for miles until he pulled into the parking lot of the Atlanta Historical Society. As soon as he got out of the truck, we flashed our badges and handed him a bullshit line about him driving through a drug surveillance area. He bought it and showed a military ID. He was a navy corpsman based at Camp Lejeune in North Carolina and said he was just sightseeing in Atlanta and was from Colorado, where his mother lived.

I needed to get inside his vehicle and used an old narc trick to obtain permission. "You have any weapons, narcotics, contraband, bazookas, or machine guns in your truck?"

"No." He laughed. So did Lang and I.

"Then you wouldn't mind if I look in it, would you?"

"Sure, go ahead. You guys really looking for a bazooka?"

While Lang kept him talking, I tore into the truck, searching for anything that might tie him to our homicide. The cab was full of fast-food wrappers, unused 35-mm film, and blank videotapes. I looked through some notebooks in which he had written. Nothing. Although he had neglected to say anything about visiting the cemetery, we couldn't do much more at this point. We had a solid ID on him and knew where he was based. We let him go. The guy was just another wingnut that Lang would later thoroughly investigate and clear.

The only other remarkable visitor was John Andrew Ramsey, who got into an altercation with a photographer.

At ten o'clock the warrant ended, and we shut down the surveillance. We retrieved the John Thomas marker and moved the wreath we had left there to the grave of JonBenét. Then a dozen GBI agents and a couple of Boulder detectives sped down Highway 41 to the Buckboard cowboy bar for some shots and beer, respectfully toasting the little girl.

I also toasted the GBI agents who had forfeited their Christmas to help us with the attitude "Whatever it takes." I had wanted to give each of them something special, perhaps personalized golf shirts or some other suitable gift that could say "Thanks," but Beckner had only authorized handing out cheap Boulder Police Department uniform patches.

I ended the night by myself at the Waffle House, feeling very, very alone and knowing the end was near.

———

While I was in Atlanta, another Christmas in Boulder was despoiled by murder. University of Colorado student Susannah Chase was beaten to death near the downtown area, in what appeared to be a random assault, someone striking out of the darkness. Chief Tom Koby put Commander John Eller, whom he had just ruined, in charge of the investigation. If another scapegoat was needed on another unsolved murder, well, Eller had already been sacrificed once and was already leaving the department. Eller did as good a job as possible on his final case in Boulder, but the Chase murder remains unsolved.

I got back to Boulder on December 29 and found a stack of accumulated Christmas cards on my desk. From Chief Koby came a department-wide e-mail that urged us to have "frequent attacks of smiling." Noting that "we have no control over what is ahead of us," he suggested that we "let things happen rather than make them happen." That lazy attitude, I thought, was what was wrong with this murder investigation.

A card from Commander Beckner stated that success in the Ramsey matter "will not depend on whether there is a prosecution." I was disgusted at the suggestion that we should be satisfied with the old college try. I wanted more than that. I wanted a killer arrested.

Hell of a way to close a hell of a year.

———

I thought a column written by Chuck Green of the *Denver Post* summed things up well for 1997.

> For millions of Americans, the Ramseys' failure to cooperate with the police has been an obscene gesture. They simply cannot understand, despite Fifth Amendment explanations by crews of defense attorneys, why the Ramseys won't talk. Yes, they have the legal right to remain silent. But they also have a moral obligation to do all they can to help find the monster who killed their daugh-

ter. They have chosen to place legality above morality, while complaining that the public just doesn't understand. Yet all the lawyers in the world, and all the public relations experts on the planet, cannot change the perception that the Ramseys are hiding something. Only the Ramseys can change that, and they need to do only one thing—something their money can't buy. They must come completely clean with the police. No conditions. No negotiations. No evasions. No lawyers' games. Only answers.

26

I was still hopeful of solving this murder as 1998 began. We had established probable cause, and in perhaps the biggest step of the past year, we were getting ready to bug the Ramsey home in Atlanta in hopes of possibly overhearing incriminating statements.

But the daring Title-3 electronic eavesdropping plan was scrubbed because, Commander Beckner told me, it had "too much of a political downside." I considered this a huge setback. The dread of scandal was driving policy in the Boulder Police Department, and once again an opportunity to gather evidence blew up in our faces.

"In a command decision such as this, one has to weigh the worst case scenario," Beckner said. "What would happen with you and Gosage inside that house if something went wrong and someone got killed? What if an armed guard was overlooked or one of the Ramseys was home and someone got shot?"

I pointed out that police agencies carry out such proactive investigative measures all the time, and it would be a perfectly legal operation with all the paperwork in order before we moved. One cannot live in fear that the absolute worst may occur.

And even if we got caught inside the house, so what? The nation would probably applaud us for trying vigorously to pursue the case. Anyway, this was just a house in Atlanta, not the Russian Embassy. The minimal risks were far outweighed by the possibility of taping implicating disclosures.

During the Christmas trip to Atlanta, I had firmed up the T-3 opera-

tion with the Georgia Bureau of Investigation and advised them that
Beckner wanted a "risk assessment." In fact, the GBI already had the
home at 4070 Paces Ferry Road under observation, and the warrants,
manpower, and equipment would not be a problem. "Not only is this
operation doable but it's necessary," said Ralph Stone, the agent in
charge. "We need to be in that house."

The tentative plan was for a GBI technical specialist to enter the
house while the Ramseys were in Boulder for interviews. If confronted,
he was to grab something valuable, take off to make it look like an
interrupted burglary, and drop the loot on the way. Any subsequent
police investigation would be dealt with quietly. With the bugs in place,
we would start listening when John and Patsy returned home after
being grilled about the vaginal trauma of their daughter and a few other
surprises. Words were sure to be said in private.

All that was needed to launch the T-3 was a sign-off by the Boulder
police, but our fearful leaders chickened out.

———

District Attorney Alex Hunter used the media again to attack us, this
time in the respected *New Yorker* magazine, saying that the case was
"unfileable."

"The cops became so convinced the Ramseys did it that they've
never been able to look at the evidence objectively," he told the author,
Lawrence Schiller. Hunter was sabotaging the case before we had even
given it to him.

"Every rock must be turned over, and if that means swabbing everyone's mouth or exhuming JonBenét's body, that's what the police will
have to do," he said. Hunter hinted that the DNA of a second person
was found on the child's body, and he gave credibility to the nonexistent stun gun by saying that an exhumation might be needed for tissue
analysis. "It wasn't a fucking stun gun!" I shouted when I read the
piece.

Upon publication, the district attorney backpedaled, smoothly claiming that he was quoted out of context, but none of us believed him,
and Schiller insisted his report was accurate.

———

The clothes that might have been worn by the Ramseys at the Whites'
Christmas party finally trickled in for testing a year after the murder, a
time delay that seriously damaged the investigation. The polite "ask the
Ramseys" approach was deadly slow in getting results.

Had the original investigators bagged the clothing on the morning of December 26, we would have had instant possession of what John and Patsy Ramsey had worn the night before. Beyond that, we could have taken the clothing with a search warrant. Instead we waited more than a year.

Beginning in January 1998, packages of clothing arrived, most of it of questionable value. For instance, we received two grocery sacks containing Patsy's clothing. The first contained a High Sierra red turtleneck. It smelled brand-new, straight off the rack. The other was a short-sleeved sweater top that was much too small for her, unless she was going for a really tight fit. She had worn neither on Christmas Day. "Gimme a break," a detective snorted.

The packages came covered with excuses. Team Ramsey said they could not be certain that any of these were the right clothes, it was impossible to determine if the garments had been worn since the date in question, and the clothing had been handled by movers and their private investigator and might have been laundered. In other words, anything that might turn up couldn't be traced back to the Ramseys.

In that they were wrong, for the labs pulled one of their biggest surprise findings of the case out of those bags.

The investigation of the black duct tape that covered the mouth of JonBenét gave every indication of being just another lost lead when it began shortly after the murder.

Originally we hoped to prove the tape was from the same roll as the pieces found on the back of several portraits in the house. By determining its manufacturer, we might be able to find where it was sold and then track it to the Ramsey house. We already thought that Patsy might have purchased a roll of such tape from McGuckin's.

The FBI lab said that both tape samples, from the mouth and the pictures, were a low grade and of low quality, possibly the Shufford Mills model PC-600, but they wouldn't call it a match.

In September 1997 Detective Gosage and I visited the Shufford Mills factory in Hickory, North Carolina, and learned that the tape was made in small quantities. In fact, it comprised only 0.4 percent of the company's product. We determined that it was sold at McGuckin's Hardware.

Shufford Mills gave us various tapes for testing, the dates when changes were made in yarn and scrim counts, recipes for various adhesives, and the different production periods, all of which we sent back to the FBI. In November 1997 the lab said the pieces of tape came from different production runs and had different yarn counts. Same brand, same type, different production run, therefore different tape. Apparently the end of the road.

A detective also found the Boulder portrait framer, who confirmed that the duct tape on the picture was his and that he bought his tape at McGuckin's. Once again we had spent a year chasing something that led to a dead end. The tape on the picture and the tape on the victim came from two different rolls.

The clue turned out to be not the tape itself but what was *on* it.

Back in February 1997, several fibers were taken from the sticky side of the tape that had been against JonBenét's face.

When Team Ramsey finally gave us the clothing purporting to be what John and Patsy were wearing on December 25 and 26, one of the bagged items was Patsy's red-and-black–checked jacket.

The Colorado Bureau of Investigation labs ran comparison tests and reported that four fibers that had been discovered on the tape were chemically and microscopically consistent with the fibers of Patsy's jacket.

John Ramsey had pulled the tape off JonBenét's mouth when he found the body and left the tape in the basement. Patsy did not go down there on the morning of December 26.

So how did four fibers apparently from her jacket get on the sticky inside of the tape that gagged her daughter?

I would leave it to the lawyers to quibble over how the fibers were transferred from Patsy's jacket to the tape, perhaps claiming she had worn the garment when she went downstairs to fetch Christmas presents, or perhaps there was a transfer to the blanket when she tucked JonBenét into bed. There were a myriad of distant possible arguments. Had the tape been removed from her mouth during the autopsy, the argument of transference would have been diminished.

But while the discovery of a single fiber might be argued, we had four!

Had the clothing been in our possession immediately after the crime, that connection would have been made in time for the April interviews. I would have sprung this on an unsuspecting Patsy Ramsey.

———

Even more devastating than the time delay on the jacket was the deal that was made to get the clothing. Beckner insisted there was no negative result, but I had watched Team Ramsey pull this trick too often, and demanded to know what we had to surrender this time. Beckner told us the asking price: the evidence photographs of the Ramseys in December, full access to all exculpatory evidence concerning the Ramseys, and for the police department to state publicly that there had been no evidence of prior vaginal abuse of JonBenét. They did get some photos out of it. We would have preferred to get the clothing through a search warrant that was already in preparation by Detective Kim Stewart, but that one never got off the ground either.

We gathered for the annual detective bureau luncheon on January 8, which was also the farewell salute to Eller. Twenty-five detectives showed up, Mark Beckner and Linda Arndt not among them. We had collected $410 to buy Eller a special golf club, a Big Bertha driver, as a going-away gift.

Eller spoke of our successes, the cases that had made a difference in the community, and, despite what had been done to him, he refused to say anything against the department. Detective Jane Harmer presented him with a plaque and a picture of his entire crew of detectives, except for me. I had been watching an Atlanta cemetery when it was taken.

A few days later in his office, Eller gave me a quiet warning. "The real reason that I was fired was for authorizing you and Gosage to meet and tape that informant," he said, referring to the Jeff Shapiro recordings about Alex Hunter. "Steve, those tapes saved you," Eller said. "Koby and Hunter were scared, and are still scared, about that."

He was packing his career into cardboard boxes, and I realized how much of a Renaissance Man he actually was, rather than the hard-nosed brute being portrayed by the media. Classical music always played softly in John Eller's office, his shelves contained philosophy books in addition to manuals on police procedures, and the walls were decorated with tastefully framed photographs. "My conscience is clear," he told me. "I tried to do the right thing."

He left Boulder soon thereafter, so totally broken that he did not even have enough money to hire a moving company. I helped him drive two trucks loaded with furniture to Miami on what we called "The Grapes of Wrath Tour."

Patsy Ramsey sent a back-channel invitation in early January for the Boulder Police to come to Atlanta for an interview without the lawyers. It sounded too good to be true, and it was. Other than duping her messenger, Father Rol Hoverstock of St. John's Church, nothing came of it.

"Why don't you meet with the Ramseys?" he had asked when I visited the church one day.

"That's what we're trying to do," I replied.

"No, no. They *want* to talk to you," said Rol. "The Ramseys want to meet privately, in Atlanta, and answer questions without attorneys present. Not as suspects, but to help with any information, such as which lights were on and that sort of thing."

"That would be a good start," I replied, and promised to run the idea by my superiors. Father Rol was trusted by both sides. Perhaps something might come of this. The next day I told him that the police department was willing, and all the Ramseys had to do was choose a time. "If they agree, we'll be out there on the next thing smoking," I said.

I did not mention that Commander Beckner had asked if it could wait fourteen days so we could get a better airfare.

A week later Father Rol showed up at our headquarters. Beckner joined us in a conference room, and I asked, "Any good news?"

Rol pursed his lips and shook his head. Team Ramsey lawyer Bryan Morgan had learned of the proposal and insisted on being at any meeting between the Ramseys and the Boulder cops. The pastor said he was "reamed" by the lawyer for becoming involved and had become so annoyed with the whole process, he vented his anger on all of us. "Enough of the bullshit," Rol said.

But instead of an interview, all he could now offer was a meeting over coffee in the Ramseys' living room. "That's unacceptable," I said. We weren't about to fly to Georgia for a coffee klatch with a lawyer. "We're back to square one."

I pushed back in my chair, confirmed in my belief that they had never intended to meet us unprotected by their wall of lawyers but had just been telling the good-hearted minister, who believed in their innocence, what he wanted to hear.

The next day the headline was "COPS REJECT RAMSEY OFFER TO TALK IN ATLANTA."

Despite the unofficial overture, we had held firm on a January 9 deadline of 5 P.M. for a response from Team Ramsey about whether their clients would submit to more interviews. At nineteen minutes before five o'clock, the answer was delivered—"No." They would not do it without seeing our evidence and reviewing the questions in advance. No police agency would agree to such terms.

Beckner put a personal letter from John Ramsey to DA investigator Lou Smit, dated December 18, on my desk. It had been mailed to Smit's house, and long weeks had elapsed before it reached us. "Patsy and I are so very thankful you came into our lives at this time," Ramsey wrote to Smit. It looked to me as if the investigator were being seduced.

Ramsey spent almost an entire single-spaced page fingering Santa Bill McReynolds as the killer. Was SBTC really supposed to be SBJC—Santa Bill and Janet Claus? Santa Bill wasn't as frail as he might seem, Ramsey suggested, and the ransom note indicated the cleverness of a real writer, such as Janet McReynolds.

I later telephoned Bill McReynolds, and again he answered all my questions. "I'll help with anything you need," he said. "I didn't do anything wrong." Although we had cleared the McReynolds family months ago, the DA's office and Team Ramsey would remain fixated on him.

John Ramsey suggested in his letter to Smit that other suspects might emerge. It could be anyone who read a newspaper article about his company passing the billion-dollar mark in sales, or someone who saw JonBenét riding in the Christmas parade, or maybe it was one of the customers of Access Graphics. That expanded the suspect list by another thirty thousand or so. For good measure, he threw in his loyal supporter Jim Marino as a possibility. Later in January, Marino received a voice mail message from his old pal, complimenting him for "doing such a good job [defending Ramsey] on TV." Ramsey ended the call with, "Love ya, brother!"

Fleet and Priscilla White, more former Ramsey friends, had stirred up a hornet's nest by openly criticizing DA Alex Hunter. Sensitive information they had given Hunter had appeared the very next week in a tabloid newspaper almost verbatim, and they were furious. They no longer believed that Hunter would ever take the case to trial and wanted him replaced by a special prosecutor. I thought that was a great idea.

These were witnesses to be prized, for Fleet had been in the cellar with John Ramsey when the body was discovered, and Priscilla had been with Patsy throughout the morning of December 26. Instead of being supported by the law enforcement officials, who needed their testimony, the couple were pilloried because they opposed the DA's office.

They had met with Chief Koby, who vouched for Hunter's integrity and competence. If the DA acted improperly, the chief said, he would be the one leading the charge to have Hunter removed from office. That one made me laugh, since the chief had ordered the destruction of the Shapiro sting tapes that had documented just such improprieties. In my opinion, Koby would be the last, not the first, to attack Hunter.

————

The Whites had been deeply hurt by the Ramseys' naming them as possible suspects in the murder of a little girl they loved almost as much as their own daughter. Then when Fleet challenged John Ramsey in Atlanta after the funeral, their friendship ended, and the Whites became targets of a savage attack. Not only did John Ramsey suggest that Priscilla White might have used a stun gun on JonBenét, but a Ramsey pit bull defender named Susan Stine slipped police thirty-one elaborate reasons why suspicion should fall on the Whites. The preposterous claims of suspicious behavior ranged from the entire Ramsey family possibly being drugged during the Whites' Christmas party to Priscilla enjoying room service at the Holiday Inn in Atlanta. The Whites were in the crosshairs of an assault designed to smear their credibility.

Priscilla and Fleet had both received kind notes from John and Patsy Ramsey, filled with cheery personal best wishes. The letters arrived just about the same time the Ramseys were pointing their fingers at the Whites as murder suspects. "I love you," Patsy wrote to Priscilla, who commented, "I only knew her for two years. We never loved each other." We would learn that similar notes were received by many other former friends who were also put on the list of suspects.

Detective Jane Harmer and I had formed a trusting relationship with the Whites over the previous months, handling them as gently as a couple of skittish thoroughbreds, but we knew they were reaching a boiling point. They asked, Why is the system failing? Why can't we get rid of Alex Hunter? Can we get a special prosecutor? Priscilla said the DA had told her he thought the Ramseys were involved in the crime.

The Whites said they would never again speak to the district attorney and if called before a Hunter-led grand jury would volunteer nothing. "What are they going to do?" Priscilla asked. "Throw a Boulder housewife in jail?" Fleet said he wanted to punch Alex Hunter "right in the nose."

Fleet told us that Ramsey lawyer Mike Bynum had called them shortly after the body was discovered. Surely he was talking about December 27, the night John Ramsey talked with Bynum at the Fernie house. White found his notes and said, "No, it was the day before, on the afternoon of December 26." You sure of that date? I asked. White checked his notes again. Yes.

The minds of two detectives went into overdrive. The body of Jon-Benét was found at 1:05 P.M., and John and Patsy left the house at about 2:30 P.M. Now White was saying that an attorney was already in play, calling witnesses, only a few hours later. WOW!

Fleet added that he was also interviewed by three people associated with Team Ramsey the following day, December 27, when he didn't know any better than to speak with them. The private investigators weren't out canvassing the neighborhood for an intruder but were pinpointing the Ramseys' best friends while the police were being stalled.

Commander Beckner was disturbed that Harmer and I would not share our information from the Whites with the district attorney. He suggested bringing Pete Hofstrom into our protective circle around the Whites. All I could do was blink. "Mark, the Whites will not cooperate with this district attorney's office, and for good reason," I said. "That, if anything in this case, is an absolute. Do not try to bring Pete Hofstrom into this equation. Absolutely not."

The Whites met privately with Governor Roy Romer and with State Attorney General Gale Norton, but neither would commit to intervening. Chief Koby said that Romer had called him to talk about "the crazy Whites." I could not believe how they were being treated.

Alex Hunter, Tom Koby, and Mark Beckner spent an entire afternoon huddling over the way Fleet and Priscilla were rocking the boat. They decided to take a hard line and send the prison guard, Pete Hofstrom, over to the Whites to "get their heads on straight." If the couple still refused to cooperate, said Beckner, then spending some time in the Boulder County Jail might change their minds. I found that suggestion outrageous.

It was ridiculous to think that someone like Hofstrom could intimidate Fleet White, and to threaten them with jail was absurd, for *they hadn't done anything wrong!* The reason for getting tough on the Whites had nothing to do with the pursuit of justice. The vendetta was the result of their openly criticizing the district attorney.

At breakfast one morning Fleet White showed me a three-page letter-to-the-editor he had written. He wanted to take the fight public. He smacked a big fist into his palm and said, "The whole thing stinks." Then he asked my opinion.

"I can't be part of any attempt to overthrow the district attorney," I replied, taking a careful sip of coffee to stall for time while my mind absorbed this idea of witnesses storming the ramparts.

"But personally?"

I didn't answer.

"None of the detectives would be sorry to see him go, would they?"

I didn't answer. Sergeant Wickman had told them earlier that we wished we could replace Alex Hunter with a special prosecutor.

A train wreck was about to happen. There was absolutely no way to stop it.

———

The Whites' two-thousand-word letter was printed in the local paper on January 16. In it they called for Alex Hunter to be replaced by a special prosecutor and cited what they viewed as indiscretions, poor judgment, improper relationships, and overall incompetence.

"There is a strong impression that the . . . district attorney has acted improperly by sharing evidence and other information with attorneys and other parties not officially involved in the investigation," the Whites wrote. They hammered at Hunter's tight relationships with defense lawyers, his historic lack of aggressiveness, and his leaks to the media and questioned his ability to conduct a successful prosecution. They wanted Governor Romer to intervene, although he had already backed away in private and now was forced to do so in public.

The Whites were responding, in my opinion, as the parents of the murdered child should have, but their claims were dismissed out of hand. Hunter suggested that Fleet White needed to be investigated further.

Two key witnesses had gone to war with the DA's office, and their battles would continue alongside the Ramsey investigation for months to come.

———

Detective Jane Harmer lay in a hospital bed recovering from surgery, and I took her some flowers. She was pale and in obvious pain, but all she wanted to talk about was the case. "I'll be back in a week," she promised, giving my hand a weak squeeze. Stress was killing us, but no one was giving up. I headed for New York.

27

I finally heard the magic words while seated in the book-lined office of Don Foster, an Elizabethan scholar and professor at Vassar College in upstate New York, who just happened to be a hell of a linguistic detective. "Steve," said Foster, "I believe I am going to conclude the ransom note was the work of a single individual: Patsy Ramsey."

Tall and trim, with wire-rimmed glasses and a slight mustache, Foster had the look of a mild professor, but if I were a criminal, I wouldn't want him after me. When only a University of California graduate student in 1984, he found an elegy to a murdered actor, "the late Vertuous Maister William Peter of Whipton neere Excster," and after several years of painstaking work, proved it to be a lost work of William Shakespeare from the year 1612. Anyone that dedicated tends to finish what he starts.

Since discovering the Bard's elegy, Foster had refined his techniques and made the news again when he unmasked the anonymous author of the highly publicized book *Primary Colors*. That led the FBI to use him to identify the Unabomber as Theodore Kaczynski. These days Foster's telephone was ringing off the hook as police and the corporate world sought his singular expertise in textual analysis. He was the best in the country at what he did.

District Attorney Alex Hunter enlisted his help in the Ramsey case, sending Foster a copy of the ransom note and the writing samples of various people, then following up with telephone calls. Foster told me that Hunter was particularly interested in Santa Bill and Janet McReynolds, and when the professor reported, "They didn't write that ransom note," Hunter seemed to lose interest.

The DA's office turned him over to the police, Beckner assigned him to me, and I ferried out to New York stacks of various people's writing samples. He explained that his work was based on much more than just one letter looking like another. Even the slightest things, such as the use of periods or the space before the start of a paragraph, could create a distinctive linguistic fingerprint. After all, it was the unconventional use of commas that had spurred his original theory about the Shakespeare fragment.

"We can't falsify who we are," Foster told me. "Sentence structure, word usage, and identifying features can be a signature."

Throughout the month, I furnished Foster with a wide range of material from a number of suspects so we would not be accused of stacking the deck. One of the first things he picked up on was Patsy's habit of using acronyms and acrostics in her communications. She often signed off with her initials, PAPR, and used such phrases as "To BVFMFA from PPRBSJ," which meant, "To Barbara V. Fernie, Master of Fine Arts, from Patricia Paugh Ramsey, Bachelor of Science in Journalism." That, I thought, might somehow link to the mysterious SBTC acronym on the ransom note.

Foster was concerned that Alex Hunter still occasionally called to introduce his own theories and ideas and had told Foster there was "no way the parents did this." To disclose such opinions to an independent examiner exposes them to attack in court, but Hunter didn't seem to care. The DA further risked tainting Foster by sending him copies of work done by other linguistic experts, but Foster refused to open those packets. In my opinion it was as if Hunter was trying to torpedo his own witness.

"Steer clear of him. You work for the Boulder Police Department, not the DA's office," I told Foster.

Foster told me, "He's just desperately trying to find an intruder. I'm not sure he has the resolve to pursue this in the direction that I'm seeing."

Team Ramsey severed all ties with the police department with a scathing communication that accused the Boulder detectives of one of the most serious charges that can be leveled at a cop, manipulating evidence in a murder case, which is a Class II felony. They said we were trying to pin the murder on the Ramseys in order to salvage our careers and avoid being sued for libel. We felt the threat was designed to have a chilling effect on our work.

But we had heard it all before. Despite the sideshows and what the defense lawyers may have wished, evidence was still coming in that indicated Patsy Ramsey was involved in the death of her daughter.

———

Detective Kim Stewart learned that the white cellar door had been painted in November 1995. That meant we could quit chasing anyone who had been through the basement before then and limit our search for the owner of the unidentified palm print to the thirteen months between that point and December 26, 1996. That still left us with about two thousand people to eliminate.

We also resolved the issue of pry marks being seen on a back door of the Ramsey home. Team Ramsey had carried on quite a bit about the marks, which they said indicated an intruder. But a witness came forward to report that she had pointed out those very marks to Patsy Ramsey months before the murder. There was no intruder entry there, and the Ramseys knew it all along.

Then, while reviewing a list of book titles from the Ramsey home at the request of Don Foster, I dug out the Polaroid photographs from the Evidence Room. Using magnifying glasses, evidence tech Pat Peck and I compared the titles on the list with what the pictures showed. Entire shelves of books had been overlooked.

When we checked the photos from a big manila envelope marked as evidence item #85KKY, I almost fell out of my chair, and Peck inhaled in sharp surprise. A picture showed *Webster's New Collegiate Dictionary* on a coffee table in the first floor study, the corner of the lower left-hand page sharply creased and pointing like an arrow to the word *incest*. Somebody had apparently been looking for a definition of sexual contact between family members.

Ever so slowly, our accumulated circumstantial evidence grew.

———

Deputy DA Pete Hofstrom met with Fleet and Priscilla White in late January, carrying out the threat to "get their heads on straight." I sat back to watch the prison guard "work his magic," knowing that Hofstrom was out of his league in the Whites' living room.

Commander Beckner had accompanied us and asked the couple to list their concerns. "I think our letter said it all," replied Priscilla.

Hofstrom launched into an oral résumé. Fifty-two years old, born and raised in New Jersey, left home at seventeen for California, attended junior college and worked as a guard at San Quentin. "I was the youngest guard ever promoted to sergeant," he boasted and unrolled a few prison stories. The Whites and I wondered when he was going to talk about the murder of JonBenét Ramsey.

Instead Hofstrom droned on about coming to Colorado, working in the Boulder County Jail, getting a law degree, and starting at the DA's office. Another San Quentin story, then how he didn't have much money and could look forward to only a small pension after committing his life to being the chief trial deputy and overseeing the felony division. The Whites glanced at me. *Weren't we supposed to discuss the Ramsey case?* He spoke of being in poor health and having to take four medications because of his high blood pressure. He called himself "an evidence man" and "passionately committed to solving the Ramsey murder."

When Priscilla couldn't stand it any longer, she pointed her finger at him. "We served that little girl her last meal. She was our daughter's best friend. We were among the last to see her alive. So don't tell us about commitment and passion," she seethed. "Don't ever think your office will carry the same kind of passion and commitment to this case that we have." The room went silent.

Hofstrom told of the hundreds of living rooms in which he had explained the criminal justice system in arranging plea bargains. He said that once the Whites understood what was happening, they would return to the fold. Fleet was unmoved. "We won't cooperate until changes are made," said White. "We want an outside prosecutor."

I made it back to headquarters just as Beckner was telling the detectives that "Pete Hofstrom did a fantastic job with the Whites." I wondered if we had been at the same house.

"They didn't like him at all, Mark, and they aren't going to cooperate without a special prosecutor," I said.

"Well, screw them. Let's just write them off," Beckner fumed. He held a thumb and forefinger close together. "The Whites are about that far away from an obstruction-of-justice charge."

The detective team briefings had grown brutal in January, filled with accusations and acrimony, and this one was no different.

Detective Harmer said she agreed with the Whites and thought a special prosecutor was needed.

"It's not even an option," Beckner said, his face turning red. "The DA has this case, and that's just the way it is." He was livid as he realized he had lost control of still another briefing. "I don't want to hear any more bitching coming from you. I'm tired of it!" he barked. Detective Kim Stewart opened the door and hung a Do Not Disturb sign on the knob.

Beckner shocked us by declaring that within three to six months the investigation would wind down. Game over. Then he told us that he wanted an alibi for *every* person involved in the case. Everybody? I considered this straight out of the Hofstrom-DeMuth playbook and quite impossible because the list would be in the thousands.

The commander had reversed his pledge to allow us to stop chasing obvious dead-end leads, causing further resentment among his detectives. Tips were still flooding in from all over the country. A former Connecticut state senator told us that a serial child killer was involved with a nationwide bomb and extortion plan. A call from California alerted us that John Ramsey's "abandoned son" worked as a restaurant short-order cook. The wackos were sucking up our investigative time. Detective Gosage demanded, "How long are we going to chase every freak and psychopath out there?"

"We've got to run these people down and clear their alibis," the edgy Beckner replied.

The detectives were getting hot too. "Don't you think we're human?" asked an exasperated Detective Jane Harmer, who had come up empty after checking out all forty-seven registered pedophiles in Boulder County and had prowled the kiddy beauty pageant subculture, where parents knew each other and any pedophile would stand out like a sore thumb. "Don't you think we'd love to find an intruder? To find that a parent didn't commit this horrible crime? With suspect after suspect we hope to find that one link that would put some monster inside the house. But that's not where the evidence is leading us."

"If we had the same evidence against an intruder, his ass would be upside down in the county jail by now," I said. "Why do we have no clear goal or clear mission or target?"

Beckner was now beet red. "There is direction in this case!" His voice rose to a near-shriek. "There is a big picture! Does anyone in this room think we have enough proof beyond a reasonable doubt?"

"That's just it," another detective responded. "We'll never get there if we keep chasing every possible intruder who comes along." He held up an anonymous letter from Altoona, Pennsylvania, that offered a screwball theory. "This stuff won't crack the fuckin' case."

Beckner admitted that he had reached a "bond of trust" with Pete Hofstrom in the DA's office and "we can share everything." Someone laughed out loud at that, goading the commander to shout at us to shut up.

The commander had decided to bypass our Dream Team and was now taking his cues from Hofstrom. The detectives felt there was no mystery about why. If Beckner wanted to become chief, he needed to work with the DA's office and was already parroting their line of "acceptable concessions" the police could make to lure the Ramseys to the interview table.

He had done a complete flip-flop, abandoned us, and in my opinion, he never came back.

On the last day of January, Day 400 of this eternal investigation, Detective Harmer discovered that only ten days before the December 23, 1996, party at the Ramsey house, there had been another function there, with caterers serving eighty people. More than six dozen new potential suspects, and Beckner's orders were to "check every one," even though we didn't know who the hell they were.

28

In the first week of February the Ramseys added their eleven-year-old son, Burke, to the stable of relatives being represented by Atlanta attorney Jim Jenkins, then went on vacation to Spain; Detective Linda Arndt sued the police department, citing emotional distress and a sullied reputation; and without warning and for no reason I could ascertain, Commander Beckner told a briefing of patrol officers that there were only two suspects and that an arrest warrant was drafted.

The detectives had consulted a couple of experts in an attempt to answer four questions concerning the DNA issues: What did we have? What did it reveal? Where do we go now? Would DNA solve this case?

A special briefing by molecular biologists Melissa Weber of CellMark Laboratories and Kathy Dressel of the Colorado Bureau of Investigation provided no miracles. The results remained frustrating and ambiguous, and even the experts did not agree on everything. Among their findings was that the DNA might not be related to the murder at all. Other results were open to interpretation.

- A head hair found at the scene appeared to belong to JonBenét.
- The primary DNA from the panties also appeared to be from her. But a secondary DNA source may have been present. If that secondary material was a mixture from two or more people, then the labs could exclude no one. Faint DNA results may have been due to "technical or stutter artifact."

It might be as simple as JonBenét having put on a playmate's underwear in which foreign DNA already existed. On the other hand, the mixture that had been found was complicated by a myriad of technical factors, including quality, quantity, degradation, and possible contamination. That meant that excluding people *might* be possible, but positive identification was unlikely.

· The fingernails of the left hand presented uncertain technical issues. JonBenét appeared to be the primary DNA source, but the experts could not exclude any male as the donor of a secondary source that was present. Issues included the possibility that multiple DNA had been under her nails for several days.

The experts noted no blood or skin tissue beneath the fingernails, as they often see when a victim has fought an attacker. However, DNA can be deposited by someone merely dragging their nails across their own cheek.

· The fingernails of the right hand were equally ambiguous, with JonBenét again appearing to be the primary donor and once again an unidentified secondary male DNA present.

· They drew no firm conclusions regarding the pubic hair. It was deemed, however, that it might not be a pubic hair at all but possibly a hair from a chest or beneath an arm. That would confuse things even more.

We would later discuss the cleanliness of the victim, including not washing her hands, wetting the bed, not wiping thoroughly after a bowel movement, and hating to have her fingernails trimmed. Weber said that the DNA beneath the fingernails could have come from anywhere, particularly if it had been there for several days, and that degradation was a concern.

They explained that obtaining additional DNA samples from any new suspects would not necessarily assist in an identification. Because of the possibility of mixtures from more than one source, conclusive determinations could not be reached.

Their results could be argued a number of ways, and defense lawyers surely would say that any unknown DNA found came from an intruder, although in fact hardly anyone could be excluded.

We could not determine whose DNA it was, when it was deposited, or if it had been degraded.

The DA's people apparently didn't hear what we heard, for Deputy DA DeMuth immediately announced that the results did not "match" John Ramsey. He said we must now locate and obtain DNA samples from any "potential suspect." Such a list would be endless. The best bet was that new equipment and DNA-testing methods might some day crack this part of the mystery.

————

With those inconclusive findings, the district attorney asked Henry Lee if he would "unravel the DNA mess," and Lee refused, suggesting that the FBI lab do that. "Adequate and complete [DNA] testing should have been done long ago," he scolded.

Hunter then asked what we should do to solve the case, and Lee replied that he was only a scientist who could advise on evidence collection, testing, and results. Figuring out what it all meant in the company of other evidence would be somebody else's job. "This case," he said, "will be a war of experts."

Trying to sound optimistic at a news conference later, Lee told reporters our chances had *risen* to fifty-fifty.

————

It had become difficult for me to get out of bed in the morning, so I would just lie there for a few minutes, staring at the ceiling and psyching myself up for another day with this ugly, sleazy case.

A talk show prattled on about the bungling cops of Boulder as I drove through a cold and snowy morning. I wanted to call in and tell them we had probable cause but weren't allowed to make an arrest.

The windowless SitRoom had taken on the oppressive feeling of a prison cell, and I felt as if I had aged ten years. "Come on in," another detective called. "This place will suck the life right out of you."

Although we had been strapped for manpower from the start, some of the detectives who had only recently been brought aboard to help already wanted out.

Detective Kim Stewart, the best investigator in the department, wanted to get back on midnight patrol duty and away from the Ramsey mess. Another detective had been screamed at and mocked as a "fucking incompetent" by Ramsey friend Susan Stine, and when he reported the incident to Mark Beckner, the commander responded, "I need to call Susan and apologize." The detective put on his overcoat and stalked away without a word. We called it Mission Impossible.

"Someday," I told Detective Gosage, "this case will be held up as a model on how not to run a major investigation."

————

I urgently needed to do more work in Atlanta. None of the palm prints submitted to the CBI matched the single unidentified one from the door to the little basement room. But we had never collected the prints of four family members who had stayed in the house—Don and Nedra Paugh and their daughters Pam and Polly.

While in Atlanta, I could also knock on the door of John Ramsey's former mistress, Jodi Roberts, and interview her. Ramsey had described her as being very emotional and claimed that she "seduced" him. In the April interviews, he described her as a vengeful person, but hadn't offered any clues as to where we could find her. I had spent a year tracking her down, and friends described her as a sweet, beautiful lady. Somebody was wrong.

Cops know that talking to former lovers can provide a treasure chest of information that the person being investigated would just as soon keep hushed up. Since we had to clear Roberts as a suspect anyway, I wanted to hear what she had to say about her affair with John Ramsey.

When I suggested going to Atlanta, Beckner asked if I could interview Roberts by phone instead. The same day I was told the budget could not cover an airline ticket, but Chief Koby hired a new consultant to provide "emotional survival training" for the police department's executive staff.

Another year would pass before detectives flew to Atlanta to talk with the ex-mistress. Agent John Lang of the Georgia Bureau of Investigation eventually obtained the Paugh family's prints, in the presence of their lawyer.

———————

Detective Gosage believed you could watch the Super Bowl in less time than it took Beckner to run a meeting, and we were in the middle of still another one.

The commander discussed an extraordinary case in Florida in which the parents had refused to cooperate with the cops, got a lawyer, and pleaded their innocence on television. Within weeks the Florida detectives were up on a Title-3 electronic surveillance and recorded the mother saying, "The baby's dead and buried . . . because you did it." The father replied, "I wish I hadn't harmed her—it was the cocaine."

I considered the irony of Beckner discussing a Title-3 that worked damned well in Florida when he had been a part of the scandal-frightened leadership that wouldn't let us try the same tactic.

Instead Beckner was now proposing that we adopt a "long view" strategy. Plan A was to wait until Burke turned eighteen years old and then "get a detective close to him." Plan B was to put a wire on Father Rol and have the minister visit Patsy when she lay on her deathbed in some future year. Terrific, hard-charging cop stuff.

"We'll document one hell of a case. Someday, someone will talk," he said, avoiding words like *solve* and *arrest*. He just wanted to check off the boxes on his beloved to-do list and hand this monster off to somebody else. The meeting droned on as we wearily covered the same names and topics we discussed day after day. When the commander went around the table for status reports on a number of individuals, we answered in monotones:

"Santa Bill didn't kill JonBenét."
"Linda Hoffmann-Pugh didn't kill JonBenét."
"Joe Barnhill didn't kill JonBenét."
"The picture framer didn't kill JonBenét."
"Jeff Merrick didn't kill JonBenét."
"Priscilla White didn't kill JonBenét."
"Tom Carson didn't kill JonBenét."

He left the room and soon afterward confided to Sergeant Wickman that he might be losing control of the detectives, who challenged him openly now. "You're right," Wickman said.

————

We had no idea what the DA's office was up to but knew they weren't just sitting over there in the Justice Center twiddling their thumbs. We gave them copies of our reports and received precious little in return. Beckner said they were taking no investigative actions until we turned over the case. That wasn't true.

A friend who was an FBI agent tipped me that a Michigan State professor was working on the Ramsey case at the request of the DA's office. The professor had talked to the FBI about crime scene photos and the ligature, had wondered if Burke Ramsey might be the killer, and admitted speaking about the case with other people. "Just thought you should know what's going on," the agent said.

They were going behind our backs and spreading evidence around the country. Hunter was telling another expert that his investigators were looking for "a third weapon, a camera tripod." Wickman punched a wall in frustration when I told him.

————

On February 25 the mayor chewed me out. This politician was meddling in a criminal investigation, probably in violation of the city charter, and didn't know what the hell he was talking about, while Commander Beckner sat there watching, doing nothing to defend his detective.

Mayor Bob Greenlee wore khakis, loafers, a blue sports jacket, and no smile when I met him in Beckner's office. "The mayor wants to ask you a few questions," my boss said and retreated to a chair.

"Detective," Mayor Greenlee began, all business. "What do you know about Jackie Dilson?" He gave me no chance to respond, and I had to suppress a grin. I knew all about Jackie Dilson, who was a regular visitor to police headquarters with her theory that her boyfriend probably murdered JonBenét.

Greenlee said he had personally met with Miss Dilson. "Did you know, detective, that her boyfriend, Chris Wolf, had Hi-Tec boots that Dilson purchased for him, that are by now undoubtedly in the bottom of some river?

"Did you know, detective, that Dilson gave the DA's investigators evidence that could be tested in this case?"

Greenlee's ruddy face was tinged with contempt, and I stole a glance at Beckner, who looked away from me.

"Detective, did you know Wolf had a flashlight similar to the one used in the murder? Detective, have you tested the rope that Dilson surrendered to you in this case? Detective, did you know Wolf was orphaned and raised by a beauty pageant queen mother whom he despised?" I was amused more than angry.

Greenlee eventually ran out of breath and let me speak.

Jackie Dilson, I told him, was nothing new. I had dealt with her for more than a year as she wove a sensational story about her boyfriend, Chris Wolf, tailoring it almost weekly to match the latest reports from the tabloids. When we decided there was nothing to it, we cut her loose, and she bounced to the DA's investigators, Team Ramsey, the sheriff's office, the district attorney's office, and back to us, always adding new tidbits of information. Now she had peddled her package to the mayor, and the sucker had bought the whole thing. Congratulations, Jackie, I thought, you've reached the summit.

I answered Greenlee's points one by one. I tried not to be insubordinate, but it was hard. "Did *you* know, *sir,* that the rope was not sent to the lab because it wasn't the same type used in the murder? Did you know, sir, that the evidence she gave the DA's office came with built-in problems such as authentication and seizure issues that make it useless in court?"

Greenlee shot back that just because I thought she might be embellishing her story did not mean we should not investigate Chris Wolf. "We need to check this out!" the mayor snorted. "We need a *thorough* investigation into this!" I guess he wanted me to cower in his presence.

Greenlee trapped himself, not me. "We *are* thoroughly investigating him," I replied. Even as we spoke, Chris Wolf was in an interview room voluntarily giving handwriting, hair, and DNA samples and a statement. The police cleared him.

Still not ready to give up, the mayor turned to Beckner with a warning. "If Dilson goes to *Inside Edition* or *Hard Copy,* you'll be embarrassed. We don't need any more embarrassment."

Commander Beckner followed the mayor out of the office, down the hallway, and into the parking lot. If Greenlee had stopped quickly, Beckner's nose would have been broken.

———

We came very close to exhuming the body of JonBenét Ramsey.

Throughout February we wrestled with that vexing question, because experts said the body might yield information on a wide range of points, from the vaginal trauma to settling the stun gun theory. The very idea was anathema to us all, and everyone agreed that before proceeding we needed assurances that vital questions would indeed be answered. Otherwise we would look like monsters.

The problem was psychological, not tactical or physical. The child had been laid to rest, and digging her up was almost unthinkable. This was one of the most shocking actions a government could take.

Commander Beckner said he was "leaning toward" doing it and assigned me to call once again upon the Georgia Bureau of Investigation for help. "No problem," said GBI special agent John Lang. He soon came back with the details from the GBI attorneys, who said the only thing they needed was a comprehensive search warrant, medically researched and specific, with the facts clearly delineated, stating why we needed an exhumation.

Legal and strategic details were worked out simultaneously. A tent would shield the site from any media or helicopters. A coroner and our forensic and medical experts would be standing by to work in a private GBI facility. Remove the body around 3 A.M., take her away in a secure convoy for the tests, return and rebury her the same day.

Lang said that Georgia law would be researched to determine if advance parental notification was needed, because the GBI would do it strictly by the book. But they would not allow it to become entangled in back-and-forth negotiations with Team Ramsey lawyers. Notification, if required, would be given by a brief call from a cell phone at the grave site, with a backhoe already in place. When the call ended, they would dig.

In a matter of days, the GBI said Atlanta was ready to go.

But the operation was then canceled because the negatives were greater than the possibility of finding conclusive evidence.

Once again, Lang was astonished at Boulder-style justice. "I may not be the most educated guy around, but hey, Mister Prosecutor, let the chips fall where they may. Either place your bet or fold, because this case ain't going to get any better."

No matter what plans fell through in Atlanta, Lang continued to help. He was now starting each day at the Moonbeam coffee shop near the Ramsey home. Patsy was in there almost every morning, sometimes with a girlfriend, and had been mentioning JonBenét. Lang told me he hoped that by becoming a familiar face, he might get close enough to overhear something worthwhile. He never gave up.

29

The DA's office called John and Patsy Ramsey "prime suspects" for the first time in March 1998 and said there was sufficient probable cause for a grand jury indictment.

I had dreamed for months of having a grand jury support the detectives with subpoena powers that would break through the wall of silence, because our hunt for the killer had stalled. Elsewhere I had worked with grand juries that were powerful bodies, headed by aggressive prosecutors who used their awesome legal powers to get major indictments.

So when I learned of the DA's change of position, I wanted to be optimistic that they might finally start acting like prosecutors. I should have known better.

First District Attorney Bill Wise had noted that a good prosecutor could indict a ham sandwich. After seeing the DA's plan, I knew the sandwich was in no danger.

I wasn't at all surprised in the fall of 1999 when the Ramsey grand jury came back empty-handed after more than a year of on-again, off-again investigation. From the very start, the whole thing troubled me and was destined to fail.

Our Dream Team had been on the sidelines but came through for us at a critical moment. When Deputy DA Pete Hofstrom proclaimed that a grand jury could not be used as an investigative body, our guys responded, "Wrong."

Bob Miller, the former U.S. Attorney, personally explained the law to Alex Hunter and his lieutenants and pointed out that grand juries were used all the time to conduct investigations. The process was used so seldom by Alex Hunter's office that the Boulder prosecutors didn't understand it. Still, Hunter was uneasy and asked, "We need to do this, huh?"

When Miller confirmed that it was indeed a necessity, he also suggested that the district attorney hire outside help to run the grand jury. Hunter agreed, tacitly acknowledging that not a single prosecutor on his staff of twenty-five attorneys was capable of doing the job. For now, however, Pete Hofstrom remained in charge, and Hofstrom had just been embarrassed. He wasn't going to make it easy.

––––––––

A few days later in the SitRoom, I sat through one of the most unbelievable briefings of the case as Commander Beckner explained Hofstrom's grand jury parameters.

The commander began with the extraordinary revelation that "people in the DA's office" were now saying that John and Patsy Ramsey were the "prime suspects," although he did not mention why they had come to that realization. Then he added that the DA's people also agreed that enough probable cause existed to obtain a grand jury indictment.

After a brief burst of hope, my heart sank as Beckner outlined their game plan.

- The grand jury might have the sole mission of helping us secure records, testimony, and evidence.
- It might not hear the entire case at all.
- It would not be used to obtain an indictment.
- And if a "runaway" grand jury somehow returned an indictment on its own, the DA would not be obligated to prosecute.

"It would be a travesty to [indict and] lose a weak case at trial," said Beckner, echoing the odious no-win outlook.

I was totally bewildered. They believed they could get an indictment against the prime suspect in a murder that had captivated the interest of the world, and were not going to do so.

In my opinion, this was just another deception to buy more time to pray for a miracle confession. They seemed willing to go to extraordinary lengths, even to distort the grand jury process, to avoid a courtroom fight with Team Ramsey.

Our next order of business, said Beckner, would be a "formal presentation" of our case to *convince* Pete Hofstrom why we needed a grand jury at all. I believe we lost both ways on this one. If we did not convince the prison guard, we wouldn't get the necessary grand jury subpoena power. If we did succeed, the police department would surrender control of the case, and the DA's office would take up to six months after our presentation to decide whether to actually call a grand jury.

The conditions were galling. In my opinion it was time to step up and take a swing. This case was for a jury to decide, not some bureaucrat in the DA's office. Who knows? You might just win! It was like watching a building burn down and being unable to do anything about it.

Hofstrom piled on stringent conditions. He wanted the specific particulars for a grand jury in writing, which our Dream Team cautioned against, because it would be "discoverable" by defense lawyers. It could be done verbally, they said, without risk.

Then he resurrected DeMuth's Five-Year Plan of interviewing everyone in Boulder County plus everyone who had passed through in the last couple of years. Had every "reluctant" witness been interviewed by police, and "if not, why not?" "Have you attached a transcript of each interview, and a copy of each report, or witness information sheet or relevant interview notes for that person to the list? If not, why not?" On and on it went. "If not, why not?" became a familiar refrain.

He wanted us to detail what each person would testify to, why we thought so, and the reason why they should appear before a grand jury. At times we had a hard time figuring out what the hell he was even talking about, such as when he wrote, "What is the relevance and materiality of that testimony to the issue of whether or not there is sufficient admissible evidence to file a charge against an identifiable person in this case?"

To get things under way, Beckner wanted each uncooperative witness "rated." I could imagine asking the Lunch Bunch in Atlanta, "Hey, just wondering, are you cooperative, semicooperative, reluctant, hostile, and if none or all of the above, how would you rate yourself on a one-to-ten scale?"

And the formal presentation idea was highly unusual and unprecedented in Boulder. A disgusted Detective Gosage stormed in with perhaps the longest speech I ever heard him make: "We've given them half a dozen presentations over the past months! Nothing has changed! We sat around and showed them how the evidence pointed at the Ramseys, and they argued that it was an intruder. I won't sit through another bullshit dog and pony show. Let's drop it in their laps and walk away. They can do with it what they want."

———

As a final insult, Hofstrom decreed that the law allowed only a couple of investigators to serve any grand jury. Wrong again, according to our advisers. In any case, none of the line detectives who had worked the case for the past fourteen months and knew it down to the last detail would be chosen.

The four being considered were DA investigator Lou Smit and Deputy DA Trip DeMuth, with the police "possibly" represented by Commander Mark Beckner or Sergeant Wickman.

I could not see Pete Hofstrom, after a career of plea bargains, pushing to get this case to trial. Now he would lead a team that included Smit, who thought the Ramseys were innocent; DeMuth, whom I thought had bent over backward to accommodate Team Ramsey; Beckner, an administrator who was trying hard to become chief of police; and Wickman, a demoralized police sergeant who hadn't even been told a grand jury was going to be called.

Eventually, at the end of April, twelve jurors and five alternates were chosen to serve on the grand jury. Among those helping to pick the panel were Lou Smit and Trip DeMuth.

———

The DA's office wanted us to admit openly that the police had "no prosecutable case" before a grand jury was summoned. That would be their life raft, for if things didn't work out, they could point to those words and say, "See, even the cops said they didn't have it."

"Depends on what you mean by *prosecutable*," Detective Gosage observed.

Commander Beckner instead offered a cautious compromise: "We agree that at this particular point in time, sufficient admissible evidence does not currently exist to reasonably expect a *conviction*."

Beckner also issued a press release stating, "We have worked well with the DA's office in the last five months, and I expect to work closer with them in the months that follow." That left the detectives shaking their heads. It was a publicity spin that all was well in Camelot.

————

On unlucky Friday the 13 in March:

- One of the first officers to arrive at one of the most colossally bungled crime scenes of all times was assigned to teach "crime scene response" to a training class of new Boulder cops.
- Sergeant Tom Wickman was by now so far out of the leadership loop that he learned of the grand jury request from reading a newspaper in the distant town of Ouray.
- And Commander Beckner told me to discontinue the thick Master Affidavit, saying it would never be used for an arrest.

A few days later we were ordered to hand over to Deputy DA Trip DeMuth all personal journals, notes, diaries, and anything else in which we may have written any observations about the Ramsey case, whether or not the documents were part of the official case file. We weren't even allowed to have personal thoughts? The police department attorney, Bob Keatley, told Beckner that Constitutional issues were involved and that there would be no such seizure, particularly in a case in which no one had been charged.

We had become the most dysfunctional law enforcement organization in America.

I could relate to the comment of the out-of-body narrator in Haruki Murakami's book *The Wind-Up Bird Chronicle*: "My reality seemed to have left me and now was wandering around nearby."

————

Sergeant Wickman finally gave the DA's office our long-held secrets about the enhanced 911 telephone call that recorded young Burke's voice although his parents insisted he had been asleep and about the grave-surveillance operations in Atlanta. Pete Hofstrom rested his chin on his chest, staring, while Trip DeMuth sat silently, "stunned" that we had done this without their knowledge, Wickman said.

During their discussion, Wickman used a term from my warrant for the covert surveillance in Atlanta, which had been to look for any "suspicious grave-site visitor." Within a week we got a call from Patsy

Ramsey's sister Pam, who wanted to report a "suspicious grave-site visitor." The exact term from my sealed warrant had found its way into Pam Paugh's lexicon. We simply could not trust the DA's office to keep anything a secret.

———

Detective Jane Harmer called the number of Patsy's parents in Atlanta to discuss the "grave-site visitor," and Patsy answered. It was only the third time that a Boulder detective had spoken to her since the murder.

Speaking in a flat monotone, Patsy said that the suspicious man in the cemetery had carried pictures of JonBenét cut from magazines, was in his fifties, from Hagerstown, Pennsylvania, and had a stuttering problem. They did not get a license plate number, and although her sister Polly rushed to tell nearby firefighters about the man, she did not call the police. Informing firefighters instead of the Marietta cops made no sense at all to me.

Patsy paused, then asked, "Are the detectives close?"

"We're very close," Harmer responded, hastily scribbling notes.

They exchanged a few pleasantries, then Patsy said, "You know I want to be out there every day" and related a dream in which she was "sitting down with the police . . . to work together."

I mouthed silently, "Ask if she will talk to us," and Harmer said, "The detectives want to talk with you, too, Patsy, and with John." The feeling was mutual, Patsy said, but the attorneys claimed the police were only trying to frame her and her husband. The lawyers, she said, would not be happy if they found out she was speaking to the police at all.

It's your decision, not theirs, Harmer parried, and Patsy replied that the lawyers were being paid to give advice, so she had to heed it. She was playing her usual coy game of offering to cooperate, then pulling away before anything could happen.

Then she ventured the suggestion that Mark Beckner could fly to Atlanta for a talk to "rebuild trust."

"Believe me, no one wants this more than me," Patsy told Harmer. "Whoever did this is sitting there laughing."

"This is absolute bullshit," I whispered to Wickman. They had avoided mentioning the mysterious grave visitor to the local cops, and she was tugging our chain with the possibility of a private meeting, the same ploy she had used with Father Rol. I knew it wasn't going to happen.

When the call ended, we told Beckner to accept the invitation immediately. Let's get on a plane, go down there, and knock on her door, we urged him. Wear a wire, ask questions. Seize the day! He declined.

Commander Beckner suggested instead that Detective Jane Harmer try to continue her "telephone relationship" with Patsy.

Meanwhile we had found out that while the Ramseys would not talk to us, they were giving interviews for a film being cobbled together by a University of Colorado journalism teacher and two *Newsweek* reporters. It became known as their "crockumentary."

Don Foster from Vassar, the top linguistics man in the country, made his conclusion firm in March. "In my opinion, it is not possible that any individual except Patsy Ramsey wrote the ransom note," he told a special briefing in Boulder, adding that she had been unassisted in writing it.

With his sterling academic reputation and a track record of 152–0 in deciphering anonymous writings, this should have been a thunderbolt of evidence, but the DA's office, without telling us, had already discredited and discarded the professor. His coming to Boulder was a big waste of time.

In our case, Foster examined hundreds of writing samples from people ranging from family members to Internet addicts, from neighbors to Chris Wolf to the McReynolds family, and a library of books, films, and videotapes.

Patsy Ramsey wrote it, he said. "Those are her words."

While Foster made that dramatic statement, Deputy DA Pete Hofstrom read a book and didn't look up. He occasionally rubbed his head and ignored the expert. I believed Hofstrom had already decided that Foster, with his definitive report, would never go before the grand jury, and he never did.

But that day in March, he built a wall of linguistic evidence before our eyes, brick by brick.

He explained that language is infinitely diverse and that no two people use it in quite the same way. They do not have the same vocabulary, use identical spelling and punctuation, construct sentences in the same manner, read the same books, or express the same beliefs and ideas. Ingrained and unconscious habits are virtually impossible to conceal, even if a writer tries to disguise his identity, he said. "Individuals are prisoners of their own language."

Foster dissected the ransom note, explained that the wording contained intelligent and sometimes clever usage of language, and said the text suggested someone who was trying to deceive.

The documents he studied from Patsy Ramsey, in his opinion, formed "a precise and unequivocal match" with the ransom note. He read a list of "unique matches" with the note that included such things as her penchant for inventing private acronyms, spelling habits, indentation, alliterative phrasing, metaphors, grammar, vocabulary, frequent use of exclamation points, and even the format of her handwriting on the page.

Chief Koby was so impressed that over lunch he confided in total seriousness, "You know, this is exactly what Hunter has thought from day one—that Patsy did it."

In the afternoon session, Foster explained why the "foreign terrorists" claim was "transparently inauthentic" and that the $118,000 ransom demand could have had its genesis from three points: the Ramsey home computer held the net liabilities figure of $1,118,000; Patsy Ramsey referred to Psalm 118 in some of her writings; and she had access to the pay stub containing that almost precise bonus figure. A stranger would not have had such inside information.

He pointed out how the odd usage "and hence" appeared both in the ransom note and in her 1997 Christmas letter.

The professor examined the construction of the letter "a" in the ransom note and in Patsy's handwriting and noted how her writing changed abruptly after the death of JonBenét.

In the decade prior to the homicide, Patsy freely interchanged the manuscript "a" and the cursive "*a*." But in the months prior to December 1996, she exhibited a marked preference for the manuscript "a." The ransom note contained such a manuscript "a" 109 times and the cursive version only 5 times. But after the Ramseys were given a copy of the ransom note, Foster found only a single manuscript "a" in her writing, while the cursive "*a*" now appeared 1,404 times!

That lone exception was in the sample that her mother had unexpectedly handed to Detective Gosage in Atlanta.

Not only did certain letters change, but her entire writing style seemed to have been transformed after the homicide. There were new ways of indenting, spelling, and writing out long numbers that contrasted with her earlier examples, and she was the only suspect who altered her usual preferences when supplying writing samples to the police.

Foster used an overhead projector to describe Patsy Ramsey's habit of creating acronyms and acrostics, which she did with astonishing frequency.

We had never found a satisfactory explanation for the S.B.T.C. sign-off on the ransom note until Foster drew our attention to John Ramsey's Bible, which was found open at Psalms 35 and 36 on his desk. Aloud, Foster read the first four verses:

Contend, O Lord, with those who contend with me; fight against
    those who fight against me.
Take up shield and buckler; arise and come to my aid.
Brandish spear and javelin against those who pursue me.
Say to my soul, "I am your salvation."

He pointed to the first letter of each verse and showed that they produced the acronym CTBS—the reversal of SBTC. Those letters appear in that arrangement nowhere else in the Bible, in either sequence. It was difficult to believe that the terrorists who killed the child had also been up in the third-floor study reading the Ramsey Bible.

On and on Foster probed, racing through numerous compelling points that left little doubt the ransom note came from Patsy's hand. The Vassar scholar explained that as people change over time, they incorporate some of what they read and experience into their language. "The Ramsey library contains many books that were sources for Patsy Ramsey's nineteen ninety-five and ninety-six writings, many of which also contain startling verbal or other detailed parallels with the Ramsey homicide and attendant staging, including language that appears in the ransom note," he said.

When Foster was done, DA Alex Hunter said he "needed time to digest" the mass of information that had been presented. Pete Hofstrom closed his book and walked away, seemingly bored.

I was totally engrossed by the presentation and thought Foster had thoroughly tied Patsy to the ransom note. It was a bombshell of evidence. So why did the DA's office seem so dismissive?

———

The district attorney continued to call Foster privately over the coming weeks, and Foster told me he was puzzled by Hunter's reluctance to move forward. "How can anyone still think this was the work of an intruder? This case appears solved. Now it needs to be prosecuted."

The answer came several weeks later when Pete Hofstrom sent over a package from an Internet junkie named Susan Bennett, who had been in contact with Lou Smit.

Her material indicated that back when Foster was just another Internet observer without access to official information, he had gotten involved in an Internet chat about JonBenét with Susan Bennett, who used the name of Jameson on the Net. Foster once guessed incorrectly that the anonymous Jameson was really John Andrew Ramsey, the oldest son of John Ramsey.

Then Foster wrote a letter to Patsy Ramsey, suggesting that he thought she was innocent. Those statements were made *before* Foster was brought aboard to look at the case file, after which he changed his conclusion 180 degrees. To me, that only strengthened his position, not weakened it, for it showed he had no anti-Ramsey bias. Once the professor had access to the actual case documents, he changed his mind.

Bob Keatley, our in-house counsel, then pointed to the postmark on the envelope, *July 1997.*

One detective yelled, "They've had these fucking documents for ten months!" It had lain in the DA's case file all year, while I was working with Foster, and Hunter himself was calling the professor with suggestions.

The DA's office knew all about the damaging information before the professor conducted his studies or came to Boulder and even while Hunter was pumping him about other possible suspects. In my opinion, Foster apparently had value until the moment he pointed his finger at Patsy Ramsey.

I believed that if Foster had said Santa Bill McReynolds or Chris Wolf or any of a dozen other suspects wrote the note, the DA's office would have been off and running after them. But now Pete Hofstrom dismissed Foster with a terse "The defense would eat him alive."

They should have fought to use Foster's expertise as the premier linguist in the nation, and explained to the jurors the totally different conditions under which he made his earlier statements. That's what courtroom argument is for. Take your best shot, and let the jury decide. The defense might have eaten him alive, but Foster might have taken a bite out of them instead.

With Foster's conclusion and the panel of doctors who confirmed prior vaginal trauma, we felt we had met the criteria set by Pete Hofstrom for prosecution.

Instead Foster was consigned to the DA's junk pile. Losing him was a devastating blow.

30

Police Chief Tom Koby was forced from office by a junta of the acting city manager, the new mayor, and the city council, and wheels were set in motion to replace him by June. He was transferred to the office of the city manager at his full annual salary of $102,353 to work on "special projects." Koby saw it differently. "I was fired," he told me.

He lashed out before he left with a department-wide e-mail, chiding officers who let "everyone else do the work" and to "grow up and join the real world." Zen had collapsed.

The firing of Koby left the entire city hierarchy in flux. The mayor had resigned, the city manager quit, the police chief and a police commander were fired, and the deputy city manager slot was vacant, as were the positions of planning director and director of human resources.

District Attorney Alex Hunter was untouched by the chaos, his position unassailable.

Lou Smit and I picked up regular coffees at Peabody's coffee shop and took a table. It was good to see him again, although he was not totally recovered from a three-week bout with meningitis. At a quiet table we went round and round on the Ramsey case, from the 911 call to the grand jury, and did not change our opinions.

For the first time I put my personal theory into words. I did not think John Ramsey was involved in the death itself, because we had found nothing to indicate that. I now viewed him as a man standing by his wife, insulating her with lawyers. There was no doubt in my mind that Patsy wrote the note. "I believe she committed the murder," I told Smit and proceeded to lay out what I thought had happened that night.

In my hypothesis, an approaching fortieth birthday, the busy holiday season, an exhausting Christmas Day, and an argument with JonBenét had left Patsy frazzled. Her beautiful daughter, whom she frequently dressed almost as a twin, had rebelled against wearing the same outfit as her mother.

When they came home, John Ramsey helped Burke put together a Christmas toy. JonBenét, who had not eaten much at the Whites' party, was hungry. Her mother let her have some pineapple, and then the kids were put to bed. John Ramsey read to his little girl. Then he went to bed. Patsy stayed up to prepare for the trip to Michigan the next morning, a trip she admittedly did not particularly want to make.

Later JonBenét awakened after wetting her bed, as indicated by the plastic sheets, the urine stains, the pull-up diaper package hanging halfway out of a cabinet, and the balled-up turtleneck found in the bathroom. I concluded that the little girl had worn the red turtleneck to bed, as her mother originally said, and that it was stripped off when it got wet.

As I told Smith, I never believed the child was sexually abused for the gratification of the offender but that the vaginal trauma was some sort of corporal punishment. The dark fibers found in her pubic region could have come from the violent wiping of a wet child. Patsy probably yanked out the diaper package in cleaning up JonBenét.

Patsy would not be the first mother to lose control in such a situation. One of the doctors we consulted cited toileting issues as a textbook example of causing a parental rage. So, in my hypothesis, there was some sort of explosive encounter in the child's bathroom sometime prior to one o'clock in the morning, the time suggested by the digestion rate of the pineapple found in the child's stomach. I believed JonBenét was slammed against a hard surface, such as the edge of the tub, inflicting a mortal head wound. She was unconscious, but her heart was still beating. Patsy would not have known that JonBenét was still alive, because the child already appeared to be dead. The massive head trauma would have eventually killed her.

It was the critical moment in which she had to either call for help or find an alternative explanation for her daughter's death. It was accidental in the sense that the situation had developed without motive or premeditation. She could have called for help but chose not to. An emergency room doctor probably would have questioned the "accident" and called the police. Still, little would have happened to Patsy in Boulder. But I believe panic overtook her.

John and Burke continued to sleep while Patsy moved the body of JonBenét down to the basement and hid her in the little room.

As I pictured the scene, her dilemma was that police would assume the obvious if a six-year-old child was found dead in a private home without any satisfactory explanation. Patsy needed a diversion and planned the way she thought a kidnapping should look.

She returned upstairs to the kitchen and grabbed her tablet and a felt-tipped pen, flipped to the middle of the tablet, and started a ransom note, drafting one that ended on page 25. For some reason she discarded that one and ripped pages 17–25 from the tablet. Police never found those pages.

On page 26, she began the "Mr. & Mrs. I," then also abandoned that false start. At some point she drafted the long ransom note. By doing so, she created the government's best piece of evidence.

She then faced the major problem of what to do with the body. Leaving the house carried the risk of John or Burke awakening at the sounds and possibly being seen by a passerby or a neighbor. Leaving the body in the distant, almost inaccessible, basement room was the best option.

As I envisioned it, Patsy returned to the basement, a woman caught up in panic, where she could have seen—perhaps by detecting a faint heartbeat or a sound or a slight movement—that although completely unconscious, JonBenét was not dead. Others might argue that Patsy did not know the child was still alive. In my hypothesis, she took the next step, looking for the closest available items in her desperation. Only feet away was her paint tote. She grabbed a paintbrush and broke it to fashion the garrote with some cord. Then she looped the cord around the girl's neck.

In my scenario, she choked JonBenét from behind, with a grip on the broken paintbrush handle, pulling the ligature. JonBenét, still unconscious, would never have felt it. There are only four ways to die: suicide, natural, accidental, or homicide. This accident, in my opinion, had just become a murder.

Then the staging continued to make it look more like a kidnapping. Patsy tied the girl's wrists in front, not in back, for otherwise the arms would not have been in that overhead position. But with a fifteen-inch length of cord between the wrists and the knot tied loosely over the clothing, there was no way such a binding would have restrained a live child. It was a symbolic act to make it appear the child had been bound.

Patsy took considerable time with her daughter, wrapping her carefully in the blanket and leaving her with a favorite pink nightgown. The FBI had told us that a stranger would not have taken such care.

As I told Lou, I thought that throughout the coming hours, Patsy worked on her staging, such as placing the ransom note where she would be sure to "find" it the next morning. She placed the tablet on the countertop right beside the stairs and the pen in the cup.

While going through the drawers under the countertop where the tablet had been, she found rolls of tape. She placed a strip from a roll of duct tape across JonBenét's mouth. There was bloody mucus under the tape, and a perfect set of the child's lip prints, which did not indicate a tongue impression or resistance.

I theorized that Patsy, trying to cover her tracks, took the remaining cord, tape, and the first ransom note out of the house that night, perhaps dropping them into a nearby storm sewer or among the Christmas debris and wrappings in a neighbor's trash can.

She was running out of time. The household was scheduled to wake up early to fly to Michigan, and in her haste, Patsy Ramsey did not change clothes, a vital mistake. With the clock ticking, and hearing her husband moving around upstairs, she stepped over the edge.

The way I envisioned it, Patsy screamed, and John Ramsey, coming out of the shower, responded, totally unaware of what had occurred. Burke, awakened by the noise shortly before six o'clock in the morning, came down to find out what had happened and was sent back to bed as his mother talked to the 911 emergency dispatcher.

Patsy Ramsey opened the door to Officer Rick French at about 5:55 A.M. on the morning of December 26, 1996, wearing a red turtleneck sweater and black pants, the same things she had worn to a party the night before. Her hair was done, and her makeup was on. In my opinion, she had never been to bed.

The diversion worked for seven hours as the Boulder police thought they were dealing with a kidnapping.

John Ramsey, in my hypothetical scenario, probably first grew suspicious while reading the ransom note that morning, which was why he was unusually quiet. He must have seen his wife's writing mannerisms all over it, everything but her signature. But where was his daughter?

He said in his police interview that he went down to the basement when Detective Arndt noticed him missing. I suggested that Ramsey found JonBenét at that time and was faced with the dilemma of his life. During the next few hours, his behavior changed markedly as he desperately considered his few options—submit to the authorities or try to control the situation. He had already lost one child, Beth, and now JonBenét was gone too. Now Patsy was possibly in jeopardy.

The stress increased steadily during the morning, for Patsy, in my theory, knew that no kidnapper was going to call by ten o'clock, and after John found the body, he knew that too. So when Detective Linda Arndt told him to search the house, he used the opportunity and made a beeline for the basement.

Then, tormented as he might be, he chose to protect his wife. Within a few hours, the first of his many lawyers was in motion, the private investigators a day later.

That's the way I see it, I said to Lou Smit. That's how the evidence fits to me. She made mistakes, and that's how we solve crimes, right? I reminded him of his own favorite saying: "Murders are usually what they seem."

————

Lou Smit totally disagreed with my version of the events that night, insisting that the Ramseys were innocent. In his intruder theory, the killer had seen JonBenét during one of her public appearances, perhaps the Christmas parade, and decided to go after her on Christmas night while the Ramsey family was out for the evening.

The pedophile intruder came in through the window-well grate and basement window, then spent quite some time roaming around the big house and learning the layout. He found a Home Tour brochure and learned more about the family. It was also during that period, while he was alone, that he came across the Sharpie pen in the cup and Patsy's writing tablet and wrote the ransom note. Then he hid, and waited.

Around midnight, when the house finally grew silent after the family went to bed, the intruder went upstairs and immobilized his victim with a stun gun, duct taped her mouth, and carried the child to the basement. He planned to remove her from the home in the Samsonite suitcase. The note was left on the spiral staircase.

Downstairs, the intruder fashioned Patsy's paintbrush handle into a garrote. Too impatient to wait, he simultaneously sexually assaulted and choked JonBenét in some sort of autoerotic fantasy. His presence in the basement also accounted for the Hi-Tec bootprint, the unidentified palm print, and the scuff mark on the wall below the window. The unidentified pubic hair was left during the attack, and the unknown DNA in her underwear resulted from the same incident, in Smit's theory.

Smith theorized that JonBenét regained consciousness, screamed, and fought her attacker, getting the unidentified DNA beneath her fingernails. The attacker struck her on the head, possibly with the black flashlight. The panicked intruder fled through the basement window, taking the remaining cord, duct tape, and stun gun with him.

That's how I see it happened, Lou Smit told me, adding, "The theory doesn't determine the evidence. The evidence should determine the theory."

"Exactly, Lou," I replied.

Smit later expanded on the theory to *Time* magazine, suggesting the garrote is a favored tool of pedophiles, and that the intruder had asked for the peculiar ransom of $118,000 because he planned to flee to Mexico, where the currency exchange rate would turn that sum of American dollars into roughly a million Mexican pesos.

I told Smit I found it hard to imagine the intruder roaming the house, writing the ransom note, sexually assaulting, garroting, and violently killing the child, apparently without fear of being confronted, while in a house full of sleeping people. CASKU had taught me one thing—ransom kidnappers kidnap for financial gain. Pedophiles kidnap for sexual gratification. But the two are mutually exclusive. Smit's hybrid pedophile-ransom-kidnapper-murderer would have been most unique.

For two hours we argued as Lou challenged my conclusions and I countered his. Neither of us could prove exactly when JonBenét ate the pineapple, but I said it came from the bowl of pineapple on the breakfast table, while he thought it was in the Tupperware bowl found in her room.

About the only thing we agreed on was that the attorneys, including the DA's office, had screwed things up, and we questioned the advice the Ramseys had received from their lawyers. As for the DA's office, Smit said Hunter was a politician.

Smit knew his position was unpopular, but that was the way he saw things. He told me that he was never attempting to do anything more than help the case, but his belief that the Ramseys were innocent was not an act.

We finally finished, shook hands, and parted as friends.

I realized that Lou Smit had become a major problem, a problem that no one would address. We'll eventually be hearing from him as a defense witness, I thought, but when I raised the issue with Commander Beckner, he said we would just have to accept that and asked if I knew how bad it would look to remove Smit from the case.

———

Detective Trujillo and Sergeant Wickman flew to Washington on April 3 to go over evidence with FBI laboratory experts, particularly the still unidentified pubic hair.

The FBI asked: Where's the pubic hair?

Only then did Trujillo realize that the evidence was sitting at the CBI lab, not the FBI lab. Such errors were maddening and becoming more frequent.

By January 1998 Trujillo had still not submitted all the prints of police officers for comparison with the palm print on the cellar room door. The paintbrush handle fashioned into the garrote took a year to finally get fingerprinted! And when the cord test results were returned, the samples I had purchased from the army store were consistent with the murder ligature.

———

Sergeant Wickman prepared my annual performance evaluation, said I was "above reproach," and Beckner signed it. I received the highest ratings in service excellence, integrity, respect for diversity, initiative, teamwork, and safety. The seventh category, "Strives to maintain physical and emotional wellness," was only a "standard" because Wickman had seen the obvious—I was not doing well balancing family, health, and social activities with work. The eighty-plus notebooks filled with the case file behind my desk bore mute witness to the reason why. No one could say I had not tried to do my job.

When Wickman asked about my future, I admitted that I was probably done with the Boulder Police Department once the Ramsey case was over. I could never file another case with this district attorney's office. I could barely tolerate being in the same room with them.

———

Something else was also going on. My lethargy, headaches, continued weight loss, and growing back pain forced me to see a doctor, although I didn't tell anyone about it. She asked if I had been irritable, depressed, or found it difficult to concentrate. All of the above, I said, and during the next several weeks I endured a regimen of intensive physical examinations and blood tests.

Finally the doctor gave me the grim news that I had something called chronic lymphocytic thyroiditis. The thyroid gland, which a person cannot live without, was failing, and my body was producing antibodies that were consuming my thyroid. It could develop into more serious problems, she said, although I thought what she had already told me was serious enough.

I can't be sick, I thought. I had never been sick in my life. I had been on the SWAT team, for God's sake, and that's about as rough as it gets. But the cold facts were right there before me. The same sort of thyroid problems that contributed to my mother's death when I was a child were in my body too.

When I was able to refocus, the doctor was telling me that new drugs were now available to counterbalance the loss of the thyroid. With lifetime therapy to stabilize my metabolism, I could return to normal, although I would have to monitor my immune system carefully in the future.

She said I could continue working without my performance being affected, but she encouraged me to make a lifestyle change. I laughed when she asked if I was under any current stress. "Yeah," I said. "I'm a detective on the Ramsey case."

––––––––

"Don't kid yourselves," Commander Beckner told a couple of detectives. "Don't think that we will ever actually handcuff somebody in this case. Should there be a charge, you can bet the DA's office will negotiate a controlled surrender."

We were all living for that big payoff, and we weren't going to get it. If a Ramsey was ever charged, they would surrender with lawyers and bail money and probably never even get out of their street clothes. "Let me tell you, we won't be putting handcuffs on anybody," Beckner reiterated. Another reason for not forcing the issue, he said, was that he did not want to get sued over "this thing."

He added that although there might be a grand jury, and probable cause existed for an indictment, the case might not get prosecuted. "Can you live with that?" he asked me. I said no, I couldn't. I told him that under those circumstances, I most likely would leave the police department. I requested a letter of recommendation, and he gave me one.

––––––––

Chief Koby told a briefing of the top people in the DA's office and police department that all roads now led toward the Ramseys. The police position was clear, he said. We believed we were working on the right suspects.

Commander Beckner agreed. He said that when he came aboard, he was open-minded on the evidence, but the investigation had led him squarely to the Ramseys. "We can't tell you exactly what happened that night, but we all agree that it's the Ramseys," he said. He drew a triangle on a grease board and marked the police at the very top of the triangle, beside the names of John and Patsy Ramsey.

District Attorney Alex Hunter picked up the marker and placed himself right there alongside the detectives. Deputy DA Pete Hofstrom marked himself halfway down the triangle, and Lou Smit was placed at the very bottom.

Hunter looked at the triangle and once again erected a wall between himself and a decision. He said his office had problems with the case proceeding and that he would have to convince them to get on board.

His wishy-washy stance of trying to be all things to all people, marking himself beside the detectives, then warning that he couldn't control his own office, was too much even for Chief Koby. "It's time to make a decision, Alex," he said. "Either pursue the Ramseys or pursue an intruder. Or take it to a grand jury. Or don't take it to a grand jury. But make a decision!"

Lawrence Schiller, who was writing a book about the case, had been reading my official police reports, and I was furious. Several witnesses called me to ask how their names and telephone numbers, which had been given to me in confidence, had ended up in the hands of an author.

I went to see Commander Beckner and protested the latest round of leaks from the district attorney's office, which was the only other place those reports were available. He later told me that Alex Hunter denied the accusation.

"That's it?" I asked. "We're just going to sit by and let confidential material go out like that?"

"I can't compete with Hunter. He's too entrenched and too politically powerful. We have to live with it," Beckner replied. "Don't you understand how many hundreds of other cases we have to file with that office? Steve, this is but one case! Look at the big picture. Do you want to see the entire system burned down?" Beckner would often remind me of his "big picture."

Schiller later told me that his source in the district attorney's office had supplied him with fifteen hundred pages of police reports, memos, and other confidential information from the case file.

Winter. Spring. Summer. Fall. Winter. Spring. Now we were almost back to summer again, and we knew we were about be thrown overboard. Detective Gosage spoke for us all one morning. "We're nothing but piss-ants," he stormed. "Let's just get this fucking thing done. They took some energetic and aggressive detectives a year and a half ago and gave us this fucked-up case, and now they've broken all of us. We have been so fucked over in this, I just want it done."

Any dreams we had of a successful prosecution had long since vanished.

In my opinion, my friends were even more trapped in this morass than I. Gosage was a family man with a wife and baby and could not afford to walk away from this screwed-up department. Harmer had other obligations and could not risk being blackballed, and we had learned from the example of former commander John Eller that finding another police job was almost impossible if you were tarred by the Jon-Benét case. Sergeant Wickman wasn't going to walk away from a long career and the potential of promotion to higher rank, although he was counting off the days he had left to retirement. Even the indefatigable Bob Keatley was thinking about resigning as our in-house attorney, which would be devastating to the entire department.

Things were different for me. My wife barely recognized in me the man she had married only two years before and had already told me that if need be, she would support us while I turned my hobby of remodeling old houses into a full-time carpentry business.

I had three choices. Did I want to resign and disappear into anonymity? Did I want to continue with this case, although I felt it had become an insult to any honor and integrity? Or did I want to leave and make a statement? The third option was the most intriguing, but if I left, I couldn't help the case . . . or could I?

The DA's office was about to make the choice easy.

PART FIVE

LAYING DOWN THE BADGE

31

We had interviewed 590 people, consulted 64 outside experts, investigated and cleared more than 100 possible suspects, collected 1,058 pieces of evidence, tested over 500 items at federal, state, and private laboratories, gathered handwriting and nontestimonial evidence from 215 people, built a case file that now bulged to 30,000 pages, reviewed more than 3,400 letters and 700 telephone tips, and contacted seventeen states and two foreign countries. And it all kept leading us in one direction. The detective team believed that John and Patsy Ramsey had knowledge of, and were involved in, the death of their daughter, JonBenét.

We endured the "Intruder Presentation" of Deputy DA Trip DeMuth in the middle of May. His justification was that he had been "asked to defense the case" and anticipate the thoughts and actions of defense lawyers and a jury. "The best way to know your strengths is to first understand your weaknesses," he said.

His tone was arrogant during the two hours he tried to weigh our case down with excruciating minutiae, couching his criticism behind phrases such as "This is what the defense will do. . . ."

What we had hoped to hear was a competent prosecutor telling us what a defense attorney would say about a critical piece of evidence or situation and then giving us advice on how a combined team of the police and the DA's office, working together, could counter their argument. This analysis by someone who, in my opinion, had hindered our investigation was the worst sort of Monday-morning quarterbacking.

The man who wouldn't sign search warrants, opposed polygraphs of the Ramseys, and had come up with the incredible Five-Year Plan seemed to think he had a crystal ball on what a jury would believe.

How do you prove the marks on her skin were not caused by a stun gun? How do you prove she did not scratch her killer? Did the work hours spent developing other suspects rival the work hours spent on the Ramseys? Did you fingerprint the Doctor Seuss book that was found in the suitcase, and if not, why not? He attacked the FBI and CBI labs. On and on and on. Before our eyes, his Five-Year Plan grew into a Ten-Year Plan. "This is the most watched case in American jurisprudence. There will be no excuse for not doing all these things I'm suggesting," he said.

Then DeMuth criticized us for "shopping experts" until we got an answer we liked. This was ironic, since his boss Pete Hofstrom would later take the 911 tape enhanced by the Aerospace Corporation down to New Mexico to let his brother-in-law, who worked in the Los Alamos scientific complex, have a crack at analyzing it. The brother-in-law apparently declared that he heard a voice say, "I scream at you." That meaningless comment managed to cast doubt on the Aerospace conclusion that Burke said, "What did you find?" and was another gift to the defense lawyers. They would now be able to point out to a jury that even the prosecutor's office and the police did not agree about what was on the tape.

DeMuth even cast doubt on Officer Rick French's version of what happened in the Ramsey home that first morning, saying that the officer could be mistaken and that John Ramsey might simply have "misspoken" about his description of events.

DeMuth maintained that we had full access to the FBI, yet at the same time he was barring the further testing of the mysterious alleged pubic hair.

When he completed his presentation, one detective noted wryly that DeMuth "forgot to tell us to compare a fiber in the Ramsey attic to a hair in the beard of General Ulysses S. Grant."

We noted that DeMuth did not prove an intruder committed the murder. He never mentioned that we had identified Patsy as the writer of the ransom note, nor did he address the confirmation of prior vaginal trauma, and some of his evidentiary points were in error. DeMuth threw a mass of little things at us, but I believed they were pebbles bouncing against a steel wall, for our macro-perspective overwhelmed his nitpicking. The main thing missing in the case was a team of aggressive and determined prosecutors.

What really irritated us was when his pettiness surfaced and he said that our fairness was skewed. About the same time, we received word from Mark Beckner that the DA's office was echoing Team Ramsey's claim that we had manipulated the evidence. What they were saying was tantamount to claiming we had committed a crime, an unforgivable piece of unfounded gossip for which none of them took responsibility.

Even after DeMuth's recital of our shortcomings, I felt we held a decent hand. Commander Beckner told me later that he felt we had gone far beyond showing probable cause. "I think she [Patsy Ramsey] did it," he said. "We should just charge them both with felony murder and aiding and abetting."

And Sergeant Tom Wickman, going behind Beckner's back in what I considered to be an attempt to reinsert himself in the leadership of the case, visited District Attorney Alex Hunter at his home. He told me that Hunter believed the intruder idea was bullshit.

But Wickman was cautious about putting much stock in the DA's comment. "I never fucking know whether to believe anything that comes out of the guy's mouth," Wickman said. The district attorney tended to tell people what they wanted to hear.

As if to underline that point, we learned that one of the prime suspects had begun direct communication with the district attorney.

John Ramsey wrote Hunter a personal letter and followed up with a telephone call. The DA would claim that he spoke briefly with Ramsey on the telephone but would not discuss the case.

The letter, however, got a warm reception and remained in the DA's office for three weeks before the police were told about it. Ramsey wrote that he resorted to the personal touch because it was difficult to communicate through attorneys who were trying to protect his rights.

Ramsey accused the Boulder Police of trying to convince others that a family member had killed JonBenét from the moment we walked into his house on December 26. We would not accept help from outsiders, he claimed, and the Ramsey family had no confidence or trust in us.

That was a rehash of lies, since those first police on the scene were investigating the alleged kidnapping of his daughter. And had they immediately focused on the family as murder suspects as soon as the body was discovered, this case might have been on an entirely different track a year and a half later.

Ramsey said in his private letter that he and his family members would meet anytime, anywhere, and for as long as needed with investigators from the DA's office. They were willing to speak before a grand jury. He referred to the murderer of his daughter as "It," wanted "maximum justice," and pledged a million-dollar reward.

The Ramseys had a track record of offering to talk openly but then retreating behind their lawyers when the time came to speak. I knew there was no way the DA's investigators would be given a meeting without involving Team Ramsey.

Hunter and Pete Hofstrom started laying plans for an interview immediately after the police presentation, saying that it would be "unethical" to refuse to talk with the Ramseys, even though the DA's office had called them "prime suspects." Lou Smit, a Ramsey sympathizer, was appointed to do the interview. The detectives would not be part of the interviews "because it was not acceptable to the Ramseys," Beckner explained.

There is nothing wrong with prosecutors talking with the attorneys of someone whom police wish to question and negotiating a deal for an interview. But for this one, I felt the timing was completely wrong.

The whole purpose of our upcoming presentation was to finally get the case to a grand jury, and from there to an indictment. Why, I wondered, should the Ramseys be allowed to waltz in at the eleventh hour and speak under conditions such as having an outspoken sympathizer like Lou Smit asking the questions?

At first glance, the mere fact that they were willing to answer questions would seem to be a break for the investigators, possibly even better than having them appear before a grand jury. A person cannot be compelled to testify before a grand jury unless they are given immunity in return for not invoking their Fifth Amendment rights against self-incrimination. In the interviews we might get something we could use. Or we might not. But John Ramsey had just written Alex Hunter a personal letter, pledging they would testify under oath in front of the grand jury. Take him up on it!

Then the Ramseys could be called to testify under oath, answer sharp questions without their lawyers advice, and with the possibility of perjury charges over any inconsistencies. The pressure would be significantly higher. They would maintain the right to exert their Fifth Amendment rights if they chose to do so.

At this point in the case, the grand jury was a better bet.

To me, it all added up to the biggest sellout of the investigation. I let Beckner have it, with a blistering response. On the one hand the district attorney was planning to convene a grand jury to hear evidence indicating that Patsy Ramsey had killed her daughter. On the other, they let John Ramsey, who was once again dangling that well-gnawed carrot of "cooperation," set the rules for a new and important interview.

Furthermore, the police were to be cut out of the picture if a grand jury was to hear the JonBenét case. Pete Hofstrom now said that only Lou Smit from the DA's office and at best one police representative would be sworn in as investigators. That critical decision reduced the rest of the detective team to a state of near uselessness.

Because of secrecy rules, the investigators who knew the case best would not be told what was happening in the grand jury room and would therefore be unable to offer guidance. Even if a cop were chosen as an investigator, he or she would not be allowed to discuss testimony with the rest of us.

This was a strategic error of some magnitude, for legally there is nothing to limit the number of detectives who can be sworn in to assist a grand jury. All of us should have been made eligible to sit in. Who better to recognize the truth and error, strong and weak points of a witness's testimony? In other jurisdictions that would have been done almost automatically. Not in Boulder, where the DA's office was cloaking its opinion as law.

We didn't yet know who the police representative would be. It might be Beckner. It might be Wickman. It might be no one. But I was told that it would not be me.

———

With that brewing in the background, the time was fast approaching when the detectives would have to deliver their presentation of the case to the DA's office. Hunter and Hofstrom said they wanted the entire case laid out, allegedly so that they could decide whether to call a grand jury.

It was an unreasonable demand and in my experience totally unprecedented. They had total access to our case file and claimed that Lou Smit knew it better than anyone, so why did we have to run it by them still again? What did they want this time? How many hoops must we jump through to get them to move?

We prepared the presentation under the guidance of our Dream Team attorneys. "Aim at Hunter," they advised. Pete Hofstrom and the usual array of advisers would be on hand, but the ultimate call had to be made by the Boulder County District Attorney.

We designed a subtle, dispassionate approach to let the facts and evidence tell the story. Instead of a who-did-what scenario, we would show that no intruder could have committed the crime and would prove a compelling need for a grand jury.

It wouldn't be just a group of detectives doing the talking, either. Our attorneys armed us with computer graphics and all the tools of the modern prosecutor to display our case. We were totally confident in our material.

Two days before we were to go onstage, we got some surprising big news when the Colorado Bureau of Investigation lab told us that the acrylic fibers found on the duct tape that covered JonBenét's mouth were a "likely match" for Patsy's blazer. We were ready.

————

Since none of the district attorney's prosecutors were deemed able to run a grand jury, there would be a welcome new face in the room for the presentation.

The DA had hired attorney Mike Kane, a former assistant U.S. Attorney who was said to be a grand jury wizard, to handle the case. Kane had deep Colorado roots and had worked for the Denver district attorney. He currently worked in Pennsylvania.

Commander Beckner told us, however, that Deputy DA Hofstrom remained in charge. Kane, a lean and studious man with a fine record in prosecuting murder cases, was no higher than number three on the totem pole, no matter how aggressive he might be. And that was only if the DA decided to use a grand jury at all, which was far from a certainty.

32

It was show time for the Boulder detectives. Everything up to now was in preparation for what we would do on June 1 and 2, 1998. We had spent weeks putting together our presentation, refining our scripts, arranging slides and photographs, running through dress rehearsals, minutely going over every detail. We knew it could very well be the last time we touched the case, and we wanted to do the best job possible. The pressure on each of us was immense, for there was no room for error. But we were ready and confident in our skills and in agreement that our material was more than powerful enough to convince the district attorney to call a grand jury. "We'll kick their ass with this stuff," Sergeant Wickman boomed enthusiastically during a final rehearsal.

The media swirled about the Coors Events Center at the University of Colorado, where we would be meeting, long before it was time to start. It was a visible reminder of how closely the world was watching.

The seats in the conference room were arranged in tiers and were generally divided between the police, primarily seated on the right side, DA Alex Hunter and his staff in the middle, and everyone else—agents from the FBI's Child Abduction and Serial Killer Unit and the Colorado Bureau of Investigation, representatives from the state attorney general, our three Dream Team attorneys, Hunter's DA advisers, lab experts, and others such as Dr. Henry Lee and DNA expert Barry Scheck sprinkled between. In all, some forty people had gathered to hear our presentation. Deputy DA Pete Hofstrom sat in the back row, ready to take notes with his legal pads and green, blue, and red pens. Our files and displays were arranged within easy reach around the stage.

I set the tone in my opening statement by flashing on the screen behind me a series of huge photographs—JonBenét with her brother, Burke, on Christmas morning, 1996; JonBenét with her Christmas bike; and JonBenét at the side of her mother, Patsy Ramsey, who was four days shy of her fortieth birthday. Patsy's fingers tightly gripped her daughter's arm. The picture remained up while I gave the overview, then gave way to a series of slides.

For more than an hour I painstakingly went over the sequence of events on the morning of December 26, pointing out discrepancies along the way, and ended with a description of how the Ramseys, for the most part, had avoided being questioned by the Boulder police while making controlled media appearances.

During a break I met Barry Scheck, the DNA expert from the O. J. Simpson defense team, and asked him to tell us if we were full of shit on this thing. Scheck replied, "To tell you the truth, I'm leaning your way. I'm more of a friend than you think." He encouraged me to hang tough in the face of the media barrage. "Until somebody has been in one of these firestorms, they can't appreciate what it's like," he said. He should know.

Detective Everett presented the biography of JonBenét, noting particularly that the girl had made thirty-three visits to the Boulder pediatrician in three years and that the doctor received three calls from Patsy on December 17, for some reason we did not know. Then Detective Jane Harmer gave the family overview, and Detective Trujillo explained the autopsy information. Trujillo carefully recited the conclusions of experts who effectively knocked down the stubborn issue of the stun gun, which the detectives believed never existed and which had become a cornerstone of the Intruder Theory.

The critical pineapple evidence was discussed by another detective. "The $118,000 question is this: When and where was that fresh pineapple consumed?" he asked. There were three theories—that she ate it before leaving the house at 5 P.M., at the Whites', or after she returned home.

If the fruit was consumed before she left for the Whites' party, then given the rate of digestion that obviously stopped with her death, the evidence would indicate that she was probably killed shortly after she arrived home. This would have been the very outside edge of the time frame for the time of death. An intruder would have been incredibly bold to do it this way as the rest of the family prepared for bed.

We knew pineapple was not served at the Whites' party, which ruled out the second option.

That would indicate that she ate it between the time she returned home about 10 P.M. and the time she died. But if that were the case, then she wasn't carried straight to bed, asleep, as her parents claimed. She ate the pineapple, it was digested, and then she was killed. This was the only way the evidence made sense.

Another part to the theory that she ate it after returning home seemed even more incredible to me. This scenario would have her awakened sometime during the night after being put to bed, eating the pineapple, digesting it for two to five hours, and then being killed by an intruder at some time before Patsy found the note.

Detective Harmer presented a surprising anatomy lesson on vaginas to a meeting attended primarily by men. She showed a picture of the vagina of a normal healthy six-year-old girl and contrasted it with a photo of the vagina of JonBenét. Even to the uninformed the visual difference was apparent, and Harmer cited the experts who said there was evidence of "chronic sexual abuse," although the detectives referred to it only as "prior vaginal trauma."

Then we presented information on the paintbrush, the handle for the garrote, the paint tray, and the matching paint on the handle and the broken brush. The splinter in the vagina had caused a disagreement among the examiners. Some examiners said it had been in the vagina as long as a week, but the detectives sided with Dr. Spitz's conclusion that it was inserted about the time of death as a part of the staging.

Doctor Lee warned us that Team Ramsey could be expected to fight back with their own expert opinions. "You get one expert to say something, defense gets two," he said.

As anticipated, Detective Trujillo's presentation of the DNA evidence led to a long discussion between Scheck, Lee, and an expert from the CBI that sounded like Latin to the rest of us. Unknown DNA was present, but it could have been from anybody, and there were serious issues of possible contamination of the samples. The use of the same clippers for all of her fingers during the autopsy, and maybe even other subjects' as well, could have caused a problem. More work clearly needed to be done, but we needed subpoena power to do it. Scheck said later that he saw a lot of potential questions but felt by instinct that some sort of "contaminant" may have caused the unidentified DNA. He said the CellMark tests raised more questions than they answered.

Trujillo presented the news that four red acrylic fibers on the duct tape covering JonBenét's mouth were consistent with Patsy's blazer. The room came to a jarring halt for a moment, since it was the first the attendees had heard of that result.

Trujillo added that fiber testing was still incomplete because we were unable to obtain Patsy's red turtleneck, slacks, footwear, and fur clothing, although we still had not identified the beaver hair from the duct tape. When the audience learned that we did not have the credit card and telephone records, one of Hunter's task force of metro DAs asked Commander Mark Beckner why. "That's some pretty basic stuff," Adams County DA Bob Grant said. Beckner, instead of laying the blame on Hunter's office, where it belonged, shrugged, "We just didn't," leaving listeners to believe it was a police screwup.

Detective Everett presented the crime scene, and we got a glimpse of the analytical mind of new prosecutor Mike Kane and liked what we saw. Questions were raised when detectives described the dispute about whether the spiderweb at the basement window was elastic enough to have been stretched. No photographs had been taken, and there were contrary opinions on whether the metal grate was moved. Kane simply asked if a police officer could testify to seeing the web intact on the morning of December 26. Everett said several could, and Kane nodded in approval.

Kane was bothered about why the unidentified pubic hair had not been tested in the past year and a half. The DA's office said the testing had not begun because the FBI would not allow Team Ramsey to be present in the lab.

Ransom note inconsistencies were discussed, and we pointed out that none of the expert document examiners, not even those hired by the defense, could eliminate Patsy Ramsey as the author. The CBI examiner explained that of the seventy-three persons whose writing had been investigated, there was only one whose writing showed evidence that suggested authorship and had been in the home the night of the killing and could not be eliminated by no less than six document examiners—Patsy Ramsey. I followed that up with a lengthy description of the findings by linguist Don Foster, who had concluded that Patsy wrote the ransom note.

Detective Gosage discussed the cord and described how the duct tape on JonBenét's mouth bore a perfect lip impression, indicating that she did not struggle against it. He also described his search for the Hi-Tec boot print and the still unidentified palm print on the cellar door. We ended the first day with the powerful review of the 911 emergency call enhancement, which proved that Burke was awake, not asleep as his parents claimed.

As we left the auditorium, the detectives could feel the current of excitement. The state attorney general's office and our Dream Team were lobbying for Don Foster to be used as a witness in court. One member of Hunter's task force of metro DAs observed that it seemed as if all the evidence that could be marshaled for a Ramsey defense could be explained away. Another of his DA advisers exclaimed, "I'd love to try this case." These were Hunter's own people talking! I walked out of there pretty optimistic.

The following day I presented the Atlanta overview, our trips to other states, and the covert grave-site surveillance operations and said we still had work to do in Georgia, ranging from getting palm prints from Patsy's parents and sisters to interviewing the former mistress about John Ramsey's infidelity. Detectives Gosage and Harmer went over the Access Graphics interviews and other suspects in the case, including Boulder County's known pedophiles, domestic help, contract workers, Santa Bill McReynolds, and Chris Wolf.

"Is anyone going to talk about Fleet White?" The question came from Bill Wise, Hunter's first assistant district attorney, who was being allowed to officially reenter the case.

"What do you want to know?" Harmer asked.

"Is he cleared?"

"Yes."

The time flew by. We hardly needed our notes as we carefully laid out the case we had lived with for so long. I had wanted to deliver my closing for more than a year, and stepped to the podium to give the first blow of our one-two punch. I would list the reasons to believe the Ramseys knew about and were involved with the murder, while Sergeant Wickman would follow with an attack on the Intruder Theory.

I said that more than a dozen points led us to the Ramseys. Prior vaginal trauma came first. Then I went through the ransom note, the pen, pad, handwriting, and practice notes, as well as the textual analysis and Don Foster's conclusion that Patsy was the author.

To that list I added the 911 enhancement, which, contrary to what the Ramseys had said, showed Burke was awake; the inconsistent statements, such as when John Ramsey challenged the independent recollections of three police officers who claimed to hear him say the house was locked and the statement that he had read to JonBenét that night; and the link between the paintbrush garrote murder weapon and the paint tote inside the home.

There was the confusing architecture of the house to consider; the staging aspects of the crime, deliberately meant to misdirect the detectives; the pineapple source and fingerprints on the bowl; the time of death in our estimate being within the date of death noted on the headstone (December 25, 1996); the scream heard by a neighbor but not by the parents in the house; the odd behavior of the parents, such as Patsy fixing her hair and putting on fresh makeup but wearing the same clothes from the day before; the parents having the opportunity no other suspects had, since they were at home all night; and finally, the fibers found on the tape.

That, I felt, established the major points. It was time to let Sergeant Wickman confront the Intruder Theory.

"The prominent red flag in the big picture is the utter illogic of such an intruder's actions and behaviors," Wickman said. "For one to believe an intruder committed this crime, one would also have to believe all of these things." Enumerating conflicting points, Wickman asked, "Would an intruder":

Have taken the time to close JonBenét's bedroom door, which Patsy said had been found closed?

Have taken the time to relatch the obscure cellar door peg that police and Fleet White found in the locked position?

Have placed JonBenét beneath a blanket and taken the care to place her favorite pink nightgown with her?

Have tied the wrists so loosely that a live child would have hardly been restrained?

Have wiped and/or redressed JonBenét after the assault and murder?

Have fed her pineapple, then kept her alive in the house for a couple of hours while she digested it? (That same fresh cut pineapple that was consistent, right down to the rind, with a bowl on the breakfast table that had the print of Patsy Ramsey's right middle finger on it.)

Have known the dog was not at home that night?

Have been able to navigate silently through a dark, confusing, and occupied house without a sound in the quiet of Christmas night?

Have been so careless as to forget some of the materials required to commit the kidnapping but remembered to wear gloves to foil fingerprint impressions on the ransom note?

Be a stranger who could write a note with characteristics so similar to those of Patsy Ramsey's writing that numerous experts would be unable to eliminate her as the author?

Have been able to enter the home, confront the child, assault and commit a murder, place the body in an obscure, concealed basement room, remember to latch the peg, then take the time to find the required writing materials inside the house to create the note without disturbing or alerting any other occupants?

Have been so unprepared for this most high risk of crimes that the individuals representing a "small foreign faction" failed to bring the necessary equipment to facilitate the crime?

Have been able to murder the child in such a violent fashion but so quietly that her parents and brother slept through the event, despite a scream loud enough to be heard by a neighbor across the street?

Have taken the pains to compliment John Ramsey's business in the rambling, sometimes irrelevant three-page ransom note, all while in the home and vulnerable to discovery?

And, Wickman pointed out, given the medical opinions of prior vaginal trauma, the night of the murder must not have been the intruder's first visit, unless the vaginal abuse and the murder were done by different people.

I followed Wickman by listing twenty-seven reasons that a grand jury was needed to continue the investigation, from questioning the parents, family members, friends, and other players to obtaining records ranging from movie rentals to complete health documents. We had yet to obtain complete phone, banking, and credit records, and still needed items of Ramsey clothing. We didn't have records from the security alarm company, nor had we been able to interview JonBenét's doctor and nurses. This was basic investigative procedure, and we needed those subpoenas.

"We feel that the unanswered questions that remain, the witnesses that have stonewalled us, the evidence that has been unavailable to us otherwise would now be best addressed through a grand jury," I concluded.

When I finished my last sentence, it felt as if a huge weight was lifted from my shoulders. We had made a strong argument on behalf of

JonBenét and left no doubt about where the detectives stood and what we were asking to be done.

During a question-and-answer period, DA Bob Grant asked us to speculate about who killed JonBenét. Commander Beckner, at the podium, said unequivocally, "I think Patsy did."

I felt we had exceeded our goal of establishing probable cause, and others agreed. One police commander commented, "The hell with a grand jury. Write an arrest warrant."

———

Beckner and the detectives gave a brief parking lot press conference, and the commander said in public for the first time that we had "an idea" who killed JonBenét. Then we filed back inside.

———

The politeness of the past two days disappeared after the presentation when everyone gathered in another conference room, where Alex Hunter wanted to discuss an "interview strategy for the Ramseys."

It was the first we had heard that an interview had been agreed to, and our friends from the FBI and the Dream Team attorneys tried to convince the DA's office that it was a bad idea.

It's a foolish move, said one of the FBI agents. They've been dicking you around for a year and a half and now want interviews under conditions that relieve them from the pressure of going before the grand jury. Don't do it, they warned.

Tension was thick in the room, and voices were raised as the meeting veered close to going out of control.

Hunter himself was all over the map. He propped his chin on his fist and asked aloud, "I wonder if Burke [Ramsey] is involved in this?" We looked at each other in disbelief. It sounded as if he had not attended our presentation. The next moment he talked tough, declaring that the Ramseys had "to fish or cut bait" now. His message, if there was one, was very mixed.

The meeting deteriorated as a lot of people shouted at each other, and Pete Hofstrom came out of his chair, waved his arms, and defended the Ramseys' "unlimited and unconditional cooperation." I sat in the back, said nothing, and just leaned against the cinder block wall. I had done all I could.

Bob Miller of the Dream Team said the time had come for Hunter to target the Ramseys officially as suspects. "You can't just wander through the grand jury," he said. "Call a spade a spade and do the right thing." When he tried to continue, Trip DeMuth loudly interrupted, and Miller barked, "Shut up and let me finish my sentence."

Bill Hagmaier, head of the FBI's Child Abduction and Serial Killer Unit, broke in with a question for the district attorney. "No disrespect intended, Mister Hunter, but is this grand jury your call?"

Hunter replied that he would work with his "trusted advisers" to reach a decision, but Hagmaier pushed until Hunter admitted that the final decision would indeed be his.

Weary of Boulder's crawl toward justice, the FBI official told the district attorney, "A little girl is moldering in the ground, and she shouldn't be. If the parents are involved, Mister Hunter, something needs to be done."

"This is a political decision," Hunter said. "I have to get with my people."

It was an astonishing assertion. I wondered how a murder charge could be a political decision. Was he really weighing votes in a criminal case?

"Our involvement in this case has become an issue at the FBI," said Hagmaier. "We want to see the right thing done, and we will continue to support this investigation. But we feel our suggestions are being ignored and our advice is not taken." The entire CASKU team was on an early flight back to Washington the next morning. Their decision to pull out of the active investigation should have been viewed as a shattering criticism of the DA's office.

The Dream Team threesome—Rich Baer, Dan Hoffman, and Bob Miller—were soon told in no uncertain terms that their services would not be needed by the DA's office, and they too were gone. Instead of being welcomed by the DA, the voices of these experienced trial attorneys were also disregarded.

The office of the district attorney was calling the plays from here on in and wasted no time exerting its strength. The police would also soon be abruptly dismissed.

When the shouting was done, the district attorney met the press and gave the reporters another serving of doublespeak. "This is all about finding the killer of JonBenét and justice," said the law-and-order DA, who immediately flipped and issued a warning of caution.

"We do not have enough to file a case, and we do have a lot of work to do," Hunter said. "I will go back to my people and analyze what we heard over a number of hours and make sure it is sensible to spend the time it takes to run a grand jury." He said he would not do anything "premature."

I put together a thank-you dinner that night at a steak house in Denver for the FBI agents from CASKU and our Dream Team advisers. Neither Tom Koby nor Mark Beckner chose to attend. "What's going on in that DA's office is a disgrace," one of the FBI agents observed during our last supper. "This case has become an embarrassment to law enforcement." We were all in agreement.

"It is terribly discouraging how the DA is handling this," said one Dream Team attorney. "Hunter is going to outsmart himself on this one."

The next day, Wednesday, June 3, I slept late for the first time in many months.

33

The detectives were suddenly adrift. After working on the case so hard and for so long, giving it up so abruptly dislocated our lives. We still talked about it all the time and were ready to do more investigating—lord knows there was more to be done—but we had no assigned role anymore. Even Commander Beckner and Sergeant Wickman were totally in the dark. "You've had this case for seventeen months. It's our turn, and it's time to get it done," District Attorney Alex Hunter told them. He confirmed that his office would proceed with the Ramsey interviews.

At the insistence of the Dream Team and the detectives, Commander Beckner drafted a letter to the district attorney to advocate that we conduct the upcoming interviews, with two detectives, the suspect, and one lawyer in the room; that the interviews be taped both by audio and video; that no lab results or other evidence or information be given up in exchange for the interviews; that a DNA adviser be consulted and testing begun; and any questions be carefully worded so as not to educate the Ramseys about what we knew. Do not forget, we warned, "At this time, it is clear the Ramseys are the prime suspects."

Beckner personally walked the strongly worded document over to Alex Hunter on June 8 and returned with his tail between his legs, explaining to me that he was sorry that he got "riled up" about the situation. Beckner said the DA really was on top of things, and he now agreed that it was best to interview the Ramseys prior to the grand jury being called. From then on, he sided with the DA's office and discarded the advice of CASKU and the Dream Team. Hunter, he said, pledged to "work through any misunderstandings."

The focus was now on the upcoming interviews with the Ramseys.

DA investigator Lou Smit was picked to question John Ramsey, even though on May 28, Smit had put in writing that the Ramseys "should be interviewed as victims." It made no sense for Hunter to bet all his chips on Smit, who went in with an obvious bias, but at least he would be paired with Mike Kane, the new grand jury prosecutor.

Deputy DA Trip DeMuth, whom I considered a Team Ramsey ally, was assigned to interview Patsy. He would be teamed with retired Denver Police homicide captain Tom Haney, whom the detectives greatly respected.

Haney would do fine as an interviewer, as would Kane. I wasn't at all sure about Smit and DeMuth.

Burke Ramsey would be questioned in Atlanta by Dan Schuller, a detective from the nearby Broomfield Police Department who held a degree in child development. Hunter told Beckner that the Boulder Police were not only to stay away from Atlanta, but the whole state of Georgia. Someone asked if we had to leave Boulder when John and Patsy came to Colorado. We had concerns about Schuller, who would soon be asking witnesses if they thought the Boulder Police had screwed up the investigation.

And John Ramsey's pledge to Alex Hunter of "unlimited and unconditional cooperation" collapsed into a flurry of bargaining between the DA's office and Team Ramsey attorneys. Smit would later tell me that Hofstrom was negotiating about whether the Ramseys could even be *asked* "the polygraph question." They weren't.

————

We spent a lot of time tearing down the SitRoom, cleaning off our walls and desks, boxing up papers, and just looking at each other. Commander Beckner told us, "We've done all we can. We gave it the best shot we could. It's time to continue with your lives now." That wasn't acceptable to me.

The photo of JonBenét that had been a fixture on the SitRoom wall had come down, which was entirely appropriate, for this was no longer about her. It was about politics. I ate a tuna sandwich at my desk and realized that I was so fucking tired of eating tuna sandwiches in the SitRoom. Although I still wanted to do something to further this case, I began to wonder why I stayed at all.

I telephoned an FBI friend who was familiar with the case and told him that I was thinking of leaving the Boulder Police Department. He was surprised at that, but the FBI had been trying to recruit me for some time. He said he would send along the papers if I was interested.

Then he surprised me in return. The FBI was watching the Ramsey case, he said, and some had even discussed the possibility of investigating the district attorney's office for obstruction of justice! I volunteered to be the first witness.

––––––––––

By the middle of the month we were officially informed that none of the line detectives would be sworn into the grand jury, over the objections of our legal adviser, Bob Keatley.

Mike Kane had said it would be impossible to move the case forward without the detectives who had done all the investigative work, and Tom Haney was even more forceful: "It would be insane to cut you detectives out of it." They didn't yet understand the hatred between the DA's office and ourselves.

One reason cited for keeping us out of the grand jury was the possibility of press leaks. But when Mike Kane suggested putting subpoenas on people to ferret out all media leakers, Hunter responded, "We may not want to go there." Probably because many of the leaks came from the district attorney himself and his top deputy. It was easier to paint the police department as the problem and leave it at that.

In a final insult, we were not to be told of the time or place of the Ramsey interviews. The DA's office had said that was part of the deal with Team Ramsey.

Instead we would be allowed to watch the interviews on videotape hours after they took place, and we could give our thoughts on the questioning to the DA's office. That would be too little, too late, in my opinion. The questioners needed immediate responses, not some late night roundtable discussion.

Sergeant Wickman picked up his briefcase that night and left, saying, "This thing is all but over for us. I don't have a fucking clue as to what they're doing anymore. I'd be pissed at Beckner for not telling me, but I don't think he has a clue either."

On the night of June 17, I made my decision to take a bunch of accumulated overtime, holidays, and leave and just get away from the madhouse.

Although I had pangs of guilt about abandoning the case, I realized that I wasn't really quitting anything because it clearly was no longer our case. I decided to simply leave quietly, and to cite my health concerns as the reason.

When I informed Chief Koby of my decision, he tried to arrange a paid leave for work-related illness. "It's time to let go, Steve," he said. "You need to get back to your life. We gave the DA a case, and if they want to screw it up, that's their decision. This is not your life."

"Steve thinks it is," said Sergeant Wickman.

———

JonBenét's brother, Burke Ramsey, was interviewed in Atlanta for two hours a day on consecutive days in early June, after Deputy DA Pete Hofstrom and Detective Schuller visited Georgia for a while to determine whether the boy was "a morning person or an afternoon person." Now eleven years old, Burke would be interviewed alone by Schuller while Hofstrom and Ramsey lawyer Jim Jenkins watched from another room. The arrangement seemed designed more to make the boy comfortable than to elicit information.

Rolling back on the idiotic order that we stay out of Georgia, Detective Jane Harmer was allowed to fly to Atlanta to represent the Boulder cops. She was kept waiting in her hotel room for hours before being contacted by Pete Hofstrom, who then refused to tell her where the meeting with Burke would take place. Harmer changed her ticket and returned to Boulder early. Videotapes of Burke's interviews were sent back to us for review.

Since I had done all the previous work in Atlanta and there was a lot left to do there, I had hoped to be included on the trip. Even if we were not involved in the interview, Harmer and I could still have covered a lot of ground. That was not to be. "There is resistance to Thomas in Atlanta," Beckner said. I wasn't well liked by the DA's office, the Ramseys, or their lawyers. In my opinion, Team Ramsey apparently had such a firm hold on the current negotiations that we could no longer even do routine police work without their say-so.

About that time, Beckner received a letter from a retired cop, who challenged him to "get some backbone, get some guts . . ." and added, "You guys should be ashamed. . . . Shame!" The hate mail was humiliating.

———

Burke Ramsey seemed to have recovered his memory, but to me his answers seemed awkward and he was clearly uncomfortable. When asked how he thought JonBenét had been killed, he replied, "I have no idea." In his first interview he had been explicit in describing what happened to her. He confirmed that her bed-wetting had been a big problem.

With his legs pulled up and his chin on his knees, Burke said he played some Nintendo on the afternoon of December 25. When showed a photograph of the pineapple and bowl, he recognized the bowl. That showed it belonged in the house and was not brought in by an intruder. He recalled nothing unusual at the Whites' party other than getting a mild shock from the electric deer fence outside.

He said that his sister fell asleep in the car on the way home but awakened to help carry presents into the house of a friend. When they got home, JonBenét walked in slowly and went up the spiral stairs to bed, just ahead of Patsy. That was quite a difference from the initial and frequently repeated story that she was carried to bed. I felt that this poor kid was confused and that he really had no idea what had happened that night.

He heard the "house creaking" during the night, he said, and when he awoke, his mother was turning on the lights and in a rush, saying, "Oh my gosh, oh my gosh," then his father turned the lights off again. Burke stayed in bed "wondering if something bad had happened." He heard his father trying to calm his mother, then telling her to call the police.

Burke told the detective he did not get out of bed that morning and that a policeman looked into his room. He recalled thinking that when the police arrived "we would probably be tied up all day" and that he was disappointed the family would not be going to Charlevoix as planned.

When the three days of interviews about his sister's murder were over, Detective Schuller asked the boy if there was anything he wanted to ask. Burke said yes and pointed to the detective's wristwatch. "Is that a Rolex?"

————

There was a new sex angle going on, of which we had been unaware, and it involved Susan Bennett, the Internet junkie known as Jameson. It was she who had sent the DA's office the early Internet communications that had turned out to be so damning for linguist Don Foster.

Now we learned that Jameson was posting confidential information on the Web, and it looked to us as if she had an inside source.

In the following days and weeks, Lou Smit admitted that he talked to Jameson "a lot" because "she has good information." Smit said Jameson claimed to have secret information about the Whites, their Christmas party, and what the children did. She passed Smit a tip about another Internet junkie who had found a Web site for child pornography and thought one of the children shown in an explicit sexual pose looked like the daughter of Ramsey housekeeper Linda Hoffmann-Pugh. The DA's office began an investigation.

I wondered why they were chasing such things. Why wouldn't they aggressively pursue the prime suspects with the same sort of zeal? When Pete Hofstrom asked the police to check out an unknown rapist and see if he was linked to the Ramsey case, I realized that they were still actively searching for their intruder and that Fleet White, Santa Bill McReynolds, and Chris Wolf were on top of their list.

Smit had not entered anything about those conversations with Jameson in the official files until we brought up the subject. Then he quickly wrote some retroactive cover-your-ass letters and pledged to stop any "direct contact" with her.

Not that it mattered anymore. They had hidden things from us all along, as if a murder investigation were some kind of "find out if you can" game, just as we dared not share everything with them if we wanted to keep it out of the media. "Alex Hunter is the biggest fucking media mouth going," I told Lou Smit in a moment of protest. Smit chewed his toothpick and agreed, "Hunter is bad about that."

On June 22 I typed up my letter requesting unpaid leave from the Boulder Police Department. Chief Koby, in his final day on the job, set up a meeting with some city bureaucrats to push for me to be granted paid medical or administrative leave due to illness. When the city representatives asked why it was related to the job, he replied, "Walk a mile in these detectives' shoes for two years, and you tell me." The city eventually said it would contest any such claim regarding my assignment to the Ramsey case.

I didn't really care, since that was Koby's idea anyway, not mine. I would just stay out for a while on a mountain of uncompensated time that had accumulated during the investigation. Then I would decide what to do next.

John and Patsy Ramsey were coming back to Colorado for their interviews, so I planned to hang around one more week and watch the delayed videotapes, then begin a long vacation. That night I dined with my family on Father's Day, and they supported my decision.

Commander Beckner and Sergeant Wickman asked if I wanted to

clear out right now instead of sitting through the interviews. No, I said, I wanted to see this show. It was the culmination of the investigation, and I wanted to give constructive observations.

But something was wrong. Beckner repeated his suggestion twice. I knew the DA's office did not want me anywhere near the Ramseys, but now there even seemed to be a problem with me watching them on a television monitor. Beckner dodged for a minute, then agreed I could stay and observe. But only that. "Don't write any reports on those interviews," he ordered. "These are the DA's deals, and I don't want you to write a report."

What an extraordinary order! They didn't want any possibility that I might document what was happening now that the DA was running the show. It was clear to me that Commander Beckner had gone over to the other side and was marching in lockstep with the DA's office and Team Ramsey. Nothing would be allowed to mar the neat picture of cooperation. The sellout was now complete.

In the final week of June, as the supersecret Ramsey interviews were held at the nearby Broomfield Police Department, Mark Beckner was named the new police chief in Boulder.

34

The June 1998 interviews with Patsy and John Ramsey defined them, in my opinion. During three days of questioning at the police department in nearby Broomfield, Colorado, Ramsey displayed a tenacious and stubborn defense of his wife and family. Patsy looked like a woman teetering on the edge. Her demeanor did not contradict my hypothesis of what happened that night.

I wished the interviews had been before a grand jury. While they could have asserted the Fifth Amendment, John Ramsey circumvented that dicey situation by letter to Alex Hunter. The DA's office allowed the Ramseys to remain safely within a negotiated comfort zone. Throughout the sessions, Ramsey referred to the district attorney and the deputy DA as Alex and Pete, while Hunter, in conferences with the police, referred to him as "Big John."

John Ramsey went on a tirade about the Boulder cops even before Lou Smit began to question him on June 23. "What the Boulder Police did to us is only exceeded by what the killer did to us," he charged, painting us as a bungling lynch mob who treated them as "hunted suspects." It was only because of our actions, he said, that their own investigation began. "These fellows were hired to protect us," he said. What rubbish, I thought. Team Ramsey was up and running shortly after the murder, and from my point of view, the Ramseys had been treated with kid

gloves for a year and a half. "The law in the hands of bigots is a dangerous thing," Ramsey declared. "And that's what we have here."

Later in the interview Ramsey would insist that "We offered and
offered and offered" to cooperate, but that the Boulder Police "were
up to no good."

Smit, who had been unable to sleep the night before the interview
thinking about what was ahead, let him blow off steam, then settled in,
with prosecutor Mike Kane also asking questions. Ramsey was accompanied by his attorney Bryan Morgan and a private investigator. The
Boulder detectives were allowed to view videotapes of the interviews
later, and briefing sessions were held each evening between the DA's
office and the police.

Ramsey stuck close to his team's theory that the murderer was someone known to the family who was angry with them. The intruder came
in through the basement window, scuffing the wall and putting the
suitcase beneath the window, then hid out and killed JonBenét.

The next morning, December 26, John Ramsey had been in the
upstairs bathroom when he heard Patsy scream his name. He hurried
downstairs while she was coming up, and she handed him the ransom
note on the second-floor landing.

As an aside, he remarked lightly that his attorneys get nervous when
he recalls exact details. They should have been nervous, for Patsy was
telling her interviewers about the same time that she did not pick up
the note, which had no fingerprints. It was a direct contradiction.

Ramsey, indicating that he took the note downstairs, said he spread
it on the kitchen floor to read it, then checked on Burke and found
him asleep. He told Patsy to call the police. Asked why he did not make
the call, he replied that it was just the way things were done in their
family.

The first big surprise came when Ramsey announced that, while
police were in the house, he used a pair of binoculars to look out of
Burke's second-floor bedroom window and saw a strange truck parked
behind a home across the road. It was the first that any of us had heard
of this. I could not believe that the father of JonBenét had waited eighteen months to reveal this information. If he thought it might be in the
least way relevant to her murder, why didn't he dash downstairs right
away and yell, "Hey, cops! There's a suspicious truck in the alley!"

He also mentioned for the first time that there was a hang-up telephone call that morning. Although it was suggestive of a kidnapper, our
records did not show such a call, and the phones were monitored.

Ramsey stuck to his original story of seeing the girl's body "clearly and instantly" when he opened the cellar door and for the first time said he did *not* turn on the light. Our tests and the testimony of Fleet White had convinced us that it was impossible to see anything in the darkness, particularly when the view was blocked by a jutting interior corner.

JonBenét, he said, was lying on the floor on her back, and the blanket was neatly folded across her body, tucked in "like an Indian papoose, like someone put her there comfortably with her mouth taped." Describing how he untied one wrist, he said the ligature was very tight around the swollen arm, although the autopsy showed no sign of a tightly bound cord. In fact, it had been so loosely tied that the knot and loop remained intact when removed.

The reason for giving the early instruction to his pilot to get the plane ready was that he wasn't thinking clearly and just wanted to take his wife and son "home to Atlanta." And when the police wanted the Ramseys to come in for interviews later that day, he said, "We couldn't."

Following up on why they yearned for Atlanta, John Ramsey replied that Patsy liked the South, enjoyed shopping and the country club life in the city, and could not find lipstick in Boulder.

He talked about his new Harley motorcycle. Returning to more serious subjects, Ramsey stumbled when Lou Smit questioned him about the pineapple. He insisted that he didn't remember JonBenét eating it at the Whites' Christmas party and knew she didn't eat it at home before going to sleep. In retrospect, he thought it "strange" that Priscilla White fixed her a plate of cracked crab. He would "guarantee" JonBenét did not eat the pineapple at home, so it had to be before they went to the Whites' or while they were there. "I don't buy that an intruder fed her pineapple," he declared, adding that he recognized neither the bowl containing the fruit nor the spoon that were on the table.

The very next day he retracted that firm statement, saying his lawyer chastised him for making it. Neither he nor Patsy fed her pineapple, he said, but then he asked, "What if she knew the intruder?" After thinking about it, he said, "It hit me like a ton of bricks." JonBenét "adored" Santa Bill McReynolds, and if he had come into her room, she would have gotten out of bed and gone downstairs with him without a problem. "She may have had a secretly prearranged meeting," he said. "Maybe he fed her pineapple." The detectives stopped the tape and watched that section repeatedly. Only the day before, Ramsey had said such a thing was impossible. Now he laid it on Santa Bill.

McReynolds also fit the profile of knowing the family, perhaps was envious of their wealth ("he didn't have two nickels to rub together"), and visited porno shops, Ramsey said. Whoa, I thought. Where'd he learn that? Then I remembered that Alex Hunter had callously joked about McReynolds and that the DA's office kept few secrets from Team Ramsey. John Ramsey had obviously been thinking quite a bit about Santa Bill. He said the old man only claimed to be frail but didn't seem that way on his television appearances and had even gone to Europe on a vacation.

(After the formal session, Deputy DA Pete Hofstrom, Deputy DA Mary Keenan, who was beginning to take a bigger role, and DA investigator Dan Schuller interviewed the Ramseys to obtain more information about McReynolds. It was as if the work we had done on the entire McReynolds family was totally disregarded. The DA's office had a target that wasn't named Ramsey, and the facts be damned.)

Over the three days of interviews, however, Santa Bill McReynolds was only one of many potential suspects named by Ramsey. Also high on the list were ex-friends Fleet and Priscilla White. He recalled that Fleet had both cord and duct tape and that instead of being comforting on December 26, Fleet had furiously scribbled notes. He said Priscilla was jealous of Patsy and used the ransom note term "fat cat." And it was Fleet and Priscilla who pressured the Ramseys to appear on CNN "to defend ourselves," Ramsey claimed. Just the opposite was true: Fleet had confronted Ramsey on the decision to appear in the media. Ramsey hedged slightly, saying that he and Patsy willingly went on the national television show because of "all the sympathy, all the outpouring of support, we wanted to thank everyone." That sounded like two opposing reasons for the same decision.

Then he offered up a smorgasbord of suspects that included a cook at Pasta Jay's restaurant, a "striking couple" from "back East" who had been seen in church, his secretary's boyfriend, other church members, business associates, "pigsty" neighbors, and assorted fringe players.

The most surprising name he turned over was that of Jay Elowsky, his friend and business partner in Pasta Jay's Restaurant, who he said possibly owned a stun gun. It was to Elowsky's home in Boulder that the Ramseys retreated after returning from burying JonBenét in Atlanta. Elowsky defended them so staunchly that he was arrested for threatening two men he believed to be photographers intruding on the Ramseys' privacy. Throwing Elowsky under the bus just about eliminated the Ramsey circle of friends in Boulder.

In view of the new suspects being named, Smit asked if Patsy might be involved in the murder, and John Ramsey snapped, "Preposterous, absolutely out of the question." In his eyes, everybody was a suspect but his wife.

"There are many who think the Ramseys did it," said Lou Smit. "I'm going to take you at your word. You're a Christian. Will you swear to God you didn't do this?"

"I swear to God," Ramsey replied. "I swear to God."

"Anyone else? Your wife? Swear to God?"

"I swear to God that what I've told you is the truth. We loved our children. Having lost a child . . . JonBenét was a gift." He began to weep. "To lose her was more than I could bear."

Kane threw Ramsey a curve on the religious aspect and asked him to recite his favorite Bible passage. John Ramsey could not do so. I felt Smit was being totally used.

Smit appeared to telegraph his questions, giving Ramsey plenty of information before asking for an answer, therefore allowing him plenty of time to consider what he was about to say. Smit even suggested that the cellar room had been recently swept and thus the Hi-Tec print was new. Yes, John Ramsey confirmed—indeed it had been recently swept.

Lou was full of unorthodox tactics, such as dropping in idle thoughts like "maybe the intruder took Patsy's bike." Patsy's bike? What did that have to do with anything? His interview, of course, was predicated on the idea that the Ramseys were innocent, and his bias was obvious.

Smit slowly leafed through notebooks filled with evidence pictures, asking Ramsey if he noticed anything different, unusual, or out of place. The common theme was that plenty of things were strange. A box of tissues did not belong there, a pillow missing here, dust and dirt disturbed elsewhere. To Ramsey it looked as though the Tupperware container in JonBenét's bedroom had something in it (the same thing Lou Smit believed). Ramsey's testimony seemed very well rehearsed. Ramsey almost seemed to know the answers before the questions were asked. A cigar box was out of place, as was his golf bag. He pointed out marks on a keyhole and noted that an Easter basket had been moved.

When Smit showed Ramsey a photo of the unidentified boot print in the cellar, Ramsey's private investigator was allowed to lean over and draw the pattern. When the detectives reviewed the videotape, Gosage threw a can of Skoal tobacco at the television screen and stormed from the room, cursing that a year's worth of work had just been handed to a prime suspect and his lawyer. Importantly, Ramsey said the "dirty" flashlight found at the scene did not belong to the family. We knew that he owned one just like it.

Smit also seemed to lose control of the interview at times and let John Ramsey question him. Ramsey asked about the stun gun, and Smit went on the videotaped record by saying that yes, he thought a stun gun had been used. It was a terrible mistake because a defense attorney would be able to show the jury that a district attorney's own investigator believed an alternate theory of the crime.

I thought I had heard it all, but Ramsey outdid himself by saying that JonBenét herself had launched the beauty pageant career and "was more insistent about it than Patsy." She had seen a newspaper advertisement, he said, and told her parents she wanted to do that. I felt it would be quite unusual for a four-year-old girl to be paging through a newspaper and reading the ads.

As a point of business, Smit asked for Ramsey's consent to obtain a complete set of credit card and phone records, which we had been unable to get because the DA wouldn't issue a search warrant. Even Ramsey was surprised the police didn't have them, but his lawyer said there were still issues about maintaining an "island of privacy." In other words, don't expect them anytime soon.

In another interview room, retired Denver homicide detective Captain Tom Haney, who was more of a street fighter than Lou Smit, was simultaneously interviewing Patsy Ramsey. He spent long hours ever so slowly pushing her into corners, pinning her down on specifics, and getting her to commit to details.

Deputy DA Trip DeMuth and Patsy's lawyer, Pat Burke, were almost invisible. Just as she had done with me, Patsy went one-on-one with Haney without hesitation. Dressed in a dark blazer, dark slacks, a scarf, and earrings, with a tissue in her hand, she would sometimes close her eyes and retreat into herself before giving her answers. She began very politely, although she was rather vague on general topics during the first two days, denying involvement and saying, "I just did my best."

Unlike her husband, Patsy saw very little out of place as she went through the photographs. She confirmed that Burke was asleep, contrary to what we knew from the 911 call enhancement, and said she had never checked on her son, although Ramsey had said she did. I thought it would have been extremely odd for a mother not to check on her other child in such a situation.

She insisted that JonBenét was taken straight to bed, and she was unable to provide any information about the bowl of pineapple, although she identified the bowl as theirs.

By the third day Haney had figured out how to push her buttons. "She's not a very good actress," he observed. He needled her by saying that the $100,000 reward they had posted was not really very much compared with the family's total wealth. It was about the price of a new boat, he noted.

As her patience became exhausted, she grew animated and aggressive on that third day, and Haney bored in. Instead of the teary victim, I saw an agitated and curt woman. I saw the southern belle vanish and a steel magnolia emerge. During the breaks she stood outside chain-smoking.

If Haney asked about her growing up or her family, she would dismiss it by demanding to know what such information had to do with the killing of her daughter. "We're wasting time," she told him.

When he brought up the prior vaginal abuse, she demanded to see the evidence. Haney pressed. "It's a fact," he said. "I want to see it," she replied. "I'm shocked. I am very distressed." Her voice, however, remained calm at that point. "Does this surprise you?" he asked. "Extremely," she said. "Who could have done it?" Haney asked. She had no idea.

But when he indicated that we might have trace evidence linking her to the death of her daughter, Patsy became indignant. "Totally impossible. Go retest it," she ordered, with a sharp edge to her voice. "I don't care what you have. I don't give a flying flip. Go back to the drawing board."

She pointed a finger straight at her questioner. "We have to start working together to find out who the hell did it! My life has been hell . . . This child was the most precious thing in my life. Quit screwing around asking me this stuff and let's find the person who did this."

Haney said they were not ready to show her evidence and challenged her further. "Pal, you don't want to go there," she warned, adding that she was a good Christian woman who did not lie. She pushed back against the couch and exhaled in disgust. "Criminy," she exclaimed.

Haney continued to be inhospitable and probed about whether the death could have been an accident resulting from bed-wetting. Patsy held up a hand, like a stop sign. "You're going down the wrong path, buddy!"

Later she said, "If John Ramsey were involved, honey, we wouldn't be sitting here. I'd have knocked his block off. Read my lips! This was not done by a family member. Didn't happen. Period. End of statement."

Still Haney came on, polite but insistent, inquiring about any family secrets, and she tired of him. "Cut to the chase," she barked.

"Oh, no," Haney responded smoothly. "That would spoil the ride."

"Then spoil my ride," Patsy said, her eyes riveting him. She didn't give an inch.

It was a spellbinding exchange. Tom Haney, with his no-nonsense style and three days in which to ask his questions, had found something I felt had to be there somewhere not too far below that polished beauty queen surface. Patsy Ramsey had, for a few moments, lifted her mask. Beneath it, I saw cold rage.

————

Each night at seven o'clock, District Attorney Hunter and his staff met with us for an hour to review the day's questioning. The police were mere onlookers, for our advice wasn't really sought. Hunter, sleeves rolled up and tie loose, was more like a bystander, and a curtain of tension hung in the room.

I was listening to the rhythm behind the words and didn't particularly like the result. No decision had yet been made on calling a grand jury, and it was clear that there was still a strong contingent in the DA's office who were obviously not for it, not even for the truncated version designed by Pete Hofstrom. I guess they didn't see what I just saw. Incredibly, they were leaning toward a brand-new investigation, starting with Santa Bill!

Lou Smit, so emotional that he shed tears, was immovable in declaring John Ramsey innocent of any wrongdoing. Hofstrom, after telling us about how he himself had married the same woman twice and idolized her when she became seriously ill, added that he realized John Ramsey felt the same way about Patsy. We pointed out that Ramsey's claim that he had supported Patsy throughout her cancer ordeal seemed at odds with some of his actions. While she flew to Maryland for treatment a dozen times, he had only been with her for two or three trips, and sometimes Patsy even went alone.

Prosecutor Mike Kane, whom we respected, said in summary that John Ramsey would be very believable to a jury. Either he is innocent, or he is blindly loyal in protecting Patsy, refusing to give up on a single point, he said. Kane said he had found a number of points that could be used effectively in a prosecution of the Ramseys, but Santa Bill alone might pose reasonable doubt. When Kane spoke, Hunter stared at him almost with a look of infatuation.

Alex Hunter said that he thought Patsy Ramsey was involved. That was more than offset by comments from his staff. Deputy DA Mary Keenan said the body language of John and Patsy Ramsey wasn't suggestive of deception and that men were not in a position to judge Patsy's demeanor. Dan Schuller, the new DA investigator, told us he had once been married to a southern woman named Patsy. "That's how people act in the South," he said. Being from Arkansas myself, I didn't know what the hell he was talking about.

When I left the final briefing, I knew that it was over for me. The inmates had taken over the asylum, and lunacy reigned. An aggressive grand jury prosecution targeting the Ramseys was not going to happen, the defense lawyers had manipulated the process to death, justice had been derailed, the DA's investigators thought the Ramseys were innocent, and the posse was saddling up to gallop off after suspects who had already been cleared.

I could no longer accept things the way they were, and I could not change them. Boulder was Boulder, and I was tired of tilting at the DA's windmills. That left only one path open for me—to resign from the police department. I had been talking with an old friend, another ex-cop from Boulder, Todd Sears, about starting a carpentry business, and that night I decided to trade my badge for a hammer.

On Friday morning, June 26, I found the SitRoom empty when I came in to clean up some loose ends and write the last of about 250 police reports I had filed on the JonBenét Ramsey case.

There was nothing more I could do on the case. I just wanted to leave quietly, and I did so by citing my health problem, although it had stabilized. I could pass any physical examination. With a couple of months' worth of accumulated leave, I would take time off to think about things, cool down, and write a brief letter of resignation at some point down the road.

I found Mark Beckner in his office, exploring the Beckner Fan Club Web site. He thanked me for all my work on the case, hardly looking away from the computer.

Detectives Jane Harmer and Ron Gosage came into the SitRoom, looking whipped after another meeting with the DA's staff. "This case is going nowhere," Gosage concluded. Harmer said the meeting was "horrible" and that I was lucky to have missed it. "It would have just made you scream," she said.

No it wouldn't. I was tired of screaming. Harmer left, and when I wrapped up my paperwork, I gave Gosage a firm handshake. We said nothing, but my partner already knew my decision. It's hard for cops to say good-bye.

Down the hall, I walked past the office of legal adviser Bob Keatley, through the corridor, and out into the parking lot. The door opened behind me, and Keatley walked with me to my car. We were a couple of battle-weary veterans who knew the war was lost. The Ramsey case would eventually cost Keatley his marriage of twenty-five years.

"You're never coming back, are you?" he asked.

"No."

"It's the best decision ever."

He shook my hand, and I got into my car and drove off, heading south, with the Flatiron Mountains on my right, leaving behind my life as a cop. I unclipped my detective shield and dropped it on the seat beside me, never to wear it again.

35

The telephone kept ringing as various cops called to keep me updated on what was happening beneath the circus tent, and I found it discouraging. The DA's office had decided to go full-out after Santa Bill McReynolds and to put him under a microscope.

A tentative plan was being drafted to assign three detectives to prosecutor Mike Kane to pursue the "Ramsey theory" and three more to Deputy DA Mary Keenan to go after the "Intruder Theory." Keenan, my sources said, was intent on entering the case by breaking it wide open and arresting the real killer. Deputy DA Trip DeMuth would be the "case manager," and Deputy DA Pete Hofstrom would be the "field general."

They had gone all the way back to square one instead of following the evidence. I wondered what part of our June presentation they didn't understand. And my sources said that the grand jury idea was looking less like an option. Even if one were called, it would play by Hofstrom's lenient, no-charge plan.

"No one will be indicted. It's going to just go away," other detectives told me. When I was in the middle of the case, I had felt that what was happening was very wrong. Now that I had left, I felt much stronger. *Goddamn, this is wrong!*

I was going to resign, and it was best to keep my profile low, but my determination to keep my temper in check eroded as I watched the continuation of what I believed to be outrageous and unprofessional conduct.

DA investigator Lou Smit tried but failed to "break" Patrol Officer Rick French from his story of what happened on the first day of the murder.

Fleet and Priscilla White were being hauled over the coals because they wanted to see their previous statements, pointing out that they were being denied the same privilege given to the Ramseys. Chief Mark Beckner declared that the Whites, who had supported another candidate for his new job, were "morally empty" and again suggested putting Fleet White in jail. "For what?" I had asked Beckner, incredulously. Beckner later asked me if Fleet could possibly be the murderer. The Whites, both of whom were crucial prosecution witnesses, had somehow maintained their dignity even while standing up to John Ramsey, being fingered repeatedly for the murder, and being mistreated by the district attorney, a couple of police chiefs, state elected officials, and the media. As one detective put it, "I've never seen two people so fucked over in my life." The Whites were thrown to the wolves because they wanted a special prosecutor to look into the murder of a little girl.

Then at the end of July Don Foster, the Vassar linguist who had helped make our case, telephoned to tell me that the DA's office had just dismissed him. Not only did they fire Foster but they informed him that he was through doing this kind of work. Citing his Internet comments to Jameson when he knew nothing about the case, they declared that his later conclusions, when he knew everything, were unreliable.

Rather than fight to use his testimony, they declared that he would be open to impeachment on that one issue. Furthermore, Foster was given the plain message that if he didn't contact the FBI and other law enforcement agencies he'd worked for and admit that he was compromised and damaged goods, then the Boulder DA's office might make the call. "He's cooked here," said one detective.

It was a ridiculous attack on the man's sterling reputation. Without Don Foster the case against Patsy Ramsey was much more difficult, but the DA's office threw him overboard. Not only did they want him off the case but it appeared they wanted to ruin his life. It was so like them, I thought, to go after the dissenters, those who didn't agree with them. The DA's office wouldn't stand up to Team Ramsey but had no hesitation about burning good people who stood in their way.

I hate bullies. A main reason I got into police work was to protect those who could not protect themselves. But how do you do that when the law itself is the bully?

Because of what was going on in secret, I was toying with the idea of blowing the whistle and letting the public see how the noninvestigation of the JonBenét Ramsey murder had become, among other things, a search-and-destroy mission against those who opposed the DA's office.

All America wanted to know why we had not solved this case, and the Boulder Police remained a national joke. What would America say if it knew the truth?

In most communities the local media would investigate and inform the public, but in Boulder the lone significant media voice was the *Daily Camera,* a small-town newspaper that befriended and defended the district attorney. The newspaper also focused its rage against critics of the system rather than examining the power elite within its own community.

"HUNTER GIVES US HOPE," the *Camera* cried in an editorial.

> District Attorney Alex Hunter has stepped up to the plate carrying a big bat and swinging it with the determination of a home run hitter. I expect justice for JonBenét Ramsey, he says firmly. And the way he says that, and the manner in which he intends to bring it about cause us to regain some of our long lost hope.
>
> It has been apparent from the get-go that Hunter is not about to make the same mistake that Boulder police chief Tom Koby and his detective force have made throughout the case. He won't let his ego—or anybody else's—stop him from getting outside help as he evaluates and readies a case for presentation to a grand jury. . . .
>
> The JonBenét Ramsey case is an exhausting 16 months old. Maybe, just maybe, our district attorney can bring closure to the Christmas Day murder of a 6-year-old beauty queen, a death and mystery that continues to captivate the curiosity and imaginations of people around the world. Now, let's give Hunter the space he needs to do the job right.

Even as the *Camera* lauded Hunter for bringing in outside help, his top outside hire was considering leaving. There was severe fighting within the DA's grand jury team, and I learned that Mike Kane was so frustrated he was about to walk away after a heated argument with Trip DeMuth. He reportedly gave Alex Hunter the ultimatum to choose between him and the Hofstrom-DeMuth team. I believed that if Kane left there would be no chance for a grand jury.

———

Things hit bottom for me with a telephone call from another detective, who gave me the news that "they're trying to hang Santa Bill."

DeMuth was on the trail of Bill McReynolds, even using undercover cops to tail him. The Dynamic Duo of DeMuth and his new investigator, Dan Schuller, pulled the trigger when they saw McReynolds loading his pickup truck at a storage locker. DeMuth confronted Santa Bill, convinced that the cord being used to lash down a tarpaulin was like the cord used in the murder garrote. McReynolds got angry, and that only fed the paranoia of the DA's people. They thought his standing up to DeMuth proved that the elderly man was not weak and frail after all, just as John Ramsey had said.

The DA's office called in a specialist from the Colorado Bureau of Investigation, and a convoy of police cars headed up the mountain to Santa Bill's house. They parked at a gas station down the road and sent my old partner, Detective Ron Gosage, up to talk because he was the only one with whom McReynolds would speak.

Gosage was met by an irate Jesse McReynolds, who said he was "sick of you guys trying to frame my dad." Bill McReynolds, distraught, weeping, and saying, "I didn't do anything," refused to come to the door. His wife, Janet McReynolds, eventually gave Gosage the cord, and Ron knew instantly that it wasn't the same type used by the killer of JonBenét.

Gosage took it back down the hill to the gas station and handed it to the technician from the CBI. She looked at it for about three seconds and agreed that was not the same cord. Gosage took the good news back to the house, but Janet McReynolds told him, "Stay out of our lives."

The embarrassed cops got into their cars, and the official convoy slunk back down the mountain. Trip DeMuth stood at the gas station with his arms crossed, watching them drive away.

Things were falling apart. My mind made up, I spent the weekend composing what would become known as "The Letter." No longer willing to go gently into the night, I decided to leave with a thunderbolt, although it meant I would never be a cop again. I no longer cared.

I called a florist and had flowers delivered to a little cemetery in Marietta, Georgia. Then I dated my letter of resignation to mark what would have been JonBenét's eighth birthday.

Aug. 6

Chief Beckner,

On June 22, I submitted a letter to Chief Koby, requesting a leave of absence from the Boulder Police Department. In response to persistent speculation as to why I chose to leave the Ramsey investigation, this letter explains more fully those reasons. Although my concerns were well known for some time, I tried to be gracious in my departure, addressing only health concerns. However, after a month of soul searching and reflection, I feel I must now set the record straight.

The primary reason I chose to leave is my belief that the district attorney's office continues to mishandle the Ramsey case. I had been troubled for many months with many aspects of the investigation. Albeit an uphill battle of a case to begin with, it became a nearly impossible investigation because of the political alliances, philosophical differences, and professional egos that blocked progress in more ways, and on more occasions, than I can detail in this memorandum. I and others voiced these concerns repeatedly. In the interest of hoping justice would be served, we tolerated it, except for those closed door sessions when detectives protested in frustration, where fists hit the table, where detectives demanded that the right thing be done. The wrong things were done, and made it a matter of simple principle that I could not continue to participate as it stood with the district attorney's office. As an organization, we remained silent, when we should have shouted.

The Boulder Police Department took a handful of detectives days after the murder, and handed us this case. As one of those five primary detectives, we tackled it for a year and a half. We conducted an exhaustive investigation, followed the evidence where it led us, and were faithfully and professionally committed to this case. Although not perfect, cases rarely are. During eighteen months on the Ramsey investigation, my colleagues and I worked the case night and day, and in spite of tied hands. On June 1–2, 1998, we crunched thirty thousand pages of investigation to its essence, and put our cards on the table, delivering the case in a formal presentation to the district attorney's office. We stood confident in our work. Very shortly thereafter, though, the detectives who know this case better than anyone were advised by the district attorney's office that we would not be participating as grand jury advisory witnesses.

The very entity with whom we shared our investigative case file to see justice sought, I felt, was betraying this case. We were never afforded true prosecutorial support. There was never a consolidation of resources. All legal opportunities were not made available. How were we expected to "solve" this case when the district attorney's office was crippling us with their positions? I believe they were, literally, facilitating the escape of justice. During this investigation, consider the following:

- During the investigation detectives would discover, collect, and bring evidence to the district attorney's office, only to have it summarily dismissed or rationalized as insignificant. The most elementary of investigative efforts, such as obtaining telephone and credit card records, were met without support, search warrants denied. The significant opinions of national experts were casually dismissed or ignored by the district attorney's office, even the experienced FBI were waved aside.
- Those who chose not to cooperate were never compelled before a grand jury early in this case, as detectives suggested only weeks after the murder, while information and memories were fresh.
- An informant, for reasons of his own, came to detectives about conduct occurring inside the district attorney's office, including allegations of a plan intended only to destroy a man's career. We carefully listened. With that knowledge, the department did nothing. Other than to alert the accused, and in the process burn two detectives (who captured that exchange on an undercover wire, incidentally) who came forth with this information. One of the results of that internal whistleblowing was witnessing Detective Commander John Eller, who also could not tolerate what was occurring, lose his career and reputation undeservedly; scapegoated in a manner which only heightened my concerns. It did not take much inferential reasoning to realize that any dissidents were readily silenced.
- In a departure from protocol, police reports, physical evidence, and investigative information were shared with the Ramsey defense attorneys, all of this in the district attorney's office "spirit of cooperation." I served a search warrant, only to find later defense attorneys were simply given copies of the evidence it yielded.

- An FBI agent, whom I didn't even know, quietly tipped me off about what the DA's office was doing behind our backs, conducting an investigation the police department was wholly unaware of.
- I was advised not to speak to certain witnesses, and all but dissuaded from pursuing particular investigative efforts. Polygraphs were acceptable for some subjects, but others seemed immune from such requests.
- Innocent people were not "cleared," publicly or otherwise, even when it was unmistakably the right thing to do, as reputations and lives were destroyed. Some in the district attorney's office, to this day, pursue weak, defenseless, and innocent people in shameless tactics that one couldn't believe more bizarre if it were made up.
- I was told by one in the district attorney's office about being unable to "break" a particular police officer from his resolute accounts of events he had witnessed. In my opinion, this was not trial preparation, this was an attempt to derail months of hard work.
- I was repeatedly reminded by some in the district attorney's office just how powerful and talented and resourceful particular defense attorneys were. How could decisions be made this way?
- There is evidence that was critical to the investigation, that to this day has never been collected, because neither search warrants nor other means were supported to do so. Not to mention evidence which still sits today, untested in the laboratory, as differences continue about how to proceed.
- While investigative efforts were rebuffed, my search warrant affidavits and attempts to gather evidence in the murder investigation of a six-year-old child were met with refusals and, instead, the suggestion that we "ask the permission of the Ramseys" before proceeding. And just before conducting the Ramsey interviews, I thought it inconceivable I was being lectured on "building trust."

These are but a few of the many examples of why I chose to leave. Having to convince, to plead at times, to a district attorney's office to assist us in the investigation into the murder of a little girl, by way of the most basic of investigative requests, was simply absurd. When my detective partner and I had to literally hand search tens of thousands of receipts, because we didn't have a search warrant to assist us otherwise, we did so. But we lost tremendous opportunities to make progress, to seek justice, and to know the truth. Auspicious timing and strategy could have made a difference. When the might of the criminal justice system should have brought all it had to bear on this investigation, and didn't, we remained silent. We were trying to deliver a murder case with hands tied behind our backs. It was difficult, and our frustrations understandable. It was an assignment without chance of success. Politics seemed to trump justice.

Even "outsiders" quickly assessed the situation, as the FBI politely noted early on: "the government isn't in charge of this investigation." As the nation watched, appropriately anticipating a fitting response to the murder of the most innocent of victims, I stood bothered as to what occurred behind the scenes. Those inside this case knew what was going on. Eighteen months gave us a unique perspective.

We learned to ignore the campaign of misinformation in which we were said to be bumbling along, or else just pursuing one or two suspects in some ruthless vendetta. Much of what appeared in the press was orchestrated by particular sources wishing to discredit the Boulder Police Department. We watched the media spun, while we were prohibited from exercising First Amendment rights. As disappointment and frustration pervaded, detectives would remark to one another, "If it reaches a particular point, I'm walking away." But we would always tolerate it "just one more time." Last year, when we discovered hidden cameras inside the Ramsey house, only to realize the detectives had been unwittingly videotaped, we allowed that, too, to pass without challenge. The detectives' enthusiasm became simply resigned frustration, acquiescing to that which should never have been tolerated. In the media blitz, the pressure of the whole world watching, important decisions seemed to be premised on "how it would play" publicly. Among at least a few of the detectives, "there's something wrong here" became a catch phrase. I witnessed others having to make decisions which impacted their lives and careers, watched the soul searching that occurred as the ultimate questions were pondered. As it goes, "evils that befall the world are not nearly so often caused by bad men, as they are by good men who are silent when an opinion must be voiced." Although several good men in the police department shouted loudly behind closed doors, the organization stood deafeningly silent at what continued to occur unchallenged.

Last Spring, you, too, seemed at a loss. I was taken aback when I was reminded of what happened to Commander Eller when he stuck his neck out. When reminded how politically powerful the DA was. When reminded of the hundreds of other cases the department had to file with this district attorney's office, and that was but one case. And finally, when I was asked, "What do you want done? The system burned down?" it struck me dumb. But when you conceded that there were those inside the DA's office we had to simply accept as "defense witnesses," and when we were reduced to simply recording our objections for "documentation purposes"—I knew I was not going to participate in this much longer.

I believe the district attorney's office is thoroughly compromised. When we were told by one in the district attorney's office, months before we had even completed our investigation, that this case "is not prosecutable," we shook our heads in disbelief. A lot could have been forgiven, the lesser transgressions ignored, for the right things done. Instead, those in the district attorney's office encouraged us to allow them to "work their magic" (which I never fully understood. Did "magic" include sharing our case file information with defense attorneys, dragging our feet in evidence collection, or believing that two decades of used-car-dealing-style-plea-bargaining was somehow going to solve this case?). Right and wrong is just that. Some of these issues were not shades of gray. Decisions should have been made as such. Whether a suspect is a penniless indigent with a public defender, or otherwise.

As contrasted by my experiences in Georgia, for example, where my warrant affidavits were met with a sense of support and an obligation to the victim. Having worked with able prosecutors in other jurisdictions, having worked cases where justice was aggressively sought, I have familiarity with these prosecution professionals who hold a strong sense of justice. And then, from Georgia, the Great Lakes, the East Coast, the South, I would return to Boulder, to again be thoroughly demoralized.

We delayed and ignored, for far too long, that which was "right," in deference to maintaining this dysfunctional relationship with the district attorney's office. This wasn't a runaway train that couldn't be stopped. Some of us bit our tongues as the public was told of this "renewed cooperation" between the police depart-

ment and the district attorney's office—this at the very time the
detectives and those in the district attorney's office weren't even
on speaking terms, at the same time you had to act as a liaison
between the two agencies because the detectives couldn't tolerate
it. I was quite frankly surprised, as you remarked on this camarade-
rie, that there had not yet been a fistfight.

In Boulder, where the politics, policies, and pervasive thought
has held for years, a criminal justice system designed to deal with
such an event was not in place. Instead, we had an institution that
when needed most, buckled. The system was paralyzed, as to this
day one continues to get away with murder.

Will there be a real attempt at justice? I may be among the last
to find out. The department assigned me some of the most sensitive and critical assignments in the Ramsey case, including search
warrants and affidavits, the Atlanta projects, the interviews of the
Ramseys, and many other sensitive assignments I won't mention.
I criss-crossed the country, conducting interviews and investigations, pursuing pedophiles and drifters, chasing and discarding
leads. I submitted over 250 investigative reports for this case alone.
I'd have been happy to assist the grand jury. But the detectives,
who know this case better than anyone, were told we would not
be allowed as grand jury advisory witnesses, as is commonplace. If
a grand jury is convened, the records will be sealed, and we will
not witness what goes on inside such a proceeding. What part of
the case gets presented, what doesn't?

District Attorney Hunter's continued reference to a "runaway"
grand jury is also puzzling. Is he afraid that he cannot control the
outcome? Why would one not simply present the evidence to
jurors, and let the jury decide? Perhaps the DA is hoping for a
voluntary confession one day. What's needed, though, is an effective district attorney to conduct the inquiry, not a remorseful
killer.

The district attorney's office should be the ethical and judicial
compass for the community, ensuring that justice is served—or at
least, sought. Instead, our DA has become a spinning compass for
the media. The perpetuating inference continues that justice is
somehow just around the corner. I do not see that occurring, as
the two year anniversary of this murder approaches.

It is my belief the district attorney's office has effectively crippled the case. The time for intervention is now. It is difficult to
imagine a more compelling situation for the appointment of an

entirely independent prosecution team to be introduced into this matter, who would oversee an attempt at righting this case.

Unmistakable and worst of all, we have failed a little girl named JonBenét. Six years old. Many good people, decent, innocent citizens, are forever bound by the murder of this child. There is a tremendous obligation to them. But an infinitely greater obligation to her, as she rests in a small cemetery far away from this anomaly of a place called Boulder.

A distant second stands the second tragedy—the failure of the system in Boulder. Ask the mistreated prosecution witnesses in this investigation, who cooperated for months, who now refuse to talk until a special prosecutor is established. Ask former detectives who have quietly tendered their shields in disheartenment. Ask all those innocent people personally affected by this case, who have had their lives upset because of the arbitrary label of "suspect" being attached. Ask the cops who cannot speak out because they still wear a badge. The list is long.

I know that to speak out brings its own issues. But as you know, there are others who are as disheartened as I am, who are biting their tongues, searching their consciences. I know what may occur—I may be portrayed as frustrated, disgruntled. Not so. I have had an exemplary and decorated thirteen year career as a police officer and detective. I didn't want to challenge the system. In no way do I wish to harm this case or subvert the long and arduous work that has been done. I only wish to speak up and ask for assistance in making a change. I want justice for a child who was killed in her home on Christmas night.

The case has defined many aspects of all our lives, and will continue to do so for all of our days. My colleagues put their hearts and souls into this case, and I will take some satisfaction that it was the detective team who showed tremendous efforts and loyalties to seeking justice for this victim. Many sacrifices were made. Families. Marriages. In the latter months of the investigation, I was diagnosed with a disease which will require a lifetime of medication. Although my health declined, I was resolved to see the case through to a satisfactory closure. I did that on June 1–2. And on June 22, I requested a leave of absence, without mention of what transpired in our department since Christmas 1996.

What I witnessed for two years of my life was so fundamentally flawed, it reduced me to tears. Everything the badge ever meant to me was so foundationally shaken, one should never have to sell one's soul as a prerequisite to wear it. On June 26, after leaving the investigation for the last time, and leaving the City of Boulder, I wept as I drove home, removing my detective's shield and placing it on the seat beside me, later putting it in a desk drawer at home, knowing I could never put it back on.

There is some consolation that a greater justice awaits the person who committed these acts, independent of this system we call "justice." A greater justice awaits. Of that, at least, we can be confident.

As a now infamous author, panicked in the night, once penned, "use that good southern common sense of yours." I will do just that. Originally from a small southern town where this would never have been tolerated, where respect for law and order and traditions were instilled in me, I will take that murderous author's out-of-context advice, and use my good southern common sense to put this case into the perspective it necessitates—a precious child was murdered. There needs to be some consequences for that.

Regretfully, I tender this letter, and my police career, a calling which I loved. I do this because I cannot continue to sanction by my silence what has occurred in this case. It was never a fair playing field, the "game" was simply unacceptable anymore. And that's what makes this all so painful. The detectives never had a chance. *If ever there were a case, and if ever there were a victim, who truly meant something to the detectives pursuing the truth, this is it.* If not this case, what case? Until such time as an independent prosecutor is appointed to oversee the case, I will not be a part of this. What went on was simply wrong.

I recalled a favorite passage recently, Atticus Finch speaking to his daughter: "Just remember that one thing does not abide by majority rule, Scout—it's your conscience."

At thirty-six years old, I thought my life's passion as a police officer was carved in stone. I realize that although I may have to trade my badge for a carpenter's hammer, I will do so with a clear conscience. It is with a heavy heart that I offer my resignation from the Boulder Police Department, in protest of this continuing travesty.

Detective Steve Thomas #638
Detective Division
Boulder Police Department

36

I had three copies of my letter delivered to the police department that morning. One went to legal adviser Bob Keatley, and another went to Commander Dave Hayes, whom I respected. Neither gave out their copies. The third went to Chief Mark Beckner.

The chief's secretary telephoned to say that Beckner wanted me to come in. Sorry, I said. I don't work there anymore. Then came a call from Internal Affairs, which wanted "to get this thing figured out." Nothing to figure out, I said. I'm a carpenter now.

About an hour later, reporter Craig Lewis of the tabloid *Globe*, whom I had never met, showed up at my front door with a complete copy of my letter of resignation. I would not talk to him. I knew Lewis had close contacts with the office of the district attorney, so I could imagine where he received his copy. DA Alex Hunter was on vacation in Alaska, and his shop was in the hands of his first assistant DA, Bill Wise.

By 5:30 P.M. my resignation was the top story on ABC World News Tonight. Cops told me that the conference room at police headquarters was packed, eyes glued to the TV screen.

The next call was not so nice. The Boulder Police Department wanted my badge and credentials immediately and also directed that I return my equipment on Monday morning, when an escort would take me through the "secured areas of the department." What a joke. One day I'm on a murder case, and the next I have to be escorted through secure areas, as if there were something in there I didn't know about.

I would not set foot back in Boulder until this was done, and I wasn't about to carry a cardboard box through a ring of reporters and sheepishly hand it over as if I had done something wrong. I said I would surrender my badge only to Commander Hayes, and within a couple of hours, not after the weekend. With the help of my friend Todd Sears, I inventoried every item of police gear I had—gun belt, leather gear, helmet, radio, vests, uniforms, the works, including all my Ramsey investigative case notes.

At 9:30 P.M. Hayes and Sergeant Mike Ready, another old friend, were waiting in an unmarked police car beneath a single streetlight at a feed store in the nearby town of Golden. Sears and I got out of my truck and shook hands with them. They were only intermediaries, and we had a history. I turned over all the gear, with Sears going over the inventory sheet. Handing my shield to Dave Hayes was one of the toughest things I had ever done.

For the rest of the night my telephone rang with calls from the media, which I didn't answer, and calls from friends and other cops who let me know they were in my corner. When I stepped outside my house, a neighbor called out from across the street: "I got one thing to say to you. Right on!"

The public relations person in the DA's office put out a statement calling my letter "outrageous" and "substantially false," although she did not say exactly what was false.

I had taken them totally by surprise, but I knew these media-savvy politicians would quickly recover, and I expected a full counterattack because it is no little thing when a cop lays down his badge and issues the kind of charges I had made. I remembered *Globe* reporter Jeff Shapiro once telling me how a gleeful Alex Hunter helped the tabloids go after Commander John Eller because "It's his time." Now, I knew, it was my time.

———————

Defense attorneys joined the fray. By attacking the office of the district attorney, I was threatening their own rice bowls. The last thing they wanted in Boulder was an aggressive DA who would vigorously prosecute criminal cases.

There was quite a bit of dissension in the police department, with line cops challenging Beckner and his command staff. Police officers had complained about the DA's office for twenty years, and this was a golden opportunity to take the challenge public, while a national spotlight shone on Boulder. My supporters were saying that the department had lost a good cop, that what I had said was true, and that the department should not play it safe on this one. Even some officers I didn't know stood up for me, demanding to know what Chief Beckner was going to do.

In response, he sent a memo to his troops saying, "It is important for everyone to know that the investigative team, myself and the Deputy Chiefs do not agree with Steve's conclusion that the case has no chance of success." The chief promised to continue working closely with the DA's office.

————

The letter did its job by getting the attention of Governor Roy Romer, who convened a team of metro district attorneys to discuss what was going on in Boulder. These were the same men who had been advising DA Alex Hunter, but now their professional reputations were on the line, so they had to find a way out of the mess while still supporting Hunter. To abandon him would indicate that they had given him bad advice all along. Hunter, the master politician, had once again placed intermediaries between himself and disaster.

The governor pledged to look into the appointment of a special prosecutor for the Ramsey case. Hunter's office promised to cooperate.

Suddenly there was a much higher priority on the table than getting even with me. I was put on the back burner while the DA tried to make the best of a terrible situation. If the governor named someone else to handle the case, it would be a devastating blow to the reputations of the Boulder prosecutors.

It was up to the governor to restore public confidence in the way things were being handled. He could no longer remain on the sidelines, and he made his official response six days after I resigned. At the time, Governor Romer was a leading light of the national Democratic Party in which Ramsey attorney Hal Haddon was also a major player. Knowing those unseen political links, I did not expect much as I watched the press conference on my living room TV.

Alex Hunter was left in place, although the governor forced him to swear in a couple of deputy district attorneys from elsewhere in the state. Being publicly forced to accept experienced outside help was a black eye for the Boulder DA, but he had survived and remained in the game.

The best part, to me, came when Governor Romer announced that a grand jury would be called to look into the murder of JonBenét Ramsey. Hallelujah!

The *Rocky Mountain News* ran an editorial that read, "The bold gamble by former Boulder Detective Steve Thomas has paid off after all. His bombshell of allegations regarding the Boulder County District Attorney's office performance in the JonBenét Ramsey case, coupled with a dramatic resignation, has prompted the governor to act."

That sounded good, and to the uninitiated it seemed that the pieces were finally falling into place. But they didn't know about Deputy DA Pete Hofstrom's rules of engagement. There was still heated opposition within the DA's office to using a grand jury at all, so it might turn out to be nothing more than window dressing. No matter what was presented, no matter how strong the evidence, no matter what Mike Kane and his new deputies wanted, the final decision on whether to seek an indictment would be made by District Attorney Hunter, who trusted and depended upon Hofstrom.

Although I liked to think my letter had something to do with the governor's decision to force the grand jury, I found it interesting that Romer never called to speak to me. He dealt only with the lawyers who had reputations and careers on the line.

While the media frenzy continued, I stayed busy with a contracting job to build a new store. A national tabloid showed up on my doorstep with a six-figure offer to sell my story. I refused. Dozens of offers to be interviewed had no appeal. I felt that I had said my piece. A month after I resigned I made a single brief television appearance. Sacks filled with mail arrived, supporting my decision to quit, giving me courage to get through one of the most trying periods of my life.

The most surprising support came from the last place I expected, a columnist for the Boulder *Daily Camera*. Juliet Whitman wrote:

> I have followed the JonBenét Ramsey case only in the newspapers, but the pattern of laziness, obfuscation and near pathological sympathy for suspects Thomas saw in the DA's office is more than familiar. Now I watch in bemusement as all the familiar rationalizations are floated, ranks close, and Governor Romer helps with damage control. Too bad for the dedicated cop who put his livelihood and reputation on the line to expose corruption. Too bad for JonBenét.

As the days passed, it seemed that things were calming after the firestorm. The police department didn't want to go to war with me and create a sideshow that would overshadow the case. They didn't deny my specific allegations and did not call me a liar. They were content to let it blow over, and so was I.

In fact, I was rather pleased with the way things were turning out. At least there would be a grand jury, and Deputy DAs Pete Hofstrom and Trip DeMuth were no longer on the case, replaced by new assistants for Mike Kane. That alone was cause for jubilation.

The ditzy scheme in which DeMuth was going to head dual new investigations of the Ramseys and "other suspects" was abandoned, and Sergeant Tom Wickman was appointed to be a police advisory witness to the grand jury. At least there would be some cop input, although Wickman had been an administrator, not an investigator, and didn't know the case as well as other detectives on the team.

I was satisfied, but the DA's office and the trash media couldn't leave well enough alone.

A source alerted me that the DA's office had gotten my confidential personnel file from the police department "to see what we're up against." Reporters told me the DA's office was using my health condition to say that my letter was only sour grapes for not being granted paid medical retirement.

Almost immediately stories appeared citing material from my personnel folder, and Bob Grant, the DA of Adams County, told a reporter, "No ill will to Thomas, but he was forced off the case by medical retirement. He wasn't there to get the job done."

Another reporter told me that First Assistant DA Bill Wise was dropping hints, not to be quoted, that I was mentally unstable. Then false reports surfaced that I was leaking case information to almost every publication and station that wanted it.

Hunter's spin was in motion. "It's his time," rang loudly in my ears. The usual systematic dehumanization of anyone who spoke against the Boulder establishment was once again in play. They were trying to take away my pride, my accomplishments, my integrity, and my reputation, and were set on destroying everything I had worked for. They were doing to an ex-cop things they wouldn't dream of doing to their pampered suspects, the Ramseys. And still I did not respond.

Jeff Shapiro of the *Globe* was waiting in ambush when I arrived home late one night in mid-August. He screeched his car to a stop in the middle of the street and flung open the door. Earlier that night he had confronted my wife when she answered the door in robe and pajamas, and tried to talk his way into our house.

"They're calling you a head case," Shapiro told me. "The DA's office wants to destroy you." So tell me something I don't already know.

Shapiro then added a warning about his tabloid employer. I would talk to them or else, he said ominously. The *Globe* had burrowed deep into my background, and "a devious little plan" had been hatched that was going to leave me with "some rather unpleasant choices to make." He started to tell me about myself.

I had studied in Sweden for a year after graduating from high school, and they had even looked up my host family there. Shapiro recounted things from my personal life that set my heart racing. "They paid a lot of money for that," Shapiro said.

Their threat would be based on the premise that my mother had killed herself because my father left her. I was stung to the core and hurt beyond belief. My mother died from a medical condition, not suicide. But I felt that a tabloid newspaper would not refrain from printing something just because it wasn't true. Facts just got in the way of a good story. And I couldn't run away. "If you move, they'll find you," said Shapiro.

He will never realize how close I came to hurting him that night. Instead I told him to get off my property and never come back. Before he got into his car, Shapiro said that I should expect another visit from Craig Lewis, his fellow *Globe* reporter, who had shown up earlier with the copy of my resignation letter. "He drives a red Explorer. Watch for it. Leave the door closed when he knocks," Shapiro warned.

When the doorbell rang a few days later, it was a Federal Express delivery. The *Globe* had dredged up ancient photos of members of my family in Arkansas, and my hands shook as I leafed through them. Photographs of my mother, my grandparents, my aunt, sisters, loved ones, navy pictures of my grandfather. They were going to drag my family into this mess, innocent people who had done nothing to bring about such an invasion of privacy. I worried about how my ill father would react when the tabloid spread lies about our family before millions of readers.

It was the most revolting, sick, and slimy thing I had ever encountered. Their intent was clear. The pictures were accompanied by a letter from Craig Lewis, saying he wanted me to "sit down and talk . . . and help me with some background information, particularly the whole conflict between the cops and the district attorney." It was carefully worded, but the warning, pictures, and letter were like some old Mafioso scheme, and to me it added up to extortion. I did not want to see my family's most private memories splashed across a supermarket tabloid, but I still refused to meet with Lewis.

This was the same tabloid newspaper that Alex Hunter was in bed with. He had almost adopted Jeff Shapiro as a pet reporter; Craig Lewis had helped deliver the *Vanity Fair* article to him; and the DA looked at *Playboy* with Tony Frost, the *Globe* editor. It disgusted me.

Later the FBI became interested in the blackmail threat after learning that Shapiro had made secret tape recordings of *Globe* meetings in which the plans were laid to pressure me. In one an editor said, "Let him stew. The pictures will freak him out."

As much as I wanted to strike back, I declined the offer of a federal investigation. If I fought them, it would just create juicier stories.

Lewis, when confronted by other media about his tactics, claimed he had innocently sent the pictures to me because he thought I would like to have them. I don't know how a dishonorable man like that can look at himself in the mirror. I don't know why any decent person would work for such a gutter publication. They are utterly beyond redemption.

In 1999 Craig Lewis was indicted by neighboring Jefferson County on charges of extortion and conspiracy for his work on the Ramsey stories and for his blatant attempt to force me to talk.

———

Only after the personal attacks did I start thinking about writing a book. Remaining a silent martyr would not work for me.

The resignation furor had been one thing, but this massive and outrageous campaign of retribution was intolerable—smearing my name by telling reporters I was mentally unbalanced, blackmail attempts by a tabloid reporter with close ties to the DA, sullying my reputation by saying I was just a pissed-off city worker who was refused a medical retirement, and claiming I was a dangerous media leak when the DA's office itself had diarrhea of the mouth. Hunter had snapped at a reporter in late 1999 when questioned once about voluminous press leaks from his office, "I am tired of these allegations!" "We leak nothing." Hunter then took himself to a new low, and declared all the memos, reports, and case information leaked to author Lawrence Schiller were from "a janitor, or a burglary, or something."

Now I had become the bad guy in the Ramsey murder investigation for exposing the flawed justice system. Anything to deflect attention from the DA's weak handling of the Ramsey case.

Things had descended to a new level, and the truth had become a casualty in this undeclared war against me.

When my plans for a book came out, even more problems arose. At one point a lawyer representing the city said, "We'll tell you what you can and cannot put in that book." My lawyer had different ideas about the First Amendment, particularly since I had signed no confidentiality agreement with the police. I was never called before the grand jury, so I was not revealing any secrets from that chamber.

As a last try, Chief Beckner appealed to my attorney, saying, "Come on, Steve is one of us." No, responded my attorney. He's not.

In my opinion, there are no secrets left in the Ramsey case, thanks to the office of the district attorney. What they were afraid of was exposure of their carefully constructed but false image that everything was fine.

I actually left Colorado to get out of the firestorm while lawyers combed through the books trying to find some way to silence me. They failed and backed off, so I came home again.

I dedicated the entire next year to writing this book.

————

As I wrote, I watched from the sidelines and talked to my cop friends to keep abreast of what was happening as the vaunted Ramsey grand jury started its sessions. Linguist Don Foster was not called as a witness. Lou Smit did testify. John and Patsy Ramsey did not. Neither did I, although I knew the case intimately. What was it they did not want me to say?

I do not doubt the abilities of prosecutor Mike Kane or his assistants, but almost two years had passed before they came on the scene, and the case they took over was already irreparably damaged. They could not be expected to magically repair what was done in the first two weeks of the case, or to repair the damage done by the sharing of evidence and secrets with the prime suspects, or to undo the special deals that had been made between the prosecution and the defense.

One of our Dream Team lawyers, thinking out loud, once wondered if having the Ramseys interviewed *prior to* the convening of the grand jury might have been part of a special deal to exclude John and Patsy from appearing officially as witnesses. Being interviewed by Lou Smit and Trip DeMuth with defense lawyers present was an entirely different experience from facing the secret proceedings with Mike Kane in charge. I thought that speculation was going too far, for surely the DA's office would not sabotage its own grand jury.

Then, from an anonymous source, I received a copy of a letter containing information on the cold case of one Thayne Smika, who had been arrested in the shotgun slaying of Sid Wells, the boyfriend of actor Robert Redford's daughter. The accused murderer is today, in cop talk, ITW—in the wind—because District Attorney Alex Hunter secretly promised the defense attorney that the 1983 grand jury hearing the case would *not* indict Smika. The victim's family, the investigating cops, and the grand jurors were not told of the deal. In the letter, an attorney named Dan Hale wrote that based on what he had seen, he reached the preliminary conclusion that "criminal acts were possibly committed during the grand jury investigation" and the stipulation agreed upon between Hunter and the defense lawyer "that certain witnesses would not be called and that no indictment would be returned . . . may be contempt of court." Dan Hale later became a judge and stopped saying bad things about Alex Hunter. Hunter insisted that the Ramsey grand jury would not be under any stipulation similar to the deal he made in the Smika case.

I remembered Pete Hofstrom's strange criteria for the possible Ramsey grand jury and how it might not even be asked to return an indictment. I once asked Commander Beckner if the grand jury was at least going to target the Ramseys and seek an indictment, and he admitted, "I don't know. Let's just see where it goes."

A Dream Team lawyer had observed that if the Ramseys were not specifically viewed as suspects, we might as well feed our 30,000-page case file into the shredder. Without targeting them, there will never be an indictment, he said.

As the months passed, the grand jury met off and on, and I stayed as far away as possible, devoting my time to this book and swinging a hammer. On the weekend before the grand jury was due to end, a friend advised me that Dr. Henry Lee told Alex Hunter, "This is a monumental decision. It all comes down on your shoulders. . . . It comes down to you. If you move forward with this, you have to confess your sins."

With that sort of warning hanging in the air, I knew where the grand jury was going. Obtaining an indictment would not have been difficult, in my opinion, based upon the available evidence and the agreement of so many law enforcement experts. The key was in Lee's comment about "moving forward," which meant an indictment followed by an arrest and a trial. These were not the strong points of our district attorney.

So after meeting for a year and a half, the grand jury adjourned in October 1999 without even issuing a report. Under law the grand jury has the option of writing a report but is not bound to do so, and the jurors usually follow the wishes of the district attorney. There was no indictment, no nothing. It was an odd, whimpering way to end this extraordinary case, and it meant that District Attorney Alex Hunter did not have to explain anything to anyone.

"I and my prosecution task force believe we do not have sufficient evidence to warrant the filing of charges against anyone who has been investigated at this time," said the district attorney.

Cloaked by the secrecy rules of the grand jury, Hunter can continue to dodge questions about what really happened. But it took fifteen years to learn of the deal that was made that crippled the Thayne Smika grand jury, and no lie can live forever.

———

The Boulder Police Department is no better post-Koby than it was pre-Beckner, although some gold circle cops are still hanging in there.

Chief Beckner continually writes editorials and posts memos about how great things have become under his leadership. But the steady exodus of good cops continues, another seven experienced officers and detectives resigning in 1999 alone. At one point the average officer on the overnight shift had less than two years of experience, including his time in the police academy.

Sergeant Tom Wickman was promoted to commander.

An Internal Affairs investigation began into tapes and material that had gone missing from the official Ramsey file, something I had brought to Beckner's attention a year earlier. Missing case file evidence is a serious matter, but nothing was done when I complained.

"Our department wasn't ready for something like this," Beckner once told me about the Ramsey investigation.

It still isn't. The recipe for a future disaster exists.

Deputy DA Mary Keenan announced as a candidate for district attorney. Among her campaign contributors was Dr. Beuf, the Ramseys' pediatrician.

Fleet White was arrested in Boulder in early 1999 for not paying a traffic ticket. He was handcuffed and taken to jail.

Tom Koby grew shoulder-length hair and a bushy beard and is occasionally seen strolling the Pearl Street Mall. He is now associated with a nonprofit venture capital firm doing worthy charitable community work.

DA investigator Lou Smit resigned shortly after the governor called the grand jury into session. He wrote in a long, public letter that "John and Patsy Ramsey did not kill their daughter [and] a very dangerous killer is still out there."

DA Alex Hunter and all his lieutenants had stuck by Lou Smit, even when we strongly challenged his ability to work in an objective fashion. They liked to say that Smit knew the case better than anyone, even better than the detectives. Lou Smit held the keys to the kingdom when he quit and returned home to Colorado Springs.

In December 1999, a few months after the grand jury came back and shortly before the third anniversary of the murder of JonBenét, Lou Smit was seen in Atlanta, praying at JonBenét's graveside with John Ramsey. He had shown case photographs to medical examiners with the Georgia Bureau of Investigation and was actively conducting an investigation, still asking stun gun questions. At this writing, he has never been challenged by the DA's office for doing so. Smit had gone over to Team Ramsey, taking all his invaluable insider knowledge with him. Hunter bet on the wrong horse.

When people ask if I believe the case will ever come to trial, if anyone will ever be arrested or convicted in this dreadful murder of a beautiful child, I sadly tell them, "No. It will never see the inside of a courtroom."

Between 1989 and 1998, there were fifty-seven homicides in Boulder County, and only a handful ever went to trial.

Alex Hunter announced in March 2000 that he would not seek an eighth term as district attorney, finally surrendering the job he held for nearly three decades. Bill Wise, his first assistant district attorney, also chose to step down at the end of the year.

I try to remain hopeful that the JonBenét Ramsey murder will be officially solved. If and when that happens, I will be the first to applaud.

But the reality of the matter is that if it gets to a courtroom, the aggressive Team Ramsey attorneys will butcher both the police department and the office of the district attorney, no matter who handles the case.

So a successful prosecution at this point is probably impossible, and it was made that way because the case was mishandled from the start, and because politics was foremost in the minds of leaders who pretended that all was well while the case disintegrated faster than sugar in water. It was the way things had been done for decades in small-town Boulder, where the system of justice is led by underzealous prosecutors who are heavily influenced by defense attorneys, and a different standard of justice exists for the rich and the poor. They should have taken a much harder line in the case from the first hours, but the police and prosecutors were untrained, unable, and unwilling to do so.

When the police botched the crime scene, they damaged the Ramsey case. When the district attorney's office started making deals, they lost it.

It was institutional idiocy, and in my opinion, there are several people in Boulder who are going to have to beg their way into heaven after this one.

I often think of the victim, little JonBenét, forever a beautiful little girl.

I believe most people are wrong about who she was, and I imagine that she would eventually have rejected the plastic Barbie doll beauty contestant lifestyle.

Shortly before her death, she participated in the America's Royale Tiny Miss pageant, which had a "come as a famous person" theme. She dressed as Marilyn Monroe, and her mother did the same. I doubt that JonBenét even knew who Marilyn Monroe was. I believe her strong-willed little spirit would have chosen her own course in life, not one mapped by a mother living vicariously through her daughter's beauty.

The more I learned about JonBenét, the more I was impressed by a child who talked about how many trips she had taken around the sun and the rhythm of the earth beneath her feet. She was an incredible little kid who loved to be tickled.

Miss America was the least she could have been.

DRAMATIS PERSONAE

So many people were involved in the Ramsey murder investigation, many with similar-sounding names, that it is difficult for a reader to keep them straight. I have attempted here to list only the major characters. BPD designates the Boulder Police Department. Alphabetically, they are:

Leslie Aaholm—City of Boulder spokesperson.
Steve Ainsworth—Boulder County Sheriff's Department investigator.
Al Alvarado—BPD computer expert.
Mike Archuleta—John Ramsey's private pilot.
Ellis Armistead—Ramsey private investigator.
Linda Arndt—BPD Detective. Present when body was found.

Rich Baer—BPD Dream Team attorney.
Ann Bardach—*Vanity Fair* reporter.
Joe and Betty Barnhill—Ramsey neighbors in Boulder.
Mark Beckner—Boulder Chief of Police, successor to Tom Koby.
Suzanne Bernhard—Child psychologist.
Dr. Francesco Beuf—JonBenét's pediatrician.
Patrick Burke—Patsy Ramsey's attorney.
Michael Bynum—Ramsey attorney.

Dan Caplis—BPD Dream Team organizer.
Tom Carson—Chief financial officer of Access Graphics.
Angie Chromiak—BPD Patrol Officer.

Laurence "Trip" DeMuth III—Boulder County Deputy District Attorney.
Jackie Dilson—Former girlfriend of Chris Wolf.
John Douglas—Former FBI profiler working for Team Ramsey.

John Eller—BPD Detective Division Commander.
Jay Elowsky—Owner of Pasta Jay's restaurant and a Ramsey friend.

John Brewer Eustace III—North Carolina prisoner with JonBenét fantasy.
Mike Everett—BPD Detective and crime scene investigator.

Barbara and John Fernie—Friends of Ramseys, summoned on December 26.
Donald Foster—Vassar professor and linguist.
Rick French—First BPD Officer on the scene.

Mike Glynn—Ramsey friend, former executive at Access Graphics.
Ron Gosage—BPD Detective.
Bob Greenlee—Councilman and later mayor of Boulder.

Hal Haddon—Ramsey attorney.
Bill Hagmaier—FBI Special Agent with Child Abduction and Serial Killer Unit (CASKU).
Joann Hanks—McGuckin's Hardware office manager.
Jane Harmer—BPD Detective.
W. Frank Harrington—Pastor of Peachtree Presbyterian Church in Atlanta.
Art Harris—CNN reporter.
Sandra and Bud Henderson—Former Access Graphics employee and her husband.
Melissa Hickman—BPD Detective.
Dan Hoffman—BPD Dream Team attorney.
Linda Hoffmann-Pugh—Ramsey housekeeper, named as the first suspect.
Pete Hofstrom—Boulder County Deputy District Attorney and chief of felony division in the Boulder County DA's office.
Rol Hoverstock—Pastor of St. John's Episcopal Church.
Alex Hunter—Boulder County District Attorney since 1972.

Greg Idler—BPD Detective.

Jim Jenkins—Ramsey lawyer in Atlanta.
Lucinda Johnson—First wife of John Ramsey, mother of Beth, Melinda, and John Andrew Ramsey.

Mike Kane—Grand jury prosecutor.
Bob Keatley—BPD attorney.
Mary Keenan—Boulder County Deputy District Attorney.
Jeff Kithcart—BPD Detective, discovered practice ransom note.
Marc Klass—Father of slain daughter Polly Klass.
Tom Koby—Boulder Chief of Police.
Pat Korten—Team Ramsey public relations specialist.
Alli Krupski—Boulder *Daily Camera* reporter.

Bernie Lamoreaux—Lockheed-Martin director of security.
John Lang—Special Agent, Georgia Bureau of Investigation.
Dr. Henry Lee—Renowned criminalist and forensic scientist.
Stewart Long—Boyfriend of Melinda Ramsey.

Mary Malatesta—Head of special capital crimes unit for Colorado Attorney General.
Jim Marino—Ramsey friend.
Larry Mason—BPD Detective Sergeant.
Bill McReynolds—Santa Claus at Ramsey Christmas parties.
Janet McReynolds—Playwright wife of Bill McReynolds.
Jesse and Tristan McReynolds—Sons of Janet and Bill McReynolds.
Jeff Merrick—Fired from Access Graphics.
Gary Merriman—Human resources director, Access Graphics.

Glenn Meyer—Basement tenant of Joe and Betty Barnhill.
Dr. John Meyer—Boulder County coroner.
Brad Millard—Friend of John Andrew.
Bob Miller—BPD Dream Team attorney.
Bryan Morgan—John Ramsey's attorney.

Fred Patterson—BPD Detective.
Don Paugh—Grandfather of JonBenét, father of Patsy Ramsey.
Nedra Paugh—Grandmother of JonBenét, mother of Patsy Ramsey.
Pam Paugh—Sister of Patsy Ramsey, former Miss West Virginia.
Polly Paugh (Davis)—Youngest sister of Patsy Ramsey.
Mervin Pugh—Husband of Ramsey housekeeper Linda Hoffmann-Pugh.

Kevin Raburn—Suspect extradited by DA's office, then released.
Burke Ramsey—Brother of JonBenét.
Elizabeth "Beth" Ramsey—Stepsister of JonBenét, eldest child of John Ramsey and his first wife, Lucinda. Died in automobile accident.
Jeff Ramsey—Brother of John Ramsey.
John Ramsey—Father of JonBenét, husband of Patsy Ramsey.
John Andrew Ramsey—Older stepbrother of JonBenét, third child from the first marriage of John Ramsey. University of Colorado student.
JonBenét Ramsey—The six-year-old victim.
Lucinda Ramsey—See Lucinda Johnson.
Melinda Ramsey—Older stepsister of JonBenét, second child of John Ramsey and his first wife.
Patsy Ramsey—Mother of JonBenét, wife of John Ramsey.
Paul Reichenbach—BPD Sergeant, patrol supervisor on December 26.
Jodi Roberts—Pseudonym for former mistress of John Ramsey in Atlanta.

Suzanne Savage—Former Ramsey nanny.
Barry Scheck—DNA expert and prominent defense attorney.
Jeff Shapiro—Reporter for the *Globe* tabloid.
Lou Smit—Retired detective hired as DA investigator.
Dr. Werner Spitz—Forensics expert.
Melody Stanton—Ramsey neighbor who heard scream.
Kim Stewart—BPD Detective.

Vesta Taylor—Former Ramsey neighbor in Atlanta.
Tom Trujillo—BPD Detective.

Chet Ubowski—Colorado Bureau of Investigation document analyst and handwriting expert.

Lori Wagner—Access Graphics vice president.
Barry Weiss—BPD Patrol Officer.
Rod Westmoreland—Ramsey best friend and financial adviser in Atlanta.
Fleet and Priscilla White—Friends of Ramseys summoned on morning of December 26.
Carl Whiteside—Director, Colorado Bureau of Investigation.
Bob Whitson—BPD Sergeant.
Tom Wickman—BPD Detective Sergeant.
Bill Wise—Boulder County first Assistant District Attorney.
Chris Wolf—Boyfriend of Jackie Dilson.
Denise Wolf—Assistant to John Ramsey at Access Graphics.